Praise for *Judgment of Paris*

"A vigorous account of the dare that made connoisseurs think differently about California wines. An intoxicating indulgence for *Sideways* fans, and an education for would-be wine sophisticates."

—*Kirkus Reviews* (starred review)

"A vivid, robust story that goes down smoothly."

—Clarissa Cruz and Paul Katz, *Entertainment Weekly*

"Taber has fashioned an entertaining, informative book. . . . This is a serious business book, too, sure to be required reading for American vintners and oenophiles."

—*Publishers Weekly*

"[A] sprightly and definitive account."

—Jerry Adler, *Newsweek*

"Detailed, evocative."

—Peter M. Gianotti, *Newsday*

"Here's the inside tale of the dramatic tasting session that transformed the wine industry. George Taber was the only reporter there, and he tells the tale with the same authority, depth, and clarity as the American wines that won. His tale has fascinating characters, great locales, and a fine bouquet."

—Walter Isaacson, author of *Benjamin Franklin*

"Although the topic may seem narrow, *Judgment of Paris* focuses a wide lens on the world of wine, and the results are intoxicating."

—T. J. Foderaro, *The Newark Star-Ledger*

"[George Taber] has written an engrossing book that puts the Paris Tasting into good historical context. . . . Even readers who know about the Paris Tasting will find plenty that's new in *Judgment of Paris*. And those who have only a vague idea about the event will get an important lesson in a watershed event for California wine."

—Laurie Daniel, *San Jose Mercury News*

"George Taber was alone among journalists to attend the wine world's Declaration of Independence from French supremacy. He tells the story of the

California wine revolution with verve showing how the upstarts managed to surprise the complacent French. This is a rare book about wine to be sipped, not gulped."

—William Echikson, author of *Noble Rot*

"Taber uses the Paris Tasting as a container for a delicious mix of Old and New World winemaking techniques, the economics and politics of wine, and an overview of worldwide wines . . . beautifully rendered. . . . It seems a shame to use a bent cliché to sum up such a well-written and cliché-free book, but *Judgment of Paris* belongs on the shelf of any wine lover worth his/her Grand Cru."

—Bob Fishburn, *The Roanoke Times* (Virginia)

"You don't have to dislike the French to enjoy this book, but it doesn't hurt. *Judgment of Paris* recalls how, in 1976, American underdogs bit the big poodle where it really hurt—in the wine culture, where France had been top dog since the Middle Ages. . . . It's a great tale, well told."

—Ralph Peters, *New York Post*

"Half the fun of appreciating wine is drinking in the history. . . . [George Taber] puts the impact of [the 1976 tasting] into perspective, offering a prehistory of things to come with globalization and corporate influences in today's wine industry."

—Gil Kulers, *The Atlanta Journal-Constitution*

"This book gets my highest recommendation for its engrossing storytelling of a tale that needs telling."

—Charles Olken, *Marin Independent Journal* (Marin, California)

"Taber recounts the story of that memorable day in a clear, well-written, and fascinating style."

—Dave Buchanan, *Monterey County Herald* (California)

"For those of us who were lucky enough to be part of the fun at Steven Spurrier's wine shop in Paris, this book is a trip down memory lane. For everyone else, Taber brings the event to life brilliantly with insightful portraits and a reporter's eye for telling detail."

—Don and Petie Kladstrup, authors of *Wine & War*

"Nearly thirty years later, Taber's book outlines an historic event that is relevant, captivating, and compelling—even for non–wine aficionados. The petty wine war that the Paris Tasting set off had one big winner: good wine. And one big loser: good wine . . . from France."
                                        —Christian Vannequé, Vannequé Publishing,
                                              Judge at the 1976 Paris Tasting

"*Judgment of Paris* is a fascinating recounting of that historic event that was like a lightning rod to the budding wine scene in California. It is a must-read for anyone interested in wine."
                                        —Daniel Johnnes, Wine Director, Montrachet,
                                              and President, Daniel Johnnes Wines

"Spirited, intelligent, and a deliciously entertaining good read. Essential for anyone who has ever enjoyed a good bottle of California wine."
                                        —Anthony Dias Blue, Executive Director of
                                        the San Francisco International Wine Competition

"I devoured *Judgment of Paris* and it is dazzling—reads like a thriller, with the added benefit that the scholarship is impeccable too!"
                                        —Orley Ashenfelter, the Joseph Douglas Green 1895
                                        Professor of Economics at Princeton University and
                                  Publisher of *Liquid Assets: The International Guide to Fine Wines*

"*Bottle Shock* supposedly tells the story of a 1976 wine tasting that is credited with putting Napa Valley on the world's wine map. . . . The event would have had little impact if not for George Taber, an American writer who was invited to attend and became the fly on the wall who recorded it in an article for *Time* magazine, which titled the piece 'Judgment of Paris.' . . . On the 30th anniversary of the tasting, Taber published a book about the event, *Judgment of Paris*. Let's just say [*Bottle Shock*] was 'inspired' by the 1976 tasting. . . . If you want to see the film as sort of wine-stained entertainment, it's your money. But if you are looking for insight into what really happened at this historic event, I suggest you read Taber's book."
                                        —Richard Kinssies, *Seattle Post-Intelligencer*

Dear Reyn & Patty,

Enjoy this read!

Merry Christmas
2010

w/love,
Kevin & Jan

JUDGMENT OF PARIS

California vs. France and the Historic 1976 Paris Tasting
That Revolutionized Wine

GEORGE M. TABER

SCRIBNER

New York   London   Toronto   Sydney

SCRIBNER
1230 Avenue of the Americas
New York, NY 10020

First Scribner trade paperback edition 2006

SCRIBNER and design are trademarks of Macmillan Library Reference USA, Inc.,
used under license by Simon & Schuster, the publisher of this work.

For information about special discounts for bulk purchases,
please contact Simon & Schuster Special Sales:
1-800-456-6798 or business@simonandschuster.com

DESIGNED BY ERICH HOBBING

Text set in Adobe Garamond

Manufactured in the United States of America

9   10   8

Library of Congress Cataloging-in-Publication Data

Taber, George M.
Judgment of Paris : California vs. France and the historic 1976 tasting
that revolutionized wine / George M. Taber.
p. cm.
Includes bibliographical references and index.
1. Wine tasting—France—Paris—History—20th century. 2. Wine industry—France—
History—20th century. 3. Wine industry—California—History—20th century. 4. Wine and
wine making—France—History—20th century. 5. Wine and wine making—California—
History—20th century. I. Title.

TP548.5.A5T23 2005
641.2'2'094436109047—dc22
2005044146

ISBN-13: 978-0-7432-4751-1
ISBN-10: 0-7432-4751-5
ISBN-13: 978-0-7432-9732-5 (Pbk)
ISBN-10: 0-7432-9732-6 (Pbk)

CONTENTS

Part Three:
THE JUDGMENT OF PARIS

Part Four:
THE NEW WORLD OF WINE

FOREWORD BY ROBERT G. MONDAVI

It was one hundred years ago that my father came to the United States and began to make wine here. And it was just nearly thirty years ago that the Judgment of Paris took place. I like to think about the advances we made over the two generations until that tasting took place and about the progress we've made since.

I always knew we had the soil, the climate, and the grape varieties to make wines in the Napa Valley that could rank with the great wines of the world. When we started, we did not have the knowledge of how to accomplish our goals, but I knew we had to begin.

It was my pleasure to have worked with Mike Grgich and Warren Winiarski, who are the real heroes of this book. They were certainly more adept than I, but I like to think that they grasped my vision of what could be done in the Napa Valley, and I know we worked and planned and dreamed together that a day like that bicentennial event in 1976 could occur.

It was also a pleasure to meet Steven Spurrier and later his associate Patricia Gallagher here at the winery. Believe me . . . there were not a great number of believers in those days and we prized every one. In London we had a few people who knew what we were doing—Hugh Johnson, Michael Broadbent, and Harry Waugh—but until Steven we had no one in France. It was a real treat to go to Cité Berryer and see California wines for sale at the Caves de la Madeleine!

I'm certainly happy to see that George Taber—who was there—decided to write the true story of the momentous event. So much of California wine history has been lost, and as he points out, the dramatic tasting sent shock waves all around the world. Although our wines were not in the tasting, it appeared at the time that we gained quite as much as our colleagues. It truly was a victory for our Napa Valley wines, California wines, and in fact, winemaking in North America. It gave us the confidence to continue what we were doing—confidence in our commitment to excel.

This is a book for every wine lover; it has a history and a very exciting story well told. And we won!

JUDGMENT OF PARIS

PROLOGUE

Author, at left, at the Paris Tasting

Was there ever a better job? In the mid-1970s, I was a correspondent for *Time* magazine in Paris. It was a small office, so I got to write stories on subjects as varied as French politics and *haute couture*. When a big story broke in one of the countries under the Paris bureau, I jetted off to Madrid to cover the assassination of a Spanish prime minister, to Lisbon to report on a revolution taking place, or to Amsterdam to check into a bribery scandal involving the Dutch queen's husband.

On May 24, 1976, I happened to be in Paris. The previous week I had suggested to editors in New York a story on a wine tasting that was doing the unthinkable: comparing some of the greatest names in French wines with new and little-known California wines. It seemed like a nonevent—clearly France would win—but as a native Californian, I had developed an interest in wine and had tried to learn something about European wines while studying or working in Switzerland, Germany, Belgium, and, of course, France.

Each week *Time* correspondents around the world suggest hundreds of stories. Only a few of the proposals are scheduled and even fewer ever make it to press. It's a fierce survival-of-the-fittest process, but the result is a lively, compelling publication. Although my story was scheduled, I knew that the odds of it getting into the magazine were long. If, as expected, the French wines won, there would be no story. But you never know, and a wine tasting—where maybe I'd get a chance to try a few of the wines myself—seemed, at the very least, like a perfectly wonderful way to spend an otherwise slow afternoon.

The event was taking place at the InterContinental Hotel, not far from the *Time* office just off the Champs-Élysées. In winter I might have taken the Métro there, but it was a beautiful spring day, so instead I walked through the immaculate gardens lining the grand boulevard toward the Place de la Concorde. I considered this the most beautiful part of the world's most beautiful city. There were monumental buildings, elegant people, and an exciting hustle and bustle. This was the epicenter of the city Gershwin put to music in *An American in Paris*. I strolled past the American embassy and the Egyptian obelisk nicknamed Cleopatra's Needle in the Place de La Concorde to the Rue de Rivoli, and then under its arcades lined with fashionable shops displaying their wares. The InterContinental, located on the Rue de Castiglione and bordered by the Rue de Rivoli and the majestic Place Vendôme, was one of the most fashionable hotels in Paris. It reeked of class and luxury.

A hotel doorman directed me to the small, elegant room off the hotel's patio bar where the tasting was to take place. As I entered, waiters in tuxedos were busily setting up the event, laying out tablecloths and distributing glasses. I knew the organizers of the tasting, Englishman Steven Spurrier, who owned a nearby wine shop called the Caves de la Madeleine, and his sidekick Patricia Gallagher, an American. I had taken an introductory wine course taught by Gallagher at the Académie du Vin, a wine school associated with the shop. Her personal plea was one of the reasons I had agreed to cover the tasting, which was designed to garner some publicity for the shop and school, but they were having a hard time getting any publications to take it seriously. In fact, I was the only journalist who showed up. After saying hello to Gallagher, I started taking notes in the brown plastic-covered book that I always carried with me.

Soon the nine judges began arriving. I knew none of them personally, but they had impeccable credentials and were among the leading wine experts in France. With the quiet formalism of the French establishment, the judges greeted each other with a handshake and then took their places along the long bank of tables. As this was going to be a blind tasting, meaning the labels of the wines would not be shown, the judges would not know which wines they were tasting. They knew only that the wines were from France and California, and that the red wines were Bordeaux-style Cabernet Sauvignons and the whites were Burgundy-style Chardonnays. Shortly after 3:00 p.m., a waiter began walking up and down a row of tables pouring wine from unmarked bottles. The judges had nothing in front of them except a scorecard, two glasses, and a *petit pain*, a small hard roll for nibbling on to clean the palate between wines. As is common in a wine tasting, the judges started with the white wines.

It was a very informal event, so I was free to roam around the room as the judges tasted the wines. They were a little chattier than is normal at a tasting, where the experts usually quietly concentrate on the work at hand.

About halfway through the white wine part of the competition, I began to notice something quite shocking. I had a list of the wines and realized that the judges were getting confused! They were identifying a French wine as a California one and vice versa. Judges at one end of the tables were insisting that a particular wine was French, while those at the other were saying it was from California.

Raymond Oliver, the owner and chef of the Grand Véfour restaurant in Paris, one of the temples of French *haute cuisine,* swirled a white wine in his glass, held it up to the light to examine the pale straw color, smelled it, and then tasted it. After a pause he said, "Ah, back to France!" I checked my list of wines twice to be sure, but Oliver had in fact just tasted a 1972 Freemark Abbey Chardonnay from California's Napa Valley! Soon after, Claude Dubois-Millot of GaultMillau, a publisher of French food and wine books and magazines, tasted another white wine and said with great confidence, "That is definitely California. It has no nose." But the wine was really a 1973 Bâtard-Montrachet Ramonet-Prudhon, one of Burgundy's finest products.

Spurrier's Paris tasting might just be an interesting story after all.

PART ONE

———◆———

A DRIVING DREAM

We could in the United States make as great a variety of wines as are made in Europe, not exactly of the same kind, but doubtless as good.

—THOMAS JEFFERSON, 1808

CHAPTER ONE

The Little Wine Shop in Cité Berryer

If we sip the wine, we find dreams
coming upon us out of the imminent night.
—D. H. LAWRENCE

O
n an autumn day in 1970, two Englishmen were walking around
Paris's posh Right Bank near the Rue Royale. Although its glory was
in the nineteenth century, luxury still reigns there as an art form in this section made up of the city's First and Eighth *arrondissements*. The area combines New York City's Park Avenue with Beverly Hills's Rodeo Drive.
Within a few blocks are found such restaurants as Maxim's, shops like Her-
mès and Cartier, and the Ritz, the quintessential ritzy hotel. The Right Bank
is a wonderful area for strolling, especially in the fall after most of the tourists
have left and the city's pace slows a little. The summer heat is gone, and the
chestnut leaves begin to fall.

The two men wandered into Cité Berryer, a street easy to miss because
it was only a block long, going from the Rue Royale to the Boissy d'Anglas.
Cité Berryer was a slightly seedy shopping arcade that seemed out of place
amid all the luxury around it. Built in the nineteenth century, it was
named after a then leading, but now long forgotten, politician. Twice a week
an open-air, fresh vegetable and fruit market took place there, and fashionable and unfashionable women alike lined up to buy produce for their
families. A small wine shop was located next to a locksmith.

As the two men passed the Caves de la Madeleine, a wine shop named
after the famous church located two blocks away, one man turned to the
other and said, "That is exactly the kind of shop I would like to buy."

Steven Spurrier was a well-to-do son of English landed gentry, who at
the age of twenty-nine was still trying to figure out what he was going to do
when he grew up. After spending several months living in Provence in
southern France, Spurrier had recently moved to Paris, where he and his

7

wife, Bella, resided on a 130-foot barge moored on the River Seine at the Place de la Concorde.

If there was a centerpiece to Spurrier's wandering life, it was wine. In his youth, when other boys were outside playing soccer, he could be found rearranging bottles in the wine cellar at Holbrook Hall, his family's estate in Derbyshire in north-central England. Spurrier worked for a short time for two leading shops in the London wine trade. One of them sent him—at his own expense—on a seven-month study tour of wine through France, Germany, Spain, and Portugal.

As Spurrier and his friend, a British lawyer living in Paris, entered the store, the owner, Madame Fougères, asked if she could help them.

"My friend here would like to buy your shop," said the lawyer with British directness.

The idea was not so crazy. The wine shop had actually been quietly for sale for two years, after the owner's husband had committed suicide. His widow had lost interest in running the business, which involved lots of heavy work lifting cases and pushing around barrels of wine. After a few minutes of conversation, the two Englishmen left.

A few days later, Spurrier returned alone to talk to Madame Fougères about buying the shop. She explained that she had a strong emotional tie to the store because it had been her husband's pride—in fact, his whole life. She was not certain if she would sell it, especially to an Englishman who didn't speak much French, despite his proclaimed interest in her country's most prestigious product. Madame Fougères told Spurrier she doubted he could "carry the torch" for her dead husband. Spurrier then made a proposal. To show he was serious, he would work for her in the store for six months at no pay, doing whatever she asked. It was a deal she could hardly refuse.

So even though he had $250,000 in inheritance money in the bank, Spurrier went to work rolling wine barrels around the store's cellar and delivering cases of wine up six flights in the service stairway of Parisian apartments because delivery people were not supposed to use the elevator. Sometimes a grateful housekeeper gave him a fifty-centimes (ten-cent) tip.

Spurrier learned the Paris wine business from the inside at the same time he was improving his French. When the six months were over, he bought the wine shop for 300,000 francs ($50,000), and on April 1, 1971, moved behind the cash register to be the new owner. Madame Fougères had been very formal up to that point, never even telling him her first name. But after he bought the business, she asked him to call her by her nickname, Timoune.

The Caves de la Madeleine was a typical French wine shop. Its core business was inexpensive *vin ordinaire,* the wine an average French family drinks with lunch and dinner. Madame Fougères bottled it out of tanks, selling four simple wines by the liter: a red with 11 percent alcohol, a 12 percent red, a white, and a rosé. The day he took over, Spurrier stopped the bottling of *vin ordinaire,* though it took him a year to sell it all off. Madame Fougères's wholesaler told Spurrier he was crazy and would soon go bankrupt.

The *vin ordinaire* crowd, however, was not what Spurrier was going after. He wanted the upper part of the market and was soon visiting vineyards all over France to buy quality wines directly from winemakers. He thought his biggest potential market was the Britons and Americans working in Paris, especially in the neighborhood around his shop. The British and U.S. embassies were only a few blocks away, and in the nearby Place Vendôme and Place de la Concorde, IBM and American law firms had offices. As the only wine-store owner in Paris who was a native English speaker, Spurrier wanted to be the wine merchant to that large and generally affluent Anglo-American community. The way to reach them, Spurrier concluded, was through the *International Herald Tribune,* the daily newspaper of Americans in Paris, which provided a diet of *New York Times* and *Washington Post* stories plus a few local articles. Spurrier began running ads in the paper's classified section for the Caves de la Madeleine's promotional events.

Given his upper-class background, Spurrier moved easily in Parisian business and social circles. He cut a dashing figure, wearing three-piece suits and with a glass of wine never far away. His hair was stylishly long, cut in an early Beatles style, and he sported a free-flowing mustache. His slight British upper-class stammer and terribly British style charmed journalists, especially women. In a profile published in the *Herald Tribune,* reporter Susan Heller Anderson gushingly wrote: "A peach-colored Englishman elegant in teal blue pinstriped suit with waistcoat and creamy linen shirt, he describes in Etonian accents how most Provençal rosés are absolutely filthy."

Jon Winroth was the *Herald Tribune*'s wine writer, and soon after taking over ownership of the wine shop Spurrier set out to meet him. Winroth had grown up in Chicago, where his father was a professor of archaeology. In a rarity of the 1940s and 1950s, Winroth's family served wine regularly with meals. He had come to Paris in 1956 on a Fulbright scholarship to study history, but wine was soon his major interest. He landed a job with the *Herald Tribune,* writing stories on topics like the year's harvest or some interesting French winery.

Spurrier sent Winroth samples of special wines he was carrying, always enclosing an invitation to stop by the store or give him a call. For months

Spurrier heard nothing in reply, so one day he walked the short distance to the *Herald Tribune* offices on the Rue de Berri. When he arrived, Spurrier got into one of those tiny Paris elevators that can hold two people as long as neither person breathes. Ever so slowly it rose to the third floor. Just as Spurrier was leaving the elevator, a thin young man, also with a mustache, was getting in.

"Can you tell me where Jon Winroth works?" Spurrier asked.

"I'm Jon Winroth," the man replied.

"I'm Steven Spurrier. I own the Caves de la Madeleine wine shop."

"So you're the guy who's been bombarding me with all those samples! I'm heading out to have a glass of wine. Why don't you come along, and we can talk?"

The two men hit it off immediately, talking for more than four hours over several glasses of wine at a table in the back of a nearby café. Spurrier told Winroth about the plans for his business. Sales were good; he was becoming better known and progressing toward his goal of becoming the wine merchant for Anglo-Americans in Paris.

Spurrier also told him about how a small but regular group of Americans came by the shop late in the afternoon after work to talk about wine. He often opened a bottle of wine and gave them some basic tips while they sipped. He'd charge them by the glass, and they seemed delighted to learn a little more about the subject in an atmosphere where they could speak English and wouldn't be laughed at because they couldn't name all of Bordeaux's famous Grands Crus. Winroth told Spurrier that he gave similar wine-tasting seminars in the back rooms of Parisian cafés to American college students on their junior year abroad. The two men mused about some day starting a wine school that would serve both their audiences.

While cultivating the Anglo-American press and companies, Spurrier did not ignore the French wine establishment. In fact, he courted it with all the subtlety of a bulldozer. With the self-confidence and impetuousness of youth, Spurrier began strong-arming his way into French wine events.

He absolutely wanted to know Henri Gault and Christian Millau, who were the hot new experts on food, wine, and travel. In 1965, they began publishing *Le Nouveau Guide,* a restaurant guide with a fresh and breezy style that quickly made it an alternative to the better-known—but hidebound—Michelin guide. The two later started a monthly magazine on both wines and restaurants that was very influential in setting French tastes. When Spurrier heard that the magazine was staging a tasting of Provençal wines at the swank George V Hotel, just off the Champs-Élysées, he showed up uninvited with several bottles of wine that he sold in his shop. At the door he said in his by now very good French, "I'm Steven Spurrier, and I own the Caves de la Madeleine wine shop. I'd like to enter these wines." The non-plussed doorman let him in, and somehow Spurrier was quickly invited to be a member of the tasting panel. The French were surprised by his knowledge of wine, and he was soon in tight with the Gault-Millau crowd, which, like him, was young and irreverent.

Spurrier also worked his way into the Foire de Paris and the Foire de Mâcon, two big agricultural shows that awarded wine prizes, and before long he was judging wine competitions all over the country.

When he heard that the prestigious wine magazine *La Revue du Vin de France* was giving a test for sommeliers, the wine stewards who work in only the best restaurants, Spurrier showed up uninvited to take the test. Officials told him the examination was for sommeliers only and not for wine merchants, but Spurrier said he still wanted to take it. Reluctantly Odette Kahn, the magazine's tall and striking-looking editor, allowed him to participate. Spurrier was the only person that day to score a perfect 100 percent on the written part. When Kahn invited him to stay for the wine-tasting section of the examination, Spurrier declined, saying he just wanted to see what the test was like. Intrigued by the young Brit, Kahn quickly took an interest in his wine enterprises.

Eighteen months after Spurrier bought the Caves de la Madeleine, the locksmith located next door went bankrupt. Spurrier bought the shop at auction, and then suggested to Winroth that they collaborate and start a wine school for Spurrier's inquisitive American businesspeople and Winroth's junior-year-abroad students. They called their school the Académie du Vin. Despite the name, instruction would be only in English.

It took about six months to turn the downstairs area of the locksmith shop, where there had been a forge, into the Académie's classroom. The ceiling was stripped to expose massive eighteenth-century oak beams. Spurrier hung maps of wine-growing regions on the brick walls and filled a bookcase with tomes on wine in both French and English. In a stroke of luck that seemed to follow all his wine ventures during the 1970s, Spurrier heard that a horseshoe-shaped mahogany bar from the Napoléon III period was for sale at a café near the famous Les Halles food market. It cost only five hundred francs (a hundred dollars), but he had to haul it away that very afternoon.

Spurrier and Winroth had to call friends around Paris to get enough students for the first class, which they taught together, just before France's traditional August vacation break in 1972. The class went well, but it convinced Spurrier that he would need help running the wine school. Serendipitously, a young American woman who loved Paris and was trying to find a way to stay happened to call him asking for a job. Patricia Gallagher had met Spurrier while interviewing him for a freelance article she had written for Delaware's *Wilmington Morning News*. But freelancing for her home state's main newspaper and doing pick-up work at the *Herald Tribune* were not going to pay her bills, so she needed a job. Gallagher went to work at the Académie du Vin almost immediately.

Although she knew little about wine when she joined Spurrier, Gallagher proved a quick study and was soon giving courses and managing the school. While Spurrier was casual and confident as a teacher, she was more serious. I can still recall her, in the course I took, carefully leading her students through an understanding of tannins, a substance found mainly in red wines. She talked about the furry sensation tannins cause in your mouth and how the students should be feeling them, until everyone in the class told her they got it.

The Académie du Vin was a big hit immediately. Early students told their friends about it, and word spread quickly through the Anglo-American community of this place where people could learn about French wines in English. The press also picked up on the unusual story of a young Englishman running a wine school in Paris. First the *Herald Tribune* and British papers ran the story; French papers soon followed.

The initial six-session course was a general introduction to the wine regions of France and cost five hundred francs. After an overview class, the following five weekly meetings concentrated on a single region, going from the Loire Valley in week two to Champagne in week six. After the school's early success, more specialized courses were offered on specific regions and various vintages. Most of the two-hour sessions were in the early evening so people could take them after work on their way home. Soon more and more students were sitting around the horseshoe bar listening to Spurrier or Gallagher talk about wine. The names of the wines under discussion were written on a blackboard behind the bar, and a platter of cheese, cold cuts, and country bread stood at the ready to accompany the wine. Conversation always became livelier as the classes and the wines progressed.

Before long even the French were calling and asking to take courses. Hard as it was to believe, the Académie du Vin was the only place in Paris that gave formal programs, in either French or English, in wine appreciation. By then Spurrier was no longer surprised at how little the average French person knew about wine, and he hired a native speaker to teach at the school. Later, the Académie also gave the official program for French sommeliers.

The Caves de la Madeleine had been a success, but the Académie du Vin put Spurrier into a new orbit. By the mid-1970s, his early Beatles look was replaced by a more conservative Savile Row style. After his mustache came off in 1975, Spurrier looked like the young banker his father had wanted him to be. His father, who had always been dismissive of a wine career, learned how successful his son had become while checking in a rental car at the airport in Bordeaux one day. The young woman at the Hertz counter asked the father, "You aren't the celebrated wine merchant, by any chance?" He proudly explained that was his son.

In the Paris of the mid-1970s, Spurrier and Gallagher were excited and exciting. They obviously loved France and all things French, especially wine, which helped them move easily in French society. They became such an item around town that people wondered if they were a couple. They were not. Spurrier's wife, Bella, was busy raising their two small children in the family's apartment at the Place de la Bastille, where they moved after they left their barge on the Seine. Meanwhile Gallagher was developing a relationship with a Frenchman she later married.

Spurrier and Gallagher traveled endlessly to the wine regions of France from Champagne to Bordeaux, talking to vintners and learning more about French wines. The more they learned, the more the French liked them. Soon they were also offering trips to wine regions, and their English-speaking customers piled into buses on Saturday mornings and traveled to Burgundy or Alsace.

Money was the least of worries in those effervescent days around the little wine shop. If Spurrier found something interesting and perhaps amusing, he just did it. He was not even taking a salary from his company, still living on his inheritance. What really mattered was having fun, and he and Gallagher were doing things that the staid French wine establishment had never done—and probably would never even have thought of doing.

In May 1972, Queen Elizabeth II made a state visit to Paris as part of warming diplomatic relations between the two countries that led to Britain's entry into the European Common Market the following year. One of the events during her stay was a dinner the queen hosted at the British embassy for French president Georges Pompidou. Shortly before her visit, Spurrier received a phone call from Major General Sir Guy Salisbury-Jones, a dedicated Francophile who had planted 4.5 acres of Seyve-Villard and Chardonnay vines in Hambledon, a town near Portsmouth in southern England. He suggested serving his dry white wine at the dinner for Pompidou. Wouldn't it be greatly amusing to serve an English wine to the president of France? Spurrier also thought it a great idea and ordered five cases of Sir Guy's wine. Dinner planners at the embassy put it on the menu.

Two days before the event, however, Spurrier got a call from customs agents at Orly Airport outside Paris. An official said the Hambledon wine had arrived, but there was a problem. With time short before the dinner, Spurrier raced to Orly to see the customs agent, who told him that unfortunately the wine could not be imported into France.

"But why not?" asked Spurrier. "It has arrived, and here are the papers."

"Because English wine does not exist," the customs agent replied. "Here is my list of goods that can be exported from England to France. There is no wine. There is no such thing as English wine, so I cannot clear it through customs. I cannot clear what doesn't exist." Spurrier was trapped in the maddening French logic that has driven the English crazy for a thousand years. Frustrated and seeing no way around this standoff with the stubborn civil servant, Spurrier reluctantly returned to Paris.

But the next day he called the customs officer for a second try. "Do me a favor," Spurrier said. "It's only sixty bottles. Let's just pretend that it's French wine. I'll pay you whatever I have to."

"I'm sorry, monsieur," said the official. "I cannot do that. We will have to send the cases back to England."

"No, don't do that! I'm coming back to Orly."

"It's no use, monsieur. There's nothing I can do."

When Spurrier returned to the airport and walked into the custom agent's office, he saw the five cases of wine on the floor next to the man's desk. "But the wine is there! You see it!" Spurrier said with growing exasperation.

"Of course, monsieur. It is physically there, but the wine does not exist because it is not on the list of exported English products."

Spurrier lost his temper and like a schoolmaster addressing a particularly dull student asked, "Does your job exist? Do you like your job?"

"Of course, monsieur."

"Well, in about two hours your job will no longer exist because this wine is supposed to be served tonight to President Pompidou and the Queen of England. If the wine is not there, you will be held responsible."

With amazing speed, the customs officer put the proper stamps on the official papers, and the wine was cleared through customs. Spurrier was soon on his way back to Paris with the nonexistent wine. That night the Queen served it to her French guests, who doubtlessly opined, "How curious! An English wine!"

About four times a year, Spurrier and Gallagher staged a special promotional event to raise the public profile of both the wine shop and the school. In the spring of 1975, Spurrier invited the vintners of Bordeaux's elite First Growth red wines—Haut-Brion, Lafite, Latour, Margaux, and Mouton—to a comparative tasting of the 1970 vintage in Paris. All but

Haut-Brion came. No one in France had ever staged such a face-off of the great wines, and the event attracted attention and numerous press stories.

Spurrier and Gallagher began thinking about holding an event around California wines because they were hearing from a wide range of people about the exciting new things being done in northern California. At a Paris dinner party in 1973 or 1974, Alex Bespaloff, an American wine writer, first tried to convince Spurrier that some California wines were actually pretty good. Bespaloff took umbrage when Spurrier said he thought California wines were "rather cooked," meaning they were high in alcohol and had a burnt taste. California winemakers visiting Paris soon began stopping at the Caves de la Madeleine and dropping off bottles of their wares. Spurrier found some of them interesting. Robert Finigan, the publisher of the influential wine newsletter *Robert Finigan's Private Guide to Wines*, and Frank Prial, the wine reporter for the *New York Times*, were frequent visitors to Cité Berryer when they came to Paris and became evangelists for the new California wine pioneers. They explained to Spurrier and Gallagher that the Americans held France up as their model of excellence and were trying to emulate the very best Bordeaux and Burgundy wines. Finigan and Prial said the California wines were surprisingly good—not up to French standards, but nonetheless interesting.

Gallagher heard similar enthusiasm for California wines from her husband-to-be, Gérard Gastaud, an electronics engineer who worked for the French telephone company and had recently spent a year in Las Vegas, where his company was installing a telephone system. During that time he made a foray to the Napa Valley and reported back that some California wines were pleasantly surprising. On his return to Paris in December 1974, Gastaud brought Gallagher a goodie bag of California viticulture: a bottle of unfiltered Robert Mondavi wine; a technical book on winemaking by Professor Maynard Amerine of the University of California, Davis; and a guide to the new wineries titled *The Treasury of American Wines* by Nathan Chroman.

Glenda Cudaback, a friend of Gallagher's who worked at the *Herald Tribune*, was also telling her about California wine. Cudaback and her husband were both from the city of Napa, where his father had a landscaping business that did work for new wineries being built in the valley.

The new smaller wineries, everyone explained, were producing far better California wine than could be bought in Paris. At the time, the only California wine easily available in Paris was Paul Masson, which was sold in screw-top bottles at fancy gourmet shops like Fauchon that carried products for expatriate Americans.

One day in early 1975, Gallagher told Spurrier that Americans were planning all sorts of special events the next year around the bicentennial of American independence and suggested that they put together something on California wines as part of that year-long celebration. Gallagher traced her family roots back to 1630 in Massachusetts and had a great interest in colonial America. The French, she noted, had played a major role in American independence thanks to Lafayette and all that. Why not have a tasting of California wines in Paris? As his earlier publicity events had demonstrated, Spurrier liked to be what the French called an *agent provocateur*. Above all, Spurrier thought it would be good fun, and in those days around the Caves de la Madeleine and the Académie du Vin, fun was all that really mattered.

CHAPTER TWO

France Ruled the World

*The effervescence of French wine reveals the true brilliance of
the French people.*

—VOLTAIRE

Alexis Lichine, a part owner and manager of Château Lascombes, a prized Second Growth under the historic 1855 classification of Bordeaux wines, opened his 1951 *Wines of France* with the categorical statement, "The greatest wines on earth come from France." For centuries no one would have seriously challenged that assertion. While grapes have been grown in Western Europe for generations, French wines were always in a league by themselves. In the world of wines, there was France—and then there was everybody else.

Archaeologists believe that wine was first developed in the late Stone Age, probably by someone who accidentally left some grapes in a jar where fermentation occurred with the help of some wandering yeast—to the person's delighted surprise. According to the Bible, Noah planted the first vineyard, but after getting drunk on his new product, he lay "naked inside his tent" (Genesis 9:20). Wine wasn't off to a good start.

Patrick McGovern, an archaeologist at the University of Pennsylvania Museum, traced the history of the beverage back eight thousand years in his 2003 book *Ancient Wine*. McGovern's more recent research shows that the Chinese made a fermented beverage out of rice, honey, and grapes about nine thousand years ago, but that had no influence on the development of western wine. Excavations in the Near East show that wine was probably first made in the western world somewhere in a broad area stretching from eastern Turkey through the Taurus, Caucasus, and Zagros mountains to northern Iran. From there, wine followed the leading intellectual and military powers of the day, moving on to Egypt, Greece, and Rome and then to the distant parts of their empires. Greek settlers brought the first wine to France in about 600 BC to Massalia, present day Marseilles, and Plato set out rules governing the use of wine in the fifth century BC.

Greek and Roman traders noted that grapes grew well relatively close to shore and also in the same place as olives did, so that's where their settlers planted vineyards. In the Old World the historic area of wine production reached from southern England in the north to northern Africa in the south, and from Portugal in the west to western Russia in the east.

Even though wine has been made in all of those places, outstanding wine has always been considered rare. British author Alec Waugh in his 1959 book *In Praise of Wine* expressed the then conventional wisdom among both wine professionals and serious amateurs when he wrote "For the real magic and mystery of wine lies in this: that though wine be grown in innumerable areas, great wines can only be produced in special places and in minute quantities."

For Waugh and many others that special place was France. Something made France unique. Soil, climate, topography, elevation, drainage, height of the sun, and a dozen other things seemed to come together best in France.

French wines were also steeped in history. A Frenchman was usually a winemaker—and until very recently they were all men—because his father and his father's father back as far as the family remembers were winemakers. In such a society tradition naturally ruled. The French winemaker had a hallowed respect for tradition. You didn't play around with success. No experiments! Thanks to centuries of trial and error going back to the Greeks and Romans, the French were certain that they had discovered the very best places to produce the very best wines. Winemakers learned from literally hundreds of vintages which types of grapes reached their highest potential and where exactly to grow them. They determined over time, for example, that Cabernet Sauvignon grapes did best in Bordeaux and Pinot Noir grapes performed well in Burgundy, so no one had to waste time trying to grow Pinot Noir in Bordeaux or Cabernet Sauvignon in Burgundy. The lessons of history had already been learned. As Émile Peynaud, a University of Bordeaux professor and the leading French wine guru of the twentieth century, said, "Tradition is an experiment that has worked."

Climatology, geology, and history all fuse in the French concept of *terroir*. There's no exact English translation for the word that combines all the factors that go into making outstanding wine. *Terroir* is founded on the conviction that there is a perfect place for making wine, where the soil and the weather and the knowledge of the ages combine to produce truly great vintages. Of the factors making up *terroir* the most important are the soil and the minerals it contains, and the French maintain that a specific *terroir*— be it Burgundy or even a particular vineyard in Burgundy—cannot be totally replicated anywhere else in the world.

In France winemaking was not just an occupation or a business. Vintners were highly respected for living close to the land and mastering the mystique of turning simple grapes into the nectar of the gods. The winemaking *paysan,* with his wine-stained hands and face weathered by too many hours in the sun, had cachet in a cachet-conscious country. Families like the Rothschilds, who had made their fortunes in other fields, got into wine as a way of raising their social stature. As the French have said for centuries, *le vin anoblit*—wine makes one an aristocrat.

The vast majority of French wine until the mid-nineteenth century was either shipped abroad by sea or drunk locally. Little made its way even to Paris, which for most of history had its own vineyards. In Bordeaux people drank Bordeaux, in Burgundy they drank Burgundy, and in the Rhône Valley they drank Rhône wines. The arrival of the railroad made overland transportation both easier and less expensive. Later roads built to serve automobiles and trucks also made it economical to ship wines to distant markets. France then became the maker of fine wine for the world.

One of the downsides of greater trade, however, was an increase in wine fraud, and inferior wines soon were passed off as higher quality ones, or good and bad wines were blended and sold under the more prestigious name at the higher price. The final series of laws to fight cheating were passed on July 30, 1935, establishing the Appellation d'Origine Contrôlée system, which was ruled by an oversight board with extensive powers. Literally translated, the term means "Naming According to Controlled Place of Origin," and the law picked up on the concept of *terroir:* a wine gets its unique character from the unique place where it is grown, and that should determine its unique name. The 1935 legislation divided France into hundreds of *appellations* or areas, and more specific regions have since been added. Today there are 450 wine *appellations*.

Although they have been modified through the years, the 1935 rules still govern French wine. Today all wines are divided into four categories: Vins de Table (Table Wines), Vins de Pays (Regional Wines), Vins Delimités (Delimited Wines), and Vins d'Appellation d'Origine Contrôlée (Appellation Wines). Very detailed regulations govern each group, with the rules getting tougher as products work their way up the quality scale to *appellation*. At that level the regulations are extremely rigid and cover such things as the type of grapes that can be used, the acceptable yields per hectare, the minimum ripeness of the fruit as determined by the percentage of sugar, and the alcoholic content of the wine. In some areas laws require that grapes be picked by hand, rather than by machine. Such stipulations determine whether a wine is a Chablis Grand Cru, which brings a high price in the market, rather than a Petit Chablis, which comes from a parcel of land only a little further up the hill in a cooler area but is worth much less. A wine-maker might be able to make great Chardonnay in Bordeaux, but under the *appellation* system he is not allowed to grow that grape there. The restrictive French wine laws certainly stifle winemaker creativity.

The system did not totally eliminate wine doctoring, but it helped safeguard the quality of French wines by keeping such practices in check. French winemakers love their system or hate it—or have both feelings at the same time.

Wine is produced in many parts of France—from the sparkling wines of Champagne in the north to the sweet Banyuls in the south on the Spanish border, but the two towering regions are Bordeaux in the west and Burgundy in the east.

Bordeaux's wine trade is centered around the city of the same name located some sixty miles up the Gironde River from the Atlantic Ocean. Its vineyards extend sixty-five miles from north to south and eighty miles from east to west, covering some 260,000 acres. Vines grow along both sides of the Gironde River and the Gironde Estuary, which is formed by the Garonne and Dordogne rivers, and also northeastward beyond the Dordogne. Bordeaux's wine-growing area is nearly five times the size of Burgundy and eight times bigger than California's Napa Valley.

The Bordeaux region has more than nine thousand wine-producing châteaux and thirteen thousand grape growers. The annual output averages about 700 million bottles, but in bountiful years can approach 900 million. Approximately 85 percent is red wine. Most of the wineries call themselves *châteaux,* although they lack the palatial residences that name implies. The properties are spread out over regions such as Médoc, Entre-Deux-Mers and St.-Émilion—and fifty-seven *appellations.* These give Bordeaux wines both their delightful subtlety and their maddening complexity. Talented connoisseurs can taste, and appreciate, the difference between a 2000 Château Lafite Rothschild from the *appellation* of Pauillac and a no-name Bordeaux of unknown vintage. That is why the first wine sells for $400, while the latter costs perhaps $5. Less discerning drinkers, on the other hand, might be unable to appreciate the differences between the two and wonder what the fuss is all about.

Warm Gulf Stream currents and prevailing westerly winds blowing over the Atlantic Ocean play crucial roles in the development of Bordeaux wines. The city of Bordeaux is located at the 45 degree parallel, at the same latitude as Minneapolis and St. Paul, but its weather is much milder than in the Twin Cities. Since Bordeaux vineyards are near the sea, an estuary, and two rivers, the weather is generally moderate and relatively stable, although there can be great variations from year to year. An old Bordeaux saying holds that the best wines come from vines that can see the rivers that lead out to the ocean.

Bordeaux soil is generally sandy or gravelly, but well drained. Much of it is alluvial, rich with the remnants of marine life from an earlier age when the area frequently flooded. Some of the land is of surprisingly low quality, and visitors for centuries have wondered how such good wines could come from such poor soil. The answer to the apparent paradox is that in those areas vines have to reach deeper into the earth to seek out nutrients and minerals that help produce superior products.

Bordeaux wines are generally not made from a single grape variety, but are blends of three or even four grapes according to the choice of the winemaker. The most commonly grown varietals are Cabernet Sauvignon, Merlot, Cabernet Franc, Petit Verdot, and Malbec.

The Roman historian Pliny the Elder recorded the earliest known reference to vineyards around the port city that was to become Bordeaux in the year 71. At that time, the local Gauls already had a profitable wine trade with England. The Gauls had been beer drinkers, but they took to the wine trade with gusto, transporting their wines in wooden beer barrels instead of the clay amphorae the Romans used. Barrels have been an integral part of winemaking ever since.

Bordeaux rose to prominence as a wine producer starting in the late twelfth century after a royal marriage between Eleanor of Aquitaine, whose lands included Bordeaux, and the future Henry II of England brought together the French wine country and the wealthy English market. Transportation from the port of Bordeaux to England was both easier and less expensive than it was for the region's competitors farther inland in France or in northern Spain. Eleanor's son, King Richard the Lionhearted, made Bordeaux his court wine and soon it was a drink of choice in England.

With exports growing rapidly, the countryside around Bordeaux was soon covered in vines. By the fourteenth century more than 75 percent of Bordeaux wine was shipped to England, where it was called claret because of its light color, which distinguished it from the darker and heavier wines produced in Spain. British wine historian Hugh Johnson has written that Bordeaux was then made like rosé is today, with the juice left in contact with the grape skins for only a short time, thus giving the wine its pale color. In the early part of the fourteenth century Bordeaux exports totaled some one hundred thousand barrels annually to England. In those days wines lasted only a few months before spoiling, and the price dropped dramatically as soon as the next year's vintage arrived.

In the late Middle Ages, however, Bordeaux wine fell into a slump.

English tastes turned away from claret in favor of heavier wines, and the Dutch, who then controlled much of world trade and were a major market, also drank mainly heavier wines. During the sixteenth and seventeenth centuries, a host of technological changes, especially improvements in glass-making, bottling, and corking, as well as the invention of the corkscrew, returned Bordeaux wines to the forefront. Dutch merchants played a major role in the comeback of French wine, and Dutch engineers used technology originally developed to drain their lowlands to turn swampy marsh-lands in the Médoc region into prime vineyards.

On April 10, 1663, English diarist Samuel Pepys spent a night drinking with friends at the Royall Oak Tavern on London's Lombard Street. The next day he wrote in his diary about the experience and gave the world the first record of a named Bordeaux. Wrote Pepys: "Drank a sort of French wine, called Ho Bryan, that hath a good and most particular taste that I ever met with." That wine is known today as Château Haut-Brion—then as now one of Bordeaux's best.

Bordeaux wine brokers as early as 1647 began periodically categorizing wines on the basis of the prices they brought. The list changed from time to time, although four properties (Haut-Brion, Lafite, Latour, and Margaux) were almost always at the top and demanded similarly high prices. Each year wine brokers set the price for those top four and then the lower wines fell into place as a percentage of the highest rate.

Planners of the 1855 Great International Exhibition in Paris asked the Bordeaux Chamber of Commerce to select some of the region's wines to exhibit at the event. The chamber, in turn, passed the job on to a trade group called the Union of Brokers Attached to the Bordeaux Market, who selected the Grands Crus (Great Growths) and put them into five categories: 4 Premiers Crus (First Growths), 15 Deuxièmes Crus (Second Growths), 14 Troisièmes Crus (Third Growths), 10 Quatrièmes Crus (Fourth Growths), and 17 Cinquièmes Crus (Fifth Growths). The classification reflected earlier ones and was based solely on recent prices. The going rate for First Growth wines at the time was 3,000 francs per tun (a storage cask that held 252 gallons), while the Second Growth ranged from 2,500 to 2,700 francs, the Third from 2,100 to 2,400, the Fourth from 1,800 to 2,100, and the Fifth from 1,400 to 1,600.

White wines were also ranked in 1855. One of them, Yquem (not yet called Château d'Yquem), received a unique honor: Premier Cru Supérieur (Superior First Growth). Another 11 white wines were ruled First Growths and 12 Second Growths.

Although Bordeaux classifications had been created before and would be made later, the ones of 1855 moved into history. Only two changes have since been made. A few months after the original determination, Château Cantemerle was added as a Fifth Growth, bringing the number in that category to 18. Then in 1973, Château Mouton was moved from Second Growth to First Growth. The 1855 group remain the Hall of Fame of Bordeaux wines, and even Fifth Growth ones of not particularly high quality usually proudly note on their labels their heritage as "Grand Cru Classé en 1855." A French journalist taken hostage in Lebanon during the 1980s kept himself sane for three years by each day rattling off the names of all 61 classified red wines.

The 1855 rankings are no longer a totally valid reference for quality since at some vineyards the skills of winemakers now may be very different from what they once were. Other Bordeaux wines that were not part of the 1855 listing, such as Château Pétrus, are today considered to be equal to First Growths and can command premium prices. Since 1855, other regions within Bordeaux, such as St.-Émilion, have set up their own classifications so that their top wines could also command top prices. Some of these listings are updated regularly and often provide a better standard of current quality. Nonetheless, the 1855 Classification remains in a league of its own.

The greatest danger ever to face Bordeaux developed in the middle of the nineteenth century, in the form of a tiny yellow insect that killed the roots of grapevines. In 1862, a friend from New York State sent 154 Native American vines to a southern Rhône Valley winemaker in the hope that they would help eradicate a fungal parasite then causing problems for French winemakers. The vines inadvertently carried aphids that reproduced and spread quickly. From the Rhône the disease began spreading north, reaching Bordeaux in 1869. From France it soon migrated over all of Western Europe. In the 1870s it spread through French vineyards at a rate of forty miles a year. French wine production fell by 75 percent, and the end of European wine seemed to be in sight.

The French set up a commission to study the disease, which the chief scientist named *phylloxera vastatrix,* and which was shortened to simply phylloxera. Every conceivable method was used, without success, to kill the insects and protect vines. Eventually researchers at France's University of Montpellier discovered that native American vines were immune to the disease. At an 1881 conference in Bordeaux, the scientists showed that French vines grafted onto American rootstock not only resisted phylloxera but also produced good wine. By the end of the century more than two-thirds of French vines were being grown on American rootstock, and the epidemic was over.

The first half of the twentieth century in France was dominated by the two world wars, which had a major impact on French wine, especially the second, when Germans occupied much of the country and controlled the business. Both wars disrupted world wine trade and encouraged new production in countries like the United States, Australia, and New Zealand.

After the end of World War II, however, Bordeaux quickly regained its prewar prestige. Starting in the late 1960s, international wine consumption, especially in the affluent American and Japanese markets, picked up, and the new wine drinkers loved their Bordeaux. The great red wines, especially the First Growths, were considered by all to be the apex of international red winemaking.

The world's most highly regarded white wine at the time was also French. It was grown further north and almost on the other side of the country in Burgundy. Red wines from Burgundy, which are made from Pinot Noir grapes, have a large and devoted following, and some connoisseurs think no wine is better than a velvety Richebourg, Musigny, or Echézeaux. Napoléon's favorite wine was Chambertin, another Pinot Noir. As he said, "Nothing makes the future so rosy as to contemplate it through a glass of Chambertin." Burgundy's white wines, though, have long been considered without equal. The French novelist Alexandre Dumas spoke for many wine drinkers through the ages when he said that Montrachet, one of the great Chardonnays, should be sipped only while kneeling and with head bowed.

The largest and most famous area of Burgundy is the Côte d'Or or Golden Slope, a string of vineyards that stretches just over thirty miles south from Dijon, a city that gives its name to a spicy mustard, to Maranges, a little-known *appellation* just south of the village of Santenay. All told, the vineyards of the Côte d'Or cover about fourteen thousand acres.

The Côte d'Or is divided into two parts, the northern Côte de Nuits and the southern Côte de Beaune. The Côte de Nuits produces mainly red wines, and the famous village Gevrey-Chambertin is located there. The Côte de Beaune, which begins just east of the city of Beaune, makes twice as much wine as the Côte de Nuits, more than half of it white. The vineyards carry some of the most famous and honored names in white wine, such as Meursault, Puligny, and Chassagne. They are all similar and of high quality, but changes in the soil and climate give each its distinctive characteristics.

As in all of Burgundy, the vineyards of the Côte de Beaune are divided into small parcels of land called *climats,* which are usually owned by many different growers. There are few *châteaux* or large estates in Burgundy of the kind found in Bordeaux.

The classifications of Burgundy wines are even more complicated than those of Bordeaux. While Bordeaux has 57 *appellations,* Burgundy has 110 in an area only one-fifth as large. It has its own classification system dating back to 1861, which was done for another Paris world's fair in 1862. The Comité d'Agriculture de Beaune, Burgundy's wine capital, asked Dr. Jules Lavalle to select the Têtes de Cuvée (Outstanding Wines). He ranked them as Grands Crus (Great Growths) and Premiers Crus (First Growths).

The Burgundian classification, which has changed over the years, was never as influential as that of Bordeaux, in part because it included so many wines—now 33 Grands Crus and 562 Premiers Crus. A Grand Cru wine carries just the name of the vineyard where it is grown; for example, Corton or Montrachet. A name of a slightly lower-grade Premier Cru gives both the village and the vineyard where it was grown, such as Pernand Vergelesses (the village) Sous Frétille (the vineyard). A third grade, Appellation Communale, has 45 *appellations* and uses the village name. Examples include Santenay and Chassagne-Montrachet. The fourth or regional level, has 21 *appellations* and gives simply a broad regional name such as Bourgogne (Burgundy) or Côte de Beaune.

The nomenclature of Burgundy wines is still more complicated because many villages have hyphenated their names to include that of their most famous vineyard. There is a great difference in both quality and price between a Chevalier-Montrachet, which is made from just one vineyard, and a Chassagne-Montrachet, which comes from anywhere in a village of that name.

The history of wine in Burgundy began with the start of trade between the Gauls and the Romans in the fourth century BC, when the Romans were shipping wine into the beer-drinking area. The Greek historian Diodorus of Sicily wrote in the first century BC that the Gauls "gorge themselves on what the wine merchants bring them, without cutting it with water. And since their passion pushes them to use this beverage in all its violence, they get drunk and fall asleep or into states of delirium."

Eventually grapes for winemaking were grown in Burgundy, and Roman wine was soon losing its market. So the Emperor Domitian in the year 92 decreed that half of Gaul's vineyards had to be ripped up. The decree fortunately was never carried out.

With the fall of the Roman Empire in the fifth century came waves of barbarians from the north and east. The Burgondes, who arrived from the shores of the Baltic, pushed out the Romans but ruled only a century before being ousted by the Franks, who dominated the area until the death of Charlemagne in 814. According to tradition, Charlemagne owned a vineyard on the Côte d'Or that had been planted at the point on the hill where the snow melted fastest, which meant it got the most sunshine. This is the famed Corton-Charlemagne vineyard, which still produces one of the world's most sought-after white wines.

Just as the English have long strongly influenced Bordeaux wine, the Catholic Church for centuries dominated winemaking in Burgundy. During the ninth and tenth centuries, Burgundy was a duchy under the Capetian kings of France and also a bastion of Christianity, with the founding of the Benedictine Abbey of Cluny and the Cistercian abbeys of Cîteaux and Clairvaux. Wine was important for the religious ceremonies of the monks and soon also became the foundation of their great fortunes. As the abbeys grew in size and power, so did their vineyards. The abbey of Cîteaux, south of Dijon, owned the famous Clos de Vougeot vineyard and many others. The monks also developed pruning, and other viticulture techniques that spread throughout the region.

In the fourteenth and fifteenth centuries, the dukes of Burgundy encouraged wine production and profited greatly from their vineyards. Among the many titles the dukes gave themselves was "Lords of the Greatest Wines in Christianity."

In 1395 Duke Philip the Bold set out rules to govern Burgundy's vineyards. He limited wine varietals to Pinot Noir and Chardonnay and prohibited the use of the local variety of Gamay, which he described as "a bad and disloyal plant." That ruling had little lasting effect, and Burgundy's famous Beaujolais wine is made from Gamay grapes. Philip also outlawed the use of certain fertilizers, including "horns, hoofs, and animal carcasses." He mandated severe pruning of the vines to limit grape production and set the exact time of harvest. A sworn inspector also had to confirm a wine's origin. So severe were the controllers that Philip's wife, Marguerite, Duchess of Flanders, who had her personal vineyard, was refused the right to brand her casks with the coveted *B* for Burgundy.

When the Dukes of Burgundy dynasty fell in 1477, the French King Louis XI appropriated many of the vineyards for himself and distributed the rest among his entourage. Burgundy wines got a big boost when Louis XIV's personal physician prescribed Burgundy as a remedy for his majesty's artery ailments. Ever since, French doctors have been prescribing wine for whatever ails you.

After the French Revolution of 1789, properties owned by the churches, abbeys, and nobles were seized and divided into small plots that were spread among many owners. The Napoléonic legal system, which parceled out property among all of a person's heirs, rather than just giving it to the oldest male as did the English primogeniture laws, resulted in further division. Despite recent land consolidation, the average holding in Burgundy today is only fifteen acres, which is the primary reason the best Burgundy wines are both rare and expensive. Clos de Vougeot, a red wine vineyard of just 125 acres, has nearly eighty owners. Because of this extreme fragmentation, the way in which each winemaker produces a particular Meursault or Puligny-Montrachet can be as important as the soil and the weather. That, in turn, leads to great differences in the quality of wines with very similar names.

With ownership so widely spread, *négociants* (wine brokers), who bought wine from many growers, blended it, and then sold it under their own names, dominated the Burgundy wine business starting in the eighteenth century. Most of the *négociants,* including Jadot and Bouchard Père et Fils, remain fixtures of the wine trade there today.

In the late nineteenth century, phylloxera hit Burgundy's vineyards, just as it did those of Bordeaux. The Montpellier solution of grafting local vines onto American rootstock, however, also stopped the infestation in Burgundy.

Because the wine-growing area is so small and the wine in such demand, Burgundy has suffered even more than Bordeaux from unscrupulous wine traders. Lesser wines from southern France and North Africa were often blended with a little true Burgundy and given a Burgundy label. The adoption of the strict Appellation d'Origine Contrôlée system in 1935, though, protected the reputation of the best Burgundy wines, making it much harder to pass off inferior ones.

A major change in Burgundy after World War II was the widespread use of the Bordeaux-style estate bottling. Rather than selling their wines in bulk to *négociants* or in barrels to restaurants, the more prestigious wineries started to control the bottling and marketing of their wines. Burgundy's famous Domaine de la Romanée-Conti had long bottled its own wine, but by the 1960s all of the great vineyards of Burgundy followed its lead.

If the world had a favorite white wine in the middle of the twentieth century, it was Burgundy Chardonnay. Consumers loved its buttery richness, and winemakers everywhere tried to match it. At its best, a Burgundy Chardonnay has a golden hue, which set the international gold standard for white wine.

The world's view of wine at that time can be seen in the itinerary of the seven-month tour Steven Spurrier made in 1965 on behalf of Christopher's, his employer and London's oldest wine merchant. Spurrier spent three months in Bordeaux, two months in Burgundy, one week in the Rhône Valley, three weeks in Germany, and one week each in Champagne, the Loire Valley, and Alsace. Then after a summer break, he went to watch the harvests in Jerez, Spain, for Sherry and Oporto, Portugal, for Port. Interestingly, he did not go to Italy at all, and only to Spain and Portugal to check out the fortified wines.

Hugh Johnson confirmed this view of the wine world in 1971 in the first edition of his *World Atlas of Wine*. In this book, France towers over the wine business like the Colossus of Rhodes, the giant bronze statue that was a wonder of the ancient world and stood at the entrance of the harbor on the Mediterranean island of Rhodes. Calling France "the undisputed mistress of the vine," Johnson wrote that it produced "infinitely more and more varied great wines than all the rest of the world."

The French section in the first edition of the *World Atlas of Wine* took up 73 of the book's 247 pages of text. German white wines got 23 pages, while Italy got just 13 pages, and Spain, including Sherry, only 10. The New World, on the other hand, received just 24 pages. Johnson gave 8 pages to California wines. The atlas had only 6 pages on Australian wine and just 2 on the whole of South America. New Zealand was not even mentioned, although a British missionary planted the first vineyard there in 1819.

Johnson and Spurrier's bosses were not simply being Eurocentric. They viewed the wine landscape at the time accurately; France ruled the world of wine.

CHAPTER THREE

The New Eden

Wine is sure proof that God loves us and wants us to be happy.
—BENJAMIN FRANKLIN

The saga began a millennium ago. The year was 1000 or perhaps 1001, and the place was somewhere about 400 miles west of Greenland. A group of explorers came ashore from long, narrow sailing ships with carved dragonheads on their bows. Their leader was Leif Eriksson, the son of Erik the Red. Standing out among the blond and blue-eyed seamen was Eriksson's foster father, Tyrker, a small and dark-complected German. Eriksson ordered his men to build a camp and divided them into two groups. Each day one group went out exploring, while the other stayed in camp.

One day the exploring group returned one man short. Tyrker had wandered off and become separated from the others. After reprimanding his men, Eriksson and several others set out to find him. They had gone only a short distance when they saw Tyrker running toward them. He was speaking German excitedly, which none of them understood, and waving something in his hands. Finally he calmed down enough to tell them in their language that he had found a place where wild wine grapes were growing. He knew what he was talking about, he said, because wine grapes were abundant in parts of his native country. The next day a large group returned with Tyrker to the place where the wild grapes grew. Eriksson was so impressed that he named the new land Vineland or Wineland, and the explorers took vines with them when they returned home.

That tale has been repeated by generations of Norsemen to their children. No matter what really happened so long ago, Europeans since the earliest days of exploration of the Western Hemisphere were always astounded by the array of wild grapes they found. Surely, they thought, this must be a perfect place to produce wine as good as, if not better than, that produced in Europe.

A century after Columbus, Giovanni da Verrazano, the Italian explorer, wrote in 1592 of the North Carolina coast he had passed: "Many vines growing naturally, which growing up, took hold of the trees as they do in Lombardy, which if by husbandmen they were dressed in good order, without all doubt they would yield excellent wines."

Captain John Smith in 1612 reported back to England: "[There is] a great abundance [of vines] in many parts . . . Of these hedge grapes we made nearly twenty gallons of wine, which was like our British wine, but certainly they would prove good were they well manured." The new colony of Virginia in 1619 promulgated a law that every man had to plant and maintain ten vines. Later every man over twenty years of age had to plant twenty vines a year. In the Massachusetts Bay Colony, wine from local grapes was made in 1630, the first summer of colonization. In 1680, a group of Huguenots, French Protestants, landed in South Carolina, intending to make wine there.

All the attempts at using local grapes to produce wine in colonial America, however, failed. The Europeans named the wild vines Fox grapes because of their foul aroma and taste. Wine made with the grapes was sour and spoiled easily. Barrels of Fox wine sent back to England were dismissed with disdain.

Gradually the colonists gave up on making wine from native grapes, but that was not the end of their attempts to produce wine. They imported European vines, believing that since those produced good wine in Europe they would do even better in the rich American soil. European vines from the grape species *Vitis vinifera,* however, could not survive in the eastern United States. They grew for a couple of years but then soon succumbed to fungus, mildew, or other diseases.

Nonetheless, the quest for American wine continued. During the seventeenth and eighteenth centuries, Americans attempted to produce wine in every part of the country. Wine was made in New York, both upstate and on Long Island. Georgia had its wine period, and Pennsylvania farmers also took a crack at making it. New types of grapes temporarily encouraged winemakers, who often had strong European backgrounds in their craft, to believe that they had finally found the secret to making good wine in America. They were all disappointed.

The most dedicated wine aficionado of this period was Thomas Jefferson, who became a connoisseur while he was the new government's envoy to Paris from 1784 to 1789. Jefferson saw wine as an alternative to corn liquor or other high-alcohol drinks, which were widely consumed in the colonies, often to excess. Wrote Jefferson: "No nation is drunken where wine is cheap; and none sober, where the dearness of wine substitutes ardent spirits as the common beverage. It is, in truth, the only antidote to the bane of whiskey."

During his five years in France, Jefferson enjoyed many glasses of France's best wines and also traveled to the major wine growing areas of Europe. "Good wine is a daily necessity for me," he wrote in a letter to his friend John Jay, the Foreign Secretary in the pre-Constitution government. When Jefferson was about to return to the United States in 1789, he sent ahead what he described to Jay as "samples of the best wines of this country, which I beg leave to present to the President and yourself, in order that you may decide whether you would wish to have any, and which of them for your own tables hereafter." Jefferson shipped home 38 bottles of Meursault, 60 bottles of Sauternes, 36 bottles of Montrachet, 36 bottles of Champagne, 60 bottles of Rochegude, and 58 bottles of Frontignan.

Back in America, Jefferson became the new country's first Secretary of State, a good position from which to continue his love affair with wine. He sent detailed instructions to the U.S. Consul in Bordeaux about the kinds and amounts of wines to send President Washington and himself.

Jefferson in 1801 became the young country's third president and moved into the White House. He spent $7,597 on wine during this first term—an enormous amount since his annual salary, including money for entertaining, was only $25,000. During his eight years as president Jefferson bought more than twenty thousand bottles of European wine. His favorites: Yquem, Chambertin, and Champagne. Jefferson, acting very much like the nation's sommelier-in-chief, calculated that a bottle of Champagne at official events would serve exactly three and one-seventh people.

Jefferson long dreamed of making wine at his beloved Monticello estate in rural Virginia. He conducted many experiments there, attempting to grow both European and native American vines. In 1807, he planted 287 vines from twenty-four European varietals. Later he cultivated two native American varietals: *Vitis labrusca,* the Fox grape, and *Vitis rotundifolia,* Muscadine. Jefferson, though, had no more success than the other would-be American vintners.

While attempts to make wine on the East Coast were failing, efforts in the Midwest in the early part of the nineteenth century had a little more success. Starting in the 1810s Nicholas Longworth produced a number of wines in the Cincinnati region using Catawba grapes. He also tried growing European vines, but they quickly died.

It was on the West Coast, though, that American vintners had their first real success. There again the first hope was that the abundant native grapes could be used. On July 3, 1769, Junípero Serra, a Franciscan priest, wrote back to a religious superior in Mexico to report on the area around San Diego, where he was to establish a mission: "We found vines of large size, and in some cases quite loaded with grapes." Father Serra looked carefully at the area's wine potential because wine plays a central role in Roman Catholic religious services and the missions would have to make their own. The Franciscan missionaries eventually established twenty-one church settlements—and vineyards—along 650 miles of a coastal road they called El Camino Real. The northernmost mission, San Francisco Solano, was north of San Francisco Bay in what is now the city of Sonoma.

Just as on the East Coast, however, the native vines produced poor quality wines. Because of its temperate, Mediterranean climate, however, Europe's *Vitis vinifera* grapes grew well in California. The Spanish padres had success, in particular, with a vine called Mission, which is of unknown origin and had been brought to California from Mexico and probably originated in Spain. Mission grapes remained a mainstay of California wine for the next century and a half. The Franciscan chain of missions and their accompanying vineyards were thriving in 1833, when the Mexican government took over church lands in an attempt to break the church's secular power. Soon after, the mission vineyards were abandoned.

Joseph Chapman of Massachusetts started the first commercial winery in California in 1826, planting four thousand vines in Los Angeles. The Frenchman Jean Louis Vignes soon followed with the city's second vineyard, this time using French vines. Vignes's wines gained a reputation for quality, and he bravely proclaimed that someday California wines might rival those of his native France. Vignes sent a barrel of his wine to France's King Louis Philippe in 1842 via a visiting French sea captain, but it was destroyed in transport.

While southern California produced large quantities of wine, the northern part of the state turned out better-quality, lighter wines that resembled those made in France. The native Indians called the area that would later be known as the Napa Valley the "land of abundance" because everything grew so easily there. George Yount, the first white settler in the Napa Valley, received a land grant of 11,814 acres from Mexican authorities and moved there in 1836. Two years later, he planted the first grapevines in the valley.

California throughout its history has been a land for dreamers and schemers, acting as a magnet for people who wanted to discover a place of easy wealth. The gold rush starting in 1849 attracted thousands of people from all parts of the world. At the end of 1848, only an estimated 14,000 non-Indians lived in California; four years later they numbered 224,000. The gold rush also helped create a moneyed class in nearby San Francisco, which was soon demanding the good things of life—including wine.

On March 10, 1852, a member of the U.S.-Mexican Boundary Commission visited the Napa Valley and was amazed at the lush vegetation he saw in this earthly paradise. He later wrote these impressions: "The hills on both sides as well as the valley were covered with a luxurious growth of wild oats, and immense herds of cattle were roaming about feasting on them. Wild flowers of varied hues were thickly scattered around."

If he had recognized it, the commission member could also have noted that the valley's soil, climate, and topography are almost ideal for growing wine grapes. The valley had been formed several million years ago by the collision of the North American and Pacific plates, which caused numerous earthquakes and volcanic eruptions. The area's still active geysers and hot springs are remnants of past geothermal action. All that geological turmoil created soils rich in minerals and sediment. The two sides of the valley are made up of oceanic crust that had thrust its way toward the sky. Some of the most complex land is found in the alluvial fans, where streambeds come down from the hills and spread out onto flatter land.

By the mid-1850s winemaking was booming in northern California. And even then, California winemakers were boasting that they could produce wines as good as those made in France. On February 2, 1854, San Francisco's *Alta California* newspaper wrote glowingly about George Yount's wine, saying, "[It] bears a good deal of resemblance to the Bordeaux wines . . . [W]ith more age, and, perhaps, a little better management, [it] would equal the best French wines."

Among the newcomers arriving in California were a large number of Europeans. After failing to make their fortunes in the gold fields, some turned to wine in the nearby Napa and Sonoma counties. Englishman John Patchett built Napa Valley's first real winery, a stone structure, in 1859. German immigrants Charles Krug and the brothers Jacob and Frederick Beringer also settled in the Napa Valley and started wineries.

The most flamboyant winemaker of the day was Agoston Haraszthy, who had come from Hungary to California via Wisconsin, where he had first tried to make wine. After those vines failed, he moved to the West Coast in 1849, first stopping in San Diego, where he was elected sheriff. Haraszthy soon traveled north, eventually buying 560 acres in Sonoma County, and in 1857 established the Buena Vista winery, a Roman-style villa that fit perfectly with a promoter who had a lot of P. T. Barnum in him. Haraszthy was variously called Count and Colonel, but deserved neither title.

Despite his extravagant style, Haraszthy helped bring California wines to their first flowering. In 1858, he wrote for the state legislature a "Report on Grapes and Wines in California," the first treatise on the subject. Haraszthy was an outspoken advocate of improving the quality of California viticulture by using better grapes. Vintners still largely depended on the lowly Mission grape, but Haraszthy argued that California wine would not achieve its full potential until winemakers began using Europe's best grapes. Haraszthy also advocated blending wines in the European style to smooth them out and help them achieve more complex flavors.

Governor John Downey in 1861 appointed Haraszthy to make a trip to Europe, asking him to research "the ways and means best adapted to promote the improvement and growth of the grapevine in California." The governor simply wanted a report, but Haraszthy had other ideas. Using Paris as a base, he roamed the Continent from Spain to Germany, spending most of his time buying vine cuttings to plant when he got back to California. He later claimed to have collected 100,000 vines from 1,400 varieties. The numbers were undoubtedly inflated, but Haraszthy had nonetheless opened California to new and better varieties of vines. In his report he advocated many of the things that in later years helped develop California wine, including the establishment of state agricultural experiment stations for viticulture research.

Novelist Robert Louis Stevenson in his short 1883 book *The Silverado Squatters* gave a colorful description of California wine at the time. He began the chapter entitled "Napa Wines" by lamenting the phylloxera-caused disaster in French vineyards: "Bordeaux is no more, and the Rhône a mere Arabia Petraea. Château Neuf is dead, and I have never tasted it; Hermitage—a hermitage indeed from all life's sorrows—lies expiring by the river . . . It is not Pan only; Bacchus, too, is dead." The future of viticulture for the entire world, Stevenson wrote, would be "decided by Californian and Australian wines." He thought, though, that California would not be ready for a while. "Wine in California is still in the experimental stage," he wrote. "Bit by bit they grope about for their Clos Vougeot and Lafite." Nonetheless, Stevenson liked what he tasted, writing, "The wine is bottled poetry."

In the 1870s and early 1880s, many immigrants and wealthy businessmen from San Francisco moved into the Napa and Sonoma valleys, anticipating that California would soon become the vineland of the phylloxera-ravaged world. In 1880 there were 49 wineries in the Napa Valley; six years later 175.

One of the newcomers was Gustave Niebaum, a Helsinki-born fur trader who had made a fortune in Alaska. He bought the land that would become the Inglenook estate in the Napa Valley town of Oakville and turned it into California's first world-class winery.

The California wine boom, however, came to an abrupt end in the late-1880s, after Europeans saved their vineyards by grafting their vines onto

phylloxera-resistant American rootstock. Following the comeback of French
wine, California was left with lost potential markets, dashed dreams, and
a huge surplus of wine. Soon wineries were closing.

Partially in appreciation for the role the U.S. played in saving French vineyards from phylloxera, the French invited California vintners to send samples of their wines to the 1889 World's Fair in Paris. To everyone's surprise
the American wines, in particular those from the Napa Valley, did very well
in competition with French wines. California wineries won 34 awards for
their wines, brandy, and sparkling wine, with Napa Valley wineries picking
up 20 prizes, including 4 golds.

It was a high point for Napa Valley wines, but it also marked the beginning of a long and steady decline. During the next forty years California
wine was hit with a series of natural and man-made calamities.

First came natural disasters—severe frosts and a California outbreak of
phylloxera, which wiped out vineyards planted with European cuttings and
required massive and expensive replanting. Then in 1893 came a depression,
after a sell-off of stocks turned into a financial panic. Thousands of businesses were forced to close, and many banks failed. Wealthy San Francisco
businessmen were drinking less wine and also leaving the wine business.

On April 18, 1906, the great San Francisco earthquake hit at 5:12 a.m.
Both the tremor and the resulting economic troubles were felt fifty miles
north in wine country. San Francisco was the center for blending and shipping wine as well as the financial capital of northern California. Wine stored
in cellars was lost when barrels and bottles broke or were crushed. The California Wine Association, a recently founded group that owned more than
fifty wineries, alone lost 10 million gallons, and the total amount that per-
ished is estimated to have reached 30 million gallons.

The most devastating development, though, was man-made. Ever since
colonial days, the U.S. had been a hard-drinking country. But in the early
twentieth century a movement to ban alcohol gathered strength, and one by
one states began outlawing its production and consumption. Beer and wine
producers tried in vain to distinguish their lower-alcohol drinks from hard
liquor, but the difference between wine with 12 percent alcohol and
whiskey with 50 percent was lost on those who wanted to ban any and all
intoxicating beverages.

Following the ratification of the Eighteenth Amendment to the U.S.
Constitution in 1919, national Prohibition officially started on January 16,
1920. Millions of gallons of California wine in storage or aging barrels was
shipped abroad, having to be on board and out of port before January 16.
Both the Drys, those favoring Prohibition, and the Wets, who opposed it,

held large celebrations to mark the end of one era and the beginning of a new. At the time 700 wineries were operating in the U.S., with 120 of them in the Napa Valley. Most people in the wine trade thought that the "noble experiment," as President Herbert Hoover called Prohibition, would be short-lived and that they would soon be back in business.

The Volstead Act, the enabling legislation for the Eighteenth Amendment, had a few loopholes that allowed limited wine production. Wine, for example, could be produced for religious and medicinal purposes, and the male head of a household could get a permit to make two hundred gallons per year for the family's own use.

Eventually some fifty wineries produced sacramental wine. The most successful was Beaulieu Vineyard, which not only survived but also prospered during Prohibition. The winery, located just south of Rutherford, had been founded by Georges de Latour, a wealthy Frenchman whose family winery in France's Périgord region had been wiped out by phylloxera. He came to the U.S. in 1883 and in 1899 began buying land to start his own winery. De Latour acquired property next to Gustave Niebaum's Inglenook, following the belief that good wine property is usually located right next to good wine property. De Latour, a leading figure of the Catholic community in San Francisco, was able to obtain endorsements from the religious hierarchy for the wine he sold to churches all around the country. Beaulieu stationery of the day proudly proclaimed it was "The House of Altar Wine."

Making wine at home was an old tradition among immigrants, especially Italians who came to the United States in large numbers in the early 1900s. The amateur production of wine picked up as early as 1915 in anticipation of Prohibition and exploded after it became law. University of California agricultural experts estimated that homemade wine production increased from 4 million gallons in 1915 to 90 million gallons in 1925. This first led to sharply higher prices for both grapes and farmland and then to overplanting and finally to the crash of grape and land prices.

Ingenious businessmen developed ways to get raw materials to home winemakers. Grape juice and concentrate were sold under names like Forbidden Fruit, Vine-Glo, and Moonmist, which often carried very specific instructions on their containers about how to turn the product into wine. Other instructions took the form of negative warnings: "Do not place container in room with a temperature over 60 degrees or contents may ferment." In some parts of the country, trained winemakers made house calls to start the fermentation of grape juice into wine.

The quality of homemade wine left many consumers yearning for a bottle of Inglenook, California's best pre-Prohibition wine. An author in the

December 1928 issue of *Harper's* magazine wrote: "There are probably few Italian-American families that do not make their own wine; but the wine they make, as a rule, can be endured only by stomachs toughened by a racial experience of hardships dating back to the Punic Wars."

Frank Schoonmaker and Tom Marvel in their 1941 classic *American Wines* wrote: "Unquestionably, most of the homemade wine of the Prohibition era was bad; it was produced by people who knew little about wine making, and less about grapes." Years later Ernest Gallo, cofounder of the Gallo wine empire, told a meeting of enologists, "Some of you may remember what homemade wine was—something like grape juice in December and something like vinegar in June."

Homemade wine had a deleterious effect on the types of grapes being grown. High-quality wine grapes like Cabernet Sauvignon do not travel well because they have thin skins and are easily damaged in transport. Home winemakers wanted large, thick-skinned grapes that could survive long railroad trips across the country. And since their wine was often watered down, home winemakers needed grapes that produced very dark juice that would still be red after being diluted.

As a result, farmers pulled out quality vines and planted hardier ones like Alicante Bouschet, the preferred shipping grape. A 1933 guide for home vintners described Alicante Bouschet as "a beautiful grape which yields a coarse wine." A minor wine grape before 1915, it became a major one just before and during Prohibition, with its acreage going from 4,394 before 1915 to 29,321 in 1940. Wine made with the similar Alicante Ganzin grapes was supposedly so dark that it could be used to paint a barn.

Many northern California farmers simply gave up on grapes, pulling out vines and planting plums for making prunes, walnuts, cherries, or other fruit that also grew well in the area's rich soil and wonderful climate. By 1926, the acreage of plums under cultivation in the Napa Valley exceeded that of grapes.

As Prohibition continued, more and more California wineries closed, with the number dropping from some 700 before Prohibition to only 130 shortly before Repeal. That did not stop Americans from drinking wine. Consumption more than doubled during Prohibition, going from 60 million gallons annually to 150 million gallons in the supposedly dry years.

After fourteen years of the "noble experiment," Prohibition ended on December 5, 1933. The parties to celebrate the end were even bigger than those thrown to start it. Martin Ray, a winemaker who had worked for Paul Masson, one of California's biggest producers, had been forced into stock trading in the dry years. In expectation of Repeal he bought a huge bronze bell from an old schoolhouse that was being torn down and hauled it to the Santa Cruz Mountains south of San Francisco where Masson lived. On the morning of Repeal, Masson woke to the pealing of the giant bell. He struggled into his clothes and staggered outside, where he saw Ray enthusiastically ringing in the new era. Turning to one of his employees, Masson, a Frenchman from Beaune who never could understand why Americans had outlawed wine, said with emotion, "When I hear that big bell I really know it is true. Good old days return now, no? I always said Prohibition was so absurd that damned if I'd ever let it outlive me."

Immediately after Repeal quick-buck businessmen reopened old wineries or started new ones in an expectation that there would be an explosion of demand for wine. There wasn't, and many of them just as quickly closed. In 1934, California had 804 operating wineries, 100 more than before Prohibition, but a decade later only 465.

American winemaking came out of Prohibition in terrible shape. Many talented winemakers and their skills had died during the fourteen dry years. Most of the surviving wineries were run-down, and farmers were growing the wrong kind of grapes for quality wine.

Worst of all, Prohibition had changed America's taste in wine. Consumers now demanded basically two types of wine, and both of them were of extremely low quality. They did not command high prices and could not provide the profits winemakers needed to pay for new vineyards and equipment. The first type was dry table wine nicknamed dago red after Italian producers who made much of it. Sold in large jug bottles and drunk largely by immigrants, it was also called jug wine. The other kind was fortified, sweet wine sold as Port, Sherry, or Muscatel, although they bore little resemblance to European wines with the same names. These were popular with winos because of their low price and high 20 percent alcohol. Before Prohibition dry wines outsold sweet dessert wines three to one, but afterward the figures more than reversed. In 1935 sweet wines made up 81 percent of total California wine production. As a result of the shift in demand, wine's center of gravity also moved from Napa and Sonoma counties south to the hotter and drier Central Valley, where both dago red and sweet wines flourished.

The American wine business in the post-Repeal years was controlled not by California winemakers but by East Coast and Midwest bottlers. About 90 percent of wine was sold in bulk and shipped east, often in railroad tank cars, where it was bottled and marketed under a myriad of local names. As late as the early 1960s, even the renowned Beaulieu Vineyard was still shipping wine east in barrels to distributors in cities like Cleveland and New York.

In the years after Prohibition, however, professors from the University of

California led a relentless crusade to improve the quality of American wine. The 1887 Pure Wine Law had directed the University of California to undertake research on winemaking, although it was many years before money was appropriated to set up a separate agricultural research center in Davis, a town near Sacramento, the state capital.

The most important research at Davis was done by professors Albert J. Winkler and Maynard Amerine, who in the late 1930s started trying to determine which grape varietals did best in California. The professors based their conclusions on studies of some 3,000 different wine samples. In 1944, they published their conclusions in *Hilgardia,* an agricultural research magazine, under the title "Composition and Quality of Musts and Wines of California Grapes." The study divided California into five climate regions and recommended the best grapes for each zone. They determined, for example, that the Yountville area in the Napa Valley was similar in temperature to the Bordeaux region of France and would be a good area for growing Cabernet Sauvignon, while the cooler Russian River Valley region of Sonoma County was more like the Côte d'Or section of Burgundy and would be well suited for cultivating Chardonnay and Pinot Noir.

The professors reached clear judgments and stated them boldly: the popular Alicante Bouschet grape received a "very poor quality" rating in all five regions. Cabernet Sauvignon, on the other hand, was the "variety of choice" for northern California, where it produced "very good quality" wine. Chardonnay grapes from the same region, wrote the professors, would produce "excellent quality" wine. Amerine and Winkler were not just theorists. They routinely tasted twenty or so wines each day before lunch and then another twenty after lunch. Amerine, though, once quipped, "Quality in wines is much easier to recognize than to define."

California grape growers and winemakers in the late 1940s recognized that their wines were inferior to the European ones they drank as points of comparison, but they didn't understand enough about their craft to know exactly why. As a result, they closely studied the "Composition and Quality" monograph and other studies from UC Davis with such titles as "Sulfur Dioxide and Metabisulfite in Wine Making" and "Clarification and Filtration of Wine." They also acted upon the professors' recommendations. Farmers who up to that point had planted grape types haphazardly began pulling out old vines and following the advice of Winkler and Amerine in their choice of new plantings. Winemakers also attended seminars and short courses at Davis, and a few full-time students made their way into the business after graduation. Gradually quality grapes began replacing the Prohibition ones in vineyards all across northern California.

World War II cut off the supply of European wines to America, which provided an unexpected opening for California wines in the large and important East Coast market, where most wealthy and sophisticated consumers lived. Respected producers like Inglenook and Beaulieu Vineyard, though, could not move fast enough to make inroads because it takes at least a decade for new vineyards to develop and for their wines to age.

In the nineteenth century German and French immigrants like Jacob Beringer and Charles Carpy dominated the California wine business. But after Prohibition and the new wave of immigrants from Southern Europe in the early twentieth century, Italian wine families took over leadership. Among them were the Martinis, the Mondavis, and the Petris.

The most powerful of the newcomers was the Gallo family in Modesto, about 120 miles south of the Napa Valley. The two Gallo brothers, Ernest, the marketer, and Julio, the production director, were a perfect match. According to legend, Ernest once told his brother, "I'll sell all the wine you can make." To which Julio replied, "I'll make all the wine you can sell." In the 1950s and 1960s upwards of 75 percent of the wine produced in California's Napa, Sonoma, and Mendocino counties was sold to Gallo and bottled under that brand. In the 1950s, Gallo's Thunderbird, a sickly sweet blend of lemonade and Port whose main attraction was that it produced a quick and cheap high, was the best selling wine in the country. While the brothers were best known for their jug wine, Gallo was also a leader in technological and production developments. The Gallo research laboratory was the best outside UC Davis. Gallo also invested heavily in equipment and built its own bottle manufacturing plant in 1958.

For the three decades after Prohibition, a small band of quality producers—Almaden, Beaulieu, Beringer, Christian Brothers, Inglenook, Krug, Martini, Paul Masson, and Wente—struggled to survive. The largest was Christian Brothers, which sold about a hundred thousand cases annually. They all depended on jug wines and sweet wines for most of their revenues. Sweet wine, for example, made up 80 percent of Beringer's production. All but Inglenook produced a line of jug wine. At the same time, though, these producers bravely continued to make small amounts of excellent table wine. But there was almost no market for it. Few American consumers were looking for good wines, and those who did drank European, mainly French. In the 1950s those top-of-the-line products made up only about 1 percent of California wine sales.

The most prestigious premium-wine producer in the Napa Valley at midcentury was Beaulieu Vineyard. Owner George de Latour liked California's land and climate, but everything else at his winery had a French accent. His daughter Hélène studied in France and married a French nobleman, Marquis Henri Galçerand de Pins, whose family also had a wine heritage. De Latour's staff was French or French-trained, and he regularly traveled to the Continent.

In 1938, Beaulieu's French winemaker retired, and so de Latour and his son-in-law headed to Paris to hire another French one. Among the people they contacted was Professor Paul Marsais at the Pasteur Institute, a research center in Paris. Marsais told de Latour that he had several good French winemakers but doubted that they would adapt well to a foreign environment like California. But he also had a Russian student who had lived in many countries and had been trained in France. Marsais thought he would work out better than any of the French.

The man was André Tchelistcheff, and he was indeed a quintessential cosmopolitan. Born on November 24, 1901, in Moscow, he traced his roots to German ancestors in the thirteenth century. During the Russian Revolution his family sided with the Whites who fought a civil war against Lenin's Communist Reds for control of the country. After the Reds won, the Whites became displaced people wandering Europe looking for a new home. Tchelistcheff first studied winemaking in the Tokay region of Hungary and then worked in the Kingdom of Serbs, Croats, and Slovenes, which was later renamed Yugoslavia.

In 1931, Tchelistcheff moved to France to further his wine studies. Growing up on the Russian family estate, he had drunk both French and Crimean wines. In fact, he got drunk at the age of eleven at a New Year's celebration, when he and his sister drank the remains of Mumm Red Monopole Champagne that revelers had left in their glasses. Tchelistcheff studied viticulture at the French Institute of National Agronomy and enology at the Pasteur Institute, where he impressed Professor Marsais. Tchelistcheff's first job in France was at the Moët & Chandon Champagne works in Épernay.

Tchelistcheff had his initial taste of California wine at an international exhibition in Paris in 1937, and he long remembered a Wente Brothers Sauterne from either 1932 or 1934. "All the Frenchmen, colleagues of mine, were just astounded that such a wonderful type of wine could be produced in California," he said later.

In view of the strong recommendation from Professor Marsais, de Latour interviewed and hired the diminutive Tchelistcheff, who was only four foot eleven inches. De Latour liked the fact that Tchelistcheff was a biochemist and thought he could help solve the problems Beaulieu Vineyard had been having with spoiled wines since the end of Prohibition. De Latour told Tchelistcheff about the shortcomings of California wine and even those of Beaulieu, allegedly one of California's finest wineries, but nothing prepared the Russian refugee for what he found when he arrived there in September 1938. The winery's equipment for pressing grapes and aging wines was badly out of date, and the vineyards were run-down. At the Pasteur Institute, Tchelistcheff had learned the importance of cleanliness around a living product like wine, and it was a shock for him to find a rat floating in a tank of Sauvignon Blanc at Beaulieu.

Georges de Latour died less than two years later, and after that Tchelistcheff worked mainly with Madame De Pins. While recognizing the need to improve the equipment at Beaulieu, she kept a tight hand on the purse strings, considering the winery a venture whose main purpose was to provide enough money for her and the marquis to maintain the lifestyle they enjoyed.

Nonetheless, Tchelistcheff was able to improve the quality of Beaulieu wines. In 1941, the year after Georges de Latour died, Tchelistcheff marketed the company's premium 1936 Cabernet Sauvignon as the Georges de Latour Private Reserve. The price was a then-high $1.50 a bottle. While it sold only modestly, for the next three decades that wine was considered the highest achievement of California winemaking.

Despite the best efforts by Beaulieu, Inglenook, and other premium producers, the American wine business in the 1950s was literally dying on the vine. The number of California wineries fell by more than one-third between 1950 and 1967. A national survey in 1956 showed that 85 percent of wine was being drunk by 15 percent of the population—and they were largely aging immigrants drinking jug wine and winos consuming sweet wine. Only a very small part of the population drank wine with meals, and when they wanted good wine, they looked to France.

Frank Prial, the long-time wine columnist of the *New York Times,* owns a 1945 wine list from the "21" club, the prestigious Manhattan restaurant then known as "Jack & Charlie's 21." It gives a vivid picture of the way Europe dominated American wine consumption at mid-century. The list contains hundreds of great wines from Germany, Hungary, Switzerland, but especially France. There was even a 1904 Château Margaux selling for $17.50. Only four California wineries—Beaulieu Vineyard, Inglenook, Louis M. Martini, and Wente Brothers—made the list. Even they were given descriptions that compared them to better-known French wines. A Wente Brothers Chardonnay, for example, was described as a "Burgundy type."

California wines had a long way to go.

PART TWO

———— ◆ ————

THE AWAKENING

In California, where the wine industry is of comparatively recent growth (a mere 200 years), really thrilling changes are taking place.

—HARRY WAUGH, 1969

CHAPTER FOUR

California Dreamer

Beer is made by men, wine by God.
—MARTIN LUTHER

The Greyhound bus pulled to a stop at the corner of Railroad and Adams streets in St. Helena, the heart of California's Napa Valley, one night in the middle of August 1958. It was just past 10:00 p.m. The only person to get off the bus was a thin man, about five foot, six inches tall and weighing some 130 pounds. He wore a black beret. His name was Mike Grgich, and he had been traveling by bus for more than a day, down the Pacific Coast from Vancouver, British Columbia, stopping in one small town after another. From the luggage compartment under the passenger area Grgich picked up two cardboard suitcases that contained everything in the world he owned—some clothes, books, and important papers like his birth certificate and university records, which were in Croatian and probably wouldn't be much help here. Grgich, though, kept in his coat pocket his most important document—his long-sought American visa.

After picking up his bags, Grgich spotted a pay phone and pulled out a piece of paper on which he had written the phone number of J. Leland (Lee) Stewart, the owner of Souverain Cellars, a small winery located on nearby Howell Mountain, on the eastern side of the Napa Valley. Grgich had put a position-wanted ad in the *Wine Institute Bulletin,* a newsletter, looking for a job as a winemaker. Stewart had answered the ad, offering him a job and agreeing to sponsor him for a permanent-resident visa.

When Grgich heard Souverain's phone ring, he held his breath. In his letter offering Grgich the job, Stewart had said to contact him as soon as he arrived in St. Helena so that he could come down and pick him up. But what if there had been some mistake? Perhaps he was supposed to be there next week—or last week! Perhaps Stewart was traveling. Perhaps he had changed his mind. Perhaps there wasn't a job! Grgich had suffered many setbacks in the four years since he left his native Croatia, then a part of

45

Communist-controlled Yugoslavia, on a student visa. If something didn't work out, it wouldn't be the first time in this long trek to California.

After a couple of rings, Grgich heard a gruff "Hello."

"This is Mike Grgich," said the new arrival in heavily accented English. "I'm supposed to start working at the Souverain Cellars. Are you Mr. Stewart?"

"Yes, I've been expecting you. But it's too late now for me to drive down to St. Helena and get you. Why don't you just go to a hotel, and I'll come and pick you up in the morning. You can find a hotel right near where you are."

Grgich said he understood, and Stewart repeated before hanging up that he'd pick him up in the morning.

Grgich looked out on the street. He had been dreaming of St. Helena for weeks, but now the real thing looked like all the other small towns he had passed through on the way from Vancouver. The few small shops were all closed.

Grgich saw a sign for the Gable Hotel and went over to it. The building was dark, so he knocked first on the door and then on the window next to it. No one answered.

"Maybe there is a night bell, and you have to ring it to get people to come down," Grgich thought to himself. "I should have arrived earlier. Then this wouldn't be happening, and Mr. Stewart would have picked me up."

Grgich walked around the hotel and looked in other windows. Everything appeared to be closed up tight. He knocked a few more times, and then waited and waited.

After a half-hour looking around the Gable Hotel, Grgich walked up to Main Street, where he saw a sign for the Hotel St. Helena. This building was also dark, except for a light shining downstairs. When he got to the light, Grgich saw it came from a bar, where a few people in groups of two or three were quietly talking.

Grgich went in and asked the bartender, "Do you have any rooms?"

"We have twenty-four rooms," he replied.

"Any empty?"

"We have twenty-four empty rooms."

"Can I get one of the rooms?"

"Two bucks. Go upstairs and take any room you want."

Grgich took out the American money he had gotten at a bank in Vancouver before his trip and paid the bartender two dollars. Then he picked up his suitcases, walked up the stairs, and opened the door of the first room at the top.

A long journey had taken Grgich from Desne, a village five miles from the Adriatic Sea, to St. Helena, a town forty-five miles from the Pacific Ocean.

Miljenko Grgich was born on April 1, 1923, into a peasant family in a rural Croatian village of about a thousand inhabitants. Wine had always been the centerpiece of his life. He was born the eleventh of eleven children, and since he was the last child his mother Ivka nursed him longer than she had the others. That made him feel special, but one day the two-and-a-half-year-old boy did something that made her angry and she snapped at him, "No more milk!"

The boy was crushed to lose his privileged position. Now he had to join the other family children and drink a mixture of water and wine called *bevanda*. Although his parents were illiterate, their folk wisdom had taught them that the combination was safe for the children to drink. The family's water came from rainwater collected from the roof into a small cistern. Ivka sanitized the water used for food during cooking, but there was no purification system for drinking water. Although the parents didn't realize it, wine sanitized their drinking water. As Miljenko learned later in college, ingredients in wine killed contaminants in the water, making *bevanda* safe to drink.

The Grgić family, like most others in the village, was virtually self-sufficient. They grew all their own vegetables, corn, and wheat and owned a few animals—horses plus cows and sheep that provided both milk and cheese. Ivka made clothes for the family from wool sheared from the sheep. There were also shoes made from the skins of animals they slaughtered. Skin of cows or pigs was used for soles, while the top was made of lamb skin.

Anyone in Desne who owned land set aside a plot for growing wine grapes. Croatia for centuries was a crossroads of Europe, and conquering Romans, Greeks, Hungarians, Italians, and others left behind their favorite grape varieties as they passed through. Miljenko later did his college thesis on Yugoslav grape varieties and found more than a hundred in use in Metković, the county where he grew up.

Wine was one of the Grgić family's few cash crops. They saved half the production for themselves, selling the other half to villagers who did not make wine. Wine was even the family medicine. If one of the Grgić children had the flu, Ivka would boil some red wine and add sugar to it. The concoction was painfully hot and often burned the inside of the child's mouth, but more often than not the next morning he or she felt better. Miljenko's father, Nikola, started his workday by gargling some *rakija*, a wine brandy.

As in any farm family in Desne, Miljenko went to work at an early age. When he was three his small feet were already crushing grapes at harvest time. The wine was fermented in a vat located in the basement of the family house. Starting at about the age of ten, when the grape juice was fermenting into wine, Miljenko would open a door in the floor above the cellar before he went to bed and lower himself into the vat by holding onto the sides. He would then stomp around to push down the crust of wineskins and seeds that had collected on the top. Breaking up the cap like that allowed carbon dioxide that developed during fermentation to escape. Then Miljenko would lift himself back up and get back into bed. First thing in the morning he would go through the procedure all over again.

The center of Grgić family life was the *ognjište,* the fireplace in front of which everything important took place. All food was cooked or baked there, and children were even born there because the fire provided the warmth Ivka needed during childbirth. At night the family gathered at the *ognjište* to talk and play. Father and mother passed along to their children the wisdom of the ages, much of it in the form of stories.

One of the greatest pleasures in young Miljenko's life was eating an egg cooked in the fireplace. Nikola would first put an egg into the hot coals and turn it round and round with a stick. The father would explain to his son that when the first drop of moisture appeared on the shell, the egg was almost ready, but the yolk was still too runny. Only when that drop evaporated and another drop appeared was the egg ready to eat. After putting Miljenko on his knee, Nikola would kiss him and then open the egg by knocking off the top with a knife. Finally, the father would take a piece of bread, dip it into the yolk, and give it to the boy. It would be delicious, and Miljenko never forgot the taste of the egg or his father's gentle kiss.

When he was about six years old, Miljenko had the chore of watching over the family's sheep. Before going to school he took them up to a nearby mountain and after school he brought them home. The best place to graze was on public land. So in the afternoon, after the government watchman had left, he often took his sheep there to forage. In the twilight when he guided the sheep back home, the animals were so full that they could hardly walk.

Religion played a very important part in the life of the Grgić family. They were Roman Catholic and always attended church on Sunday and holy days and regularly went to confession and communion. Just as the children never challenged their parents, no one ever doubted the village priest.

Miljenko was a good student, first attending primary school for four years in Desne. The education of most village youngsters ended there, but since the boy seemed eager to learn his mother sent him to the nearby town of Metković to stay with his sister, Stana, so he could get four more years of business schooling. After eight years of education and at the age of fourteen,

Miljenko got his first degree, the Mala Matura. Anyone with that much book learning was considered something of an intellectual, and that was enough education for a while.

A cousin, Srečko Grgić, had opened a general store in Desne, and Miljenko was put in charge of it. The shop, which was open seven days a week, sold everything from food to clothing. The boy still lived at home and helped each year with winemaking.

This pleasant, simple, and orderly life ended in 1939, when Miljenko was sixteen. The winds of war began blowing across Europe, and they were felt particularly intensely in the Balkans, where a ratatouille of rival ethnic groups had been fighting for centuries. The war provided another opportunity for them to restart the killing. Ethnic groups split into Fascist, Communist, Royalist, and pro-Western factions that battled each other for the next five years almost as much as they fought the occupying Germans and Italians.

In 1943, the Communists took control of the region around Desne and carted away everything from the store that Miljenko was still running. He then escaped to a neighboring village, which the Communists did not control. That same year Italy capitulated and the Italian army moved out of Dalmatia, but the German army soon moved in and started a brutal search for resistance fighters. German troops devastated Desne, destroying nearly every house in the village.

When the war ended in the spring of 1945, Miljenko had just turned twenty-two, and the Communists, led by Marshal Tito, controlled the country. The young man knew he wasn't going to do well there. He had seen what happened when Communists confiscated his cousin's store and had also read about what took place when they conquered other countries. During the Communist seizure of power he saw them steal anything of value from the peasants and kill two women. Miljenko, though, still had to make a life for himself. He could have become a Communist and gotten a government job, but his experience running the general store and books he had read about American businessmen like Henry Ford, John D. Rockefeller, Andrew Carnegie, and Thomas Edison had turned him against Communism.

Miljenko thought for a while about becoming a scientist. He knew that in the Soviet Union scientists enjoyed a somewhat better life because the Communists needed them. He also noticed that there was plenty of work for bookkeepers in the new Communist country to keep track of things in the heavily centralized economy. So a year after the war ended, Miljenko went to a business school in the town of Split to learn bookkeeping.

Life was tense in the Communist-controlled country. Once while studying in Split, he ran into someone he had known before the war who was
now a Communist and an officer in the Yugoslav army.

"What are you doing?" asked the old friend.

"I'm going to business school," answered Miljenko.

"Who gave you permission to do that? Only Communists can go to university." That, however, was not actually government policy.

After finishing his business studies, Miljenko worked for a year as a
bookkeeper of a state-owned co-op in Metković.

Wine, though, which he had been drinking since his mother stopped
providing breast milk, had a hold on him. During the war Miljenko had
seen wine become almost as valuable as gold. In bad times people drank
wine to forget their troubles. Winemaking, he concluded, was a trade
that would always serve him well. Miljenko had regretted pulling out
some grapevines at home in the early days of the war and replanting the land
with wheat, corn, and vegetables because his father thought food would be
more important than wine in the tough times ahead. It would have been
smarter, Miljenko thought, to have left the grapes, which the family could
have made into wine that could have been exchanged for food.

In 1949, Miljenko decided to study viticulture and enology at the University of Zagreb in the capital of Croatia. Only twelve students were
allowed each year into the program, but he thought that if he arrived at the
university early on the sign-up day, he might be able to get one of the coveted spots. Since he didn't have a bicycle, much less a car, and the streetcar
didn't start running until 5:30 a.m., Miljenko had to walk. He got up at
2:00 and walked the seven miles to the university with a friend. When they
arrived, the two found a woman already ahead of them. But no other students came until about 5:30, when the streetcars began to run. Soon a hundred students were vying for those twelve spots, but only the first twelve
students in line were accepted. The rest went home unhappy.

While studying in Zagreb, Miljenko also held down two jobs: one
working on genetic experiments to make new varieties of corn, wheat, and
other cereals; the second doing research on new varieties of fruit. He lived
far from the university in the center of Zagreb near the Opera House in a
tiny upstairs maid's room. The building was more than a hundred years old,
the rooms narrow and dark. His room had no heat, running water, or even
a table. In winter it was so cold and the light so poor that Miljenko often
studied in nearby cafés. He would order a glass of water and read from two
to six in the afternoon, when he had to leave because dinner customers
started arriving. For the first two years Miljenko took courses in general agri-

culture and such sciences as microbiology, climatology, and botany. During his second two years, he studied viticulture and enology.

It rained frequently and heavily in Zagreb, and Miljenko rode the streetcar to classes. One day he forgot his umbrella on the streetcar, but when he went to buy a new one he didn't have enough money, so instead he bought a beret to keep his head dry. He's been wearing a beret ever since.

During his last year at the university, Miljenko got into trouble when he joined a protest movement against the administration for firing a popular professor, Marko Mohaček, just two months short of full retirement. Mohaček had dared to voice complaints about Communism, and the firing reduced his pension by 25 percent. After the protest a friend told Miljenko, "Be careful. The secret police are following you." Grgić decided he had to leave Yugoslavia as soon as possible.

One day in early 1954, the life of the now thirty-one-year-old student changed. A professor at the University of Zagreb had just come back from a six-month sabbatical in California, and a group of students including Miljenko asked to meet with him to talk about life in the United States. They wanted to know what it was really like there. The Communist-controlled Yugoslav media reported regularly on how racial injustices and worker exploitation were rampant in the U.S., but people knew there was more to life in America than that propaganda.

"What does California look like? What is it like?" the students insistently asked.

The professor talked for a long time. At one moment almost in passing he said, "In California where there is no water, it's a desert. But where there's water, it's paradise." Paradise. The word echoed in Miljenko's mind that day and for years to come.

"And what about the farming equipment?" asked a student.

"Almost all farmers have a tractor," the professor replied. "But every five years they get a new one because the new model is so much better than the old one and more efficient."

"Everyone has a tractor!" the students said in disbelief.

Miljenko had been thinking of leaving Croatia for a while, and after the meeting with the professor he knew for sure that he wanted to go to California. An older sister, whom he had never met, had married a Croatian-American. They lived in the state of Washington, and their son was a Catholic priest. Perhaps they could help him get a visa so that he could go to that place that was paradise if there was water, and where every farmer had a tractor.

Shortly before he was due to graduate, Miljenko applied for a United

Nations fellowship to go on a two-month student program to West Germany. He knew that he would not be allowed out of the country if he had finished his academic work, so he deliberately did not complete his thesis on the grape varieties in the Metković region.

Miljenko got the fellowship and in August 1954 hurriedly left Yugoslavia with a passport valid for only four months. Before departing he went to a shoemaker and had him put an extra sole on his shoe under which he hid thirty-two dollars in American money that he had obtained on the black market. Miljenko hoped that thirty-two dollars would take him to California.

His first stop, though, was Schwäbisch Hall, a small town located between Frankfurt and Stuttgart. He arrived by train in the middle of the night and slept on a bench in the station waiting room. In the morning, a clerk at the station telephoned Hannfried Franck, a farmer in the Oberlimpurg section of town, where Grgić was to stay under the UN program. Franck picked him up and took him to his farm about one mile away.

Miljenko was warmly received and both worked and lived with the family. The common language among them was English, which Hannfried's wife, Gertrud, had learned when she lived in New York City in the 1920s. The family had five children, three girls and two boys. The younger boy, named Peter, who was fifteen soon regarded Miljenko like an older brother.

Schwäbisch Hall was beautiful, with the Franck farm standing in the shadow of the Limpurg Castle. The farm was a research station that employed some thirty people and did studies on new varieties of cereals, which Hannfried Franck also sold.

The other Yugoslav students who came to West Germany returned home at the end of the summer, but Miljenko stayed on and began trying to get a visa to enter the U.S. After his Yugoslav passport expired, Miljenko officially became a refugee in West Germany. Schwäbisch Hall was in the American occupation zone of West Germany, and he was taken to an internment camp in Nuremberg. Hannfried Franck, though, paid the required money to get him released.

Miljenko ran into severe frustration trying to get an American visa. His hopes soared early on, when he received a letter from New York City's Cardinal Francis Spellman telling him that a job had been found for him and that his transatlantic trip by ship would be paid for. The letter told Miljenko that in two months he would be in the U.S., but he never heard anything more from Spellman.

The months dragged on with no action on a visa, while Miljenko continued working at the farm. The number of U.S. visas in those days was based on the percentage of a nationality currently living in the country. Since the number of Yugoslav-Americans was small, there were few visas. Miljenko soon realized that he might be waiting years to get one.

After he endured eighteen months with growing impatience, one day in December 1955, a friend suggested that Miljenko emigrate first to Canada, and then see if he could get into the U.S. from there. He went to the Canadian consulate in Munich and that very day received a visa. When a Canadian official asked him where he wanted to go, Miljenko pointed on a map to Vancouver because it was close to the state of Washington where his brother-in-law, Vide Domandich, lived.

As soon as Miljenko received a Canadian visa, he called Domandich, and asked him for two hundred dollars to pay for his passage, adding that he should send it as soon as possible. Miljenko then began making reservations for the train trip from Schwäbisch Hall to Hamburg, the northern German port city where he would board the ship *Italia,* which was to take him to Halifax, Nova Scotia, in Canada.

All the tickets together cost about $150, but as the day of leaving approached, no money had arrived. The day before departure, Hannfried Franck paid for the tickets, and Miljenko promised to repay him as soon as he could. The morning Miljenko was to leave, the money finally arrived, and he immediately repaid Franck. Grgić, though, never forgot the man who was ready to give money out of his own pocket to a refugee so that he could make a trip to start a new life.

The Franck family threw a going-away party for Miljenko that included not only family members but also people working on the farm. During the party Miljenko became very emotional. He told the elder Franck privately that although he was happy to be leaving, he was also scared about his venture into the unknown. At the end of the party, as many people as could squeezed into the family's gray Mercedes-Benz to take Miljenko to the train station for a tearful good-bye.

Miljenko's spirits picked up when he boarded the *Italia.* It had been very depressing being a refugee in West Germany, even though people had been nice to him. But once headed for Canada he dared to have his first flirtation with hope. Seas were rough during the nine-day-long winter crossing, and most people on board got seasick. Miljenko, though, was so heady dreaming about his future that he had no problems.

As soon as the *Italia* docked, the passengers had to go through Canadian passport control. Miljenko received immigration papers, but since he had no relatives or job he was assigned to work cutting logs in the Yukon. The information was put on a tag on his jacket that resembled the one on the lost teddy bear in the childhood classic *Paddington Bear*. Before he left Nova Scotia, Miljenko sent a telegram to Anthony Domandich, his nephew who was a priest in the Seattle area, asking him if he knew anyone to contact once he arrived in Vancouver.

Then Miljenko boarded a train bound for Vancouver. He was told that a Canadian immigration official would meet him there and arrange for transportation to the Yukon.

The first night on the train Miljenko went to the dining car. A week before leaving West Germany, he had gone to a local shoemaker and had him remove the false sole under which he had hidden thirty-two dollars two years earlier in Croatia. Now that money had to last him until he got to Vancouver and could get a job. Looking at the menu, Miljenko pointed to the lowest price he saw—seventy-five cents—even though he had no idea what he would get for that money. A waiter brought him one piece of buttered toast on a plate. He never went back to the dining car again, buying food instead in stores at stops along the way.

Two days out of Halifax, a man boarded the train and sat down next to Miljenko. After a period of awkward silence, the man, who was dressed in a dark suit and looked like a businessman or civil servant, started up a conversation. The exchanges were slow because Miljenko's English was halting. The stranger started by asking all the standard questions about where he was from and what he was going to do. Uncertain about who the man was, Miljenko told him he was going to the Yukon to cut trees.

As the train traveled across the flat and vast Canadian prairies, the man in a fatherly tone told him that he should start his own business. Miljenko had already started thinking about his secret dream of owning a winery in California, but he didn't tell that to the Canadian. Instead he said, "Oh, no. I have none of the skills that would make me successful in business."

The stranger insisted that he should save his money and run the operation on the cheap, with family members doing most of the jobs. Owning your own business was the way to really succeed, he said. Miljenko listened intently and then carefully put the idea in the back of his mind.

The train finally arrived in Vancouver on the evening of February 6. Fortunately no one from Canadian immigration was there to meet the train and send Miljenko to the Yukon to cut trees. By now, he had only about fifteen dollars in his pocket and no idea what he was going to do. It was ten o'clock and snow was falling. Miljenko found his way to the railroad station's information office, where there was a telegram from his nephew telling him to go to Vancouver College, a high school run by the Christian Brothers, a Roman Catholic religious order, where he could get both a job and a place to stay.

One of the first things Miljenko Grgić had to do in Canada was change his name. His first boss at Vancouver College asked him if had a nickname because everyone had a hard time pronouncing Miljenko. The newcomer said his mother used to call him "Mee-lay" for short, but that would end up being spelled "Mile," which seemed a strange first name, so he simply took the name Mike. No one could pronounce Grgić either, so he anglicized the spelling. By the end of his first month in Canada, Miljenko Grgić had become Mike Grgich.

Living in a country where he knew almost no one and spoke the local language poorly was a struggle, and for the next two and a half years Grgich did what he had to do to survive. He washed dishes and was a waiter at the school for a year. Then he was a clerk in a grocery stored owned by a fellow Croatian. He frequently wrote letters to the Franck family, telling them that his life in Canada was difficult. Once he sent the Franck's daughter Anne Marie a birthday card and enclosed a Canadian dollar bill.

One day Grgich heard that MacMillan Bloedel, a paper company, was building a factory on Vancouver Island in Port Alberni, a fishing town surrounded by forests. He got work there as a waiter, while the factory was under construction. At the same time he applied for a job doing quality control of paper, which he got thanks to the technical training he had in Croatia.

For the first time since he had left Croatia, Grgich felt that he had a real future. He was doing chemical analysis of rolls of paper and finally putting to work his education. He stayed at MacMillan Bloedel for more than a year and enjoyed the work, but the lure of making wine in the California paradise still kept pulling at him. Grgich looked into the possibility of making wine in western Canada, but at the time there were only two wineries—one in Victoria and another near Lake Okanagan—and neither produced the quality wine that he hoped one day to make in the Napa Valley.

As the months drifted by, Mike talked frequently with his nephew, Anthony Domandich, telling him that he still hoped to move to California. The nephew contacted the Christian Brothers, who ran a winery in St. Helena, and asked them how his uncle might get a job in the Napa Valley. One of the Christian Brothers suggested that Grgich put a position-wanted ad in the *Wine Institute Bulletin,* offering his services as a winemaker and outlining his education in winemaking and his experience. Lee Stewart of Souverain Cellars saw the ad and gave Grgich the job guarantee he needed to get an American visa. He quit his quality-control job at the paper mill, and a few days later boarded the Greyhound bus headed for the Napa Valley, carrying with him that precious and all important job guarantee.

As Mike Grgich sat on his bed at the Hotel St. Helena that night in

August 1958, Desne and his former life seemed far away. He was all nerves, worried about whether he would be able to make it in California. Grgich was now thirty-five, which was old for someone making such a life-changing move. His age and travails, though, had given him great determination. Grgich was convinced he could succeed if he got a chance. Years before in the evenings sitting at the *ognjište* his father had told his children, "Every day do something just a little better." His son would put that maxim to practice in California just as he had in Croatia, Germany, and Canada.

Grgich was excited, but as he tried to go to sleep that first night in the Napa Valley, he allowed himself to dream a little. Wouldn't it be great if he could find a winery that nobody wanted? One that was rundown and that he could buy at a good price. He couldn't afford anything now. But he'd save his money, and maybe within a year he would be able to have his own winery. It was a dream good enough to sleep on.

CHAPTER FIVE

Starting Over in America

Wine can of their wits the wise beguile,
Make the sage frolic, and the serious smile.
——HOMER

As Lee Stewart drove Mike Grgich across the Napa Valley and then up the winding mountain road to Souverain Cellars, the newcomer looked around at everything with amazement. He was surprised by how rural the valley was and enjoyed listening to birds singing and watching deer run. He was also shocked that most of the farmers weren't growing grapes. They were cultivating plums for making prunes or even walnuts in what was supposed to be America's wine country.

When they arrived at the winery, Stewart showed his new employee around. From Stewart's house Grgich looked across the valley at tree-covered mountains and down at a lake made by the Bell Canyon Reservoir. Directly in front of the house were grapevines.

Stewart then showed Grgich the small cottage where he would be living. It had just a bed, a table, and a hot plate, as Grgich would be having most of his meals with Stewart and his wife during the harvest. Grgich would earn a hundred dollars a month, half of that going back to Stewart for food and lodging.

At the end of the first day on the job, Stewart treated Grgich to two of his most prized wines: a 1951 Cabernet Sauvignon and a 1954 Zinfandel. Aged wines were something new to Grgich, and he had never before enjoyed a seven-year-old wine. Back in Croatia people drank all the wine they made one year before the next year's harvest. He thought both of Stewart's wines were outstanding.

As the two savored the wines, Stewart began telling Grgich about himself and about the winery. Stewart was born in 1905 and grew up in Fresno and San Francisco. His mother was a member of the wealthy and influential

Leland Stanford family, which was the origin of his first name, but he hated the pretension and insisted that people call him Lee.

Stewart played professional baseball for a year, then worked for Armour, a large meatpacking company where he handled exports to the Far East from San Francisco. He found, though, that he was temperamentally ill-suited for working in a large corporation and was soon looking for something else. He toyed with the idea of being a freelance writer, but soon discovered that the work was difficult and his talent limited.

Long interested in wines, Stewart during Prohibition brought wines illegally into San Francisco. Then in 1943, he bought thirty acres of land plus a house at an altitude of about nine hundred feet on Howell Mountain. The property included a stone-and-redwood winery that had not been used since Prohibition. Built in 1875 by immigrants from Northern Italy, it was originally named the Rossini Winery. Stewart at first grew chickens on the property. But he soon tired of lugging around hundred-pound sacks of chicken feed and decided to switch to wine.

Stewart thought the winery ought to have a French-sounding moniker, so he named his new property Souverain. The name was one of several suggested by his printer's daughter, who was studying French at a local high school. With the new name in place, Stewart set out to run a business. In 1944 he made his first wine even though he knew next to nothing about how to do it. He crushed the grapes and put the juice into barrels so porous that it leaked out through the staves. Unaware of what really should be happening with the developing wine, he only hoped it wouldn't turn into vinegar. Eventually Stewart sold the 1944 wine in bulk to the Mondavi family winery, which mixed it with its own production.

That and other haphazard experiences led him to hire as a consultant André Tchelistcheff, who in addition to his work at Beaulieu Vineyard had an independent research company. Robert Mondavi, whose family the year before had bought the Charles Krug winery and who was always willing to help other winemakers, also taught Stewart the basics of making wine.

The early years at Souverain were tough, and many times the only things Stewart and his wife had on the table for dinner were bread and beans. Even in January 1947, nearly three years after the first vintage, Souverain's sales for the month totaled $1.25, the price of one gallon of the wine he called Red Burgundy.

Stewart ran a very small operation and was slow to spend money on either staff or equipment. He often said, "Being of Scottish descent, I am tight with the dollar." Dozens of stories were told around the Napa Valley about Stewart's frugality, which he seemed to enjoy playing up. Once in the early 1960s he was particularly appreciative of a part-time worker who had put in lots of extra hours, so he gave him a Christmas bonus of exactly one dollar. In order to save money Stewart had generic labels printed in large quantities for his Cabernet Sauvignon and then wrote the year on each bottle by hand.

With the help of Tchelistcheff and Mondavi, Stewart developed into a highly regarded winemaker, and his wines regularly won medals at agricultural fairs. Between 1947 and 1957, Stewart won thirty-four prizes just at the California State Fair. He produced the Napa Valley's first Green Hungarian wine, which was made from a grape that grew easily in California but had a bland taste and never gained much popularity. He also had a small vineyard of Petite Sirah, a lackluster French grape know as Durif. Petite Sirah had once been extremely popular in California but hadn't been grown much in the Napa Valley after Prohibition. Stewart was well known for his Zinfandels, and many people said he made the best Johannisberg Riesling in the Napa Valley. Although Tchelistcheff was considered the dean of California wine, some thought Stewart the better winemaker.

When Grgich arrived at Souverain, the winery was about to begin its peak of activity. The crush, when grapes are harvested and then made into wine, is an exhausting time for everyone involved. Although the fundamentals of winemaking were the same as what Grgich had first learned from his father in Croatia, the Stewart operation was both bigger than what he had seen at home and more technically advanced than what he had learned at the University of Zagreb.

Like most California winery owners, Stewart grew many different kinds of grapes on his thirty acres of vineyards. When he bought the property in 1943, Zinfandel, Grenache, and Petite Sirah were growing there. Later he added Carignane, Cabernet Sauvignon, and some more Petite Sirah. French winemakers over generations learned which grapes did best in which particular location and specific type of soil. In California viticulturists knew far less. Professors Winkler and Amerine in their classic study of California's wine-growing regions had set out broad planting suggestions, but thousands of acres of old vines, such as those at Souverain, had been planted without the benefit of their research. Stewart and many other growers didn't see any reason to tear out producing vines just to plant the ones the professors recommended. Souverain grew only a small proportion of the grapes that went into its wines and bought others from farmers as far away as Sonoma County. Stewart had a Zinfandel vineyard next to his winery that was used for that wine, but he bought additional grapes for his Cabernet Sauvignon and for all three of his whites: Johannisberg Riesling, Chardonnay, and Green Hungarian. The winery produced only about four thousand cases a year.

Once the harvest started, day laborers, mostly Mexicans, went through the Souverain vineyard picking bunches of grapes and putting them in wooden crates that held about forty-five pounds. They were paid by the box. The older, more experienced laborers knew how to quickly spot the biggest clumps of grapes amid the plethora of leaves. They usually earned more than the young workers who might be stronger but were not as adept and didn't work as fast. Each laborer had his own rows, and the ones who picked fastest earned the most money. Grgich and Stewart collected the boxes of grapes, loaded them on a flatbed truck, and then brought them from the vineyard to the winery, where they would be crushed, pressed, and fermented. Farmers also delivered the purchased grapes to the winery in wooden boxes on flatbeds.

When they were inside the winery, the grapes for white and for red wines went through different processes. The white grapes were crushed, pressed, and then fermented. Red grapes, on the other hand, were crushed, fermented, and only after that was finished, were pressed.

Stewart and Grgich dumped the grapes—one box at a time—into a crusher. Inside the crusher were fingerlike projections, and when a motor was turned on, the inside of the crusher began rotating the fingers and slightly crushed the grapes. One of the men caught the grapes in a bucket at the end of the crusher and dumped them into a basket press located about five feet away. Some golden juice drained immediately down into a receiving container and was then pumped into the settling tank. Crushing continued until the basket press was full. While the press was being filled, juice was draining out through the slits in between the staves because of the weight of the grapes added on top. Stewart explained to Grgich that this juice was called free run and was the best quality juice.

The basket press was made of a series of wooden staves held together by galvanized hoops. In the middle of the press was a metal screw. On top of that screw was a heavy metal block with a handle. When the press was filled, a heavy wooden top was added that covered the fruit inside the press. At this point, all the juice that had been collected was free run.

Stewart or Grgich began the pressing by taking the handle and screwing the heavy metal box downward. Juice then seeped out of the press between the slots of the staves and drained down into a metal dish at the bottom of the press. There were two levels of pressing, depending on the degree of pressure on the grapes. At the beginning of the pressing process, the first 10 to 15 percent was called light press and was added to the free run juice. This mixture would be kept together and sold as a varietal wine such as Johannisberg Riesling, Chardonnay, or Green Hungarian at a premium price of between $1.25 and $2 a bottle. The wine that resulted from the heavier pressing was kept and processed separately and sold as Dry Sauterne for $2 a gallon. Stewart's Dry Sauterne contained no Sémillion, the dominant grape in the sweet Bordeaux wine called Sauternes, which is spelled with an *s* at the end.

When the pressing was finished, the hard residue in the press containing the seeds, skins, and stems was collected and spread in the vineyards as mulch and fertilizer.

Pressing a ton of white grapes yielded about 150 gallons of juice, and Stewart crushed white grapes on one day and red grapes the next. The white juice produced in a day would go into one tank. That juice was then analyzed in the laboratory, usually by Grgich, for the amount of sugar and acid. If the acid level was low for that type of wine, some tartaric acid would be added. At the same time, sulfur dioxide was added to prevent oxidation or browning of the juice. The next step was to cool the juice with the help of a pump that lowered the temperature to 50–55 degrees. Everything was then mixed and the juice was left to settle overnight.

The next morning the clear juice from the top of the tank was moved to another tank or puncheon. The sediment was then moved to a smaller container for further settling. Selected yeast obtained from the University of California at Davis was then added to the juice to start fermentation. In two or three days, the fermentation started bubbling and releasing carbon dioxide. The yeast was splitting molecules of sugar into wine alcohol and carbon dioxide gas. The gas escaped from the fermentation tank through a wet bung, a device that lets carbon dioxide gas escape from the tank but does not permit oxygen into it. Wine fermentation is an anaerobic process.

White wine finished fermentation in about forty-five days. Every day during the process, Grgich checked the temperature of the liquid as well as the sugar level with a hydrometer. The wine was cooled to maintain the temperature at around 50–60 degrees, and the sugar level fell as the alcohol level rose. Cooling the wine slowed fermentation and also protected the delicate aromas and flavors from being driven off.

After fermentation, the white wine was pumped into another tank and fined with bentonite to eliminate proteins, so that no undesired change in the wine would take place if it got warm after leaving the winery during transportation or storage.

After another three weeks, Grgich and Stewart racked the wine, a procedure that pumped the clear wine at the top of the tank into another wooden tank, while the sediment at the bottom was discarded. The wine was then aged in oak for an additional four to five weeks. After tasting and analysis, Stewart would decide when to bottle the wine. During the bottling, the wine was sterile filtered. The wine was then aged for an additional six to twelve months in bottles before being released.

Grapes to make red wine were loaded into a crusher just like those for white wine. Then the winemakers transferred the mixture of grapes, seeds, and skins, which Stewart called the must, using its French name, into open redwood tanks for fermenting. Fermenting the juice for red wines while it is still in contact with skins and seeds gives the liquid color and character. The winemakers again added yeast to start fermentation, which took place at a temperature of about 80–85 degrees. Because of the higher temperature during fermentation, there was no need to heat stabilize the wine.

Carbon dioxide, a byproduct of fermentation, pushed the seeds, skins, and berries to the top of the tank, where they formed a hard crust called the cap. It was important, though, to keep the liquid in contact with the solid material since that gives it color, tannin, and taste. Twice a day during fermentation, Stewart or Grgich climbed a wooden ladder to the top of the tank and used a pole with a flat disk on the end to break up the cap and mix the liquid and solid material. In the morning and evening the men also pumped over the tanks of red wine to keep the cap moist and to further increase the contact between liquids and solids. They first attached one end of a hose to the bottom of the tank and put the other end at the top. Then they pumped the juice from the bottom of the tank to the top and sprayed it over the cap. Punching down the cap and pumping over are the very soul of red winemaking.

Because of the higher temperature, the red-wine fermentation took much less time than that of the white—only about a week. When the process was finished, the wine was allowed to settle. Stewart kept the Zinfandel in wood for a year and the Cabernet Sauvignon there for two years. Just as with the whites, the oak added flavor and character to the reds. Stewart sold this better-quality Zinfandel or Cabernet Sauvignon for $2 a bottle.

The remaining pulpy mixture in the tanks was moved to the basket press, which squeezed out the liquid, leaving behind a thick solid mixture of seeds and skin called the cake, which was discarded. The heavily pressed Zinfandel and Cabernet were blended with some Petite Sirah and Grenache, aged a few months in oak, and sold as Red Burgundy—although it contained no Burgundy-style grapes—in jugs for $2 a gallon. The quality reds got twelve months in the bottle before release.

Grgich watched Stewart closely as he controlled the whole process. The newcomer was impressed with Stewart's attention to detail and the way he faithfully followed a program set out for him a decade before by André

Tchelistcheff. Stewart kept notes of everything he did, comparing them to records from previous years. He was almost obsessive about cleanliness, carefully and frequently sterilizing the pumps used to move juice or wine from one container to another.

Stewart and Grgich worked sixteen hours a day during the crush, and everything had to be done precisely the way Stewart wanted. If a hydrometer test wasn't done the first time as Stewart specified, Grgich had to do it again and again until the boss was satisfied. Work at the winery was deadly serious. One day Stewart was complaining about his ulcers but added, "At least I've never had any heart problems." William Kirby, a retired army colonel who sold wines for Stewart, replied, "How could you have heart pains, Lee? You don't have a heart."

Many things were new and puzzling to Grgich. On his first morning he went out into the vineyard before everyone else was awake. There he saw some vines that reminded him of home. The leaves and grapes looked just like those of a variety that he knew back in Croatia called Plavac Mali. When Grgich mentioned this to Stewart, the American corrected him saying that those were Zinfandel, probably the most widely planted grape in California. Grgich, however, remained unconvinced by Stewart's explanation. In 2000, scientists from Croatia and California concluded with the help of DNA tests that the origin of Zinfandel was Crljenak Kastelanski, the father of Plavac Mali. Forty years later, Grgich was proven right.

One evening during his first week, Grgich was sitting on the porch looking at a newspaper, when he noticed a snake curling up a yard away from him. Just at that moment Stewart walked out of the house and saw the snake as well. Without saying anything, Stewart went back into the house, got a gun, and shot the snake. Then Stewart told Grgich about rattlesnakes, which the foreigner had never seen before.

Despite Grgich's respect for Stewart, personal relations between the two men were never very good. From the ad that had appeared in the *Wine Institute Bulletin,* Stewart had expected to get a European who had plenty of experience in current European wine techniques. Someone perhaps like Tchelistcheff—only younger and cheaper. Stewart considered Grgich more of a wine chemist than a winemaker. In addition, Grgich hadn't made wine in the four years since he left Croatia, which was not exactly on the cutting edge of world wine trends as it was.

After about four months at Souverain and after the basic winemaking was completed, Grgich began feeling uncomfortable. There wasn't as much to do now. Things were also not going well personally with Stewart, and Grgich felt isolated living halfway up the mountain surrounded by nothing but trees and vines. He didn't own a car and public transportation was infrequent. As a result, he had to depend on Stewart to take him to St. Helena once a week to shop. Grgich felt he had learned a lot from Stewart, but it was time to move along. Stewart was not unhappy to see him leave.

Since the Christian Brothers had opened the door to the Napa Valley for Grgich, he called Brother Timothy, their well-known cellar master, and asked if he might have a job for him. The Christian Brothers were a Roman Catholic religious order founded in the seventeenth century in France with the mission of educating poor children. The Brothers started making sacramental wine in California in 1882, and in 1931 bought a winery and vineyards on the western side of the Napa Valley. After Prohibition the Christian Brothers made both premium and bulk wines, but their real success came from selling brandy and a sparkling wine marketed as Champagne.

The religious order, in 1950, bought one of the most famous buildings of the Napa Valley—Greystone, located two miles north of St. Helena. The magnificent building was built in 1889 and for a while laid claim to being the world's largest stone winery. It was also a wonderful showpiece for the wines and brandies Brother Timothy promoted in national advertising.

The Christian Brothers didn't have a winemaking job for Grgich, but they offered him one in Champagne production paying two dollars an hour. Nearly half his pay went for a room he rented in a hotel in St. Helena. He walked one mile to work every day and lived frugally, cooking his meals on a hot plate in his room. He owned just one knife, which he had bought for thirty-five cents shortly after his arrival. He used the knife for both preparing food and to cut bread and meat.

Grgich had been living in the hotel for about five months when his brother-in-law, Vide Domandich, who was a fisherman in Aberdeen, Washington, came to visit. Mike's sister had died, and the widower wanted to take a break from fishing. Domandich was shocked to see his relative's austere living conditions and immediately bought Grgich a second knife for five dollars. The brother-in-law also tried to buy him a garbage can, but Grgich explained that there was no garbage. Just as back in Croatia, nothing was thrown away. He used up everything in one way or another; all the food was consumed; there were no such things as scraps. Domandich did manage to convince Grgich to move out of the hotel, however. The two found a duplex in St. Helena for sale for $8,500. Domandich loaned Grgich $2,500 for the down payment and later bought him a refrigerator and a table. After staying for six months, Domandich left, convinced that his relative had achieved at least a minimum standard of living.

Despite his poverty, Grgich found money to continue his winemaking education at UC Davis. While working for the Christian Brothers, he took a week off at no pay to take a course on the latest developments in wine production. The night before the program started, Grgich checked into a hotel near the campus and learned that the price would be $2.50 for a night. Back in Croatia the price of everything was fixed. Since a hotel room cost $2.00 a night in St. Helena, he assumed it would also be $2.00 a night in Davis. That fifty cents extra a night meant a lot to Grgich, but the clerk told him he could go back to St. Helena if he wanted a $2.00 hotel room. Grgich reluctantly paid the higher amount.

At Greystone, Grgich did a bit of everything in the Champagne production department on the third floor, working in both bottling and shipping. But after less than a year, Grgich didn't feel that he was progressing toward his goal of making wine or someday owning his own winery. Members of the Christian Brothers order held most of the top jobs, and they had made a commitment to the order for life. Grgich didn't think he'd ever have a chance there to be either a wine chemist or a winemaker. He had a job, but his career wasn't going anywhere.

So on one of his days off in mid-1959, Grgich went to Beaulieu Vineyard to see André Tchelistcheff. He didn't know Napa Valley's most famous winemaker, although he was very familiar with the basics of his biography. Grgich felt Tchelistcheff might help him because they had so much in common. Both had been blown about by the winds of history before finally landing in California. Grgich hoped that Tchelistcheff might offer him a job or at least give him some advice about what to do or where to go next. One day Grgich simply picked up the phone and got an appointment to see the man who had become his idol. As the Greyhound bus took him from St. Helena to the Beaulieu winery in Rutherford, Grgich kept saying to himself, "He was a refugee—like me. He knows what it means just to survive—like me. We're both Slavs. He's even lived in Croatia—like me. Maybe he will understand me."

When they met, however, Tchelistcheff immediately told Grgich that he didn't have any openings. Nonetheless, Tchelistcheff suggested that he fill out an application anyway. Grgich left after asking Tchelistcheff to keep him in mind if he ever had an opening.

Two months later, Grgich unexpectedly got a phone call from Tchelistcheff, who told him that his wine chemist had been diagnosed with leukemia and might never come back to work. Tchelistcheff asked Grgich to come in for another interview. At the end of the second talk, Tchelistcheff explained that the job of wine chemist paid three dollars an hour, but Grgich would first have to pass a two-month probation. Tchelistcheff gave him a textbook on wine chemistry to take home for the night. The next day the cellar foreman gave Grgich twenty-five samples of red wine and asked him to analyze them to determine the levels of sugar, alcohol, and acid. Tchelistcheff wanted to make sure Grgich knew the fundamentals of being a wine chemist and could do the lab work needed during winemaking. The new hire asked for some help, but Tchelistcheff replied, "Mike, I am very busy. I gave you the book. Read it and do it yourself."

Working alone in the Beaulieu wine lab, Grgich set to the task. Every day he got the six o'clock bus from St. Helena that dropped him off in front of the winery, rather than the eight o'clock one, so that he had two hours to work on the twenty-five samples before everyone else arrived. It took Grgich a week to analyze all the wines, and Tchelistcheff approved the results.

Grgich counted down the days and hours to the end of his probation period. When the end of two months arrived, he went to Tchelistcheff and asked, "Can I stay?"

"Yes, congratulations," replied Tchelistcheff. "You've done a good job. I'll even give you a raise to $3.25 an hour." Grgich would later say that the twenty-five-cent raise was the most important one he ever got because it gave him a job with a future in wine.

Grgich usually worked in a white lab coat while doing his wine analyses and even took off his trademark beret. With a camaraderie born of their similar backgrounds, Tchelistcheff and Grgich worked well together. Tchelistcheff spoke some Croatian from his days living there, and the two men sometimes talked to each other in that language.

Only three months into the new job, Grgich showed Tchelistcheff that larvae of fruit flies were living around the barrels' bung holes in the tops through which they are filled or emptied. Not all that much seemed to have changed at Beaulieu Vineyard since 1938, when Tchelistcheff had discovered the rat in the Sauvignon Blanc. Tchelistcheff immediately named Grgich sanitary inspector in addition to wine chemist.

Grgich quickly felt at home at Beaulieu. On November 17, 1962, he married Tatjana Čizmić, also a native of Croatia, in a ceremony at Madame de Pins's residence in Rutherford. The couple soon had a daughter, Violet.

Tchelistcheff gave his new assistant ever-increasing authority, and he was soon in charge of quality control for the whole winemaking operation from grapes in the field to bottled wine in the warehouse. That gave him the opportunity to learn the whole winemaking process in a way that few winemakers ever get. Tchelistcheff told him, "Mike, you have to be my eyes. I cannot be everywhere. Look at everything and report back to me."

Grgich became obsessive about checking every barrel of wine at Beaulieu once a week. He told himself that a good winemaker had to learn to communicate with his wine in the same way that a mother interacts with her children. A winemaker can know all the techniques, he believed, but if he doesn't develop a way to converse with his wine, he'll never make really fine wine. Grgich would go into the vineyard during the growing season and squeeze the berries to see how they were progressing. Winemaking, Grgich believed, is a feeling, and you have to use all your senses—seeing the wine, smelling it, listening to it, touching it. To Grgich winemaking was not just chemistry; it was an emotional and spiritual experience. Grgich spoke little with other employees at Beaulieu. He preferred to walk the fields and the winery, visiting with his vines and wines.

CHAPTER SIX

A Revolution Begins

When there is plenty of wine,
sorrow and worry take wing.
—OVID

Louis M. Martini, founder of the Louis M. Martini Winery, in 1945 organized the Napa Valley Vintners group with just seven members. They met once a month for lunch at the Miramonte Hotel in St. Helena. The meals lasted three or four hours, and in addition to the food there was lots of wine tasting and singing in French and Italian. With a cooperation rarely seen in other fields of business, the leading winemakers in the Napa Valley readily exchanged information, helping each other turn out better wine. They might compete with each other on the shelves of shops around the country, but they were allies at home. They traded winemaking experiences, both good and bad, and were always ready to lend a hand, whether it was to crush grapes or provide a place to store wine. During harvests in the late 1950s, Peter Mondavi, the winemaker at the Charles Krug Winery, routinely stopped by rival Beaulieu Vineyard late at night for a snack of French bread, salami, and Cabernet with winemaker Joe Heitz. The two discussed any problems they were having with the harvest as well as their new experiments. Robert Mondavi wrote in his autobiography *Harvests of Joy,* "We all understood that the more the whole valley succeeded, the better it would be for each of us in it."

By the early 1960s, the pace of change in California winemaking was picking up, abetted by research coming out of UC Davis and the free flow of information among grape growers and winemakers. A revolution in winemaking was starting. Its birthplace was in Sonoma County at Hanzell, a small hobby winery started by James D. Zellerbach, the chairman of Crown Zellerbach, the second-largest forest-products company in the world. A knight of the Confrérie des Chevaliers du Tastevin, an organization that celebrates Burgundian wine, Zellerbach had particular affection for that region's two most prized products, Pinot Noir and Chardonnay. He particularly liked Romanée-Conti Pinot Noir and Meursault Chardonnay, a taste he developed while working for the Marshall Plan that rebuilt Europe after World War II.

Zellerbach and his wife, Hanna, owned a weekend retreat in the town of Sonoma named Hanzell, which combined parts of her first name and his family name. After returning from Europe, Zellerbach came up with the idea of trying to see if he could produce his two favorite wines in California. He told people his goal was to "make California wine as good as the best of Europe." As a symbol of the French inspiration, Zellerbach had his architect model the winery after the wooden, slate-roofed building in Burgundy's Clos de Vougeot where the Tastevin group held banquets.

Zellerbach enlisted top people in California wine. Ivan Schoch, a leading grape grower in the Napa Valley who owned the famed To Kalon vineyard and whose grapes went into Beaulieu Vineyard wines, helped plant the Hanzell vineyards starting in 1953 and later sold grapes to Hanzell. R. Bradford Webb, a Berkeley-trained biochemist and former winemaker at Gallo, directed the winery with the French title *maître de chai* (cellar master). André Tchelistcheff became a consultant on winemaking, and Davis professors were all over the place.

Hanzell wanted to combine the best of French techniques with the best of Davis research and adapt both to the California soil and climate. The clone for Hanzell Pinot Noir, the specific subtype of that grape, came from the Napa Valley, but had been originally imported from France by Martin Ray. Webb also started fermentation with Burgundy yeasts. Zellerbach followed the advice of Burgundy's Louis Latour and insisted on aging his wines in small French Limousin oak barrels, rather than the larger redwood or American oak ones then commonly used in California.

Professors from Davis offered a steady stream of suggestions, and Hanzell became, in effect, their laboratory. Researchers, for example, had been trying to get winemakers to lower the temperature at which fermentation took place in order to protect a wine's fruity characteristics. Since California is generally much warmer than Burgundy during the harvest, its wines often had a burnt taste because fermentation at a higher temperature was robbing the fruit of its natural flavors. As a result, the people at Hanzell had to introduce a way to cool the liquid. The objective was to ferment wine at roughly the same temperature in Sonoma as in the cooler Burgundy. To achieve that, Zellerbach commissioned the manufacture of twelve double-walled stainless-steel tanks, where chilled water, which was kept at a steady 55 to 58 degrees, circulated between the walls and cooled the wine. Each rectangular tank held exactly one ton of crushed grapes. A ten-ton refrigerator located in the winery's basement chilled the water. Tchelistcheff and Harold Berg, a UC Davis professor, designed the tank.

Davis professors were also warning winemakers about the oxidation of white wines, which occurs when there is excessive contact with air and causes the wine to lose its fruity flavors and turn brown. The researchers suggested engulfing the grapes and young wine in nitrogen in order to keep air away. Hanzell achieved that by blanketing the wine in tanks with a layer of nitrogen.

The biggest breakthrough at Hanzell, though, was the introduction of controlled malolactic fermentation, the secondary fermentation that converts the harsher malic acid into lactic acid and carbon dioxide. This smooths out the wines and makes them mellower. Malolactic fermentation occurs naturally as the wine ages in barrels in all Burgundian Pinot Noir and most Chardonnay wines during the fall and winter after the alcoholic fermentation. In California wines in the 1950s, it was taking place haphazardly—if at all. Sometimes it occurred after bottling, giving wines an effervescence that could make the bottles explode. The first Hanzell vintages did not undergo malolactic fermentation, but Tchelistcheff and Berg told Webb that it was essential if Zellerbach was going to achieve Burgundy-style wines. Webb, though, developed a way to induce the process and make sure it took place even when nature didn't cooperate.

John L. Ingraham, a UC Davis professor, first isolated several lactic acid bacteria, the most promising of which came from the Louis M. Martini Winery and was named ML34. In January 1959, Webb conducted the first induced and commercial malolactic fermentation in California by adding the malolactic bacteria to wine fermenting in a glass-lined, stainless-steel tank. The procedure was repeated in the 1959 Hanzell Pinot Noir, which is believed to be the first wine in history with induced, rather than spontaneous, malolactic fermentation.*

Zellerbach was not around the winery to follow the historic developments taking place at his property. In November 1956, President Eisenhower named him ambassador to Italy. Zellerbach, though, kept in close contact with his *maître de chai*. After Webb successfully accomplished controlled malolactic fermentation, he quickly shot off a message to the ambassador.

---

*France's Émile Peynaud was also doing research on controlled malolactic fermentation at about the same time and may have achieved it earlier. Wine technology did not travel very fast between France and California at the time, however, and the men were unaware of each other's work.

Webb also shipped bottles of Hanzell wines to Rome, which Zellerbach served at his embassy dinners and sent to European wine friends without telling them the origin. They told him the Chardonnay was obviously a white Burgundy from the Côte d'Or, but they couldn't tell which vineyard!

In an interview in the January 1960 issue of the California publication *Wines and Vines,* Zellerbach insisted that Hanzell was not "just a pastime" but a "serious business enterprise." With its output of only about a hundred cases of 1956 Chardonnay, though, it was hard to consider Hanzell a commercial winery. Zellerbach priced his wines at exactly what it cost him to make them: the then lofty price of $6 a bottle.

James Zellerbach never had the chance to see the impact of his experimental winery. After a very brief illness, he died on August 3, 1963, in San Francisco. His wife had never shown any interest in the winery and she did not even produce the 1963 vintage, selling off the grapes, wines still in barrels, and bottles to other wineries who marketed it under their own labels. Two years later, Mrs. Zellerbach sold Hanzell to a retired businessman.

Developments at Hanzell, though, were not lost. Given the free flow of information in northern California wine circles, and because Zellerbach had hired so many consultants as well as professors from UC Davis, word of Hanzell soon spread to leading Napa Valley wineries.

Hanzell was not the only winery breaking new ground. Another leader in new technology was the Charles Krug Winery, where Peter Mondavi was the winemaker. A UC Davis graduate, he did extensive experiments under the tutelage of William Cruess, a Davis professor, on cold fermentation of white and rosé wines. He also did trailblazing work on new methods for pressing grapes and filtering wines.

André Tchelistcheff adopted lessons from both Hanzell and Krug, where he was also a consultant. In 1962, Beaulieu became the first large-scale winery to introduce malolactic fermentation for all its red wines. At a UC Davis seminar that year Mike Grgich gave a presentation demonstrating how winemakers, with the help of a specially treated paper— chromatography paper—could see the progress of the procedure as it was taking place.

In addition, Tchelistcheff and Grgich were introducing a way to protect vineyards from frost, which could wipe out a year's crop on a single chilly night. Tchelistcheff had a hard time convincing Madame de Pins to spend money to install a frost-prevention system, but finally succeeded when he showed her that the winery would be more profitable if he could eliminate frost damage. Tchelistcheff and Grgich initially tried burning hay and then old tires to fight off frost. They had the most success with return stack heaters, which burned diesel fuel and were widely used in southern California to protect citrus trees from cold weather. In addition, Tchelistcheff installed wind machines that looked like propellers on a tower to mix relatively warm air with the colder air near the surface of the soil to supplement the heaters.

Grgich played a major role in introducing a very fine filter that trapped small amounts of yeasts and bacteria that slipped through the filters then being used just before the wine was bottled. These particles sometimes contaminated wine. Grgich and Tchelistcheff were spurred on to find a solution to the problem after Beaulieu had to dispose of ten thousand bottles of spoiled rosé. A company named Millipore Corp. made a filter for the pharmaceutical industry to assure sterile manufacturing of medicines. It proposed using the same technology to eliminate even the smallest yeast particles and bacteria in wine just before bottling. Gallo had first tried the new process, but had discontinued the experiment. Tchelistcheff learned about that from his son Dimitri, who was then working for Gallo, and asked the Millipore Corp. people to do another test at Beaulieu. They spent several weeks in 1962 at the winery working with Grgich to develop, install, and test a double filtering procedure that first put the wine through a traditional filter and then through a microscopic one. The filters worked and were soon adopted by many wineries.

All the technical advances being made in California wine production resulted in much better wine, although even those doing the work didn't always realize how much they were accomplishing. In 1964, UC Davis professor Maynard Amerine visited Beaulieu to talk with Tchelistcheff before going to a wine symposium in Bordeaux. It was quite an honor for him to be asked to address the group, and he asked what he should talk about to this major international wine gathering. Amerine knew that Tchelistcheff read French technical wine publications and so was very familiar with developments there.

"What can I tell the French about winemaking?" asked Amerine.

"Don't be so humble," Tchelistcheff replied. "We are now doing many things in California that they don't know about. Tell them about controlled malolactic fermentation and tell them about microfiltering wine to stabilize it biologically. Those are two things we are doing here that even the French do not fully appreciate."

CHAPTER SEVEN

The Swashbuckling Wine Years

Making good wine is a skill, fine wine an art.
—ROBERT MONDAVI

Rodney Strong came to California winemaking via Broadway. He grew up on a farm near Vancouver, Washington, discovering at an early age that he loved the theater and dancing. For a while he worked as a between-acts comedian at a Portland burlesque show, keeping audiences laughing while the girls prepared for their next performance. After a year at the University of Washington, Strong went to New York City in 1946 and studied with dance legends George Balanchine and Martha Graham. He was also in the chorus of long forgotten Broadway shows like *Toplitsky of Notre Dame*. Successful as both a dancer and choreographer, he earned a then lordly $100,000 a year.

A Paris nightclub owner in 1948 saw one of Strong's shows and offered him the choreographer's job at the Lido, a new nightspot he was opening in Paris. Strong jumped at the opportunity and lived in Europe for the next four years, where he grew to appreciate good wine and good food. It was an idyllic life. He was well paid, and his theater connections gave him an entrée into French society.

A dancer, though, has to think about life when the music stops. Like a football running back, a dancer's legs begin to go at a certain age. So while he was enjoying fine French wine, Strong began thinking about making wine his second career. Before returning to New York City in 1952, he picked up odd jobs at harvest time in family wineries in Bordeaux and Burgundy. The work was hard and he was usually not paid, but he learned Old World winemaking techniques from the vineyard up.

In 1959, Strong married and decided it was time to put away his dancing shoes. While performing with traveling shows in California, he had looked at breaking into the wine business there as well as buying property for a vineyard. He first worked at a small winery in Santa Clara, south of San

Francisco, and then opened Tiburon Vintners, a wine shop in a town of that name north of San Francisco. It operated out of a rundown Victorian house, where Strong and his wife received free rent in exchange for repairing the place. He bought wine in barrels from vintners in Sonoma and Napa counties and bottled it in the cellar, while his wife handled sales upstairs. First-year sales totaled ten thousand dollars. In order to survive, Strong taught dance at San Francisco State College three days a week and choreographed shows like *West Side Story* for the tony Bohemian Club.

Sales at Tiburon Vintners eventually took off, and Strong set out to buy land for a vineyard. From his European experience, he was convinced that the location and quality of land was the key to great wine. The French had taught him that the vintner played only a secondary role; the vineyard had the starring role. Strong looked for a cool area, fearing that Europe's leading grapes like Chardonnay and Pinot Noir would not do well in the hot California sun in places like the Napa Valley. He also worked with professors at Davis on soil and temperature studies, looking for the best location for a new vineyard.

Finally Strong found his ideal in Sonoma County, where the chalk-colored soil reminded him of the vineyards he had seen in the Champagne region of France around Épernay and Reims. In 1962, Strong bought a sixty-acre vineyard, complete with a winery dating back to 1898, and renamed it Windsor Vineyards.

Strong pulled out the poor-quality, Prohibition-era grapes and replaced them with quality ones. Soon he was producing wines that had a cult following. He also brought new ways of doing business to the local wine trade. He called his first property Chalk Hill after the vineyard's location. Since distributors were reluctant to handle his little-known wines, Strong sold them by mail, often to the same clients he had in Tiburon and to members of the Bohemian Club.

Strong's business exploded, with annual sales going quickly from $300,000 to $3 million. Financial institutions like Bank of America and Prudential Insurance were anxious to lend money to a promising winery because it had good collateral—its land—and promising sales thanks to growing wine consumption. Strong was soon buying up plum orchards and turning them into vineyards. By 1970, his company owned five thousand acres in Mendocino and Sonoma counties. Strong later called this period "the adventurous, swashbuckling wine years in California."

Rodney Strong was just one of a new breed of winemaker who started arriving in northern California's wine country in the 1960s. Sometimes a person came alone; more often they were a couple. Some were millionaires;

others were a pittance away from poverty. They came from all parts of the country and from all walks of life. There was a dermatologist, a securities analyst, engineers, bankers, and professors. Some were young people seeking adventure; others were going into retirement. Many were escaping the riot-filled and declining American cities of the 1960s and were seeking a simpler life close to nature. Just as the first settlers who came to California nearly two centuries before, the newcomers hoped to get some land and carve out a great future for themselves.

Many of the new breed had spent time in Europe, often an extended stay, where they had discovered a more interesting and exciting lifestyle than they had experienced in America. Wine played a central role in that culture, and they returned to the U.S. looking for a way to make wine part of their lives. The wannabe winemakers were usually just gifted amateurs who knew little more about wine than that they enjoyed drinking it. But they also didn't want to make just any wine; they shared a determination to make world-quality wine.

Unlike the French, the new California winemakers had no tradition or handed-down wisdom. They couldn't pass along a wine heritage because they didn't have one. As a result, they became experimenters, borrowing ideas where they found them and trying different ways of turning grape juice into wine. The lessons from Hanzell—fermenting in temperature-controlled stainless-steel tanks, induced malolactic fermentation, using inert gases to eliminate oxidation, and aging in small French oak barrels—became gospel. In addition, though, they did their own thing. At one point, for example, winemakers at Trefethen Vineyards in the town of Napa decided they were getting too much color from the Pinot Noir grapes going into its sparkling wine, so they and other growers tried harvesting at night when it was cooler to see if they'd get less pigment. The experiment worked and produced a wine with more freshness and vibrancy. The new winemakers also tried different ways of marketing, selling direct to consumers at their wineries and through mail order.

Not all their trials were successes, and some experiments were more popular with novice wine consumers than with connoisseurs. When a batch of Zinfandel got stuck during fermentation and all of the sugar did not convert successfully into alcohol, the vintners at Sutter Home in St. Helena decided to market the slightly sweet, pink wine as White Zinfandel. Soon Sutter Home was selling millions of cases annually.

The newcomers had a model for the wines they wanted to achieve: the great French wines. They studied French techniques closely, trying to ascertain exactly what made the great French wines great in hopes that they could then reproduce that taste. They drank them regularly alongside their own wines to see how theirs stacked up against what they considered to be the world's best. The staff at Hanzell regularly tasted the great Burgundy Pinot Noirs and Chardonnays. After drinking them they placed the empty bottles on a shelf in their bottling room almost like sacred offerings to Bacchus. Among the remembrances of wines past: a 1952 Bâtard-Montrachet, a 1959 Grands Echézeaux, a 1935 Clos de Vougeot, and a 1959 Romanée-Conti. Only the best.

That search for quality led the new generation to plant different grapes than those that locals called "the standards"—Zinfandel, Petite Sirah, Carignane, and Alicante Bouschet, which had been grown in California since the nineteenth century and were popular largely because they grew easily and crops were large. In their place the new winemakers followed the direction of UC Davis research and concentrated on what became known as the "four noble grapes"—Cabernet Sauvignon, Pinot Noir, Chardonnay, and Riesling. In the Napa Valley in 1961 there were only an estimated 387 acres of Cabernet Sauvignon, but by 1973 that number had increased to 2,432 acres. Pinot Noir grapes in the same period went from 166 to 1,013 acres, Chardonnay increased from 60 to 785 acres. On the other hand, acreage in Alicante Bouschet, the old reliable red from Prohibition days whose main attribute was its thick skin, dropped from 228 to 58 acres.

The new winemakers respected the old and strong California tradition of sharing the knowledge they acquired and helping each other. Most of them closely followed the new techniques and technology that had been developed at Davis and Fresno State College, which set up its own wine program in 1958. There were few trade secrets as all of them struggled to find their own style of winemaking and advance their technical skills.

Jack and Jamie Davies were living in San Francisco in the early 1960s, when they became interested in the California wine country. Jack had attended Stanford, received an MBA from Harvard Business School, and then worked for a variety of companies, including Kaiser Aluminum, McKinsey, and Fibreboard. After being the president of two companies, Davies decided he wanted to have his own business.

The couple first learned something about wine through the San Francisco Wine and Food Society, and then from Martin Ray, who had previously worked for Paul Masson in the Santa Cruz Mountains but now had his own winery there. One memorable session of good food and good wine with Ray started at noon and ended thirteen hours—and many bottles of wine—later. Jack and Jamie invested in Martin Ray's wine ventures and also listened to his suggestion that they buy a winery.

Jack's business background led him to look for a niche market and he quickly zeroed in on a California version of Champagne. A few local sparkling wines were being produced, the best-seller being Almaden Blanc de Blancs, which was made in the Santa Cruz Mountains. Kornell in the Napa Valley and Korbel in Sonoma were also making sparkling wine. But none of those were using the French techniques developed by the monk Dom Pérignon and others. Davies said later, "We picked Champagne because we thought nobody was paying any attention to it in California."

The couple in 1965 bought a rundown Victorian manor in Calistoga. The price was about $500,000, and they had to put down just $10,000 in cash. In a quintessential example of the naïveté of so many of California's new winemakers, they bought land in the wrong place for growing grapes needed for sparkling wine. According to the research done by Professors Amerine and Winkler, Calistoga, the hot area in the northern Napa Valley, is best suited for growing Cabernet Sauvignon grapes. Carneros, the cooler southern Napa region, is a better place for the Chardonnay and Pinot Noir grapes they would need for sparkling wine.* Location didn't matter, though. They both fell in love with the old house built by German immigrant Jacob Schram, and they decided to buy the property as soon as they saw the house. The Schramsberg winery, which Robert Louis Stevenson visited in 1880, was one of the most famous of the "ghost wineries," as dormant facilities were called.

Since the Davies couple knew virtually nothing about making wine, much less the more complicated Champagne, they asked Maynard Amerine to be their teacher and consultant. He declined, but recommended André Tchelistcheff's son Dimitri, who had graduated from Davis and was then working as a winemaker in Mexico's Baja California. Over a shrimp lunch on the beach in the fishing town of Ensenada, Dimitri agreed to be their consultant. His father, who happened to be visiting his son at the time, said that he would also help.

Since no grapes of any kind were then growing at Schramsberg, Jack and Jamie set out to buy fruit on the open market. There weren't any of the Chardonnay that they would need for Champagne, so they purchased five tons of Riesling grapes from a local grower and then exchanged them with the Charles Krug Winery for the same amount of Chardonnay to make

---

*It took more than three decades to correct that mistake. In the 1990s, Schramsberg replanted forty-two acres of vineyard and experimented to see which grapes did best there. It turned out to be Cabernet Sauvignon, and in 2001 the winery produced its first vintage of J. Davies Cabernet Sauvignon, which immediately won high marks with critics.

their first vintage of sparkling wine. Aware that old-timers were laughing at the idea of making a French-style sparkling wine in the Napa Valley, the entrepreneurial couple made only 250 cases the first year. But veterans still had their doubts, and a rumor got started that Jack knew so little about agriculture that he put plants in upside down in his new Schramsberg vineyard.

The reputation of Schramsberg grew quickly, however. When President Richard Nixon made his historic trip to China in 1972, he took along fourteen cases of Schramsberg sparkling wine, and at a formal dinner in Beijing he toasted his host Chou En-lai to a new era of relations between the two countries with Schramsberg Blanc de Blancs.

In 1968, Eugene Trefethen, a recently retired president of Kaiser Industries, the company that built the San Francisco–Oakland Bay Bridge and the Grand Coulee Dam, bought Napa Valley's old Eschol winery and ranch, which was started in 1886 and included 600 acres of prime vineyards. Trefethen's son John, who had done his undergraduate studies at the University of North Carolina and was working on an MBA at Stanford, became more interested in the possibilities of winemaking at the family's new property than following his father into corporate America. While he was learning about the wine business, John met Janet Spooner, who had recently returned from nearly a year of living in Europe, mainly in Besançon, France. She came back to California determined to get a job in wine and eventually landed at the Winegrowers Foundation in St. Helena.

John produced small batches of homemade wine in 1971 and 1972. It was pretty primitive stuff: he crushed Chardonnay grapes in plastic garbage cans. He had heard around the valley about the importance of cold fermentation of white wines, so he put the fermenting juice in an air-conditioned house on the ranch and turned the thermostat down as far as possible. Fermentation, which had been expected to take perhaps a week, lasted a month. His first tank of fermenting Pinot Noir erupted late one night like an exploding volcano because he had overfilled it. Trefethen, though, learned from his mistakes, and the quality of his wines soon improved.

As part of his studies at Stanford, John produced a business plan for the winery. One of the biggest problems he addressed was distribution. Like Rodney Strong before him, Trefethen had run into problems getting distributors to sell his wine. They wanted to deal with big-brand companies such as Gallo that moved millions of cases, rather than the little-known new ones that sold perhaps a few thousand. Trefethen's solution was the same as Strong's: go around distributors by selling direct. He proposed setting up a sales office in the tourist town of Carmel, California, and selling to residents and visitors. An added advantage of direct sales was that profit margins would be higher since he didn't have to go through a distributor.

Things moved fast for Trefethen in 1973. He married Janet in August before the harvest of his first commercial wine crop. Later that year, he reached an agreement with Moët & Chandon, the French Champagne company, to make its first California sparkling wine at the old Eschol winery, now Trefethen Vineyards. Moët had spent two years roaming the world looking for a place outside France to make sparkling wine and had decided that the best location was the Napa Valley. The company had quietly bought up land for vineyards in the central and southern Napa Valley, but while their own vines were maturing it wanted to jumpstart its operation by buying grapes from Trefethen and using its facilities to make its wine. For a while the historic Eschol building contained two separate, bonded wineries: Trefethen Vineyards on the ground floor, and Domaine Chandon, the French firm's American subsidiary, on the second floor. Working in such close proximity with the French, the Trefethens learned a lot about winemaking—and also showed the French a few new things such as mechanical harvesting, which was anathema at home.

Basking in the glory of having worked with the French, Trefethen went on to develop one of the most extensive wine lists in the Napa Valley that included Gewürtztraminer, a spicy wine produced mainly in Alsace. Trefethen was also one of the California pioneers in growing Merlot, which he did at the suggestion of his mother, who was very familiar with French wines and knew that Merlot was blended with Cabernet Sauvignon in many of Bordeaux's most famous brands.

By the early 1970s, many of the ghost wineries had been reopened. The influx of the ambitious amateur winemakers continued, but the new arrivals had to buy land from farmers who were grazing cattle or growing plums and other fruit. The newcomers shared the same eclectic background as the first arrivals. Two engineers from the Silicon Valley, Thomas Cottrell and Thomas Parkhill, started the Cuvaison Winery in 1970 on the Silverado Trail near Calistoga. In 1972, seven new wineries changed hands or were opened. Tom Burgess, a retired Air Force pilot, bought Lee Stewart's old Souverain Cellars. Albert Brounstein, a pharmaceuticals wholesaler in Los Angeles, purchased property on Diamond Mountain in the northern part of the Napa Valley and in 1972 released his first Cabernet Sauvignon. Francis Mahoney, who had planned to be a history teacher, launched Carneros Creek Winery.

Jack Cakebread and his wife, Dolores, in the early 1970s owned Cakebread's Garage, an auto-repair shop in Oakland. In his free time Jack was also a professional photographer. In 1973, he got an assignment to shoot pictures for *The Treasury of American Wines* book and traveled to the Napa Valley to see Jack and Helen Sturdivant, family friends who were raising cattle and growing a few grapes. As he was leaving, Cakebread told them that if they ever wanted to sell their property, he'd like to buy it. No sooner had he gotten home to Oakland than he got a call from the Sturdivants saying that they wanted to sell.

The Cakebreads drove up to the valley, all the while thinking that it was a wasted trip because they didn't have money to buy anything. When they arrived, Jack candidly told the Sturdivants that all he had was the $2,500 advance he was getting for taking pictures for the book. The Sturdivants said they'd take the money as a down payment. While continuing to run their Oakland garage, the Cakebreads became winemakers. They took classes at UC Davis and sought the advice of local savants like Robert Mondavi and Louis M. Martini. Slowly the Cakebreads began selling their wine—almost bottle by bottle. The Cakebreads led their double life at the garage and the winery for nineteen years until they finally sold the garage.

Social changes that had been taking place at a rapid pace in America in the late 1950s and early 1960s created a new market for the young California wineries. Americans were becoming wealthier, better traveled, and more sophisticated about food and wine. Economist John Kenneth Galbraith in his 1958 book *The Affluent Society* pointed out that the country was enjoying "quite unprecedented affluence." The number of American families in the then top category of federal income statistics (earning $15,000 or more per year) jumped from 1.2 percent in 1951 to 22.3 percent in 1970. One of the first things the newly affluent Americans did was travel. The number of passengers departing from the U.S. jumped from 1 million in 1951 to 9.4 million in 1970, and about 40 percent were Europe bound.

Flying on the new Boeing 707 jet, which made its first transatlantic passage on October 26, 1958, on a trip from New York to Paris, Americans arrived carrying Arthur Frommer's *Europe on $5 a Day*, first published in 1957. While there, they were exposed to a lifestyle that many saw as less harried and more enjoyable. And wine was an integral part of that lifestyle from Paris to Madrid, Rome to Lisbon. The footloose Americans often tried to reproduce some of the things they had enjoyed in Paris, France, when they returned to Paris, Texas. The first and easiest way to do that was to drink wine with special meals.

Another consequence of European travel was a new interest in food.

Americans who had previously considered well-done roast beef to be the epitome of haute cuisine were now making *carbonnade de boeuf* on Saturday night. First Lady Jacqueline Kennedy in 1961 hired a French chef for the White House. That same year, Julia Child, Louisette Bertholle, and Simone Beck published *Mastering the Art of French Cooking,* a book dedicated to making fine cuisine accessible to American home cooks, and two years later Child started her popular public television series *The French Chef.* On November 25, 1966, she was on the cover of *Time* magazine with the headline "Everyone's in the Kitchen."

Wine was also the drink of preference for members of the counterculture revolution of the 1960s. Hippies and their followers were rebelling against everything that reminded them of the lifestyle of their parents, including the hard liquor they generally preferred. So instead of drinking a martini or scotch on the rocks, young people were reaching for a glass of wine.

All these trends came together to create a significant increase in American wine sales in the 1960s and also a change in the type of wine people were drinking. The breakthrough year was 1967, when sales of dry table wines surpassed those of high-alcohol sweet wines for the first time since Prohibition, and annual per capita consumption went over 1 gallon, a 16 percent increase in the previous decade.

Few of the new wine connoisseurs, however, were paying much attention to what was taking place in California wines. The state's reputation for producing only low-quality jug wine was tough to kick. When it came to wine, the new American sophisticates ordered French. While living in New York City in the late 1960s, I wanted to drink California wine to support my home state. But the merchant on Madison Avenue where I shopped always steered me toward French or Italian wines, saying that California only produced "cooking wine."

One of the very few people who recognized that something important was happening in northern California was Harry Waugh, a British wine writer and one of the major players in the global wine business. Waugh started in wine in 1934 and introduced Bordeaux's then little-known Pomerols, in particular Château Pétrus, to the English market. He worked for Harveys of Bristol, a liquor importer, and was its representative on the board of directors of Château Latour, a Bordeaux First Growth.

Waugh first learned of the new small California wineries in June 1964 at a tasting in New York City. The next spring he made an extensive trip through the California wine country and shipped back to England cases of Souverain Cellars Cabernet Sauvignon and Heitz Cellars Chardonnay. At the end of his trip he wrote in his diary that he was "sticking my neck out rather dangerously" but thought that the best California Chardonnay and Cabernet Sauvignon were equal to "good estate bottled" French wines.

For the next few years, Waugh traveled to California nearly every spring and his enthusiasm for California wines grew exponentially, sentiments he recorded in his diaries. During his 1969 visit he wrote, "To my mind, at this particular period of time, these vineyards of California must be among the most exciting of all." In April 1971, he wrote that the Napa Valley had become "the most fascinating, the most exhilarating grape-growing district of the world." He credited that to "the vitality, the enthusiasm, the expertise, and the thirst for knowledge of the winemakers, [and their] willingness to experiment and try out new ideas increases from year to year." Three years later, Waugh wrote, "This is what is so fascinating about California, the growers have such open minds and are adventurous enough to try almost anything."

It was not enough, however, for the new breed of winemakers just to make good wine. The world's wine connoisseurs had to recognize the quality coming out of the new California wineries. In the early 1970s, Waugh was the exception.

CHAPTER EIGHT

In Search of a Simpler Life

Nothing more excellent or valuable than wine
was ever granted by the gods to man.

—PLATO

Warren Winiarski in 1952.

The white Chevrolet station wagon pulling a U-Haul trailer filled with books, clothes, furniture, household goods—and more books—was barely able to get up the hill on Route 66 in western Arizona just before the highway goes into California at the town of Needles. The temperature under the stifling desert sun of August 1964 was over 110 degrees. Driving the car was Warren Winiarski, a University of Chicago lecturer in the liberal arts program and a graduate student in political science. Accompanying him in the car were his wife, Barbara, and their two children, aged four years and eighteen months.

The car chugged and coughed its way up the dry and barren Arizona hills, while the passengers sweltered inside. The station wagon was on its second set of valves, having blown its first on the initial day after the family left Chicago. Warren pushed the gas pedal to the floor, but the car sputtered its way up the steepest grades at no more than five miles an hour.

With the Chevrolet dying in slow motion, Warren and Barbara agreed that she and the children should get out in order to lessen the load over the last two major crests. As they approached the top of the first one and the car inched forward, Barbara jumped out and walked alongside the car for a while before it got ahead. When Warren was over the crest, he stopped, and Barbara got the children out of the car. Warren also off-loaded some of their luggage to further lighten the load. They then waited until he flagged a trucker carrying a load of oranges, who stopped and told them that after the next crest they were near a major downhill slope. He offered to take Barbara, the children, and the luggage to meet Warren further along the road. Barbara never asked the trucker where he was coming from, but thought it was lovely to ride into California accompanied by oranges.

The family was reunited after the last crest. Warren stopped at the next small town, where he found a garage that rented him space to unhook the trailer and store it until he got back later with a stronger vehicle to pull it. The family, now unburdened by the weight of the trailer, was able to continue on its way toward the Napa Valley.

Born in 1928, Warren had grown up in the large Polish section on the northwest side of Chicago during the Depression, when a quarter of American workers were unemployed. His father ran a livery business that had been started by Warren's grandfather in the late nineteenth century. He delivered coal to homes in the winter and ice in the summer. The transportation of goods eventually evolved into the transportation of people, and by the time Warren was grown, his father was providing cars for weddings, funeral services, and other rites of passage for Chicago's Poles.

Winiarski means "son of a winemaker" in Polish and, sure enough, his father made honey, dandelion, and fruit wines in the family basement. One of Warren's earliest memories was of putting his ear to the side of a wine barrel stored in the family's basement and listening intently to the blub-blub-blub sound of fermentation taking place. To the young boy, the barrel seemed magically alive.

The Poles were a small, tightly knit society inside the big city. The Winiarskis lived across the street from the Polish National Catholic Cathedral, a centerpiece of Polish life and source of local pride. Services at the cathedral were conducted in the native language. Religious and social events bonded the people together.

The Polish neighborhood was a place where everyone knew your name—and probably your father's and mother's as well. Whether you were born in the old country or only spoke a smattering of Polish, you were never a stranger in your section of town. Whenever something happened, whether it was a happy event like a wedding or a sad one like an automobile accident, people would immediately ask, "Was it someone from the community?" The sense of people, place, and purpose meant that no matter what happened, it would be a lot easier to accept if you had the support of your people. Warren would later devote his life to trying to re-create the sense of solidarity and family that he had first experienced in Chicago.

Warren began to move beyond Chicago's Poles when he went to high school, but he never totally left the neighborhood until college. As a young student, he was hard to categorize. He had to repeat the seventh grade, a rattling experience in a family that stressed education and achievement. But Warren wasn't a slow student—quite the contrary. He was very bright, but had to get his arms around ideas or problems and shape them in ways that he could understand.

After high school he entered the University of Chicago, home of the Great Books program fostered by its president Robert M. Hutchins. The liberal-arts curriculum centered around the great writers and thinkers of Western civilization from Aristotle to Zeno. A truly educated person, Hutchins maintained, had to be at home with the fundamental thinkers of the Western tradition. Warren stayed there only a short time before going off to a school of agriculture and mining at Fort Collins, Colorado, thinking that he might be at home in forestry. Studies there, though, showed him he was really more interested in the world of ideas than in technical subjects.

While he was in Colorado someone gave Warren a book about St. John's College in Annapolis, Maryland. St. John's, like the University of Chicago, centered its curriculum on the Great Books, and so he transferred there. The school was small, with less than three hundred students, and both teachers and students lived an intimate, intellectual life. In many ways, St. John's offered Warren the kind of enlarged family atmosphere he had enjoyed growing up in the Polish section of Chicago. He also felt at home in a college where philosophic thoughtfulness was more important than rote memorization. A picture taken of Winiarski at St. John's shows a young man with a serious demeanor, wearing thick black-rimmed glasses.

In his senior year, Winiarski met a freshman who shared many of his interests. Her name was Barbara Dvorak, and she had grown up in nearby Baltimore. Her family had been in farming, although there were also artists and musicians in her heritage. Barbara was well read and could keep up with Warren when his brown eyes grew distant and his ideas jumped from one thought to another like a ball bouncing around a squash court. Warren became Barbara's guide through the Great Books, and the couple began sharing their dreams for the life that spread before them.

After graduating in 1952, Warren went back to the University of Chicago for graduate studies in political science. He soon drifted into political theory and the ideas of Niccolò Machiavelli, a contemporary of Christopher Columbus who advised members of the ruling Medici family in the Republic of Florence. In addition to power politics, Machiavelli advocated a civic spirit and solidarity among people, which laid the foundation for Italian nationalism. That sense of cohesion appealed to the Chicago grad student.

As part of his graduate work in political theory, Winiarski went to Italy in 1953 for a year of study at the Croce Institute in Naples. Winiarski did more than just read Machiavelli in the original Italian. He also discovered an attractive European way of life built around wine and food. While his family in Chicago had drunk wine for festive occasions, this was the first time he had been around people who enjoyed it as a daily experience. Winiarski loved the long luncheons and dinners, where a sense of intimacy was reinforced over a lingering glass of wine or cup of espresso. Winiarski admired the way people came together at mealtime in an aesthetic experience that seemed to give their lives a structure.

Warren returned to the University of Chicago in the fall of 1954 to take up a position as a lecturer in the basic program of the Great Books studies, where he taught for the next six years. He was on track to getting a Ph.D. and then a life as a college professor. Warren, though, couldn't get the Italian experience out of his mind. Life abroad contrasted so starkly with what he and his new wife, Barbara, saw around them. At the time all the sinews holding American society together seemed to be breaking. U.S. cities were decaying, as millions of people took advantage of the new Interstate highways to begin fresh lives in the suburbs. There was little sense of community in the static housing developments being built on the edges of old cities. Ethnic enclaves in places like Warren's Chicago and Barbara's Baltimore were atrophying. The couple also had disdain for the power of television, which was becoming the center of family life. American family dining was becoming fast food, as Ray Kroc spread McDonald's golden arches across the country from their beginnings in San Bernardino, California.

The Winiarskis, who were living in faculty housing, talked a lot about those changes. They soon had two children, Kasia and Stephen, and wondered about the atmosphere in which they were growing up. The couple dreamed of a simpler life, closer to nature, where children might come of age in a family surrounded by books, rather than in front of a television set.

Always a voracious reader, Winiarski began poring over books about people living the kind of life to which he aspired. One of them was written by Philip Wagner, an editor at the Baltimore *Sun* and a winemaker. The son of a University of Michigan professor of romance languages, Wagner had grown up drinking wine with meals. Prohibition forced him into making his own wine, and he wrote a how-to book telling Americans the way to make wine at home. For Wagner, wine was part of a way of life, just as it was for the people Winiarski had met in Italy.

In 1945, Wagner opened Boordy Vineyard, a winery in Riderwood, Maryland, where he set out to produce quality American wine. Although others had tried and failed to make French-style wines not far from there, Wagner used new French hybrid vines, which adapted better to the mid-Atlantic soil and climate. Wine historian Leon Adams described a Boordy white wine as "fresh and delicate" and a rosé as "soft and fruity." Each year Wagner easily sold out of the four wines he produced. Winiarski had first heard about Wagner while a student at St. John's. The more he learned about Wagner, the more Winiarski liked, so in 1962 he wrote him a letter and then visited Boordy Vineyard.

One of Winiarski's main concerns at the time was whether he could get started in winemaking by working at a winery and picking up the needed skills as he went along. As a father with a new family and limited financial means, he couldn't simply drop everything and go back to school for a couple of years. Winiarski had run cross-country when he was in high school, and he considered winemaking to be like running long distances. You didn't need a degree in anatomy to run two miles. And in order to make wine, he felt, you didn't need to become a chemist.

When he visited Wagner in Riderwood, Winiarski was entranced by the way of life he found there. It was a small operation and had the elements of food, wine, and family he was seeking. Wagner was intrigued by the question of whether someone could still get into winemaking as Winiarski suggested, and so he wrote his UC Davis friend Maynard Amerine. Not surprisingly, the academic dismissed Winiarski's idea, saying it was impossible for someone to learn everything on the job; a person needed the foundation of university study. Wagner relayed the letter to Winiarski in Chicago, but it had scant influence on the college lecturer, who was becoming more and more determined to grow grapes and make wine.

Winiarski started making wine in his Chicago apartment, just as his father had before him. Once when he was visiting his wife's family in Baltimore, he drove to rural Westminster County and bought some Baco Noir grapes from a farmer who sold the same grapes to Wagner. Winiarski continued on to an antique store, where he bought an old crock. He crushed the grapes in Baltimore and carried them in his station wagon back to Chicago, where fermentation took place. At first, the station-wagon wine was okay— in fact, it was almost pleasant. Soon, though, a problem developed. Crocks like the one he had bought were used in rural Maryland to pickle or ferment all sorts of things. The one Winiarski purchased had probably been used for making sauerkraut or pickles. The crock's tiny cracks contained remnants of life from its earlier uses, and soon he was drinking pickled wine. It was an inauspicious introduction for Winiarski to the mysteries of microbiology.

Winiarski explored agricultural options other than wine. In the spring of 1963, he set out alone for New Mexico to look at the cultivation of both grapes and apples there. Living out of the family station wagon, he drove around the Rio Grande Valley examining the agriculture and looking at the way people lived. What he found was raw and rough. Outside of irrigated areas, the land was arid and unavailing. Lecturers in Chicago were not affluent, but the apple farmers he saw in New Mexico were dirt poor.

One day during the trip he pulled the station wagon to a stop along the highway and looked at a nearby abandoned adobe house. Picket fences still stood around the fields. Cornhusks left from the last harvest lay on the ground. The tumbleweeds carried depression in their wake as they rolled across the countryside. Winiarski looked around and wondered why he was even considering moving there, saying to himself, "Your ancestors would curse you for having left what you left to come back to something like this, and your descendants will curse you for having opportunities and then bringing them to this."

Warren bought some grapes in New Mexico and carried them home to Chicago, where he made a second batch of wine. Increasingly Machiavelli was taking a backseat to wine in Winiarski's studies and life. He began devouring all the books and articles on the subject he could find. He studied classics like *American Wines* by Frank Schoonmaker and Tom Marvel, which had been published in 1941, as well as Wagner's *American Wines and Wine-Making*. A book by John Storm entitled *An Invitation to Wines* introduced Winiarski to new small wineries in northern California that carried names like Hallcrest Vineyard, Mayacamas Vineyards, and Souverain Cellars. According to Storm they were producing good, European-style wines. The Martin Ray winery in the Santa Cruz Mountains south of San Francisco appealed particularly to Winiarski because it seemed to incorporate the simple life close to nature that he was seeking.

Winiarski wrote Ray, asking him for an apprenticeship. In his response Ray held out the possibility of a job, but asked Warren first to go to Ann Arbor, Michigan, for a preliminary screening by Peter Martin Ray, a stepson who taught at the University of Michigan. While there, Winiarski tasted his first Martin Ray wine, a Chardonnay that was better than anything he had ever experienced.

Winiarski passed the interview and was invited to the winery for a week to see the operation. The week with Martin Ray was like living in a dream. Here was everything: the bucolic location amid pines; communal dining; intelligent conversations. Food was prepared as simply as possible, with only a few seasonings added to enhance the natural flavors. Ray and his wife spent hours preparing rustic and robust meals, and fowl was cooked over an open spit. For a special occasion, the large school bell—the same one Ray had used to celebrate the end of Prohibition—rang out to call everyone to table. There was almost a sacramental character to life at the Martin Ray winery.

Winiarski joined in with gusto. He put on boots and tramped behind a tractor breaking ground for a new Chardonnay vineyard. Since Ray produced only about a thousand cases a year, everything was done on a small scale. Wine, for example, was bottled with a siphon hose. Winiarski put one end of a small hose into a barrel of wine and the other end into an empty bottle. Then he sucked the air out of the tube in order to start the flow of wine. When the bottle was full, he pinched the hose to stop the wine and then moved the hose to another bottle and filled it. Winiarski looked at a place where Ray said the family might live and chalked out on the floor where each child would sleep. At the end of the week, Winiarski left with high spirits and dreams of a new life.

On his return to Chicago, he wrote Ray an enthusiastic letter, thanking him for his hospitality and expressing his interest in moving to California. But for a long time he didn't hear back. When a response finally arrived, Ray explained to Winiarski that he seemed too independent to be part of the Martin Ray world.

Winiarski was crushed. Only later did he realize that life on Ray's mountaintop might not have been the paradise he had originally envisaged. It would have been difficult for Winiarski and his young family to live in Ray's forced togetherness, and he probably *was* too independent to adjust to the winemaker's strict, almost militaristic, way of doing things. Ray, he later recognized, had the traits of a benign despot. It had been magic for that week, but what would have happened when the magic faded?

The rejection slip from Ray, however, did little to diminish Winiarski's obsession with winemaking. Someway, somehow he had to get back to California. Martin Ray's approach was not the only way. The positive aspects of Ray's lifestyle could be preserved without replicating the less attractive side.

Soon Winiarski was doing what he had done before: writing letters and reading more books. He wrote to other small wineries mentioned in the Storm book. Several did not bother to reply. But finally he got a bite. Lee Stewart at Souverain Cellars offered him work as the number two man in a two-man winery. It was basically the same job that Mike Grgich had held six years earlier. Stewart told Winiarski that he and his family should arrive in the middle of the summer so that he could help with the grape harvest and crush.

On August 1, 1964, the Winiarskis packed up the station wagon and headed off to a new life on the West Coast. It was an exciting, if stressful, journey. Problems with the car put them far behind schedule, and Warren was concerned about getting to Souverain Cellars in time for harvest. He drove each day for as long as he could, but eventually fatigue would set in and the family would have to stop for safety's sake. Some nights they camped by the side of the road, with Warren and Barbara sleeping outside under the stars while the children slept in the car. One day they drove long after dark to a mountain mesa campground in Arizona and were not sure exactly where they were when they parked for the night. The next morning they awoke at dawn's first light and realized that if they had taken another twenty steps in the dark, they would have stumbled off the edge of the mesa. From that flat tabletop they looked across miles of red-rock desert toward other mesas as far as the eye could see.

Warren kept pushing forward through small towns toward the Napa Valley. When the family reached the recently completed Interstate 80 highway east of San Francisco, Barbara grew worried. The hills around San Francisco Bay were desolate and parched. Only a few trees could be seen in the small arroyos; everywhere else there was only dry grass and scrub bush. Warren tried to reassure her, telling his wife that the Napa Valley, which was now only about fifty miles away, would be beautiful.

A week after leaving Chicago, the Winiarskis finally made their way into the Napa Valley and up Howell Mountain to the Souverain Cellars winery, where Warren had a job waiting for him. Lee Stewart had arranged for the family to rent a small house below the winery on Crystal Springs Road. The cabin dated back to California pioneer days and had a wood-burning stove and a screened porch all around it. Just across the road were trees, where the family could pick its own fruit. A stream went through the property, and the sound of the wind blowing through the pine trees resounded like a symphony. It was a long way from Chicago.

CHAPTER NINE

An Apprentice Winemaker

Give me wine to wash me clean
of the weather-stains of cares.
—RALPH WALDO EMERSON

(Above left) Warren Winiarski in the summer of 1970,
irrigating the vines that, once budded, would produce
the 1973 Stag's Leap Wine Cellars Cabernet Sauvignon.
(Above right) The Winiarski children (from left to right),
Julia, Stephen, and Kasia, in the vineyard in the spring of
1973, with the wild mustard cover crop, which will be tilled
and returned to the soil as fertilizer.

When the Winiarski family arrived at Souverain Cellars, the grape crush had already started and Warren went to work immediately, slipping easily into the rhythm of the place. In the two-man winery, he did a bit of everything, but spent most of his time at first stacking onto a truck the fruit boxes filled with grapes that day laborers had picked. Warren and Lee Stewart drove the truck out to the vineyard to pick up the containers and then carried them to the winery for crushing. It was hard work, and every night Warren returned home exhausted.

Souverain Cellars was a much bigger and better-equipped operation than Martin Ray Vineyards, Warren's only other close experience with a winery in operation. At Souverain, for example, they were no longer filling bottles using a siphon hose. A machine allowed several bottles to be filled simultaneously, although an operator still had to manually run it. There were also 1,500-gallon oak tanks for aging wines.

Souverain had developed a lot in the six years since Mike Grgich had worked there, thanks in large part to André Tchelistcheff, who was still a consultant to Stewart. The Beaulieu winemaker was passing on what he had learned in the Hanzell experiment as well as innovative things winemakers like Peter Mondavi were doing. Stewart learned from Tchelistcheff about controlled malolactic fermentation, which greatly improved the complexity and finesse of his red wines. Stewart was also at the cutting edge of new technology that used selected yeasts to achieve low-temperature fermentation of white wines.

While Grgich left Stewart after only the basic winemaking was completed at the end of four months, Winiarski stayed there for two years and was able to watch the development of the entire annual wine cycle twice. After the initial fermentation was completed in late September, the clarification of the wine began. The process of turning sugar into alcohol had left behind in the liquid lots of small particles. As the wine sat in its holding tanks, those gradually fell to the bottom. Stewart showed Winiarski how they pumped the clear wine from one tank to another, leaving the sediment, called the lees, behind to be discarded. The procedure was called racking, and they did it several times in the early fall for both the red and white wines.

In October, the secondary or malolactic fermentation of the red wines began. Stewart had kept some of the lees material and introduced that along with malolactic bacteria into the wine to start the later fermentation. This process took much longer than the first fermentation, and the goal was to have it finished by Thanksgiving, before it became so cold that the process would simply stop. The malolactic fermentation again stirred up the wine and left residue behind, and so again it had to be clarified by racking.

Then the wine was stabilized. Stewart explained that they didn't want any surprises in the bottle after it left the winery: the wines would have to be able to withstand cold and heat fluctuations during travel and on store shelves. First the wines went into barrels or tanks where any remaining carbon dioxide, which could make the wine fizzy, escaped. Then the temperature of the white wines was lowered to about 40 degrees so that tartar crystals, which occur naturally in wine at low temperatures and could be unwelcome remnants at the bottom of a bottle, formed and then fell down in the tanks. After the cold stabilization, the clear liquid was siphoned off and the tartar crystals left behind.

Red wines did not need to be cold stabilized because this process of having the crystals settle to the bottom would take place naturally while the wines were aging for two winters in tanks or barrels. Bentonite, a clay compound, was added to the whites and acted as a coagulant, attracting protein and other substances before falling to the floor of the tanks. Finally the wines were filtered to remove yeast and any other microorganisms that might later harm the wine.

Soon after the beginning of the new year, Stewart and Winiarski were out in the vineyard pruning the vines. The two men cut back the plants while leaving only a few stubs, called spurs, that would bear fruit in the coming year. Stewart showed Warren examples of his own pruning and how to choose the correct number and orientation of the buds left for new growth. When the pruning was finished, only the skeleton of a plant remained.

As the weather warmed up in the spring, the two men were back in the fields tending to the vines again. Now the plants, acting as if they had minds of their own, were sending out stray shoots called suckers. These could take vitality away from the shoots that Stewart and Winiarski had meticulously selected. In addition, the suckers would produce unwelcome additional leaf cover that would later block the sun from getting at the clusters of grapes. Two or three weeks after the first buds appeared, the two men walked down the rows of vines pinching off the stray suckers. They returned one more time to remove new ones that had appeared.

With spring progressing, Stewart and Winiarski began applying sulfur on the new growth on the vines to prevent mildew. Whenever there was another six inches of growth on the plants, the two men walked the rows of vines applying a fine sulfur dust. They repeated the procedure three or four times during the rapid growing season.

The vines had developed nicely by early summer, and it generally took about 180 days from the first bud burst to the fruit's full maturation. In midsummer, though, Stewart told Winiarski that they needed to thin out the crop. The two men then went through the vineyard picking off poor clusters or removing parts of damaged ones to eliminate any imperfect grapes that would lower the quality of the final product. All during the growing season winemakers fight an endless series of battles that nature throws up against them: extreme weather, poor fruit set, insects, mildew, wandering animals, and more. If the grape growers are successful, they will reap bigger harvests. Each ton of grapes will produce about sixty cases of wine.

By August the grapes at Souverain were ripening rapidly, and it was time to begin preparing for another harvest and winemaking. Most wine that still remained in barrels or tanks from the previous year was bottled, so that the containers would be empty and ready to receive the new vintage.

Winiarski had an insatiable appetite for information about what they were doing both in the vineyard and the winery, constantly asking Stewart about why this or that procedure was being done. At one point Stewart seemed to get suspicious that Winiarski's plethora of questions was a sign that he would soon be leaving, perhaps to start his own winery. Stewart said there were about a dozen wineries in Napa Valley and that there might be room for another two. Even the quality wines Stewart was producing were selling for only about $3 a bottle, and there just wasn't the demand to support more wineries.

Stewart drilled into Winiarski the same attention to cleanliness and detail that he had taught Grgich. The boss was extremely fastidious, watching closely over every last detail. For example, when Stewart put a bung, a wooden plug, into the top of a small barrel, he carefully aligned the grain of the bung with that of the barrel to assure a tight fit. He demanded that Winiarski do it exactly the same way.

The veteran showed the younger man how to stack cases of full bottles fourteen high, pointing out the way to interlock the containers so that they were perfectly straight, with the stack not leaning in the slightest. When the cases were in place, Stewart would step back and quietly admire his work just as Michelangelo must have gazed at his *David*.

As he watched him work, Winiarski realized that Stewart was not as big physically as he seemed at first, but was powerfully built. Stewart sometimes climbed out the top of an open tank by lifting himself up by his arms much like a gymnast raising himself on parallel bars, a feat that required tremendous arm and shoulder strength. When equipment or tools were exchanged on the job, Stewart simply tossed them to Winiarski, who quickly learned how to catch things on the fly. Winiarski got along with Stewart better than Grgich had. In the intense atmosphere of a two-man winery, the two

Americans had more in common and no language barrier to complicate communication.

While Winiarski was learning a lot from Stewart, he wasn't accepting everything as dogma and began developing his own views of winemaking independent of his boss. Warren didn't think much of Lee's Green Hungarian wine, which he thought was made with inferior grapes. Winiarski also didn't approve of his leaving a small amount of sugar in white wines, which made them slightly sweet. Winiarski was surprised that all Souverain reds, whether Cabernet Sauvignon, Zinfandel, or Petite Sirah, were treated the same way during the fermentation. He also thought fermentation of reds was done at too high a temperature, which diminished their natural flavors.

Near the house where the Winiarskis were staying was a ghost winery, where Warren began doing his own winemaking. After working with Lee Stewart during the day, he would have a quick dinner with the family and then go out to check on his various wine experiments. There was no electricity in the barnlike structure, so the only light came from flashlights or candles. Bats emulating dive-bombers added to both the fun and the fright. In his second season with Stewart, Winiarski made a half-barrel of Zinfandel. When the main harvest was in, he handpicked small, second-crop clusters that grew on lateral shoots that had been passed over in the regular picking. Winiarski then crushed and fermented the grapes at Souverain with help from Stewart. Winiarski brought the half-barrel of Zinfandel down to the ghost winery, where he and his daughter Kasia carefully racked and clarified it. Few wines have been made with more loving attention and study.

When Warren Winiarski had headed west in 1964, owning a winery had not been part of the plan. But the idea began to take root in the California soil. In August 1965, Winiarski paid $15,000 for fifteen acres of uncleared land higher up Howell Mountain at about 1,900 feet. The plan was to plant three acres of grapes on the nearly flat part of the property. He had been able to get money together for a down payment from his savings and by borrowing money from Barbara's parents. He took out a bank loan for the rest.

In the spirit of the young winemakers, Winiarski was experimenting and taking risks. Most people in the valley didn't think quality grapes would prosper at so high an altitude, but Winiarski was determined to give it a try. At the time, the highest Cabernet Sauvignon vineyard on Howell Mountain was on Stewart's property at about nine hundred feet. The sparse quality of the soil on Howell Mountain, Winiarski thought, would restrain the normally vigorous grape from growing too fast in the spring and accelerate the ripening of the fruit in the fall. If only spring frost did not turn out to be too much of a problem, he thought he could make it work. Winiarski felt like a pioneer. At the same time, he recognized that it might be a long time before he would know whether he was right. He recalled an old adage he had first heard in Italy: *Vedremo in Cent'Anni* (We'll see in a hundred years).

The land where the vineyard would go was covered with poison oak and scrub brush, and Warren and Barbara immediately set out to clear it. Then Warren installed a fence around the area where the vineyard would go to keep out wandering deer.

In the fall of 1965, Warren hired a man from the valley who owned a Caterpillar tractor to come in and prepare the land that had never been tilled. The earth was densely compacted and parched. In a procedure called ripping, the farmer pulled a sharp, wedge-shaped steel blade three feet through the earth at five-foot intervals. Then he went across the land in the opposite direction and made a final pass diagonally across the area where the vineyard was to go. The action reminded Warren of a pick being thrust into a block of ice. When the ripping was finished, the land was littered with large clumps of earth and rock. Hired hands removed the rocks, while Warren and Barbara broke up the remaining soil. The goal was to have the ground to a consistency where plants could grow easily, but not to the texture of a fine soil. Old-timers in the valley said that the ground should be worked until you could push a stake into the ground to the depth of one foot. The ripped ground was then left in that open condition so that fall and winter rains would penetrate deeply into the fractured earth.

At the end of the year, the Winiarski family left its first house below Souverain Cellars and rented a place near the top of the mountain in order to be closer to their new property. Their new house had the romance of the Old West, having previously been a resting place for Wells Fargo wagons on their way between the Napa Valley and Pope Valley to the east. Olive trees grew all around, and there was an olive press in the basement. The house was built into the hillside, so its cellar was cool even on the hottest days. Behind the structure was a forest of Douglas fir trees, and in front was a meadow, walnut trees, and a lake. The family had a large garden, where they grew their own vegetables and fruit. They also had sheep, a young bull, and a pony. The house faced Pope Valley, so in the morning the rising sun smiled in on them. The evenings were cool.

By the spring of 1966, Warren was ready to lay out his vineyard. Following the strictures of UC Davis, it was to be eight feet by twelve feet— vines eight feet apart in rows that were twelve feet apart. Professor Winkler from UC Davis had determined that those dimensions provided the most efficient use of land, allowing a tractor to travel easily between rows and giving each vine plenty of space to gather nutrients from the soil. This density is much less than that found in France, where vines generally grow only three feet apart.

In a bigger vineyard the viticulturist would have laid out blocks of vines with clear demarcation lines to divide the property into smaller units by soil type or climatic conditions. In that way he could monitor how different blocks were producing and perhaps pick one block earlier or later. But there was no need for blocks in that three-acre vineyard since there was little soil variation.

From an agricultural supply store in the valley, Winiarski bought lines of steel wire on which nuts had been welded at eight-foot intervals. He then laid the wire on the ground for the entire 325-foot length for a row, pulled the wire tight, and fastened it at both ends. Then day laborers Winiarski had hired to help him drove a redwood stake into the ground at each point where there was a nut. That was the spot where they would plant a vine. There would be exactly 413 plants per acre in the vineyard. The peg was later replaced by a rot-resistant, six-foot post to which the plant would be staked while it was growing to the desired height. Wires would be attached along the row of stakes to form the trellis. As the plant grew, the arms of the vine would be tied to the lowest wire of the trellis.

After the vineyard was laid out, Warren and Barbara plus two other couples, who were their best friends from the valley, held a ceremony to mark the beginning of the new vineyard. They planted the first three vines—one for each couple—and Warren asked heavenly powers to watch over and care for the plants.

The first living thing to go into the ground was the rootstock. This was a phylloxera-resistant plant that would provide the foundation for the vine. Winiarski selected St. George rootstock, which was then widely used and reportedly resisted drought. The rootstock came in dormant, dry bundles of fifty from a valley nursery. After the rootstock was severely trimmed so there were only one or two spurs sticking out the top and short stubby roots at the end, the rootstock was planted with five inches above the ground and ten inches below. Six weeks later, in front of each planted rootstock, the workers dug basins into which water was placed to provide irrigation. Warren drove a truck carrying water through the vineyard. His day laborers took a bucket of water to each plant to irrigate it, a process they repeated every few weeks during the next five months. This vineyard, like nearly all those in the Napa Valley at the time, would be dry farmed, which meant that this would be the only time the plants would be irrigated. After that, the vines were on their own and had to survive on the area's modest rainfall—perhaps only a couple of inches during the spring part of the growing season.

After two years with Lee Stewart—the harvests of 1964 and 1965—Winiarski felt he had learned most of what he could at the place that brought him to California. He increasingly felt that he was not working toward his goal and felt it was time to move on. He was not content to remain the number-two man at a two-man winery. That was not the reason he had come to California. Stewart must have sensed this also, and he told Winiarski he was going to make a change. In mid-summer 1966, when Winiarski left Souverain, he did not have a new job but felt he could live on savings for a while until he found work. He also supplemented the family income by starting a small business serving farmers, spraying fields by hand that were overrun with poison oak and wild blackberries.

In the fall of 1966, Winiarski was ready to bud his Howell Mountain vineyard. In this process the desired grape variety, in this case Cabernet Sauvignon, would be grafted onto the rootstock that had now taken hold. The grafted vines then produce the grapes that go into wine. Winiarski had obtained the Cabernet Sauvignon cuttings from the Larkmead vineyard north of St. Helena.

Then the serious work began. Warren had hired budders, day laborers who did the budding for the whole vineyard, to do the main work. The window of opportunity for budding was short because it all had to be accomplished before fall weather set in. First the workers made a V notch on the rootstock, sliced a bud away from a piece of Cabernet Sauvignon wood, and joined the two so that the bud piece fit into the notch on the rootstock. Then they wrapped the two parts with a strip of rubber to bind them tightly together. Finally, the plant was covered with soil to prevent it from drying out in the heat and sun and so that the two pieces could grow together in the semimoist, cool earth.

The moment of truth came in the spring of 1967, when Winiarski went from plant to plant removing the bands of rubber to see whether the bud had grown into the root. In a major disappointment for the fledgling viticulturist, some 90 percent of the buds had not taken. Because of the soil's dryness and the difficulty of providing enough hand-carried buckets of water, the rootstock had not gotten enough moisture to grow actively and fuse with the buds. Winiarski, though, was not easily discouraged. He considered it just a learning experience, and the next fall he budded the vineyard again, this time being careful to have the rootstock well irrigated in advance, and achieved much better results. The roots were also now a year older, which meant they were stronger and easier to bud.

All this time, Winiarski continued learning about winemaking from a variety of sources. He took a course on wine taught by Professor Amerine at the St. Helena Wine Library and also read voraciously. Warren called the Amerine and Winkler pamphlet on California wine regions his "bible" and each night studied a short section. But despite the idyllic setting high on Howell Mountain, life there was tough. The Winiarskis were isolated, and money was short. The family bought second-hand clothes for vineyard work and lived off their land. In addition to harvesting vegetables from the garden, Warren shot deer during the hunting season—and occasionally out of season when they got over or under the fence and into the vineyard. Barbara froze the meat and served it throughout the year. The family entertained itself with games and plays, and on Saturdays listened to opera on the radio. They might have been poor, but they were very happy.

CHAPTER TEN

The Rise of Robert Mondavi

Let us have wine and women, mirth and laughter,
Sermons and soda-water the day after.

—BYRON

In the mid-1960s, the California wine business was going through a shift in generational leadership. The people who had led the drive for quality wine for the three decades since the end of Prohibition were retiring, and a new group was taking their place.

Inglenook, the grand old winery founded by Gustave Niebaum in 1879 that had been the most prestigious, high-quality California wine producer both before and after Prohibition, was sold in 1964 to United Vintners, a huge cooperative that vied with the Gallo brothers for leadership of the low-end, jug-wine trade. John Daniel Jr. had inherited Inglenook in 1939 and had resolutely protected its heritage of outstanding wines through the 1940s and 1950s, when there was almost no market for such products. He was broken by that Sisyphean effort, however, and resigned himself to selling the winery. Only four years later, Inglenook was sold again, this time to Heublein, the giant East Coast liquor company, and the transformation of the proud Inglenook brand from quality wine to jug wine soon took place at an accelerating pace. To the valley's winemakers it was like a death in the family. Everyone felt somehow diminished, even violated.

Across Route 29 from Inglenook at Beaulieu Vineyard, the Napa Valley's other showcase brand, André Tchelistcheff still reigned, but things were slowly going downhill. The parsimonious rule of Hélène de Pins was taking its toll; Beaulieu was not keeping up with the latest advances in equipment and technology. Tchelistcheff was very aware of research being done at the University of California, Davis, and in France, but Madame de Pins vetoed most of his requests to spend money to improve conditions at Beaulieu. While Tchelistcheff had helped install the very latest technology at Hanzell in the 1950s, he had not been able to make the same upgrades at Beaulieu. The winery was still using redwood tanks to ferment wine, and not aging it in French oak barrels as Tchelistcheff had told private consulting clients to do.

The new pacesetter for quality California wines was the Mondavi family. Founding father Cesare Mondavi had immigrated to the U.S. in 1906 from Sassoferrato, Italy, a village ninety miles northeast of Rome. He worked first in the mines on Minnesota's Iron Range, but when Prohibition started, members of the local Italian Club designated Mondavi to go to California and buy grapes for them to use in their home winemaking. Two years later, Mondavi moved permanently to California and started a produce company in Lodi in the Central Valley.

The family business did well shipping grapes east to Italian communities, but after Prohibition ended, Cesare moved into the wine business. He initially produced bulk wine at the Acampo Winery in Lodi. Then in 1937, Mondavi bought the Sunny St. Helena Winery in the Napa Valley. Acampo and Sunny St. Helena produced so-called tank-car wines, which got their name from the railroad cars that carried them to the Midwest and East Coast, where the wine was bottled and distributed. In 1943, Mondavi also bought St. Helena's Charles Krug Winery, which had been opened in 1861 and was the oldest operating winery in the Napa Valley. Soon Mondavi was selling several qualities of wine under three brand names: Charles Krug, Napa Vista, and CK Mondavi. While the bulk of the business was still jug wine, the family was moving into quality products that had higher profit margins. Starting in the late 1940s, Krug wines began winning medals at the California State Fair and in other wine competitions.

Cesare Mondavi's two sons, Robert and the younger Peter, were both active in the family business. But as in the Bible's story of Isaac's twin sons Esau and Jacob, there was an intense rivalry between the boys. Robert was Mr. Outside, directing the marketing and traveling the country to promote Krug and Mondavi wines. Everybody loved Robert. Outgoing and affable, he was always ready to help newcomers to the wine business by buying up their surplus grapes or letting them use the family's equipment. Anyone holding a party in the Napa Valley dreamed that Robert would come because he could make it a success. He had star power and was a visionary. Peter, on the other hand, was Mr. Inside. He stayed at home to make wine and develop new technology. Peter, the worker bee, was studious and practical. He was not as gregarious or as much fun as his older brother. No one in the valley thought Peter would be the life of a party. The two brothers were even opposites in stature. Robert, who played soccer at Stanford, was tall and athletic. Peter was built like his father—short and solid.

The Mondavis hired Tchelistcheff as a consultant before they relaunched the Charles Krug brand as a premium wine. With Tchelistcheff's guidance and Peter's research, the Mondavi family moved into the leadership of California wine technology. Krug was the first large California winery, for example, to age wine in French oak.

Sibling rivalry between Robert and Peter Mondavi was kept in check and out of the public eye as long as Cesare lived. Papa ruled the family, and no one dared challenge his decisions. After his death in late 1959, however, tensions slowly started to surface.

Robert made his first trip to Europe in 1962 and returned with a passion to make wines that could match the best of France. By 1965, the Mondavis were having trouble keeping up with the demand for quality Krug wines and took out full-page ads in newspapers under the headline "Not Enough Charles Krug Wines." For a while at least, Peter and Robert Mondavi had a good division of labor, much like the successful partnership between Ernest and Julio Gallo.

A split between the Mondavi brothers, however, was unavoidable; it seemed only a question of time. Each brother was struggling to get control of the company and put members of his own family into key management positions. Peter thought Robert was spending too much money on travel and promotion, while Robert thought Peter was working with his mother to block the rise in the company of Robert's oldest son, Michael. Valley residents began to chuckle at how the two brothers were no longer even pronouncing their family name the same. Peter pronounced it in the Americanized way: Mon-day-vi, while Robert used the original and more chic Italian pronunciation: Mon-dah-vi.

Tension culminated at a family gathering in November 1965, when a fistfight broke out between the two brothers. According to the story that made its way around the valley, trouble got started with a disagreement over a mink coat that Robert's wife had bought to wear to a dinner at the White House. Robert won the fight but lost the battle, since their mother, Rosa, thereafter sided with Peter on questions of who should lead the company. Robert was banished from the business where he had worked all his life, but soon found backers who would support him financially to start his own winery.

The explosion in the Mondavi clan was an opportunity for Warren Winiarski. Shortly after he had left Souverain, Winiarski had visited André Tchelistcheff to ask him if he knew of any openings in the wine business. Winiarski knew him only casually but thought he would be aware of opportunities in the valley. Tchelistcheff said there might be an opening at

Robert Mondavi's new winery in Oakville, a Mexican hacienda–style structure set far back from Route 29, Napa Valley's Main Street and just south of both Inglenook and Beaulieu Vineyard. This was clearly going to be a showpiece property. Before he knew it, Winiarski had a job paying five hundred dollars per month. He would be a *deus ex machina* for Mondavi, whose grand plan was for his son Michael to be the winemaker. The Vietnam War was under way, though, and Michael had gone into the National Reserve. While Michael was on military duty, Winiarski would be the winemaker.

For Winiarski, Souverain Cellars and the new Robert Mondavi Winery were studies in contrast. While Souverain was small and orderly, Mondavi was big and chaotic. Winiarski quickly realized, however, that his two years' experience made him the only veteran winemaker around. Robert had spent most of his life marketing wine, not making it. Most of the others on staff were new hires with limited training.

Building the Robert Mondavi Winery was a lot like setting up a traveling circus. Things were going on everywhere. New equipment was constantly rolling in, though often no one knew how to operate it. Sometimes one new machine wouldn't work with another. Huge tanks were bought, but no one remembered to order the fittings to make them useable. Equipment would arrive before the place where it was to be used had been built, so it ended up sitting outside exposed to the weather. Electricians and plumbers worked above, below, and around people making wine. When Winiarski didn't have things to do as a winemaker, he picked up a hammer and became a carpenter. People from Peter's Charles Krug Winery helped the Robert Mondavi crew, and Krug grapes even found their way into Robert's wines. Peter put differences with his brother aside long enough to crush Robert's first batch of Chardonnay.

Top managers and owners from Louis M. Martini, Beaulieu, and other wineries were also ready to help Mondavi get off the ground. The whole valley was elated about the founding of a new large winery after the dejection caused by the sale of Inglenook. Other winemakers admired the ambition of Robert's goals. He had the vision to be a category builder. Some business people start companies, and that can be a great achievement. Others create a whole category of enterprise that is bigger than just their single company. Henry Ford did that with the automobile, and Steve Jobs of Apple Computer created the personal computer category. Says Vic Motto, a modern-day wine business consultant: "Robert Mondavi didn't just make great wine; he created the category of Napa Valley wine starting in the mid-1960s."

Robert Mondavi himself had many jobs at his new business—raising money, hiring new staff, ordering barrels and presses, as well as overseeing

construction and buying grapes from other producers. He had a strong intu-
ition born from a lifetime spent around wineries, which often helped
solve problems. In his new company Mondavi was combining his vast experience with the best new technology available anywhere in the world. He
bought all new equipment and only the best tanks, crushers, and barrels.
Winiarski was particularly impressed by the new jacketed stainless-steel fermenting tanks that allowed winemakers to determine more easily the
exact temperature during fermentation. France's Haut-Brion had introduced
the tanks in 1961, and these were the first in the Napa Valley. He was also
intrigued by the new Coq pumps from France, which moved the must from
the crusher to tanks much more gently than the older types did.

The Robert Mondavi Winery offered Winiarski a tremendous opportunity. While he had learned the meticulous, small-scale artisanal way of
winemaking from Lee Stewart, Mondavi gave him the big picture and a
glimpse into the future of both viticulture and enology. Mondavi was
open to new ideas and swung quickly from one project to the next. Not
everything he tried worked, but he was innovative and gave Winiarski a
chance to be on the cutting edge of international wine production.

When the first harvest in 1966 began, walls on the main Mondavi
building had been built, but there was no roof, so it was like making wine
in the outdoors. Fortunately for the Mondavi crew, the harvest was late. In
the early fall, the morning fog often hung around until 1:00 or 2:00 in the
afternoon. As a result, the grapes ripened later than normal. The last
Cabernet vines were not picked until November 11. Mondavi didn't have
a lab technician on staff, so Winiarski did many of the tests during fermentation and directed the blending of wines. Mondavi and his partners
anxiously followed the progress of the wines and held frequent tastings either
at the winery or at Mondavi's home in St. Helena. The late harvest had, fortunately, let them spread out the winemaking process.

The harvest and crush the following year were a little less hectic than they
had been in 1966. Systems and equipment were now in place, and everything went much smoother. The staff was larger, and Winiarski was able to
turn some of his duties over to lab technicians and others. Michael Mondavi had now returned from military service and was acting as winemaker
and head of production.

As dynamic and exciting an environment as the Mondavi winery had
been, Winiarski knew he wouldn't stay there long. The thrill of the new
had faded, and routine had set in. He had learned a lot from Robert Mondavi, but wanted to do his own thing. Just as at Souverain, in two years he
had learned most of what there was to learn at Mondavi. It was time to

move again. Shortly before the beginning of the 1968 harvest, Winiarski left Mondavi to strike out on his own. For some time he had been fielding offers to do consulting work, and he decided to become a freelance winemaker and consultant. Other wineries desired the skills and experience Warren had acquired as well as the knowledge of new technology his time at Mondavi had given him.

CHAPTER ELEVEN

Launching a New Winery

Wine is like the incarnation—it is both divine and human.
—PAUL TILLICH

In the late summer of 1968, Warren Winiarski's mother, Lottie, made her first visit to the Napa Valley. She was anxious to see her three grandchildren, especially her new granddaughter, Julia, who had been born in California. Near the end of her weeklong stay, Warren and his mother were sitting on the large veranda on the front of the family's rented house on Howell Mountain, enjoying the panoramic views. As they talked, she told him that she had accumulated some money and that if he ever wanted to buy more land or start a winery, she would be willing to help. Warren was surprised, grateful, and above all enthusiastic. His mother's offer opened new vistas.

A disappointing episode the year before had showed him that he couldn't do much without money. In his spare time Warren liked to wander all over the valley, seeing where grapes were grown—or had been grown—and where he might someday plant his own larger vineyard. One day he was on Spring Mountain, on the western side of the valley. He was attracted to one particular area that he could tell had been a vineyard before Prohibition, perhaps as far back as the 1880s. Walking through the young forest he had even found some still standing redwood stakes left over from the vineyard days. As he entered a clearing, Winiarski spotted a spring in the distance. In a flash he thought it would be a great place for both a vineyard and a winery. The area was stunningly beautiful, and it had all-important water. Since a vineyard had already once been planted here, a new one would certainly succeed.

Winiarski rushed home and brought Barbara back to see the property, and she too thought it was beautiful and had great potential. Research turned up that it belonged to the widow of one of the owners of the Freemark Abbey, an old winery that had recently been restarted. Warren tried to interest her in selling, but she died before any action was taken. He also asked an old Chicago friend to invest with him, but that too failed.

The land eventually went into an estate sale, where another buyer got it before Warren could get his financing together. The whole experience was disappointing, but now with his mother's support, another opportunity like that might turn out differently.

It was also becoming clear to Winiarski at this time that there were severe limitations for him to develop the land and the vineyard he was working on Howell Mountain. Without adequate water on the property, no winery could be built there. It was also becoming clear that the vineyard needed something like drip irrigation because the soil on the property drained very rapidly. Finally, access was over a road that needed to be paved. All those improvements would take a lot of money—more than even his mother could offer.

Warren had to ask himself the tough question. Would the Howell Mountain property ever make it for him? Experience and romance were beginning to run into reality. A new approach had to be taken, and so Warren and Barbara decided to cut their losses, sell the property, and look at other alternatives.

Things worked out well, however. The owner of a San Francisco furniture store bought the property in October 1968, made the investment to drill a well that produced fine crystal-clear water, and hired Warren to manage the vineyard he had planted. That helped bring in some money for the family to supplement what he was making as a consultant winemaker. His first such job was with Dr. Gerald Ivancie, a Denver periodontal surgeon. Ivancie loved wine and had come up with the idea of buying Napa Valley grapes and fermenting them in Denver. Winiarski bought Gamay and Cabernet Sauvignon grapes in the valley and shipped them to Denver, where they were made into wines that were sold as Ivancie Beaujolais or Ivancie Cabernet Sauvignon.

Winiarski also did work for Parducci Wine Cellars in Ukiah, about eighty miles north of Napa in Mendocino County. Parducci had been making bulk wine since just after the end of Prohibition. Every other week or so, depending on the time of year, Winiarski drove to Ukiah to help John Parducci with everything that needed to be done to transform the winery from a bulk operation to one that produced bottled wine.

While working for Ivancie and Parducci, Winiarski also farmed the three-acre vineyard on Howell Mountain. The Cabernet Sauvignon vines were beginning to produce small crops of grapes, but it would still be a year or two away before they would be large enough to make significant amounts of wine.

Winiarski in late 1968 and 1969 was something of a professor in residence in the Napa Valley, carefully studying the whole wine district, looking for where he could buy land for another vineyard. From one side of the valley to the other, Winiarski looked carefully at soil types and microclimatic weather conditions. One objective was to determine the areas susceptible to spring frost, which damaged grapes. So, for example, every time there was a frost he rushed out to discover the pattern of how tiny ice crystals covered the land, examining it on mountains, midrange slopes, and flat ground. He had to observe all this before the sun's warmth melted the frost, which meant getting up at 4:00 a.m. in order to get to spots on the mountaintops facing east, where the sun hit earliest. Winiarski was like a scientist in his lab, only the lab was the entire Napa Valley.

Winiarski's winemaking philosophy continued to evolve during his consulting years, and he was striking out on his own. At the time, the conventional wisdom among valley winemakers was that 100 percent varietal grapes made the best wine. As Robert Finigan wrote in the widely read newsletter bearing his name in October 1973, "Most California winemakers consider a 100 percent varietal the highest form of their art." At the same time, however, the Californians freely mixed Cabernet from different vineyards often miles apart to make the final product, and few wines carried a vineyard specific name. One exception was the very popular Heitz Martha's Vineyard Cabernet Sauvignon.

This emphasis on 100 percent varietal and mixing wines from several vineyards is very different from the practices of the best French producers, especially those in Bordeaux. All the First Growths of Bordeaux are blends of wines from several grapes, at least Cabernet Sauvignon and Merlot, and often others as well. Given the French concept of *terroir*, the leading French wineries would not dream of freely mixing wine from a wide variety of geographical sources in their leading brands.

As his winemaking concepts took shape, Winiarski found himself coming down more on the side of the French rather than with his fellow Californians on both blending and *terroir*. He believed that the 100 percent varietal purists were unnecessarily limiting their abilities to make the best wines possible. He was open to blending some Merlot with the Cabernet in the Bordeaux style, if that was needed to soften the Cabernet. Winiarski also became convinced that specific sites in the Napa Valley produced different expressions of Cabernet Sauvignon, and he was attracted to the concept of a vineyard-specific wine.

While looking for the best *terroir* in the Napa Valley, Winiarski consulted with his old boss Lee Stewart about the land where he grew Zinfandel grapes, since Souverain Zinfandel was considered one of California's best. It was the red volcanic mountain soil of Howell Mountain, Winiarski concluded, that gave Stewart's Zinfandel its special soft texture, and he was sure the right land in a good microclimate would produce a great Cabernet Sauvignon. He was looking for something like the vineyard at Bordeaux's famed Château Mouton Rothschild, one of his favorite wines. It had a slightly higher location than neighboring, and lesser, vineyards.

Winiarski's experience transporting water to new plants at the vineyard on Howell Mountain had fostered in him an interest in irrigation. For his next round of planting he was determined to find a more efficient way of watering young plants. In early 1969, Winiarski heard that Nathan Fay, who grew grapes in the southern part of the Napa Valley on the Silverado Trail, five miles north of the city of Napa, had come up with a new irrigation system. He called Fay and asked to come by and talk. Fay, a friendly man who hardly ever turned down anybody for anything, agreed.

Fay had come to grapes late in life. The son of an engineer from the San Francisco Bay area, he dropped out of Michigan Tech in the early days of the Depression when he ran out of money and took a construction job in Los Angeles. After military duty in World War II, Fay first sold farm equipment and then got into farming. In 1953, he bought 205 acres of pastureland located under the Stag's Leap Palisades on the eastern side of the Napa Valley. Most farmers in the area were growing plums, cherries, and walnuts. Some also cultivated grapes, but they were mainly low-maintenance and high-yield varieties like Carignane, Alicante Bouschet, Petite Sirah, and Zinfandel.

In 1961, with help from an advisor from UC Davis, Fay began planting Cabernet Sauvignon grapes. It was a bold move from the point of view of both the location and the type of grape, and other farmers in the area thought Fay was crazy. Conventional wisdom at the time, supported by the Amerine-Winkler research, held that Cabernet grapes did best from the northern Napa Valley south to Rutherford, about nine miles north of Fay's property. Cabernet Sauvignon is also a high-maintenance grape, with a yield of three to four tons per acre, as compared with the thirteen tons an acre for the easier-to-grow Alicante Bouschet.

Nonetheless, Fay pushed ahead in 1961, pulling out fifteen acres of plum orchards and planting them with Cabernet Sauvignon grapes. Each year thereafter he planted a few more acres of Cabernet until he had cultivated about seventy acres. Fay did almost all the work himself, which slowed down the development of his vineyard. He sold his first Cabernet grapes to the Mondavis, who used them in their Charles Krug Cabernet Sauvignon, and later Heitz and Carneros Creek also bought Fay grapes.

One afternoon in the spring of 1969, after Winiarski and Fay finished a discussion about irrigation at the Fay property, Winiarski was a bit disappointed because his method seemed to have limited potential. The visitor was about to leave when Fay invited him to try some wine he had made with his Cabernet grapes. Many grape growers in the valley kept some of their production for themselves to make homemade wine. Fay produced twenty-five or so cases each year, crushing the grapes in thirty-gallon trash cans. Home winemakers were always anxious to show off their product, so Fay and Winiarski drove down to a building across from Fay's own residence on Chase Creek. In an annex built out from his guesthouse, Fay stored winemaking equipment as well as a few barrels and bottles of wine.

The wine they were going to taste had been made the previous year, 1968, and was still aging in wood. Using a wine thief, a tube used to extract a small amount of wine from a barrel, Fay took out a sample of the Cabernet. He wanted to get it from the center because he didn't want it to pick up excessive flavors from the oak. Fay put his finger on one end of the wine thief and put the other end into the barrel. When he lifted his finger, wine filled the tube, and then he put his finger back on the end, which trapped the wine by vacuum in the tube. Fay pulled out the wine thief and released the contents into a glass, which he gave to his guest.

Winiarski swirled the liquid around in the glass to release and concentrate the aroma and then smelled the wine. It was wonderful—like black cherries, with a host of spicy and mysterious characteristics. He took a sip and was again deeply impressed. The wine had a complex, layered structure that provided a progression of flavors as the wine moved across his taste buds. It didn't pass through his mouth smoothly like silk. It was more like linen, with an extremely fine-grained texture of intertwined tastes that could be savored and enjoyed slowly. The aftertaste was excellent—long and lingering.

"This is fabulous, just fabulous!" Winiarski thought to himself. Even though the wine was less than a year old and wouldn't be ready for bottling for perhaps another year, here was the Cabernet Sauvignon taste he had been looking for during his two years of tasting wines up and down the valley. "This is it!" he thought excitedly. "This is the best Cabernet I've ever tasted! It's complex. It has a strong regional character, but also a classical Cabernet character. It combines suppleness and strength."

In the room's dim light Winiarski did not let on to Fay what he was thinking. When his host asked what he thought, Winiarski said simply, "It's very good." Shortly after, he left.

Almost immediately a plan began to take shape in Winiarski's mind to raise money and buy more vineyard land. He remembered his mother's offer of financial help and now wondered whether he might be able to buy land very close to Fay's vineyard that would produce the same kind of outstanding wine he had tasted.

By chance or providence, the property located right next to Fay, the fifty-acre Heid Ranch, was for sale with an asking price of $120,000. The owners had farmed the property since 1928, growing a hodgepodge of plums, apples, cherries, and high-yield, low-quality grapes. Without saying anything about his intentions to anyone except his wife, Winiarski negotiated the price down to $110,000 and then began putting together a plan to get the needed money. Winiarski's mother put in $20,000, which together with Warren's savings and money still left from selling the Howell Mountain property was enough for the $50,000 down payment. Finally on February 22, 1970, nearly a year after he had first tasted the Fay wine, Winiarski closed the sale on the Heid property. The day before, he had registered the terms Stag's Leap Vineyard and Stag's Leap Wine Cellars with Napa County and the state of California, naming his new ventures after the rocky hills above his property.

Winiarski immediately set to work. Confident that the soil on the Heid land would be similar to that on the adjacent Fay farm, he had not done any soil samples before the sale. But soon after the deal was done, he had the U.S. Soil Conservation Service do a complete study. He was delighted with the results. The earth was a mixture of volcanic and alluvial material. The volcanic consisted of coarse particles, while the alluvial was very fine in texture, having been deposited there over thousands of years. The different soils would give the grapes and wine different characteristics. The area where the Alicante Bouschet and the plums grew was Bale gravelly clay loam, and Winiarski pulled those plants out and planted that section first. Believing that some of the best French Merlot grew in rocky soil, he grafted Merlot in a rocky block of soil and Cabernet Sauvignon in the gravelly block. Winiarski thought he was the first person to plant Merlot that far south in the Napa Valley.

In the spring of 1970, Winiarski planted his new vineyard, drawing heavily on his experience on Howell Mountain. He put the rows of vines on an east-west orientation, fearing that the grapes would get too much sun during the hottest part of the day if planted in a north-south pattern because they would be exposed all afternoon on the western side of the vine. He installed a four-wire trellis system, which opened up the leaves to the sun and provided a more even exposure to sunlight.

Winiarski first planted phylloxera-resistant St. George rootstock, the same kind he used on Howell Mountain, buying it from Frank Emmolo, a nurseryman in the valley. Then in the fall he grafted Cabernet Sauvignon and Merlot buds onto the rootstock. The choice of bud wood for the new vineyard was crucial. The understanding of grape clones, the specific variation of a grape type, had progressed tremendously in the six years since Winiarski had arrived in the Napa Valley, and he knew exactly what he was looking for when he set out to get vine cuttings. He wasn't looking to make blockbuster tasting wines, but ones that showed balance and moderation. In addition, he wanted vines that produced loose clusters with small berries. The loose clusters would let in plenty of light on the berries during the growing season, while the small berries would give the wine a rich, intense taste.

Two-thirds of the first vineyard would be given over to Cabernet, with one-third for Merlot. Winiarski got enough buds from Nathan Fay to make twenty rows of Cabernet Sauvignon vines and material for another twenty rows of Cabernet Sauvignon from Martha's Vineyard in nearby Oakville. He obtained buds for twenty rows of Merlot from Zuckerman Island in the Sacramento Valley because he thought that clone produced better Merlot grapes than those then being grown in the Napa Valley. The vineyard spacing, just as on Howell Mountain, followed the UC Davis stricture: rows twelve feet apart and vines eight feet from each other along the rows.

Winiarski decided to leave the Petite Sirah vines, which were located closer to the foothills. The plants were producing well, and he could sell the grapes to other winemakers. That would help his cash flow, while he waited at least three years for the Cabernet Sauvignon and Merlot vines to produce enough grapes for a marketable vintage.

Making wine may be a work of art, but Winiarski also had to run a business. As an academic and then an apprentice winemaker, he had never concerned himself much with such matters. Now he had to learn fast. Winiarski calculated that he needed to raise another $100,000 for working capital. Hoping to get ten investors, he decided to offer $10,000 shares in the new limited partnership he formed. Meanwhile he worked with an accountant to produce a financial plan that would impress potential investors.

With a passion for his cause, Winiarski first talked about his vision and his winery to friends whom he felt might be interested in becoming partners. The first investor was Hilde Strobell, a neighbor who had become a close acquaintance. She came from a prominent German family that had diverse financial interests. When Warren and Barbara traveled, she cared for the Winiarski children, who called her Aunt Hilde. The second was Peter McGhee, a long-time friend of the family and Barbara's classmate at St. John's College. He was then an independent film producer in New York City who did documentaries for public television. He invested inheritance money that he had received from an aunt.

Friends of friends also became partners, and fairly quickly five people had put up money, but Winiarski still needed more. An advertisement in the magazine *Wines & Vines* brought interest from potential investors who were both more skeptical and more demanding than friends and family.

Winiarski gave all of them a Bank of America report that presented rosy prospects for wine consumption and investments. Eventually Winiarski got his ten backers. He would certainly need more capital later, but this was adequate for the time being.

To help cover operating expenses, Winiarski decided also to borrow some money. Wells Fargo Bank turned him down, but Equitable Agricultural Lending, a part of Equitable Insurance, loaned him $80,000. During the closing, Winiarski was surprised to learn that he would have to guarantee the loan personally, meaning that if the business failed the lenders could repossess any assets he had. It was nothing personal, simply standard business practice. But it was new to Winiarski.

Despite the family's money worries—he paid himself just three hundred dollars per month—Winiarski jumped rather quickly at a second financial venture when an opportunity unexpectedly appeared. One day in the summer of 1972, he visited Marian Backus, a long-time Napa Valley resident and real estate broker who handled grape sales for winemaker Louis M. Martini. Winiarski had come to talk about grapes he was buying for Ivancie. They met at the Backus house, which was located near the property Winiarski had purchased. A Napa Valley pioneer family named Parker had built the house in 1910 atop a knoll called Parker Hill. Sitting on the porch in the afternoon, you could feel cooling breezes at about four o'clock, even in summer, blowing up from the distant San Pablo Bay. The house was simple, but had great charm. It had a cedar-shingle exterior, and each bedroom had its own sleeping porch. Winiarski was enthralled by the house and the site, which commanded a panoramic view of the surrounding Napa Valley and the Stag's Leap Palisades. While they talked grapes, Marian Backus mentioned in passing that the house and thirty acres around it had been for sale for five years.

The following day Winiarski returned to discuss a few more details of the grape purchase. While there, he asked David Backus, Marian's husband, what they were asking for the house and land. David had a speech impediment, and Winiarski understood him to say $37,500, which set off a flood of enthusiasm: "We can do that! We could put together a down payment and then get a loan."

Winiarski was almost mad with excitement. It was like the moment when he had first tasted Nathan Fay's wine. He rushed back to the Wells Fargo house on Howell Mountain and told Barbara that he had just seen "the most fantastic house." It was located less than a mile from the vineyard. They had always rented before, but now was the time to buy. And this was the right place.

A few days later, Winiarski went back for a third visit to the Backus house, and this time he brought along Barbara. She fell hopelessly in love with the property, calling it a "house where every day is Christmas." But the Winiarskis discovered there had been a misunderstanding about the price. It was not $37,500, but $137,500. No wonder it had been on the market for five years!

From their enthusiastic high, the Winiarskis came crashing down. They couldn't pay that kind of money for a home at a time when they were already carrying a heavy debt load with the vineyard and Warren was earning only a little money from consulting. The dream was about to evaporate when Warren had another idea: the property would be ideal for other purposes besides just housing his family. They could build the vineyard's winery there, and the house could also be the place where Warren and Barbara entertained merchants, journalists, and others in the wine trade. Warren knew that schmoozing was an important part of the business, another lesson he had learned from Robert Mondavi.

They would need more financial backers, so Warren went back to looking for partners. He figured he needed to raise an additional $100,000 and began selling shares this time for $20,000. He hoped to have six partners in the second venture and would use the additional money for equipment and other startup costs. Three of the original vineyard partners also came into the winery project. In addition, he found new ones. One of the two new investors was Dick Rainey, who had just left RAND, a defense think tank located in southern California. Rainey went on the payroll for two years and was helpful in formulating a new business plan and running financial projections. He remained an investor after he stopped working at the winery. Winiarski also got a $120,000 loan from Bank of America. By then he had become adept at putting together business deals.

In the spring of 1972, the Winiarski family moved from their Wells Fargo House on Howell Mountain to Parker Hill. There was a shower the day of the move, but the heavy rain was over by late afternoon, when the family was making the last trip carrying goods down to the new house. At one point as they drove down the mountain, Warren looked across the valley below and turned to Barbara, saying, "Look at the rainbow. The end of it is falling right on our new home."

It might have looked and felt romantic, but the Winiarskis were literally putting their lives on the line. They had three young children and were now deeply in debt. They also had partners who were looking for a return on their money and would be unhappy if things didn't go well. College professors are usually not gamblers, but Warren had placed a huge bet on his own abilities as a winemaker at the future Stag's Leap Wine Cellars and the future of California wine.

CHAPTER TWELVE

A Case of Industrial-Strength Burnout

Wine in moderation—not in excess, for that makes men ugly—has a thousand pleasant influences. It brightens the eye, improves the voice, imparts a new vivacity to one's thoughts and conversation.

—CHARLES DICKENS

Jim Barrett, circa 1975.

One Saturday morning in the late spring of 1971, Jim Barrett, a southern California lawyer, climbed into his twin-engine Aztec plane at the Torrance Airport near Los Angeles. Barrett was an experienced pilot who frequently flew to Mexico on medical mercy missions and to Idaho to go fly-fishing. After takeoff he flew over LAX, the Los Angeles Airport, and then up the coast over Ventura, Santa Barbara, and the Santa Ynez Valley. When he approached SFO, the San Francisco Airport, Barrett got on the radio to Bay Approach and asked the tower for permission to land

at Santa Rosa, about sixty miles further north. As he flew over San Francisco, Barrett could see the rust-colored Golden Gate Bridge below. On his
right in the east the sun shone brightly, hanging over the sharp, snow-
capped Sierra Nevada Mountains. Off his left wing was open ocean. A little farther north the land below looked parched. Barrett then banked the
plane out over the Pacific Ocean and made a perfect landing at the nearly
empty Santa Rosa Airport in Sonoma County. Leonardo, as Barrett had
named his guardian angel, had once again taken care of him.

Barrett lived with his wife, Laura, and their four children only about a
hundred yards from the Pacific Ocean in the fashionable Palos Verdes
Estates just south of Los Angeles. He was suffering from what he called "a
case of industrial-strength burnout." In his early forties, he was a very successful lawyer whose name came first on the door of the Torrance law firm
Barrett, Stearns, Collins & Gleason. But after nearly twenty years of torts and
retorts, he wanted to do something different with his life. He was particularly
tired of all the personnel issues he had to deal with in running a business.

The lawyer loved language and spoke colorfully. He called himself the
"Papa Bear" of his law firm and the northern California town where students
at the University of California always seemed to be protesting "Berserkley."
Both of his parents were born in Ireland, and he was proud of his heritage.
His mother, he told people, was born "hard by Blackwater Bridge," five miles
outside the village of Kenmare on the Ring of Kerry. Mom was a peasant
girl, who herded the family cow—"not cows, a cow." Dad was from Water-
ford and became an American citizen by joining the U.S. Navy during
World War I, when any foreigner going into the military got automatic and
immediate citizenship. He later worked for Sears. Mom was proud of the
fact that she was a chambermaid at the famous Waldorf-Astoria Hotel in
New York City. That position put her high in the pecking order of Irish
immigrant girls working in America and gave her certain bragging rights
among the Mollies of New York City.

In 1937, when Sears transferred Jim's father to Los Angeles, the boy was
nine. The family lived near the intersection of Santa Monica Boulevard and
Vermont Avenue not far from downtown Los Angeles. At age eighteen, Jim
joined the Navy as an apprentice seaman in a program that was turning out
newly minted officers in ninety days. He finished the Naval Reserve Officer Training program at UCLA, where he graduated with a Bachelor of Arts
degree and was commissioned an officer in the navy the same day, June 1,
1946. Barrett went on active navy duty for twenty-four months, serving on
the USS *Adams,* a destroyer, in the Pacific. He left the navy in 1948 for civil-
ian life and went to Loyola University Law School in Los Angeles. But when

the Korean War broke out in June 1950, Barrett was recalled to active duty, serving in the Pacific for two years in the submarine service aboard the USS *Sea Devil*. After his second tour of duty ended in 1952, Barrett opened a law office with a notary seal, and not much else, in Hawthorne, where bean fields were rapidly being given over to new housing developments.

Barrett slowly built a one-man law firm into an organization that had twenty-three lawyers and more than seventy employees. Its main business was real estate law, and the major client was Ernest Hahn, an entrepreneur who had started a small construction company in Hawthorne, where he had grown up. When they met, Barrett was working alone, handling mostly civil cases from a modest office that resembled one of those drab cubicles where a car salesperson takes a buyer to nail down the final price.

Hahn, who was four years older than Barrett, started building shopping centers to serve the thousands of people moving into the new housing developments growing up in southern California. Large tracts of orange groves and lettuce fields were being cleared for new houses built and sold in rapid succession. In 1959, Hahn put up the $2 million Montclair Shopping Center near Riverside, California, and soon he was one of the biggest developers of those properties in the country. Barrett was his *éminence grise* and lawyer. With Hahn as a client, Barrett became a specialist in the legal work related to developing and operating shopping centers.

By the late 1960s, however, Barrett was bored with land-development law and yearned for something different, ideally something that would bring him closer to nature. But it could be anything. "Maybe I can sell frozen chocolate bananas," he said. Barrett told friends that his guardian angel Leonardo was going to find him a place to start a new career, where he could "watch the sun come up in the morning and go down at night."

Barrett had a long-standing interest in wine, having had his first taste when he was a law student in the late 1940s. The height of his culinary adventure in those days was to cook some chicken and buy a bottle of Louis M. Martini Barbera for $1.25 to go with it. Barrett ventured into foreign territory with Portugal's Lancers rosé, a slightly sweet, sparkling wine—just right for Americans making the switch from Coca-Cola to something more sophisticated. As his law practice prospered, Barrett graduated to France's great wines like Château Lafite and Château Pétrus.

Barrett had been looking in northern California for about eighteen months for an investment having something to do with wine when he made that trip north to meet with Lee Paschich, a local businessman. Paschich had moved from San Francisco to the Napa Valley in the late 1950s. He built a house on Picket Road in Calistoga, a sleepy town that had just one of everything—one shoe repair shop, one dry cleaner, one restaurant—where he made window shades using materials imported from Korea, China, and Japan. Paschich also owned a winery named Chateau Montelena.

After driving through the mountains from Santa Rosa to the Napa Valley, Barrett turned off Route 128 onto Tubbs Lane. There wasn't another car on the road. Ahead of him stood the two peaks of Mount St. Helena. The taller one, the highest in the region, rises to 4,343 feet and was considered the noblest mountain in the San Francisco Bay area. It dominates the northern end of the Napa Valley. Farms stood on both sides of Tubbs Lane, and cattle grazed in the fields. A mile down the road, Barrett passed a small geyser on his left, Calistoga's own Old Faithful. A short distance beyond was Paschich's factory, where the two men were to meet.

After introductions, Paschich and Barrett walked a couple hundred yards down Tubbs Lane to the winery. Barrett's first reaction was that Leonardo had brought him to a very special place. The main building was impressive, with two turrets and a beautiful façade, although there were also touches of early Disneyland kitsch: two knights in dented armor stood guard next to plaster-of-Paris cannons in front of the chateau. The property was overrun with weeds, and disrepair hung around the building along with the spiderwebs. A small pond was filled with snakes and frogs. Behind the chateau was a rundown vineyard. Grapes from the poorly maintained vines were sold to Gallo.

Chateau Montelena dated back to the glory days of early California wine. In 1880, Alfred L. Tubbs, a successful San Francisco businessman who had come west from New York City in 1850 to start a rope company, traveled the new train line in the Napa Valley all the way to its end in Calistoga. There he bought 275 acres as a site for a winery. He named it Chateau Montelena in honor of the mountain located directly behind the property.

Tubbs didn't know a lot about making wine, but he was determined to learn and he went first class. He traveled to France and bought cuttings from some of the great vineyards. The model Tubbs had in mind for his winery was Bordeaux's Château Lafite. Tubbs hired a French architect and French masons to build a chateau replica, complete with walls forty-two inches thick made of imported European stone. In 1886, Tubbs hired Frenchman Jerome Bardot to be his winemaker.

Chateau Montelena produced very good wines, particularly reds. The land, which includes alluvial, sedimentary, and volcanic soils, was ideal for viticulture. Temperatures are warm during the day and cool at night with 50-degree swings between afternoon and evening, giving red wine the complexity that winemakers seek and serious consumers appreciate.

Tubbs died in 1897, and Chateau Montelena passed to his son William and then in 1919 to grandson Chapin Tubbs, who had the unhappy experience of seeing the chateau through Prohibition. Many of the Montelena grapevines were pulled up and replaced with pear and plum trees. Chapin led the Napa Valley campaign to repeal Prohibition and was ready to restart the winery in 1933, when it again became legal to make wine.

But his efforts were jinxed. Along with many winemakers at the time, Tubbs overestimated the American public's interest in fine wine after Prohibition. In September 1934, Chateau Montelena went bankrupt. In later years, the Tubbs family stopped making wine, although they continued to work the vineyard and sold grapes to other wineries and amateur winemakers. The winery, though, had mostly stood silent since Prohibition.

Paschich bought the chateau and an adjacent 15.2 acres in the mid-1960s with plans to construct a new building on the property for his blinds business. But like many newcomers to the Napa Valley, Paschich caught the wine bug. He began making his own wine as a hobby and was soon producing fifty cases a year, which he drank himself or gave to friends. He didn't actually want to own a winery, though, and so he put together a real estate package that included an additional 135 acres of property that he bought from the great granddaughter of Alfred Tubbs. Paschich figured that some wealthy surgeon or lawyer from San Francisco or Los Angeles would buy it, and he'd walk away with a nice profit.

As Paschich recounted the history, Barrett could hardly contain his enthusiasm, but also saw that it was a great place to commit financial suicide. Barrett had done enough land deals for Hahn to know that if he showed too strong an interest, the price would immediately go up. As it was, Chateau Montelena was on the market for $1 million. Trying to appear blasé, Barrett told Paschich that he was looking at three or four other wine properties in the Napa Valley and suggested that they meet for dinner a few days later.

Over the next six months, Barrett would escape from his law practice for a few days, fly up to the Santa Rosa Airport, and drive over to Calistoga for dinner with Paschich to talk about the property. In the process the two men discovered that they enjoyed each other's company as well as talking about and drinking wine. Normally, they picked up a good bottle of wine and dined at the Silverado Bar and Grill in Calistoga, where the Wednesday-night specialty was Prime Rib on the Spit, or at the Abbey, a restaurant close to St. Helena. It was—and still is—common in the Napa Valley for customers to bring along their own wine for dinner even though the restaurant might have an extensive wine list. Barrett and Paschich were not trying to save money, but rather they wanted to taste the best products from Napa wineries. If Heitz, Freemark Abbey, and Robert Mondavi were going to be Barrett's competition, he wanted to know what he was up against. Barrett and Paschich usually drank Cabernet Sauvignon, although they occasionally shared a bottle of Chardonnay.

The dinners gave Barrett a quick education in the issues of owning and running a winery. Barrett was well aware of the fact that liquor was the most controlled business in the country. The Department of Alcoholic Beverage Control regulated it in California, and at the federal level the Bureau of Alcohol, Tobacco, and Firearms governed it. He was more concerned about water issues. The two men talked about the possibility of damming up a creek to create a reservoir on the property to provide a guaranteed source of water. Barrett wanted to master the details of the business if he was going to invest $1 million.

Over these dinners, Barrett sketched out for Paschich his basic concept for the winery. Barrett said he wanted to produce world-class Cabernet Sauvignon, and his role models were the famous First Growths of Bordeaux, just as Château Lafite had been the goal for Alfred Tubbs. Those were mainly family-operated wineries that year after year turned out great wines. As the winery was being brought back to full production, Barrett might compromise on a lot of things, but not on his vision.

The entire property now consisted of 150 acres of land with about 100 acres useful for vineyards, but nearly all the existing low-quality vines needed to be ripped out and replaced with Cabernet Sauvignon. Only 10 acres of Zinfandel were worth saving. In addition, the winery had to be gutted and all the old equipment thrown away. Concrete slabs had to be poured. Tanks, crushers, must pumps, barrels, lines, presses, and on and on had to be bought. A bottling line had to be set up, and warehousing had to be prepared. Barrett wanted the equipment to be top of the line. Wine barrels, for example, had to come from France—Limousin, France, to be exact. You don't make world-class wine with second-rate equipment, Barrett maintained. He was also going to use the latest technology and techniques developed by Napa Valley vintners and researchers at UC Davis. It would be a big job to get the winery up and running for the 1972 vintage, Barrett's goal.

The financials Barrett prepared showed that he needed $1.4 million—$1 million for the purchase price and $400,000 for start-up costs. This second-career dream was turning into a giant risk! He was starting a new business in a field where he knew almost nothing. In addition, he was going to be an absentee owner, spending most of his time on his law practice in southern California. Barrett was planning to continue working there to help pay the family bills, which were large and would be getting bigger when his four children went to college. He clearly needed a financial partner, and his thoughts naturally turned to his client and old friend Ernie Hahn.

The first week of December 1971, Barrett visited Hahn at the E. W. Hahn corporate offices in El Segundo. The two men often met after working hours to discuss key projects. They had just wrapped up the day's business when Barrett said, "Ernie, you know I want to do something else. My firm is doing a great job for you, and I know you're pleased and very comfortable with the work my lawyers do. They're hardworking and fast. I want to turn everything over to them. They are every bit as experienced as I am—only smarter."

"You got that right," quipped Hahn.

"Well, what do you say, boss? I won't do it unless I have your okay."

Hahn looked at Barrett for a long moment and then said, "Go for it, Jim. It's okay with me."

Hahn got up to leave, but Barrett stopped him, saying, "*Uno momento,* pal. Have I got a deal for you!"

"What kind of deal?"

"It's a roll of the dice, but it's exciting, romantic. I want to make a world-class wine like Château Lafite or Château Margaux, and I've found this winery and vineyard in the Napa Valley. It's called Chateau Montelena." Barrett gushed with enthusiasm as he told Hahn about his great find.

When he finally finished, Barrett said, "I need you to come in on this because I can't do it alone. Why don't you take half of the action? We'll be equal general partners. I'll do the work for free—*gratis.*"

Hahn, who thought big and loved a gamble, immediately replied, "Sounds great, Jim. Let's do it."

The following week, Barrett and Paschich had another of their dinners at the Silverado Bar and Grill in Calistoga to talk about the deal. That night, though, the dinner ended differently. When the food—and the bottle of wine—were finished, the two agreed that they didn't have any more outstanding issues. They had the framework of an agreement. So Barrett took out a sheet of paper and began writing down the various terms. When he was finished, the two agreed that Paschich's lawyer would draw up the final document. Contracts would be signed before the end of the year, but for tax purposes would be dated January 2, 1972.

A few days later, Paschich flew down to Los Angeles ready to sign the papers and close the deal. He was shown into the conference room in Barrett's offices, where the lawyer was already waiting for him. After the two men exchanged pleasantries, Paschich gave Barrett the contract his lawyer had drawn up. Barrett quickly scanned it and saw it was exactly the same as the working papers they had agreed upon. He handed it back to Paschich, who signed and gave it to Barrett for his signature.

But instead of signing, Barrett looked Paschich in the eye and said, "Sorry. No can do."

"What?" asked Paschich in disbelief.

"Leland, we've had a lot of fun and drunk a lot of good wine these last few months. Why don't we just keep it up? Let's face it. I still don't know the wine business, despite all I've learned in the past couple of years. The Napa Valley is going to consider me a blue-suede shoe guy from L.A. You know the locals, and I need you. It's no deal unless you agree to be my representative and the local manager for two or three years."

Barrett wasn't following the script.

"Ernie Hahn and I will be the general partners and will each have forty-five percent of the deal," Barrett continued. "You'll be a limited partner with ten percent. And I'll give you a three-year put agreement. That means if you want to leave at any time in the next three years, we'll be obligated to buy back your one-hundred-thousand-dollar share plus pay seven percent interest for as long as your money is tied up. You can't lose. You'll have no financial exposure."

"Let me think about it," said Paschich. But after only a few seconds, he said, "Okay, let's do it."

"I'll draw up amendments to these papers, and then fly up to Santa Rosa the day after tomorrow," said Barrett. "After we sign them, we can go out for dinner and talk about what you've got to do. The very first thing is to find a winemaker. Get me at least three well-qualified people to interview."

CHAPTER THIRTEEN

The Rebirth of a Ghost Winery

*Wine is one of the most civilizing things in the world and one of
the natural things of the world that has been brought to the
greatest perfection, and it offers a greater range of enjoyment
and appreciation than, possibly, any other purely sensory thing.*
—ERNEST HEMINGWAY

*Clockwise from left: Ernie Hahn, Jim
Barrett, Lee Paschich, and Mike Grgich,
circa 1975.*

One morning in the fall of 1968, Mike Grgich got into his white Plymouth Valiant and drove two miles down Route 29 from Beaulieu Vineyard in St. Helena to the still new Robert Mondavi Winery in Oakville. Like everyone in the valley, Grgich had been impressed with both the beautiful low-slung adobe building sitting back from the highway and the wines Mondavi was producing. Grgich was also looking to make a change. He had been very happy at Beaulieu working for André Tchelistcheff and once had perhaps unrealistic hopes that he could succeed him as winemaker. But one day a fellow worker told Grgich that André's son Dimitri had already applied for the job. Grgich concluded that Dimitri would probably get it and therefore his future would always be limited at Beaulieu. The Robert Mondavi Winery thus looked very attractive.

As Grgich pulled into the Mondavi parking lot, he could see that the staff was in the middle of harvest. Only weeks before, Warren Winiarski had left to start his new life as a wine consultant. It was one of those beautiful days in the valley that make so many people who visit the area decide to stay. Sitting on a wooden bench in front of the main building, Mondavi and Grgich talked about what each was doing—and dreamed of doing.

In the small world of Napa Valley wine, Grgich and Mondavi knew each other and also each other's reputations, so there was little need for polite chitchat. Mondavi asked Grgich what specifically he did at Beaulieu. The visitor explained that in addition to making wine he had done research on things like malolactic fermentation and was proud that Beaulieu in 1962 had done the first large-scale malolactic fermentation in the valley. Grgich also discussed using Millipore filters to stabilize wines. He talked at length and with great pride about making the Georges de Latour Private Reserve Cabernet Sauvignon, which had earned a reputation of being California's best Cabernet.

Then with his ever-present and infectious enthusiasm, Mondavi sketched out the goals for his new winery. He was going to make great, French-style wines and had equipped his facility with all the latest equipment and technology. He was going first class—and right to the top. This was going to be America's premier winery. Mondavi also explained that his son Michael had come back from his military service and was now the winemaker, but added that Michael was only in his early twenties and didn't yet have much experience.

Grgich was clearly interested, and Mondavi knew how to close the deal. He put his hand on Grgich's shoulder and said, "Mike, I'm going to make you a little André Tchelistcheff."

That was exactly what Grgich wanted to hear. After Lee Stewart, Tchelistcheff had been his second mentor in the valley. But it was time to move, and this was the place to come. The problem of a successor son remained and he would not have the top job, but Mondavi was a place where Grgich could grow. His title would be that of head of quality control, but he would be doing a lot more than that. He would be working directly with Robert and Michael and helping make wines.

Grgich stayed on at Beaulieu to finish that year's harvest, but then started working for Mondavi. He got a raise, going from six hundred dollars a month at Beaulieu to seven hundred dollars a month. Things remained a bit helter-skelter at the winery. Many of the wine tanks were still located outside, as they had been when Winiarski was at Mondavi, and experiments were constantly taking place. But it was an exciting place to work.

Grgich contributed to the winery what he had learned from Stewart and Tchelistcheff. Stewart was particularly good with white wines, while Tchelistcheff was stronger in reds. Everything, of course, was more modern at the Robert Mondavi Winery than at Souverain or Beaulieu Vineyard. Mondavi, for example, was using the same small oak barrels as those of the top French châteaux. The new winery was also buying the best grapes it could find in the valley.

Every Monday afternoon the Mondavis, Grgich, and a few people from production and sales got together and tasted Mondavi wines against the best French wines, their standard of international excellence that Robert was determined to beat. With good equipment, good grapes, and good winemakers, the result was not surprising. Robert Mondavi wines, both white and red, soon showed the classical style Grgich had learned at Beaulieu and quickly began attracting attention.

Robert Lawrence Balzer, the wine writer for the *Los Angeles Times,* put together a blind tasting of nine of the best 1969 California Cabernet Sauvignons. The judges were some of California's winemakers, including Tchelistcheff and Robert Mondavi, plus the heads of such wineries as Concannon Vineyard, Christian Brothers, Heitz Wine Cellar, and Rodney Strong Vineyards. The judges had themselves made most of the nine wines they tasted. The Robert Mondavi Winery Cabernet came out on top. That brought a flood of favorable publicity, and Mondavi's wines were immediately considered in the top rank of California wines, on a par with those of Beaulieu Vineyard.

Robert personally got all the good press, but Grgich enjoyed the afterglow just as much in private. This was the first of many important wine competitions where a wine he had made, or helped make, had won, and it felt good. "This is proof that I can make better wines and that I should continue doing that," Grgich told himself over and over after the Balzer tasting.

As much as he enjoyed the excitement at Mondavi, Grgich grew to be uncomfortable with the direction the winery was going. The lack of rules and procedures began to bother him. From Lee Stewart he had learned that everything had to be done rigorously by the book. From Tchelistcheff, Grgich had seen and learned that you improve wines by doing an experiment, following up to make sure the results were repeatable, and then doing another experiment and more follow-up. At Mondavi the attitude was: Just do it.

"Robert has twice as many ideas as I do," Grgich told friends. "I have some, but not as many as he." Mondavi was charging ahead faster than Grgich was comfortable following.

Mondavi's goal was to build a very large winery that would produce wines at various levels of quality and price. The winery was crushing five hundred tons of grapes a year when Grgich arrived; four years later it would be crushing five thousand tons. One day in 1970, Grgich went to Robert Mondavi and told him that he could no longer control all the wines being produced. Grgich suggested hiring another winemaker to handle lesser wines, while he would continue to work on just Chardonnay and Cabernet Sauvignon.

Mondavi turned down the request, telling him, "Mike, I know you can handle it."

Grgich responded, "I know I cannot. I will not be happy if some mistake happens, and I cannot control it. I want to have total control and perfect wines."

Eventually Grgich was allowed to hire an assistant, Zelma Long, but still the work was overwhelming. During the harvest and crush Grgich and Long worked virtually around the clock.

The pace and the size of the Mondavi operation continued to bother Grgich so much that he began listening to job offers from other wineries, often at much higher salaries. All of the offers, though, involved Grgich being just another hired hand. They didn't get him closer to his goal of one day having his own winery. So he decided to stay at Robert Mondavi. Despite the problems, it was still the best winery in the valley.

Winter in the Napa Valley is particularly beautiful. Wild mustard plants grow among the vines on the valley floor, turning the area into an explosion of yellow. In some spots the tightly packed mustard plants make it look as if someone has thrown down a huge yellow carpet. On one of those winter days early in 1972, when flowers were in bloom, Lee Paschich showed up at the Robert Mondavi Winery, ostensibly to get some yeast to use for his homemade wine.

Paschich met with Grgich, and it didn't take him long to get to the real point of his visit. "Mike, I now have partners at Chateau Montelena, and they wanted me to talk to you," he said.

"About what?" asked Grgich.

"I've sold the vineyard and the winery to two investors from Los Angeles, but I'm still involved as a partner. They need a winemaker and are wondering whether you'd be interested in talking to them. My partners want to make quality wines. We like Cabernet Sauvignon, and that's what we want to make. Why don't you come up, and we can talk further?"

With Michael Mondavi and even his younger brother Timothy Mondavi ahead of him at their father's business, Grgich thought that the Paschich proposal was worth at least further discussion.

Grgich met first with Barrett and Paschich at the offices of the window-shade company next to Chateau Montelena. Grgich arrived wearing his trademark dark-blue beret, and the meeting went well. Grgich told them about his experience making Cabernet Sauvignon and Chardonnay. Barrett described his vision of making a world-class Cabernet that would be as good as the best wines of Bordeaux. In order to keep the quality high, the output of the winery would remain small—no more than forty thousand cases a year. That smaller-scale approach appealed to Grgich after his experience with Robert Mondavi.

Barrett offered Grgich the job, with an unexpected fillip. The lawyer wanted to get some golden handcuffs on his winemaker, so he offered him the chance to eventually own 10 percent of the business. For starters Grgich would sign a five-year contract that gave him a salary plus 1 percent ownership per year. If Grgich ever left the company, however, he'd have to sell back his shares. The possibility of some ownership hit the right button with Grgich. After working for others around the Napa Valley for fourteen years, here was a chance to own a part of something.

Grgich was excited at the prospect, but told Barrett that he first had to talk with Mondavi. "I'm almost part of the family," Grgich explained.

The next day Grgich went to Mondavi. "Bob, I'd like to take a one-month leave of absence. It's still early in the year, and there isn't that much to do here. Some people are starting a new winery, and they want me to be the winemaker. They are willing to give me part ownership."

"Mike, if that's true, it's a big improvement over what you have here. I can't give you a partnership. I have two sons and a daughter. I can't match that offer."

"I'm not asking you to match it. I just wanted to tell you that I have this opportunity."

"Take the month off, and good luck. If it doesn't work out, you'll always be welcome back."

Two weeks later and after further talks with Barrett and Paschich, Grgich was back in Mondavi's office. "Bob, these people want me to go ahead."

"That's fine. But don't do a thing until you have everything on paper and signed. Get a clean-cut agreement about the percentage you will get and get it in writing. Otherwise, don't do it!"

On May 8, 1972, Grgich started his new job. Not much had been done since Barrett had bought the property nearly six months before. The winery was still little more than a beautiful pile of rocks with a lot of useless old equipment. The first day on the job Paschich gave Grgich a pad of paper and a pencil and told him to design a winery and come up with a five-year budget.

Grgich had never designed a winery, but a friend who had been a consultant with Mondavi helped with the layout. When Grgich returned with his design and budget, Barrett was alarmed: there was no income for five years.

"What's going on here?" he asked.

"That's the minimum of how long it's going to take to get any income from Cabernet. We first have to rip out the old vines and plant Cabernet grapes. Then for the first couple of years, you won't get much of a crop, and after that the wine will have to age in oak barrels for about two years."

"Mike, we're going to be broke before that happens. We haven't got that kind of money. We've got to figure out some other way of doing it."

"We could make white wines first. We'll buy grapes for the white wines from growers. Robert Mondavi buys his grapes. Only a few wineries like Beaulieu grow all their own. We can buy the grapes and get some cash flow while we wait for the Cabernet to develop. Lee Paschich loves Riesling. We could crush Riesling grapes in October and sell it in March. Chardonnay takes a little longer. It has to age in barrels for about eight months, but you'll be selling it about two years after we crush the grapes."

"Okay, let's give it a try. But don't skimp on the price for grapes; pay what you have to in order to get the best. You can't fool people. If we cut corners to save money, they'll know it."

Although he spent little time in Calistoga, Barrett gradually became intimately involved in all aspects of the business. About twice a month he flew up to Napa Valley for some hands-on work, which often involved visiting a grower from whom they might buy grapes. On these trips Barrett camped out at the winery in a room equipped with a single bed and a hot plate for making morning coffee or heating up dinner.

Once new winery equipment was bought and new vines were planted, Barrett turned his attention to marketing. Americans were demanding better cuisine when they went out to eat, and good restaurants, the kind where you might order a great bottle of wine to go with a great dinner, were opening in San Francisco, Los Angeles, and other cities. Believing that fine wines follow fine food, Barrett decided to target the restaurant business, which meant getting Chateau Montelena on wine lists and before influential people. He hired a salesperson to work San Francisco–area restaurants. Barrett also wrote a chatty newsletter that he sent to friends and customers. Someday, he wrote, Chateau Montelena wines would be "recognized as being among the finest in the world." He added: "The wines of Chateau Montelena will be instantly recognizable by the distinctive style of the wines when you taste them."

In the vineyard and the winery, Grgich was experiencing both failure and success. In 1972, he crushed 12,147 gallons of Cabernet, made with grapes bought from the Redwood Ranch in Sonoma County's Alexander Valley and the Lee Paschich vineyard in the Napa Valley. But rain fell for twelve consecutive days during the peak period for picking the Cabernet and mold developed on the grapes. Looking at the mold, Barrett, Grgich, and Paschich knew they would not produce wine of the quality they wanted as their first Cabernet on the market. Early tasting in the spring of 1974, while the wine was still in barrels, confirmed their fears. They all agreed that it wasn't what they had hoped for. Barrett told Grgich and Paschich: "You don't go to a ball in a torn gingham dress." They later sold this wine under a second label, Silverado Cellars.

The Chateau Montelena white wines, on the other hand, enjoyed early success. Grgich put to work what he had learned at both Beaulieu Vineyard and the Robert Mondavi Winery to make his own Johannisberg Riesling, the new winery's first product on the market. Beaulieu's Riesling was a little bitter because it was totally dry. The wine, Grgich thought, was not food friendly, and as a result sold poorly. The Riesling from Robert Mondavi Winery, on the other hand, had about 1 percent residual sugar and sold much better. Grgich left 2 percent residual sugar in his first Riesling in 1972 and called it a Late Harvest, a term used by Germans to signify a slightly sweet wine.

The 1972 Chateau Montelena Johannisberg Riesling, the winery's first wine on the market, captured the attention of critics perhaps because its touch of sweetness appealed to American tastes. It picked up a Golden Eagle award as one of the ten best California Rieslings at a tasting done by the *Los Angeles Times*. In October 1975, wine critic Robert Finigan wrote of Chateau Montelena's 1974 vintage, "Intriguing flavors combine with an elegant style and an exceptionally long finish to produce what I consider one of the finest California Rieslings currently obtainable."

The Chateau Montelena Chardonnays also did well in tastings, although less well with critics. Grgich aged his first 1972 vintage in French oak barrels, but since they were being used for the first time, the barrels gave the wine an overly oaky and tannic taste. Grgich attempted to compensate for that with extra bottle aging, which gave the wine a good bouquet and fruitiness. Since only 800 cases were made, it was not widely distributed. In September 1974, the *Robert Finigan's Private Guide to Wines* rated the Chateau Montelena Chardonnay only as "above average." Finigan wrote that it had an "attractive smaller Chardonnay nose," damning it with faint praise as "nice enough but not especially deep or complex; lightly oaky aftertaste."

Chateau Montelena wines were doing well with new tasting groups that were starting to be fashionable in the early 1970s. Many Americans became acquainted with good wine through such clubs as the Berkeley Wine and Food Society or the many chapters of Les Amis du Vin. The members often used a scoring system designed by professors at UC Davis and brought a very systematic approach to wine tasting. It wasn't good enough to say that you liked this wine better than that one; you had to explain why and describe the tastes. The most important organization was the San Francisco Vintners Club, which held its first tasting on June 21, 1973. An eclectic collection of wine professionals and amateurs met every Thursday afternoon at 4:30 for a blind tasting of usually twelve wines of a given category such as Zinfandel or Sauternes. The 1972 Chateau Montelena Johannisberg Riesling was part of a tasting on June 16, 1974, that noted its "small but elegant nose." The following month its Chardonnay was center stage and gained the comment "excellent Chardonnay nose."

As reported by the *San Diego Grapevine* newsletter, the Feisty Friends of the Vine at a meeting on October 27, 1974, at Zolezzi's Restaurant in San Diego compared ten easily available California Chardonnays. The 1972 Chateau Montelena came in first. The same group at another meeting that year in San Diego blind tasted just two wines: a 1972 Bâtard-Montrachet, one of the most famous white Burgundies, and the 1972 Chateau Montelena Chardonnay. The French wine was then selling for about $17.50 a bottle in stores, while the California wine was $6.50. By a margin of three to one, the tasters preferred the Chateau Montelena.

Barrett, Hahn, and Paschich were delighted with the results the Grgich wines were receiving. They were off to a very good start and things would only get better once their own vineyards were producing their own grapes. As a gesture of their appreciation for the progress that they were making, the owners sent their winemaker for a week's vacation in Hawaii. In addition, Hahn gave Grgich 800 shares of his shopping mall company. At the time the stock was worth only three cents a share, but in 1977 Grgich sold them for $45,000.

CHAPTER FOURTEEN

Making the 1973 Stag's Leap Wine Cellars Cabernet Sauvignon

A glass of good wine is a gracious creature and reconciles poor mortality to itself, and that is what few things can do.
—SIR WALTER SCOTT

*The 1973 Stag's Leap Wine Cellars
Cabernet Sauvignon aging in oak barrels.*

André Tchelistcheff's most prized possession was his yellow 1971 Datsun 240Z sports car, which he normally drove too fast along the Napa Valley's narrow roads. He was again going too fast on a warm afternoon in late September 1973, as he pulled off the Silverado Trail and into the driveway of Stag's Leap Wine Cellars. He was there to take a look at the ripening grape crop. In just a few days Warren Winiarski would have to make the crucial decision about when to pick his grapes. Nature had just about finished with its work in the vineyard, and the winemaker would soon be start-ing his job of turning the ripe grapes into wine.

The 1973 growing season in the valley had been nearly perfect, with lots of warm, dry days. There was a heat spell in late June and early July, and the temperature in nearby St. Helena hit 107 degrees and in Yountville was 105 degrees on June 26. There was another heat spike in late July with another 106-degree day in St. Helena. But for most of August temperatures were slightly below normal. Both July and August were also almost dry, and by mid-September less than an inch of rain had fallen during the growing season.

Winiarski had been trying to lure Tchelistcheff, who was much in demand as a consultant, to help him at his new winery, and at a meeting of the American Society of Enologists in San Diego Winiarski had pressed him hard to agree. Only four months before, Tchelistcheff had finally cut all ties with Beaulieu Vineyard. He had stayed on after Heublein, a liquor company, bought the winery in 1969, but felt increasingly like a showpiece for the new owners and finally left in protest after he was reprimanded for giving an interview to a reporter without permission from his corporate bosses. The parting was bitter and whenever Tchelistcheff drove from the southern Napa Valley to the north he took the less traveled Silverado Trail to avoid Route 29 and having to drive past Beaulieu.

Winiarski wanted Tchelistcheff's experience to help him in particular with tasting his wines; the young winemaker recognized that he needed an independent expert to check on his impressions and restrain his enthusi-asm. It was too easy for a winemaker to be blinded by his attachment to a certain style, and when it came to tasting wine, Tchelistcheff was *nonpareil*. Drawing on his education in the classics, Winiarski compared the rela-tionship the two winemakers might have to that of the two great philoso-phers of ancient Greece: Tchelistcheff could be the Plato, and he would be the Aristotle.

Winiarski and Tchelistcheff were indeed a good match. Tchelistcheff had the ability to dramatize what to science was merely prosaic and taken for granted. He was the first person who talked with Winiarski about wine in terms of beauty and poetry. Some of the valley's winemakers poked fun at Tchelistcheff's grandiloquent language, saying with a sigh, "There goes André again." Winiarski, though, admired his style and verve. In turn, Tchelistcheff had great respect for the younger man, calling him "one of the best winemakers in the Napa Valley, maybe even the best." Tchelistcheff had noted that Winiarski minutely watched over each step of grape growing and winemaking, hovering over every row of vines and every barrel of wine.

While he usually displayed a European formality, Tchelistcheff that September afternoon was relaxed and wore an open shirt. His wife, Dorothy, accompanied him, and the two Tchelistcheffs and Winiarski went out immediately into the vineyard to a section Winiarski had labeled Block Two, which was located midway between the foothills of the Stag's Leap Palisades and the Silverado Trail. The soil is brownish gray close to the highway, but turns reddish gray near the eastern side of the valley. In this section of the vineyard the alluvial soil of the valley floor meets the volcanic soil of the hills, and it was the first area where three years earlier Winiarski had pulled out plum trees and planted grapevines.

The Tchelistcheffs and Winiarski started at the block's eastern end and walked toward the Silverado Trail. The vines were trained in what the Italians called a spaghetti-plate style, with the trunk sticking up and the arms of the plant spreading out to form an almost flat surface. The vine should be so flat that you can put a plate of spaghetti on it. The plants were still very young, and the grapes small, enabling loose clusters to get lots of sunlight— just as Winiarski had hoped when he grafted the Cabernet Sauvignon and Merlot onto the rootstock three years earlier.

Picking grapes and tasting them as he walked, Tchelistcheff was very soon walking ahead of his wife and his host. Winiarski was nervous but proud of his vineyard, which had developed this year just as he had wished. For the last ten days he had been walking through the property alone, picking grapes at random and tasting them. He thought the crop was good, but he was anxious to hear the view of a respected outsider. Like a son hoping to win approval from his father, Winiarski waited for Tchelistcheff's opinion.

The small berries Tchelistcheff picked were a deep purple, with a light gray, waxy coating that rubbed off easily. The seeds of a wine grape make up a larger part of the fruit than those in a table grape and have a strong, woody taste. Tchelistcheff, though, did not bite down on the seeds. He tasted the pulp, chewed the skin, and then spit out the remnants. The quality of a wine grape is determined in large part by the taste of the skin, in particular the fuzzy inside, which breaks down during winemaking, more than by the fruit's tough, leathery outside. The skins give tannin, the grainy substance that provides the platform for the sweet taste of the pulp. Picking grapes first from one side of the row and then the other, Tchelistcheff began to comment about what he tasted, although speaking to no one in particular. "Honey. This tastes like honey," he said. "Divine honey."

Winiarski was so elated that he grabbed Dorothy and hugged her. As the three kept walking, Tchelistcheff continued making similar comments. When they finished surveying the field, the three chatted for a while and then Tchelistcheff and his wife departed. As Winiarski watched them drive away, he had a great sense of pride and satisfaction. The master had just passed judgment on his product. Moreover he didn't just say it was good; this year's crop had the potential to make a great wine.

Shortly after that visit, Tchelistcheff agreed to be a consultant, and the two men were soon kindred spirits. Part of the bond was a shared Slavic background. The Russian-born Tchelistcheff felt a kinship with the wine-maker of Polish heritage, whose wife's family was of Czech background. For several years after, the two families spent Christmas Eve—one of the most important holidays of the year in a Polish household—together.

Once he had the blessing of Tchelistcheff, Winiarski knew the harvest was not far away. He kept a close eye on the weather, always concerned about the possibility of heavy rains, which could cause mold and damage the crop. Another danger was excessive heat, which can dehydrate the grapes, and in extreme cases turn them into shriveled raisins on the vine. If the damaged grapes are not removed, the resulting wine will have a burnt-fruit taste. As he watched the weather and the vineyard, Winiarski felt as if he were on the edge of a knife, trying to eke out the most he could from the fruit. Winiarski used a hand-held refractometer to measure the percent of sugar in a drop of juice, giving its reading in Brix. In normal weather, the Brix goes up about a degree and a half a week. If the weather turns hot, however, the Brix will shoot up. Winiarski knew he was near harvest when the Brix went over 23 degrees.

No instrument, though, is better than a winemaker's sense of taste, and as the grapes continued to mature, Winiarski sampled more individual berries and sometimes clusters of grapes. Fields do not mature uniformly and berries at the top of a cluster taste different from those at the bottom. So he crisscrossed the blocks picking and tasting along the way. By the end of September, the berries seemed to be reaching their flavor peak. Winiarski also noted that the juice was developing both the structure and the softness he sought.

Like a general deciding whether to launch an invasion the next morning at dawn, Winiarski alone had to take the decision on when to harvest. No one was there to help him. On the afternoon of September 22, everything seemed to indicate that it was time: the flavors were good, promising the wine would have layers of tastes; the skins had a wonderful grainy texture from the tannin, foretelling structure and a long life for the wine; and finally the weather was warm, so waiting any longer would produce more sugar and thus more alcohol later, which would make the wine too powerful and alcoholic. From a logistical point of view, the pickers Winiarski needed were available for the next few days, but perhaps not after. If he didn't act now, he might miss this window of opportunity. So Winiarski decided that the harvest would start the following day.

Winiarski's idea of when to pick, indeed his whole philosophy of wine-making, by now differed greatly from that of his fellow valley winemakers. The so-called big wines they produced repelled him. He thought the alcohol was too heavy and the tastes overpowering. If some Cabernet varietal character was good, other winemakers were saying, more had to be better. Winiarski, by contrast, stressed harmony and balance in his wine.

No other vintner has probably ever used the ancient Greek concept of the Golden Rectangle to describe his winemaking. To the Greeks, beauty comes from a harmony that results from the dynamism of opposites. To them a square is perfection because all sides are equal, but it is not particularly interesting because it lacks dynamic tension. The Greek mathematicians Pythagoras and Euclid identified the Golden Rectangle as more intellectually attractive. In a Golden Rectangle the ratio of the short side to the long side is the same as the ratio of the long side to the sum of the short and long sides together. The Parthenon in Athens is an example of the Golden Rectangle in architecture. Classicists also see this golden mean relationship of opposites in music and even in such natural forms as sunflowers and seashells.

Winiarski looked for the classical harmony of opposite elements in his Cabernet Sauvignon. The fruit, he felt, should be soft, while the tannins are hard. Sweetness and acidity were another point of balancing opposites. The soil of the Stag's Leap vineyard, he thought, had the gentle qualities from the alluvial soil and the tougher ones from the volcanic soil. The blending of Cabernet Sauvignon with Merlot, which Winiarski always favored, unlike most California winemakers, produces that same point and counterpoint. The Cabernet Sauvignon provides strength and structure, while Merlot is fleshy and soft. Winiarski believed that all these factors come together in a tense harmony that would give his Cabernet Sauvignon an exciting taste.

Determining the peak moment for the harvest was an early case of achieving harmony. The crop must have the appropriate ripeness—but not the most he could get. The ripeness and richness of the Cabernet had to be combined with restraint in what Winiarski called directed understatement.

Picking began early in the morning of September 23, and by mid-afternoon 8.3 tons of grapes had been harvested—4.5 tons of Cabernet Sauvignon and 3.8 tons of Merlot. The picking continued for five more days, following the ripeness of each of the different blocks of grapes and even sections within a block. The final 1.8 tons were picked on October 3. The 1973 harvest totaled 32 tons.

The main work was done by Mexican laborers who walked the rows using sharp, crescent-shaped knives to snip off clusters of grapes with a quick turn of the wrist. The harvested fruit was then gently dropped, so as not to bruise it, into wooden lug boxes that held forty-five pounds. After all the clusters were cut from one vine, the picker moved his box to another vine and snipped off more fruit until his box was full enough to transfer the contents into a gondola, a large open-topped container that sat on wheels. A tractor dragged the container through the fields.

When the gondola was full, it was towed to the winery, located 200 yards away near the Silverado Trail. During the months before the harvest, Winiarski had bought a collection of some new, but more often used, equipment. The hoist that lifted the gondola filled with clusters of grapes and dumped them into the crusher had been bought used from another winery. The crusher, though, was new and had been designed by someone who had previously been in the prune business but was now making equipment for the new wineries.

When the grapes arrived from the field, they were dumped into a hopper that had a giant screw at the bottom. The screw took the grapes into the crusher and destemmer, which separated the grapes from the stems. The mass of berries, skins, seeds, and a few stems that had slipped past the destemmer were pumped into twelve-foot-high stainless-steel fermenting tanks. Each tank held up to ten tons of crushed fruit, but a maximum of only eight tons was put in to leave room for the material to expand during fermentation and for pumping over to keep the juice in contact with the skins and add color to the wine.

Winiarski had designed the tanks himself, basing the height-to-width proportion on pictures he saw in a magazine that showed new steel fermenting tanks being used at France's Château Latour. These were creating quite a stir in international wine circles. The Latour tanks pictured in the magazine seemed to Winiarski to have the right relationship between width and height. If the tank were narrow and tall, the cap of skins would be too thick and the pump-over process would not extract the required substances from the skins. As a result, the wines would be poorly endowed with color, tannin, and flavor. If the tank were too wide and flat, there would be too much contact and extraction, resulting in an overly powerful and harsh wine. The Château Latour design seemed just right.

The vast majority of French winemakers at that time used almost exclusively wooden fermenting tanks, so California winemakers like Winiarski who were installing new temperature-controlled stainless-steel equipment were leapfrogging most French wineries in adopting next-generation technology.

At about 10:00 on the evening of the first day of picking, Winiarski heaved a bucketful of yeast through the opening in the top of the tank to start fermentation in the first tank. He had propagated the yeast himself, using material given him in the valley's cooperative spirit by Beaulieu Vineyard. The starter made the wine a living organism, and Winiarski carefully followed sterilization procedures to make sure that no contamination developed, techniques he had first learned from Lee Stewart at Souverain. The must pumps, hoses, and other equipment were repeatedly sterilized to stop any microflora from being introduced into the fermentation process and spoiling the wine.

Fermentation took place over a six-day period. During that time Winiarski got little sleep. He wanted nothing to go wrong and monitored the process like an obstetrician delivering his first baby. He carefully controlled the temperature in each of the seven tanks, cooling the liquid if it got over 90 degrees. He also regularly read all of the wine's vital signs, such as the sugar level, tasting each tank in the morning and then again in the afternoon.

Fermentation finished at different times for different tanks depending on when it was started. When the sugar level fell to approximately 6 degrees Brix, Winiarski drained the first juice, or free run, out of the tanks and put it into a separate container. Then he removed the skins and pressed them to get the so-called press wine, which went into another tank.

Dying yeast cells and other suspended solid material in the juice fell to the bottom of the tanks and formed the gross lees. Then he racked the wine, removing the liquid and leaving the sediment behind.

Winiarski's only help during the winemaking process came from Wes Schramm, who had first started making wine with him when the Winiarski family was living on Howell Mountain. Schramm, a Seventh-Day Adventist who abstained from drinking alcohol for religious reasons, monitored the grape juice and must along the way with Winiarski until the point when it became alcohol. Then he stopped tasting.

In the fall of 1973, the wine underwent malolactic fermentation, which gave it a smoother taste by converting malic acid into lactic acid. Winiarski was very familiar with the still relatively new process, having used it at both the Souverain and Robert Mondavi wineries. He also got the fermentation starter from the lab at Beaulieu and propagated it into the amount he needed. He began the malolactic fermentation in generally the same way as the primary fermentation, although it required much less starter material to begin the process.

The malolactic fermentation, though, takes longer than the primary one, and only occurs at a reasonably warm temperature of 45 degrees or so. By now, though, the nights in the Napa Valley were cool, and the Stag's Leap winery building was not heated. Winiarski did not have a way of heating the tanks by circulating warm liquid through the cooling jackets, as he had circulated cold liquid to lower the temperature during primary fermentation. So he bought some electric blankets at a department store in nearby St. Helena and wrapped them around the tanks to keep the wine at a temperature where malolactic fermentation would continue. Since he was worried that the process would stop if air reached the wine, the tanks were filled to the top and large cotton swabs were plugged into the opening there. The cotton allowed carbon dioxide, which was created by the malolactic fermentation, to escape but stopped air from entering the tank.

From mid-October to late November, Winiarski periodically tasted the wine and checked the cotton swabs. As the rate of malolactic fermentation slowed, he began taking samples of wine and putting a drop on a special paper that measured the amount and type of acid remaining. When the paper tests showed that the malolactic fermentation appeared to be finished, Winiarski took a wine sample to a lab in St. Helena, which confirmed his conclusion.

Shortly after Thanksgiving, it was time to give the wine some air. During malolactic fermentation, it had not been exposed to oxygen, which was now needed to start the wine's evolution and aging. The liquid was pumped through a splash tank that had a screen over it to break up the stream. A fan over the tank also increased the volume of air exposed to the wine. Then Winiarski did a first fining, a procedure that introduces a product, in this case a small amount of gelatin, into the wine and absorbs minute particles before falling to the bottom of the tank. In February 1974, the wine went through a second fining before being pumped into another tank, leaving the settled materials behind.

The next month, the Cabernet Sauvignon wine was moved out of the stainless-steel tanks and into 225-liter (59-gallon) barrels made of French Nevers oak. The barrels came from Dick Graff, the winemaker at Chalone, a winery located south of San Francisco, who had a sideline business importing French barrels. All the barrels were new and had been very slightly smoked inside in a procedure called light toasting. Winiarski had treated the barrels with water to make them watertight and also with a citric acid solution to stop any organisms from growing in them.

The Merlot, which had gone through the primary fermentation and then malolactic fermentation on its own separate from the Cabernet Sauvignon, went into puncheons, 500-liter (132-gallon) barrels also made of Nevers oak. The softer, milder Merlot did not need as much direct contact with oak, which is why Winiarski put it in the larger barrels.

For the next year, the Cabernet and Merlot aged in the winery. The Cabernet barrels were stacked several high, while the larger Merlot puncheons stood alone. From time to time, Winiarski topped off the barrels, putting in new wine to replace what had evaporated, and once a month he tasted. Before the wine went into barrels, he had put some in five-gallon glass containers, so that he could compare the original wine with that aged in oak. Gradually he noted how the oak was performing its magic. The French have aged wine in oak since Roman times, and for a good reason. Oak imparts subtle tastes, texture, and aroma that lift a good wine to a whole new level of enjoyment. Try as they have over the centuries, winemakers have never been able to find any other wood that can match oak in winemaking.

During that year the wine in each barrel was developing slightly differently in the cellar. A sample from a barrel at the top of the stack did not taste the same as one from a barrel at the bottom, partly because the slightly warmer cellar temperature of the higher barrel caused it to evolve and absorb the oak a little faster.

The next milestone in the wine's progress was separating it from the oak. The question for the winemaker at this point is how much slow oxidation through the cells of the wood is required to bring the wine to its peak before he moves it to bottles, where evolution in the presence of oxygen is terminated. How much oak can be added to the wine's identity before that identity is lost? Only the winemaker's vision and sense of taste could answer that question.

In the spring of 1975, Winiarski began taking four-ounce samples of wine from different barrels. Evenings after his wife and children were asleep and there were no distractions, he retired to the family living room with the specimens. At first he tasted wine from all the barrels and then later from only certain barrels. Winiarski poured it into separate glasses, carefully noting its origin. Then he tried the samples one by one. He examined the color and swirled it around in the glass to open up the aroma. He smelled it deeply and then carefully wrote down his observations about the aroma. Winiarski recorded his impressions in an attempt to both clarify them and also make them more precise. He then sipped a small amount of wine. He moved the wine around in his mouth, making sure that it touched all the points of sensual sensation on his tongue—the tip, the back, and the sides. Finally he spit out the wine and tasted another sample.

At first Winiarski worked alone, but he eventually asked Tchelistcheff to join him in order to get a second opinion. For several afternoons the two men tasted wine from the barrels, as the late-day sunlight shone in through the living-room door. Tchelistcheff offered his opinions candidly but not dogmatically, leaving the final decision to his pupil by making nonjudgmental statements like, "Maybe you should consider . . ."

After tasting all the barrels of Cabernet, Winiarski and Tchelistcheff agreed that the wine needed some Merlot to mellow it and give it more finesse. Cabernet Sauvignon in French means savage or wild Cabernet, and it can sometimes be quite astringent and rough. Merlot can smooth out Cabernet's harsh edges. Winiarski and Tchelistcheff decided to add 10 percent Merlot to the Cabernet, which added softness without weakening the wine's structure.

The barrels of both Cabernet and Merlot were then pumped into the stainless-steel tanks for blending. Winiarski also did a third and final fining, this time using egg whites, a common agent for this procedure that combined with any suspended material. Both fell to the bottom of the barrel, leaving behind the perfectly clear wine. The egg whites also imparted a very subtle taste that Winiarski liked.

Finally, the wine was pumped from the holding tanks to the bottling machine. Warren and Barbara Winiarski plus their three children, who were now 13, 10, and 7 years old, all helped out on the bottling line, where everything was done by hand. First new bottles were taken from cardboard boxes and inverted, two at a time, over spouts that sent a shot of nitrogen gas into them to remove not only any dust that had gathered during transport but also air, which could potentially spoil the wine. Then the bottles were placed under spouts that filled them with wine, but at different speeds so it took some juggling to make sure they did not overflow. Next the bottles were handed off to the person doing the corking, who pulled down the handle on a device that forced a cork into the bottle. The next person on the line placed the metal foil cap on the bottle and rolled the cap tight. The bottle then went to the Winiarski's older daughter, who had mastered the rhythm of putting glue on the label, placing it on the bottle and then rolling it on a curved surface to spread the glue as it dried. After the bottle was labeled, it went into an empty carton.

It took several days to bottle the 1,800 cases of wine, and when the procedure was finished the cases were moved to a storage area under the family living room. They remained there for five months of bottle aging. At last in July 1975, Winiarski released his second vintage to the market.

Determining the price for a wine is more art than science. Winiarski could have set it simply by looking at the shelf prices of other Napa Valley wines and figured out where he would be competitive. Instead he blindtasted several other wines to find what those that were comparable to his in quality and style were charging. Based on those tests, he thought the final retail price should be about $6 a bottle. That was less expensive than the wines he blindtasted, but since he was still a newcomer to the market he thought he should underprice his product. Of course the final price was in the hand of wine shops that could mark it up or down as they wished. Then he worked backwards to determine the price for distributors, retailers, or restaurants. Distributors got the so-called six-bottle price, meaning they paid the retail price for six bottles in a full, twelve-bottle case: $36. Restaurants and retailers paid the eight-bottle price for a case: $48.

The 1973 Stag's Leap Wine Cellars Cabernet Sauvignon stood out among its California counterparts, in many ways, by what it was not. In one of his diaries, the English wine critic Harry Waugh quoted Winiarski as saying that he wanted to produce a "sufficiently powerful wine which, while not too massive, would combine both style and elegance." This, wrote Waugh, represented a swing away from the California's "huge Cabernet Sauvignons" to a wine of "more finesse and elegance, in effect more along the lines of the Médocs from Bordeaux."

CHAPTER FIFTEEN

Making the 1973
Chateau Montelena Chardonnay

God made only water, but man made wine.
—VICTOR HUGO

*Mike Grgich using a wine thief
to extract Cabernet Sauvignon
from the barrel.*

On September 6, 1973, John Hanna, a grape grower whose ranch was located two miles north of Napa city near the southern end of the Napa Valley, drove a flatbed truck pulling a gondola filled with four tons of Chardonnay grapes into the driveway of Chateau Montelena. Hanna had grown the grapes under contract for the winery, selling them at $725 a ton. He was greeted by a small crowd: Jim Barrett, Lee Paschich, Mike Grgich, and the three cellar workers—Roam Steineke; Bo Barrett, Jim's son; and Ron Sculatti. Also present was Father Vincent Barrett, Jim's brother, who was a priest in the Los Angeles diocese. In a nod to an old European tradition, Father Vincent blessed the grapes as well as the people, and prayed for a successful and safe harvest. After prayers were said and holy water was sprinkled on the grapes, a hoist lifted the gondola off the truck bed and tipped the contents into a hopper. The 1973 harvest and wine crush, only the second since the new owners had taken over the winery, had begun.

Chateau Montelena was a much larger operation than Stag's Leap, which was located some twenty miles to the south. Chateau Montelena had some one hundred acres planted in a variety of grapes ranging from Aligoté to Zinfandel. Most of the grapes, though, were sold to other wineries. Barrett and Grgich wanted to build a premium wine label and didn't want to damage their brand by selling inferior products. Gradually they were shifting the vineyard over to higher-quality grapes. In 1972 they pulled out Chasselas, Alicante Bouschet, and Carignane vines and replanted the fields with phylloxera-resistant St. George rootstock, budding it with Cabernet Sauvignon. The budding material came from a premium Cabernet Sauvignon vineyard owned by Wallace Johnson in the nearby Alexander Valley. John Rolleri, an experienced vineyard manager, supervised the planting and cultivation.

While waiting for the Cabernet vines to produce, Chateau Montelena bought grapes for its Chardonnay from local growers. Just over forty tons of Chardonnay grapes in 1973 were purchased from four suppliers: Charles Bacigalupi from Sonoma County's Russian River Valley, Lee Paschich, whose vineyard was located about a mile from the winery; Henry Dick from the Alexander Valley in Sonoma County; and John Hanna. Bacigalupi provided 14 tons, Paschich about one ton, Dick about 20 tons, and Hanna four tons. The Chateau Montelena Chardonnay was thus made with predominantly Sonoma Valley grapes, although it was produced in the Napa Valley. While the Chardonnay was Chateau Montelena's prestige white wine, the Johannisberg Riesling brought in the sales. In both 1972 and 1973 Chateau Montelena produced more than twice as much Riesling as Chardonnay.

Starting in the spring of 1973, Grgich regularly visited the three vineyards where the Chardonnay was being grown. Although it was not his property, he believed the old saying, "The best fertilizer for a vineyard is the owner's footsteps." Relations between growers and winemakers are often tense because their goals are fundamentally different: a grower wants to produce big clusters of grapes that have a lot of weight, since he is paid by the ton; the winemaker wants smaller clusters that have more intense flavor. Grgich, though, sought good relations with all his growers, realizing that both had to work together to get the best possible final product. All through the spring and summer he and the growers walked the vineyards inspecting the crop. Grgich checked the vines in April to see the buds opening and was back in May and June to see the flowering and the setting of the berries.

Monitoring the vineyards intensified starting in the second half of July. Now every week Grgich visited each growing site, examining the grapes and talking with the farmers. Accompanied by them, he walked through the rows picking a berry here and there, tasting it and then spitting out the skins and seeds. The growers and the winemaker talked about whether they should put sulfur on the vines to protect them against mold. The UC Davis professors urged growers to spray sulfur as a protective measure whether it appeared to be needed or not. Grgich tried to interfere as little as possible with nature and did not agree with that preventive approach, especially in 1973 since the grapes showed no signs of mold or mildew. He also disagreed with the recommendation of the professors to irrigate the vineyard once a week. Early in the season, Grgich told his growers to water the vines only once—in the middle of the summer. Limiting irrigation, he thought, would make the vines work harder and intensify the flavor.

Grgich always had with him a refractometer to test the amount of sugar in the grapes. And while visiting a grower, Grgich usually collected between two hundred and five hundred berries from different spots around the vineyard and put them in a plastic bag. He then took the berries back to the laboratory at Chateau Montelena and did more extensive studies on the amount of sugar and acid in the grapes and most importantly their taste. The readings in the lab were more accurate than he could ever get in the field.

By the middle of August, Grgich was visiting each vineyard every two or three days, still going through the ritual of walking the rows of vines, collecting berries, and tasting. Temperatures now reached the high 80s and 90s almost every day, and the sugar level of the grapes was rising rapidly. As his Brix readings climbed closer to 20 degrees, the Chardonnay grapes changed from green to golden brown. They also became translucent, and if Grgich held a cluster up to the sun he could see the seeds through the skin and pulp. Sagging on the vine under the weight of the cluster, the grapes seemed tired. Another way to tell that crush was near was the arrival of starlings that fed on the ripening grapes to prepare for their journey south for the winter. Chattering birds swarmed into a vineyard and ate the ripest fruit. As soon as the first starlings arrived, Grgich knew that the harvest was not far behind.

In addition to using his sense of smell and taste, Grgich listened to the grapes. He had noticed over the years that when Chardonnay grapes have 23 degrees or more sugar he could squeeze them together between his fingers and hear a squeaking sound, almost as if tiny pieces of sugar were rubbing against each other. When the refractometer readings started hitting 21 degrees Brix on a consistent basis, Grgich alerted his crew at the winery to get everything ready for the arrival of the grapes. Machines were washed and sterilized. In late August, Grgich started to see on some vines an occasional shriveled grape that looked like a raisin. That and the refractometer readings showing an average of 23.5 degrees Brix indicated the harvest was at hand, so Grgich set up a schedule for the grapes to be delivered. Once they reached their peak of flavor, he knew that he had about four days in which to pick and crush the crop. After that, they would start to lose their delicate chemical balance and begin to decline.

Grapes were picked mainly by migrant Mexican laborers who started working at dawn when the grapes were still cool and finished at about two o'clock because afternoon heat could damage the recently picked grapes before they were crushed. Chardonnay berries are more sensitive than Cabernet Sauvignon ones, so growers watched their workers closely during picking and transport. In much the same way as Cabernet picking, workers put the grapes into forty-five-pound boxes, throwing the contents into a gondola that held four tons or into bins that held two tons. Tractors pulled the gondolas and bins through the twelve-foot-wide rows of vines. Once they were filled, the gondolas were slowly pulled to the Chateau Montelena winery. During August and September, traffic along Route 29 and the Silverado Trail, the Napa Valley's two north-south highways, was heavy with gondolas carrying grapes to wineries.

The staff at the winery was not of Grgich's choosing, and he and they did not always get along. Grgich tried hard to keep the cellar hands in line, but there was a significant age and cultural gap between them. The winemaker was fifty and had a serious demeanor. Grgich internalized many of his emotions, undoubtedly part of the reason he had developed ulcers. Grgich's doctor ultimately told him that to get rid of his stomach pains he had to give up either wine or coffee. Not surprisingly, the winemaker gave up coffee and began drinking weak tea laced with half and half for breakfast.

The three cellar workers, on the other hand, were in their early twenties and were caught up in the student rebellion and Vietnam War protests of the day. Two of the three were related to owners, who hoped that some hard manual labor at the winery would show the kids what the real world was like. Bo Barrett was between his freshman and sophomore years at the University of Utah, where he spent more time skiing than studying. His father,

Jim, was not amused by his son's approach to learning and refused to pay for more than his tuition and books. Bo had a blond Afro haircut, and his father called him Brillo because the bushy hair reminded him of a steel-wool pad. Roam Steineke, who also wore his hair long, was married to Ernie Hahn's daughter. The young couple had spent time among the hippies in the Haight-Ashbury section of San Francisco.

The young men worked hard, often putting in eighteen-hour days with few complaints. Bo usually worked the winepress, often going to sleep for a few hours on bags next to the machinery and then getting up and pressing again. After Grgich left at the end of the day, the cellar hands often broke out a bottle of tequila. Working at the winery was great fun—and best of all they were getting paid for it.

One day in the fall of 1973, Robert Mondavi and two friends from Hawaii came to visit his former employee's new operation. It was an honor for Chateau Montelena to have Mondavi visit, and the young cellar hands were nervous. At one point the Mondavi group walked over to where Steineke was holding a hose that was filling a two-thousand-gallon tank with Zinfandel. Instead of keeping an eye on the top of the tank, Steineke watched Mondavi and his group standing nearby and forgot what he was doing. When the tank was full, the wine started spurting out from the top. Mondavi and his friends were suddenly showered with beautifully red Zinfandel.

When the Chardonnay grapes arrived in gondolas from the growers there was serious work to be done. A hoist lifted the gondolas off the trucks and dumped the grapes into a hopper. A screw conveyer at the bottom of the hopper carried the grapes to a crusher, which removed the berries from the stems and let the berries drop to the bottom of the crusher. The stems exited the crusher onto the cement floor. There a workman with a pitchfork picked up the stems and put them onto a truck that took them to the vineyard, where they were spread between the rows of vines as mulch.

The berries were then pumped from the crusher into a 2.5-ton stainless-steel press. The crusher had been bought used from the Inglenook winery, but the press was new and had been built to specification by the Valley Foundry in Fresno. The press used the new bladder-squeezing technology, which was replacing the old screw press that used a grinding pressure to extract the liquid. The bladder press consisted of a rubber tube that was slowly inflated by compressed air, which squeezed the grapes gently against a screen. Grapes were pressed in 2.5-ton batches. Grgich told his cellar hands that everything had to be done gently. "It is like hugging a friend," he said. "You don't want to squeeze so hard that you break your friend's ribs."

In the case of the grapes, you didn't want to squeeze so hard that you crushed the seeds inside the grapes because that would release tannins, which in sufficient quantities would make the Chardonnay bitter. When the pressure in the bladder press reached fifteen pounds per square inch, it was released, the bladder was rotated, and the pressure was again raised. The whole process of pressing a bladder full of grapes took about ninety minutes. After that initial pressing of up to fifteen pounds of pressure, a secondary one was done under greater pressure. The juice from the secondary pressing, which had more tannin extracted from the grape skins, was isolated from the primary juice in separate tanks throughout the winemaking process.

All during this procedure, Grgich protected the liquid to keep it away from oxygen, which is the enemy of good white wine. Contact with too much air can oxidize the juice, turning it dark and taking away its freshness.

Once the pressing was finished, the juice was immediately pumped into stainless-steel tanks, while the skin and the seeds were removed and sent to the vineyard to be mulch. The clear juice was immediately cooled to a temperature of between 45 and 50 degrees, and it remained in the tanks at that temperature for four days, while pulp in the juice settled to the bottom. The tank was cooled by propylene glycol, a dense liquid often used to prevent freezing that circulated in pipes located between the inner tank and an outer skin. Grgich had first used the jacketed stainless-steel tanks at the Robert Mondavi Winery.

Grgich kept a close eye on the grape juice during that period, and when it appeared that most of the sediment had fallen to the bottom, he racked it by pumping the juice out from the top of the tank, leaving the pulp fragments behind. Getting rid of the pulp sediment prior to fermentation gives the wine a fruitier taste. The decision on when to pump out the juice is based on experience. Nothing in a book can tell a winemaker when it's time to rack the wine into another tank.

Once the wine was in a new tank, Grgich tested it for acidity and sulfur dioxide. Ideally the juice should be between 0.7 percent and 0.75 percent acid. If it's not, some tartaric acid may be added, but the 1973 vintage did not need any additional acid. At this point the Chardonnay grape juice was ready for fermentation. Grgich used a granular yeast developed by the Pasteur Institute in Paris, which was named simply French White, to start the fermentation process. He had worked with six different strains of yeast while at Beaulieu Vineyard and liked French White the best. He dumped buckets of it into the tanks through openings in the top to begin the process.

Following procedures advocated by the staff at UC Davis, which he had also used at Beaulieu, Grgich kept the temperature in the tanks during fermentation at between 40 and 50 degrees. So while Winiarski's primary fermentation of the Cabernet Sauvignon took only six days and the temperature hit 90 degrees, Grgich's fermentation of the Chardonnay took a month and a half at temperatures half as high. Fermenting Chardonnay at a higher temperature would have evaporated the wine's aroma and destroyed its fruitiness.

During fermentation, Grgich put a one-gallon jug filled with water at the top of each of the tanks. A tube went into the tank to carry carbon dioxide, a byproduct of transforming sugar into alcohol, out of the tank without letting in any oxygen. Again he was struggling to keep oxygen away from the wine. While fermentation was taking place, the spent yeast fell to the bottom of the tanks. Once the process was finished, the wine was again racked, and the yeast and sediment at the bottom were removed.

Although Grgich used malolactic fermentation for red wines, he did not use this procedure for his white wines. A malolactic fermentation, he thought, would make the Chardonnay flabby and take away the crispness found in the very best French Chardonnays. "Don't monkey with God in making wine," Grgich said. "God is the best winemaker. Leave nature alone."

Next came heat and cold stabilization. Bentonite was first added to the wine to remove any proteins. The bentonite fining prevented protein haze if the wine were later heated up during shipment or storage. Then the temperature of the wine was lowered to 30 degrees and kept there for four weeks. Lab analysis finally showed Grgich that both heat stability and cold stability had been successfully achieved. The wine was then filtered and moved to another tank, and the sediment on the bottom of the first tank was discarded.

By mid-November the Chardonnay was ready to go into barrels. All the stabilization was finished. Grgich's testing in the lab showed that the alcohol level was 13.2 percent, while the residual sugar was 0.1 percent and the total acidity was 0.68 percent. It was an ideal balance for a crisp, aromatic Chardonnay.

The wine was then moved into French Limousin oak barrels. Grgich had bought the 225-liter (59-gallon) barrels the year before and used them for the 1972 vintage. Wine had been in the barrels for only eight months, but the first use had mellowed the wood, taking off some of the rougher edges from the tannins and smoothing out the oak taste. The oak the year before had been something like a slap in the face to the Chardonnay, but now the year-old oak enveloped the wine like a gentle cloud. After they were filled, the barrels were stored along the inner wall of the winery, which was partially underground on three sides. The point where the cellar went underground was clearly visible because of water seepage that discolored the cement and rocks that formed the cellar walls. The cellar temperature was fairly constant during the eight months of barrel aging, ranging from only between 50 and 60 degrees.

While the wine aged in oak, pulling in the hints of oak extractives and mild tannins from the wood and giving the clear wine a golden hue and rich aroma, Grgich topped off the barrels every two weeks, replacing wine lost to evaporation through the pores of the wood and the bung at the top of the barrel. Grgich tasted the wine as it aged, and by early spring he was very pleased: it was the best wine he had ever made. The bouquet, the buttery taste, the crispness seemed to be coming together in perfect balance.

The Chardonnay was still in barrels on May 4, 1974, when the British wine writer Harry Waugh visited Chateau Montelena on one of his periodic trips to the California wine country. This was another big event for the still young winery. Waugh met both Paschich and Grgich, who were anxious to show him around. The Chinese junk that the former owner had put in the lake he built near the winery particularly amused Waugh. When they were in the cellar, Grgich removed the bung from a barrel of Chardonnay and used a wine thief to extract some wine.

Waugh looked at the straw-colored wine, smelled it, and then took a sip. He smiled and said, "Mike, I haven't tasted such a good wine even in France."

Grgich flashed a broad smile. He thought it was good, but what a compliment! He could hardly believe what he had heard.

Waugh also tasted Grgich's Zinfandel and Cabernet Sauvignon wines and told him that all of his wines had a good acid level, adding, "That is not the case with many other wines from the Napa Valley." Grgich liked wines with good acidity because they activated a person's taste buds, making the wines food friendly.

Following his visit, Waugh wrote in his diary, "Mike Grgich is a true perfectionist and we can expect exciting things from the Chateau Montelena."

By December 1974, the winemaker had decided that the aging in oak had given the wine the exact character he wanted. It was time for the master blend. Grgich wanted his wines to have a consistency from year to year, which he achieved by blending wine from the various barrels together in tanks. The same proportion of wine from each of the three growers was put in each tank to standardize the final taste. Then Grgich put the wine through Millipore filters to remove the last organisms and bottled it.

While bottling was done mainly by hand at Stag's Leap Wine Cellars, it was more mechanized at Chateau Montelena. Grgich was still passionate to keep oxygen away from the wine. After the bottles were filled and corked, a small machine glued on a label. Despite the new equipment, only 300 cases could be bottled a day, and so it took just over a week to complete the 2,200 cases.

After bottling in December 1974, the cases were stacked in the cellar for aging. Bottle aging is the anaerobic process when the aromas of the grapes and the aromas and extractives of the oak are married into the bouquet. Grgich called this process, which takes one to two years, "the wine honeymoon." The 1973 wine was scheduled to be released to wineshops in September 1975.

According to Barrett, however, something unexpected happened before the Chardonnay reached store shelves. In early 1975, only weeks after bottling, Barrett arrived at Chateau Montelena for one of his periodic visits. He was feeling a little down because his wine business had not taken off as he had hoped. He and Grgich were coming to the conclusion that they would have to sell off 12,000 gallons of 1972 Cabernet Sauvignon under the Silverado Cellars label because the quality was not good enough to sell it under the Chateau Montelena brand.

As Barrett tells what happened next, when he arrived at the winery, he sampled a glass of the Chardonnay, only to discover that while its bouquet was appealing and its taste excellent, the wine had a distinct copper color. Barrett then went into the storage room and began pulling bottles of wine at random out of cases and opening them. He discovered that every bottle had the same copper color. He felt like someone who had just had a thousand cases of wine fall on him. He thought to himself, "First the Cabernet; now this. I'd better not quit my law practice anytime soon."

Barrett figured they'd have to sell off the wine to someone just to get rid of it and salvage at least a little of his investment in that year's vintage. Barrett says Darrell Corti, a wine merchant in Sacramento and also one of the most respected wine tasters in California, was contacted to see if he would buy it. Barrett recalls being told that Corti could probably put together a group that would buy the 2,200 cases of wine at $2 a bottle, but that he couldn't buy it until he got his group together.

In early spring, Barrett returned to the winery for another routine visit. As he often did, he brought a piece of chicken with him that he planned to cook at the winery. On the way to the kitchen, he stopped and picked up a bottle of the 1973 Chardonnay. Walking back to the living area, Barrett mused, "I'm going to carve out a hundred cases of this for me and my buddies. We'll put blindfolds on and drink it. It tastes terrific; it just looks terrible."

After he cooked the chicken, Barrett opened the wine and poured a glass. Something was different. The copper color seemed to be gone. The wine now appeared to have a beautiful straw color—just like a good Chardonnay.

"Maybe it's just the lighting," Barrett thought. The room was dimly lit since it had only one small window. Nonetheless, Barrett went down to the storage area and began opening random bottles. The copper color seemed to be gone from all of them.

Barrett hoped against hope that this was not just some *trompe l'oeil*, but he still feared the poor lighting was playing tricks on him. He couldn't be sure until morning, when the sun came up and he could see the bottles in natural light, which would be late because it was early spring. Barrett slept fitfully that night, but finally woke shortly after 6:00 a.m. and looked at the wine.

There was no doubt. The copper color had disappeared. Barrett was ecstatic. Something had happened to the wine; he didn't know what. But his first thought was that he didn't want to sell that wine to Darrell Corti for $2 a bottle. So Barrett says he sent Corti a telegram that was written in the telegram style of the day, which used the word "stop" in lieu of punctuation and was all in all capital letters. It read:

DEAR DARRELL STOP WE AGREED TO SELL YOU TWO THOUSAND TWO HUN-
DRED CASES OF CHARDONNAY AT TWO DOLLARS A BOTTLE STOP WE HAVE NOT
HEARD FROM YOU STOP YOU HAVE TWENTY-FOUR HOURS TO SEND US THE
MONEY OR WE ARE WITHDRAWING OUR OFFER STOP JIM BARRETT

The next twenty-four hours was the longest day Barrett ever lived. By the deadline, though, he hadn't heard back from Corti. Corti recalls being offered the wine at a low price before it had been bottled, but doesn't recall the telegram or any discoloration of the wine.

Mike Grgich, for his part, says that the 1973 Chateau Montelena Chardonnay was "perfect from the very beginning" and that the events Barrett recounts never occurred. He recalls that there was some temporary discoloring of the 1972 Chardonnay when an old bottling machine let in some extra air into the bottles, but not of the 1973 one.

So-called bottle shock, when unexpected developments in the wine took place after bottling, was fairly common even at some of the most famous and technically advanced wineries. Experts describe a phenomenon like the one that Barrett says happened as "pinking in the bottle," and in the still early days of the California wine revolution the process was not widely understood. Napa Valley wineries in the early 1970s had not yet completely mastered their technology, and were sometimes so anxious to protect Chardonnay from air that they overprotected it. Wine has a natural browning enzyme that disappears when it comes in contact with oxygen, but wineries at that time wanted to make sure no oxygen ever touched their white wines in an attempt to protect their freshness and clarity. If the browning enzyme has no contact with air prior to bottling, a temporary discoloration sometimes turns up in the bottle but then soon naturally disappears.

In his July 1975 newsletter Jim Barrett announced that the 1973 Chateau Montelena Chardonnay would be released in September 1975 and sell for a suggested retail price of $6.50 a bottle. Because of the limited supply, customers could buy only one case.

PART THREE

———◆———

THE JUDGMENT OF PARIS

No matter how fine an average American wine might be, the American snob does not praise it highly, for fear of being thought naïve, or even chauvinistic. . . . There are two ways to cope with wine snobbery. One is to compare wines with their labels hidden. . . . The other way is to send American wines to Europe and challenge the imports on their home grounds.
—LEON D. ADAMS,
THE WINES OF AMERICA, 1973

CHAPTER SIXTEEN

Voyages of Discovery

A glass of wine is great refreshment after a hard day's work.
—LUDWIG VAN BEETHOVEN

In the summer of 1975, Patricia Gallagher was making plans to visit her sister in Palos Verdes Estates, the wealthy coastal community south of Los Angeles. Gallagher and Steven Spurrier had been talking for months about staging the tasting of California wines in Paris to show the French that interesting things were happening in the new, small California wineries—and of course to publicize their wine shop and school. But they faced two problems getting the project off the ground. First, they did not know that much about what was really happening there. American wine journalists Frank Prial and Robert Finigan had told them about the new California wines, but Spurrier and Gallagher had little firsthand experience with them, having tried only an occasional bottle. Second, none of the really good California wines were readily available in France. Fauchon, a fashionable shop in Paris that carried some American products for expatriates anxious for things from home, sold a few Paul Masson wines mainly out of curiosity, but they were of low quality and came in screw-top bottles. Clearly either Spurrier or Gallagher had to make a trip to California's wine country and see what was really happening there and also to come up with a way for getting the wines back to Paris.

As Gallagher made plans to visit her sister, she got the idea of extending her trip by a few days to make a scouting trip up north. When she suggested the side trip, Spurrier immediately agreed and phoned Robert Finigan to ask if he could make some introductions on her behalf. It was decided that Gallagher would stop in San Francisco to meet with Finigan before proceeding into the wine-producing area.

In early August, Gallagher arrived on Finigan's doorstep a few blocks from San Francisco Bay. The weather was cold. Finigan gave her a rundown of the wineries he thought most merited a visit. He recommended about a dozen places both north and south of San Francisco, paying little attention to well-known ones such as Beaulieu Vineyard, Inglenook, or even the new Robert Mondavi Winery and concentrating only on lesser-known places, where newer and more exciting things were taking place. Finigan called ahead to several wineries to introduce Gallagher, and that night they dined at Chez Panisse, a notable San Francisco–area restaurant. Her Paris friend Glenda Cudaback had suggested she stay with her family while visiting the Napa Valley and also put her in touch with Joanne Dickenson, the wife of a leading lawyer, who had started a company called Wine Tours International that ran wine trips to exotic ports of call.

Dickenson took Gallagher to several wineries on Finigan's recommended list, where Gallagher tasted wines and talked about winemaking styles. None of the California winemakers had ever heard of the Caves de la Madeleine—much less the Académie du Vin—but they all readily opened their doors and their bottles. Gallagher was impressed by the intensity the mostly young winemakers had for their craft, noting that many wineries were family owned and operated. Joe Heitz had one of his three children working with him in the field the day Gallagher visited Heitz Vineyards.

The morning she visited Stag's Leap Wine Cellars, Gallagher and Warren Winiarski hit it off quickly, and she ended up staying for lunch. Since he had taught political science, which was Gallagher's major in college, the two had many interests in common.

Gallagher also visited Chateau Montelena and talked with winemaker Mike Grgich. She was struck by the beauty of the setting at the base of Mount St. Helena and Jade Lake, located only a few hundred feet from the winery.

Gallagher returned to Paris convinced that the new generation of winemakers in California was indeed doing exciting things. The plan to hold a tasting of their wines in Paris as part of the American bicentennial was eminently feasible from the quality point of view. Gallagher carried back to Paris three bottles as samples: a 1973 Chateau Montelena Zinfandel, a 1968 Mayacamas Zinfandel Late Harvest, and a 1973 Chalone Chardonnay.

In September, Joanne Dickenson went to Paris to make arrangements for a wine tour of France she was organizing that would be led by André Tchelistcheff. It was being billed as "André Tchelistcheff's Tour of France," and he had already contacted many old friends from his days in France, lining up a nonstop tour of wineries from Champagne to Bordeaux. The tour was scheduled to last from May 6 to May 28, 1976. Tchelistcheff's presence and a program that took the group to some of France's best châteaux attracted many Napa Valley winery owners, including Louis M. Martini and Jim Barrett.

Dickenson brought along to Paris a bottle of Chateau Montelena Chardonnay for Gallagher, which was soon uncorked. Bottle by bottle Gallagher and Spurrier were becoming more familiar with California wines. Thanks to Finigan and Dickenson, they had now tried wines from many of the new wineries and from several different areas.

On December 30, 1975, Gallagher scribbled a note to Dickenson, thanking her for the wine and saying that the California wine tasting was going to be one of the top priorities of the new year at the Caves de la Madeleine. "The only problem involves getting the wine over here without great expense," she wrote. "If you have any ideas, please let me know."

Early in 1976, the pace of correspondence between Gallagher and Dickenson picked up. In a February letter, Gallagher proposed holding the tasting of California wines while the Tchelistcheff group was in Paris. But that suggestion never got very far. The tour had its own very tight itinerary, and no one was anxious to complicate things.

Then in March Spurrier went to California with his wife, Bella, to make the final selection of the wines that would be tasted in the bicentennial event. It was his first trip ever to California. By this time, Spurrier already had some definite ideas about the wines that he wanted to include. He had been particularly impressed when he tasted wines from Ridge and Chalone, two wineries located south of San Francisco. He also wanted to meet some of the California wine people who had stopped in the Paris shop over the previous few years.

Staying at the Alta Mira, a luxury hotel in Sausalito just north of the Golden Gate Bridge, Spurrier and his wife made forays into Napa and Sonoma counties as well as into wine-growing areas south of San Francisco. He surprised some of his hosts because unlike many people in the wine trade, who are always looking for a wine handout, the very proper Englishman always paid full retail price for his wines. He didn't make any fuss about what he was planning to do in Paris, and David Bruce, whose Chardonnay would be included in the tasting, didn't even know until years later that Spurrier had visited his winery.

The reception Spurrier received at the various wineries was good—except at Heitz Wine Cellars. Joe Heitz was well known in the Napa Valley as a charming curmudgeon, and when Spurrier called to make an appointment to see him, he got the classic treatment.

Heitz first barked at him, "I don't receive people. Are you a journalist?"

"No," Spurrier replied, a bit taken aback.

"Are you a wine merchant?"

"Yes."

"Well, I don't export. And anyway, I don't have time."

"Mr. Heitz, I'd like to come and see you anyway. You are a great name in California wine, and I'd like to meet you."

So with his style of just showing up that had worked so well in Paris, Spurrier went uninvited to Heitz's winery on the Silverado Trail east of St. Helena, hoping his charm would get him by.

After a few minutes of casual conversation, Heitz offered his visitor a glass of his Chardonnay and then quickly asked, "What do you think?"

"It reminds me of a Meursault Charmes," Spurrier said, referring to one of the great white Burgundies.

"Meursault Charmes is my wife's favorite wine, and that's what I try to make," replied Heitz.

Suddenly the doors of Heitz Cellars flew open, and Spurrier went on to taste several other wines. Heitz the curmudgeon had turned into Heitz the charmer.

During his California travels, Spurrier kept picking up bottles of wine, and by the time he was ready to go he had more than he could carry with him as luggage on his return trip. He had already decided to have six California Cabernet Sauvignons tasted with four Bordeaux red wines and six California Chardonnays matched with four Burgundy whites. He figured he needed two bottles of each wine, which meant he needed at least twenty-four bottles. Only one would probably be enough for the tasting, but he wanted an extra in case a bottle broke or the judges asked for retests. Plus there were some other wines he wanted to take back.

By this time Spurrier had also determined that if the wine were shipped to Paris via a normal transportation company, it could be stopped at customs. He didn't want a repeat of the troubles he had getting the English wine into France for Queen Elizabeth II's dinner for President Pompidou. Finally Spurrier decided the safest way to get the wine to Paris was to have people on the Tchelistcheff tour bring it along as accompanying baggage, so he called Dickenson to see if she could handle it.

After agreeing to help, Dickenson phoned a TWA representative with whom she was working on her upcoming tour and asked if that would be okay. TWA was then trying to establish a relationship between the wine-producing areas of the world that it called a "Wine Bridge," and the representative said he would be delighted to handle it.

Several days later, Spurrier's wine was delivered to Dickenson's home and left in a hallway. Then two days before he was leaving California, Spurrier phoned Dickenson again and inquired if she could also bring two bottles of Chalone Chardonnay. Dickenson called the winery and asked that the wine be brought to the Napa Valley. A company representative said she would have to pick up the bottles at the company's San Francisco office. So on her way to San Francisco Airport to start the trip to Paris, Dickenson made a detour to pick up the Chalone wine.

Once back in Paris, Spurrier, with the help of Gallagher, scurried to get everything together for the event. The date was set for May 24, and there was a lot to do. The classroom at the Académie du Vin was too small to accommodate the tasters, so they looked for a bigger location. Ernst van Dam, the food and beverage manager at the Paris InterContinental Hotel on the Rue de Castiglione, was a friend and client of Spurrier. The hotel was only a few blocks from the Caves de la Madeleine, so Spurrier asked if he could use a room. Van Dam told him that on May 24 between 3:00 p.m. and 6:00 p.m. he could have a room located next to an interior courtyard where drinks and light food were served. But the group had to be out by 6:00 because after that the room was booked for a wedding reception. Van Dam then corrected himself and said they would have to be out of the room a little before 6:00 because the staff would need time to set up for the reception.

Now that he had selected the California wines, had a way to get them into France, and had a location and firm date for the tasting, Spurrier set out to get the judges. He relied on the connections he had built up so assiduously over the years to get an outstanding group of French wine experts, and their participation reflected the prestige he had achieved with influential members of the French wine business. It would have been hard to come up with a better group of judges; with only one exception, they were widely known and respected. When Spurrier invited them he told them it was for a tasting of California wines; he did not say that they would be tasting both California and French wines at the same time. The tasting panel:

- Pierre Bréjoux, Inspector General of the Appellation d'Origine Contrôlée Board, which controls the production of the top French wines. Bréjoux was also the author of several books on French wine.
- Michel Dovaz, teacher of wine courses in French at the Académie du Vin and the supposed president of the Institute Oenologique de France. There is actually no such organization; Dovaz made up the name as a joke to look like he belonged to the august group. He was invited because of his connection with Spurrier but would later go on to write several books on wine as well the chapter on Champagne for the annual *Hachette Guide des Vins*.
- Claude Dubois-Millot, sales director of *GaultMillau*. Dubois-Millot was the only inexperienced judge. In fact, this was his first wine tasting.

Despite the slightly different spelling of their names, he was the brother of Christian Millau, one of the cofounders of *GaultMillau*. Dubois-Millot had spent twenty years in the automobile industry before joining his brother's business in 1973. Spurrier had tried to get *GaultMillau* to cover the California wine tasting, and the publication at first had agreed. Later, though, the editors changed their mind and sent Claude Dubois-Millot as a gesture to their friend Spurrier.

- Odette Kahn, editor of the *Revue du Vin de France* (Review of French Wine) and also of its sister publication *Cuisine et Vins de France* (Food and Wines of France). The *Revue du Vin de France* was started in 1927 by Raymond Baudoin, a former wine dealer whose goal was to "instruct and defend the consumer." His crusading magazine carried stories about wine scandals and unscrupulous wine merchants that helped foster the Appellation d'Origine Contrôlée system. Kahn was named editor of the two publications in 1970.

- Raymond Oliver, chef and owner of Le Grand Véfour restaurant. Spurrier chose Oliver because he came from Bordeaux, where his mother had a famous restaurant. Le Grand Véfour, then and now, was one of France's great restaurants, dating back to the late eighteenth century. Located under the arcades of the Palais Royal, it has long been a favorite of French politicians and artists. Napoléon ate here, as did Voltaire, Colette, and Sartre. When Victor Hugo dined at Le Grand Véfour, which was often, he always ordered the same meal: vermicelli, breast of mutton, and white beans. Oliver took over the restaurant in 1948, and in 1976 was at the apex of his career. Le Grand Véfour had three stars in the *Michelin* restaurant guide—the highest possible rating—and an 18/20 score in the rival *GaultMillau* guide. Oliver also hosted a very popular cooking show on television. Le Grand Véfour naturally had an outstanding wine cellar.

- Pierre Tari, owner of the Château Giscours and Secretary General of the Association des Grands Crus Classés, the organization of the wines classified in 1855. Château Giscours is a Third Growth. Tari's father bought the property in 1955 and together with his son brought it back from near oblivion.

- Christian Vannequé, head sommelier of La Tour d'Argent, another three-star restaurant. Probably the most famous restaurant in Paris, La Tour d'Argent also has an extraordinary wine cellar, which privileged guests can visit after a meal. The building where it is located was built in the thirteenth century and has a tower constructed of stone laced with mica that glitters in the sun, hence its name La Tour d'Argent or "The Silver Tower." The royalty of nations, Hollywood, and politics have all dined at

La Tour d'Argent. The restaurant is famous for its roast duck and has been keeping track of the number of people ordering it since the 1890s. The one millionth duck was served with great fanfare in 2003.

Vannequé was only twenty-five years old at the time and had been at La Tour d'Argent for seven years. He had gotten to know Spurrier in Paris wine circles and they were talking about starting a business that would sell wines under the brand Académie du Vin Sélection. Vannequé had been introduced to California wines in 1971 by the movie director John Frankenheimer, when he was then making *The French Connection* in France and living in the same building as La Tour d'Argent. The two often discussed wine, and when Frankenheimer left Paris he gave Vannequé about 150 bottles from leading California producers, including Clos Du Val, Freemark Abbey, and Chalone.

- Aubert de Villaine, co-owner and co-director of the Domaine de la Romanée-Conti. Some of the world's most expensive—and most sought after—wines are produced on the four-and-a-half-acre patch of stony, dark red soil of the Domaine de la Romanée-Conti. The vineyard has been held in almost sacred awe for centuries. When La Romanée-Conti was auctioned off after having been seized during the French Revolution, the catalog described the vineyard as "the most excellent of all those of the Côte d'Or and even of all the vineyards of the French Republic." Aubert de Villaine, who was married to an American, also had some experience with California wines.

- Jean-Claude Vrinat, owner of the Taillevent restaurant, another of the stars of French gastronomy. The restaurant was started in 1946 by André Vrinat, his father, and won its first star in the *Michelin* restaurant guide in 1948. It picked up its second star in 1954, and its third in 1973. Taillevent, which is named after the court chef to King Charles V in the fourteenth century, has long been considered the epitome of Parisian cuisine. The decor is classic and restrained, with wood paneling and deep blue velvet banquettes. Jean-Claude Vrinat began working at his father's restaurant as a sommelier and had taken over direction of the restaurant in 1973.

After the judges were selected, Spurrier and Gallagher set out to get the press to cover the event. A very simple press release went out to the leading media organizations in Paris announcing a tasting of California wines and inviting coverage. They paid special attention to invite the wine writers from the two most important Paris newspapers, *Le Monde* and *Le Figaro*. *Gault-Millau* received a personal invitation from Spurrier.

On May 7, Spurrier drove out to Paris's Charles de Gaulle Airport to meet the Tchelistcheff group on the overnight flight TWA 810 from Boston's Logan Airport. The flight was due to arrive at 9:25 a.m. The weather was unusually hot for Paris in May, so Spurrier wore a white summer suit. He was very anxious to get his hands on the California wine the tour members were bringing. The event was now only two weeks away, and without that wine there would be no tasting.

The tour group had flown first from San Francisco to Boston, and the wine traveled with them in the cabin. In Boston they changed planes, and the wine was transferred to the baggage compartment.

Joanne Dickenson had no trouble spotting Spurrier in his white summer suit when he arrived at the baggage area with a cart to pick up the cartons of wine. Before long Spurrier and Dickenson saw three boxes coming around the carousel with the other luggage. Spurrier was elated; Dickenson was horrified. Spurrier saw his wine; Dickenson saw a case with a red stain all over it. At least one bottle had obviously broken during the flight or in the baggage handling.

Later when he examined the contents of the cases, Spurrier discovered that a bottle of Freemark Abbey Cabernet Sauvignon had broken. There was still the extra bottle of that wine, which was enough for the tasting. No winery was going to be excluded because of a broken bottle.

After the members of the group retrieved their luggage, Spurrier helped them through customs where officials, as expected, stopped them to ask about the wine. Spurrier explained to the customs agents that the group consisted of thirty-two people, and together they were carrying less wine than they were legally allowed to bring into the country. French customs allowed travelers to carry one bottle of wine, and the officer waved them through. The group had actually slightly more bottles than the legal limit. They had thirty-six bottles—or more correctly thirty-five bottles and one broken bottle. But the customs officer didn't count.

Spurrier and the group left for the Chemin des Vignes, the wine storage cellar on the outskirts of Paris that Spurrier co-owned, where they tasted several French wines and had a light lunch. After that the Californians went to their hotel. The next day they started their study trip.

Two weeks later, and a little more than a week before the planned tasting, Spurrier and Gallagher sat in the Académie du Vin offices and discussed a serious problem. No one from the press was going to attend their tasting! Not *Le Monde,* not *Le Figaro,* not *GaultMillau*! A tasting of California wines? No one in the French press saw a story there.

How could they get some journalists to attend, they wondered? After all, publicity was the main purpose for staging the tasting. It then occurred to Gallagher that I had taken their wine course and might be interested in covering the event.

She picked up the phone and called me at the *Time* office, located just off the Rond-Point des Champs-Élysées.

I had received the press release but paid little attention to it. People were always trying to get *Time* reporters to come to events in the hope that they would have stories written about them. This appeared to be just another one of these nonevents: it seemed almost absurd to compare the best French wines with California unknowns.

After Gallagher explained more about the tasting, however, I reconsidered and said I'd try to get there, without promising anything. The Inter-Continental Hotel was not far from the *Time* office, so it wouldn't be a major time commitment. A wine tasting was always interesting and I knew little about the California wines. If something more important—or interesting—came up that day, I could always drop out.

Gallagher put down the phone and turned to Spurrier, "That's wonderful. Taber will come."

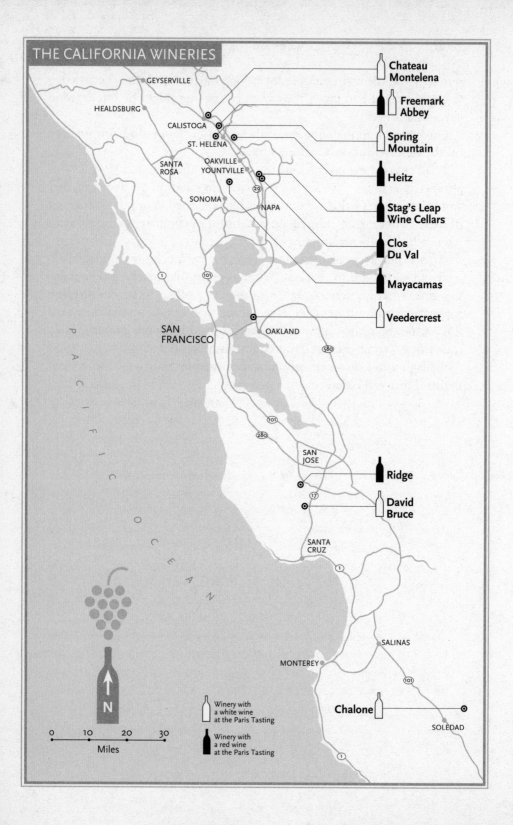

THE CALIFORNIA WINERIES

GEYSERVILLE

HEALDSBURG

CALISTOGA

ST. HELENA

SANTA
ROSA

OAKVILLE
YOUNTVILLE

SONOMA

NAPA

Chateau
Montelena

Freemark
Abbey

Spring
Mountain

Heitz

Stag's Leap
Wine Cellars

Clos
Du Val

Mayacamas

Veedercrest

SAN
FRANCISCO

OAKLAND

SAN
JOSE

Ridge

David
Bruce

SANTA
CRUZ

PACIFIC OCEAN

SALINAS

MONTEREY

Chalone

SOLEDAD

N

0   10   20   30
Miles

Winery with
a white wine
at the Paris Tasting

Winery with
a red wine
at the Paris Tasting

CHAPTER SEVENTEEN

California Wines at the Tasting

To take wine into our mouths is to savor
a droplet of the river of human history.
—CLIFTON FADIMAN

The twelve California wines—six Chardonnays and six Cabernet Sauvignons—that Steven Spurrier selected to participate in the Paris Tasting all came from wineries started or reopened in the 1960s and early 1970s. Nine of the twelve wines came from the Napa Valley, and three came from mountain areas south of San Francisco. Grapes that went into some of the wines, though, were also grown in Sonoma County. The wines came from a total of eleven wineries: Napa Valley's Freemark Abbey was the only one with entries in both the red and white categories.

The wineries were all very representative of the new age of California wine. They were generally small operations still run by the founders, who were often on a second career. Most of the winemakers had been strongly influenced by the work done at the University of California, Davis, but they didn't just slavishly follow the dictates of professors. They were always experimenting, trying to discover what could be done with their unique land and the northern California climate. They freely shared their successes as well as their failures. These new wineries concentrated primarily on just two grapes: Cabernet Sauvignon and Chardonnay, although they might produce some others as well. And in their search for excellence, France was their model. They tasted the best French wines regularly and candidly compared their own to them.

The other California wineries in addition to Chateau Montelena Winery and Stag's Leap Wine Cellars:

CHARDONNAY

Chalone Vineyard, 1974

Chalone is located about a hundred miles south of San Francisco and two thousand feet above the Salinas River on an unusual geological formation known as the Gavilan benchland. A million or so years ago, when the land mass that geologists call the Pacific plate started sliding under the North American plate, marine deposits were trapped between the plates and various hunks of geography were shuffled around. That monumental shift and the prehistoric eruptions of the Pinnacles Volcano left a large tract of soil rich in limestone and calcium carbonate.

The Frenchman Charles L. Tamm in the 1890s thought the soil was very similar to that found in Burgundy and planted some grapes, although he didn't stay around long enough to harvest them. During the next several decades, the land passed from owner to owner. The property's history of fine wine began in 1923 when Will Silvear, a sickly rancher, came to the mountaintop because he had been told its dry clean air would be good for his health. His brother planted a vineyard that included high-quality French varietals—Pinot Noir, Pinot Blanc, Chardonnay, and Chenin Blanc. After Silvear died, however, Chalone went back to revolving ownership as new owners tried their hand at winemaking and failed. Severe, near-drought conditions made the harvests small, and the grapes were usually sold to other wineries.

In 1965, Dick Graff, a young banker, bought into the winery, obtaining a 47.5 percent share. He had landed in California winemaking after being a music major at Harvard, a navy officer, and a banker. R. W. Apple Jr., a *New York Times* reporter and friend of Graff, in a preface to the book *Chalone: A Journey on the Wine Frontier,* called Graff "an odd combination of a woolly-headed dreamer and a practical man who could build things with his hands." Graff was also given to philosophical musings and published a treatise on decision making entitled *The Technique of Consensus.*

A chance encounter with wine had led Graff to leave his $450-a-month banking job to be the chief winemaker and boss at Chalone Vineyard, even though he then knew nothing about winemaking. As part of his signing agreement, though, Graff agreed to spend a year at UC Davis studying both viticulture and enology. True to his eclectic nature, while at Davis he also took courses in French and orchestra conducting.

Not far away in San Francisco, the flower children at the time were preaching love and peace, and some of them found their way to Chalone, especially at harvest time. One was Captain John, whom Graff met in jail. Graff was there for speeding; Captain John was in for writing bad checks. After they got out, the Captain became a member of the extended Chalone family. He found people to lend money to the winery, purchased equipment on credit, and even bought 160 acres for $10,000 by guaranteeing payment of $1,000 a year.

The 1969 vintage was Graff's first, and conditions were primitive. Wine was made in a converted chicken coop and the capacity was only about two thousand cases a year. Everything from picking the grapes to labeling the bottles was done by hand. Despite the rustic environment, Graff produced very good wines. André Tchelistcheff knelt down in front of Graff after tasting his 1969 Pinot Noir, saying that he had reacted that way to a great Pinot Noir two or three times in Burgundy, and this was the first time it had happened in California.

Graff took up cooking to go with his wines and in a bold move invited TV chef Julia Child to visit Chalone. He was shocked when she actually came, and was even more pleased when she proclaimed that Chalone made the first non-French wines she had ever liked.

Before the 1974 vintage, Chalone built a new winery, with Graff doing much of the plumbing and electrical work. The new facility could handle twelve thousand cases, and the harvest that year was both large and of good quality. The company's official history recounts: "They were heady years— 1973, 1974, 1975. We were getting shareholders. We were getting money. We had three good vintages. We were right on track."

In October 1975, *Robert Finigan's Private Guide to Wines* took notice of Chalone, writing, "The wines of Chalone, that aerie near Soledad, enjoy a certain cult appeal based at least in part on their unavailability. To be sure, what has trickled down from the mountain has indeed provided ample evidence that climate, soil and winemaking skill are admirably suited to production of California Chardonnays and Pinot Noirs matched in quality only by very great Burgundies."

The 1974 Chalone Chardonnay tasted in Paris sold for the rather high price, at the time, of $9 a bottle; most of the others in the competition were in the $6 to $7 range.

David Bruce Winery, 1973

David Bruce grew up in a teetotalling family, but while he was a medical student at Stanford University in the early 1950s he became interested in good cooking and then in wine, because the two always seemed to go together. At the time, Bruce had a summer job on a ranch in the mountains, and one day ventured into the hills with his two-year-old son Karli to repair a broken water pipe. He had located the pipe and was working on it, when his son let out a scream that brought a couple hiking nearby rushing to see what had happened. The boy was fine, albeit a bit bored. It turned out the couple owned a small winery in the hills, and they invited father and son to come and see it. Bruce was amused by the winery's slogan lifted from Oscar Wilde: "Work is the ruin of the drinking class."

Bruce began reading classic books like John Melville's *Guide to California Wines* and Alexis Lichine's *Wines of France*. Lichine intrigued him with the description of Richebourg, one of the great Burgundy Pinot Noirs, as wearing a "noble robe." Bruce simply had to get a bottle. He finally found one in San Francisco, but the price was a stunning $7.50—at a time when most premium wines cost about $2. Nonetheless, Bruce put his money down for the 1954 Richebourg and always remembered the way the wine's aroma filled the room when he pulled out its extremely long cork.

While a medical resident in Oregon in 1956, Bruce made some wine using Concord grapes and a unique way of crushing. He put the grapes on a large piece of plastic, folded it over the grapes, and finally put wooden planks over the whole thing. He then drove a car over the boards. Bruce ended his grape crush by pouring the juice into gallon jugs and starting fermentation with Fleischmann's yeast, a product normally used for making bread.

After his residency, Bruce returned to California and began looking to combine his love of winemaking with his work as a dermatologist. In 1961, he bought a forty-acre plot above the town of Los Gatos, which seemed ideal for growing the grapes used in Burgundy's great wines— Chardonnay and Pinot Noir. The land was sandstone and had good drainage. It was located at 2,200 feet on the ocean side of the mountains, which Bruce called the Pinot Noir side, as distinct from the inland side, where Cabernet Sauvignon seemed to do better. The property was above the fogline and only a short distance from the San Andreas Fault, the fracture in the earth's crust where earthquakes regularly occur. Bruce gave his winery the slogan "Wines of elegance and distinction from the dangerously beautiful Santa Cruz Mountains." Annual rainfall was heavy, averaging sixty to eighty inches.

In addition, the property was just a mile from Martin Ray's vineyard. As others had reasoned before him, great wine could probably be made on land near where great wine was already being made. Martin Ray was then making the best Pinot Noir in California, and Bruce's goal was to make a world-class Pinot Noir just like that Richebourg with the "noble robe." Although the two men never became personally close, Bruce followed Ray's strictures of sticking as closely as possible to nature's way of doing things, going against conventional thinking at the time and using no insecticides or preservatives.

Bruce replanted the old vineyard on the property with Chardonnay, Cabernet Sauvignon, Riesling, and Pinot Noir grapes, which were not readily available from local farmers. His own grapes, though, provided only about 10 percent of the total amount he needed. He got most of his grapes from farmers in the Santa Cruz Mountains and the Santa Clara Valley.

Bruce's medical training came in handy for wine chemistry, and he was constantly trying new methods as he learned winemaking by the books. He produced seventy different wines in 1971, including twenty-two types of Zinfandel. Bruce got wide attention with a White Zinfandel that he called Blanc de Noir and also with a sweet, late-harvest Zinfandel that tasted like Port. He left the 1969 Chardonnay in French barrels for five years to see what would happen to the color and was surprised when longer aging made the wine lighter.

The dermatologist by day and winemaker by night and weekend was best known in the 1970s for his Chardonnay, which had a big oaky taste that came from the French wood Bruce used for aging. Following Martin Ray's dictum, Bruce did not use sulfur dioxide to protect his wines. The absence of that made them more susceptible to spoilage, but he thought it also made them more robust, helped them develop faster, and gave them a distinctive amber color.

Wine critic Robert Finigan in 1976 rated the 1973 David Bruce Chardonnay as "outstanding," writing, "The flavors of this exotically rich wine are sufficiently intense to suggest Pinot Noir rather than Chardonnay, and the finish is dramatically long." Finigan called it the "essence of Chardonnay."

Freemark Abbey Winery, 1972

Freemark Abbey had a long history in the Napa Valley and was staffed primarily by people who had deep roots there, rather than by newcomers to the wine business. In 1967, St. Helena grape growers Charles Carpy and Laurie Wood purchased the old stone winery just north of St. Helena. Although its name would suggest otherwise, it has never had any religious affiliation. Josephine Marlin Tychson founded the winery in 1886. She had brought her sickly husband, John, who suffered from tuberculosis, to the Napa Valley in the hope that the drier air there would help him recover. She paid $8,500 for 147 acres where a few grapevines had already been planted but no wine had been produced. After her husband died, Josephine built a thirty-thousand-gallon facility, naming it Tychson Winery. She made Zinfandel and Riesling for eight years before selling the property to her ranch foreman.

The winery had several owners and a variety of names until 1939, when three southern California real estate developers—Charles Freeman, Markquand Foster, and Albert (Abbey) Ahern—bought it. Using a bit of each of their names, they called it Freemark Abbey. The three were better at coming up with a good name than they were at making wine, however, and the winery soon fell into decline.

When Carpy and Wood bought it, Freemark Abbey was dormant, and the main business of the owners was selling wine jelly and candles to passing tourists. Carpy and Wood had been following developments in the Napa Valley wine business and the shift to quality grapes, and in 1964 they planted a vineyard with Cabernet Sauvignon and Pinot Noir; the following year they put in one with Chardonnay and Riesling. They also closely studied the work being done at UC Davis that had turned Chardonnay from a grape plagued with disease and a poor producer into a healthy and major product.

The two growers eventually recruited five more partners. The most important was Brad Webb, and it took Carpy a year of wooing and the promise of a partnership to get him. After the Hanzell winery was sold, Webb couldn't find a winemaking job that interested him and ended up as a biochemist at the Sonoma State Hospital working on brain research, doing only a little wine consulting on the side. Building on the expertise of the grape growers in the partnership and his own experience making wine at Hanzell, Webb quickly moved Freemark Abbey into the premier ranks of California wineries. In 1969 Webb hired Jerry Luper, a recent graduate of the wine program at Fresno State College, to be the winemaker.

Freemark Abbey produced its first wines under the new management in 1967. The grapes came mainly from Carpy's vineyards, although Wood contributed some Cabernet Sauvignon. In the cooperative style of Napa Valley, the sixty tons of grapes were crushed at the new Robert Mondavi Winery seven miles south on Route 29. By the next year's harvest, however, Freemark Abbey had its own new equipment.

Freemark Abbey quickly earned kudos for its Chardonnay. *Robert Finigan's Private Guide to Wines* gave an "outstanding" rating to the 1969 vintage. Wrote Finigan: "A nearly faultless wine in a fairly big style. Among generally distributed Chardonnays, my strong first choice."

That same 1969 Freemark Abbey Chardonnay came on the radar screen of the small group of American wine connoisseurs in March 1973, when it won a major taste-off of twenty-three California, New York, and French Chardonnays in New York City. The tasting was organized by Robert

Lawrence Balzer, the wine writer who the year before had staged the Cabernet Sauvignon tasting Mondavi won and now published *Robert Lawrence Balzer's Private Guide to Food & Wine*. He brought together fourteen wine experts, including Sam Aaron, a New York City wine merchant; Paul Kovi, a manager of the Four Seasons restaurant in New York; and France's Alexis Lichine. The event took place before 250 members of the New York Food and Wine Society, who were shocked when California Chardonnays received the top four scores. In fifth place was the 1969 Beaune Clos des Mouches Joseph Drouhin. Other French wines at that tasting: 1970 Corton-Charlemagne Louis Latour; 1971 Pouilly-Fuissé Louis Jadot; and 1970 Chassagne-Montrachet Marquis de Laguiche Joseph Drouhin. California wines were starting to get attention, but news of the Balzer tasting didn't travel much beyond a small circle of wine aficionados.

The 1972 Freemark Abbey Chardonnay was a classic Webb-Luper product and followed in the tradition of the award-winning 1969 wine. The grapes came from the Carpy Ranch and the Red Barn Ranch in the Napa Valley. The wine had an oakiness that came from nearly seven months of aging in small French barrels.

Spring Mountain Vineyard, 1973

When Mike Robbins grew up during the 1930s in Iowa, no one he knew drank wine. He left Des Moines to go into the military and then went to the Naval Academy in the last months of World War II. While an Annapolis cadet, he dated a stunning blond named Grace Kelly, who lived in nearby Philadelphia and later went on to capture the heart of Hollywood as well as that of the prince in Monaco. Robbins was still on active duty in the navy when the Korean War broke out and he eventually served three tours in the Pacific.

In 1954, Robbins retired from the navy and settled in San Francisco. He went to work for the real estate broker Coldwell Banker and earned a law degree and an MBA from the evening division of the University of San Francisco. His first introduction to wine came through the friend of a friend in San Francisco, and a leisurely tour of Western Europe in 1959 confirmed his interest. Robbins got started in the wine business the following year, when he invested in Mayacamas Vineyards, where he also did some marketing work while continuing his real estate career. But after three years he sold his stock, telling owners Jack and Mary Taylor that they were producing a weak-tasting "Cabernet Rosé that was a waste of outstanding Cabernet Sauvignon grapes."

Combining his interest in wine and his knowledge of real estate, Robbins in the early 1960s began buying land in the Napa Valley. There was plenty of property for sale, and the prices were low since land was mainly used for cattle grazing or plum orchards. Good property cost only $2,500 to $3,000 an acre, and Robbins bought some of the best available. In 1962, he purchased a Victorian home with a small winery and vineyard north of St. Helena. Founded in 1884, it was named the Johannaburg Vineyards. Robbins renamed it Spring Mountain after the hill on the western side of the valley where the property was located.

Robbins took a year off from real estate in 1968 to get the winery started, while learning about his new field from members of the local wine brotherhood: Robert Mondavi, Joseph Heitz, and André Tchelistcheff. For the next seven years he experienced the life known to many entrepreneurs—holding down two jobs. Weekends he was a winemaker, while during the week he was a real estate broker, working on projects like the Golden Gateway Center in San Francisco and Century City in Los Angeles.

The early years at Spring Mountain were haphazard. Robbins blended Cabernet Sauvignon from his first two years and marketed the wine as the 1968–69 vintage. Originally he bought all the grapes he used for winemaking and did his crushing at other wineries. But as money became available, he restored the Victorian mansion, replanted the vineyard, and bought his own equipment.

Robbins hired Charles Ortman to be his winemaker. Once a commercial artist, Ortman learned much of his winemaking while doing pick-up work for two years at Heitz Cellars on the other side of the valley. He used both his old and new talents at Spring Mountain, designing its wine label and also becoming a master maker of Chardonnay. Ortman and Robbins had an iconoclastic approach to winemaking. They weren't out of the UC Davis school and thought the work of the professors was more applicable to the large Central Valley wineries than it was to the Napa Valley's smaller ones that were producing more refined wines. Robbins adopted the French view that growing grapes under stress improved their quality. One of his maxims was never to irrigate his vineyard after May 20, even in the driest of years. Stressed vines, he thought, produced a more intensely flavored harvest.

In the early 1970s, Robbins was used to coming home from wine tastings with the gold prize. His 1969 vintage won at a tasting of thirteen Chardonnays put on by the Los Angeles/Beverly Hills chapter of Les Amis du Vin. The competition included not only Freemark Abbey and Heitz Cellars from the Napa Valley but also Corton-Charlemagne Remoissenet and Puligny-Montrachet Leflaive from Burgundy. *Robert Finigan's Private Guide to*

Wines gave "outstanding" rankings to Spring Mountain's Chardonnay for its 1970, 1972, and 1973 vintages.

Finigan put the 1973 Spring Mountain Chardonnay into a special class with the Freemark Abbey and Heitz Chardonnays. Finigan wrote that all three reached "a special level of quality," adding that he couldn't pick out one as the best. Then after pointing out some shortcomings in both the Freemark Abbey and Heitz wines, he wrote: "I suppose that leaves the Spring Mountain as my narrow favorite, but choosing among these classic California Chardonnays really involves senseless hairsplitting."

Veedercrest Vineyards, 1972

A. W. (Al) Baxter, the winemaker at Veedercrest, was a home winemaker with serious ambitions, who started the winery with a group of investors. Its first bonded location was the basement of Baxter's home in the upper-middle-class Berkeley Hills area northeast of San Francisco, where he had three fermentation tanks.

Baxter was a man of many tastes and a colorful background. A Stanford philosophy student, he went on to get a master's degree in the subject at the University of California, Berkeley, and then became a professor of philosophy there. Later he was an assistant to Clark Kerr, the chancellor of the University of California. Baxter wrote poetry and mystery novels in his spare time. A book of his poems was published under the title *Carneros Cantos,* and his mystery, *Slay Me with Flagons,* is set in a winery and opens with a dead body in a fermentation tank.

After a failed attempt to get into wine imports, Baxter found several partners and bought three hundred acres of land for a vineyard on Mount Veeder on the western side of the Napa Valley. The property had been a vineyard during the nineteenth century heyday of California wine, and Baxter replanted fifty acres in 1974. The 1972 vintage that competed in the Paris Tasting came from grapes bought from the Winery Lake Vineyard in Carneros, in the southern part of the Napa Valley.

Baxter did his winemaking in the industrial section of Emeryville, a town located an hour's drive from his vineyard. "We're a neat little urban vineyard," he told visitors. He added that "the grapes don't care that they are crushed in Emeryville." The building had been constructed originally for Shell Development, a research arm of the oil company, and had housed an atom smasher. The basement laboratories had heavily insulated walls four feet thick, which turned out to be a very good place to store wine. Baxter had heard about the building from partners who had worked for Shell

Development but left the company when their operation was moved to Houston.

Although a self-taught winemaker who got his first experience at home, Baxter easily adapted to leading-edge technology: stainless-steel tanks and oak barrels. But he always considered himself a craftsman, saying, "There's no question that the best wines are artistic in nature." He thought a wine-maker needed a scientific foundation for his work but added, "That doesn't give you the lofty mating of oaks and wine, aging and wine, vineyard pro-duction and winemaking style."

Like most California wineries at the time, Veedercrest made a host of wines, ranging from Cabernet Sauvignon to Gewürztraminer. Its first commercial crush was in 1972, when Baxter made five wines: Cabernet Sauvignon, Merlot, Pinot Noir, Riesling, and Chardonnay. The Veedercrest Chardonnay that competed in Paris was part of Baxter's very first vintage.

CABERNET SAUVIGNON

Clos Du Val Winery, 1972

John Goelet and Bernard Portet, the two men behind Napa Valley's Clos Du Val, were both born into the French wine business. Goelet's mother, Anne Marie Guestier, was a descendant of François Guestier, who in the eigh-teenth century worked for decades for the Marquis De Ségur, the owner of two of Bordeaux's First Growths, Château Lafite and Château Latour, plus the then Second Growth Château Mouton. The son of François, Pierre François Guestier, was the owner of Château Beychevelle, a Bordeaux Fourth Growth. The family was also a partner in Barton & Guestier, one of France's leading wine exporters.

Portet was born in Cognac into a family that has been making wine for more than six generations. His father was the technical director at Château Lafite, and Bernard grew up playing in the vineyard there. He went on to study at two of France's leading wine institutes, Toulouse and Montpellier. At the age of twenty-six, Portet went to work for Goelet, who was looking to expand his wine holdings. At the time, he was negotiating to buy a French winery and planned to have Portet manage it. While waiting for the talks to conclude, Goelet asked the new hire to look for other areas in the world where he might buy land and begin producing Bordeaux-style wine. The château deal eventually fell through, but Portet spent 1970 and 1971 traveling the world studying wine regions in South Africa, Australia, Argentina, Chile, and the United States. Two sites particularly impressed him—Napa Valley, California, and Victoria, Australia, twenty miles north-west of Melbourne.

Portet was especially taken by the Stag's Leap section of the Napa Valley. The coarse, rich soil reminded him of Bordeaux's St.-Émilion. Although he liked the wines of leading valley wineries, Portet thought he could do better. He considered Napa wines a "bit hot on the palate," since the alcohol level was often higher than what he was used to in French wines.

The heat of the Napa Valley also worried him, particularly the temper-atures during the summer growing months. As he drove south on the Sil-verado Trail toward the city of Napa in the late afternoons with the windows of his car open, however, Portet noticed how the temperature dropped significantly at Parker Hill, about five miles north of Napa. That was only a few hundred yards south of where Nathan Fay was growing Cabernet Sauvignon grapes and where Warren Winiarski had recently planted a vineyard. This Stag's Leap area had cool nights, despite the hot days, so Portet thought this could be the special spot he wanted.

In November 1971, Goelet leased 120 acres of land on the Silverado Trail. Portet returned to France in December, but by April he was back in the valley, now with the charge of building and running a winery that would produce wines to rival those of his native Bordeaux. Goelet named the winery Clos Du Val, which translates as "the valley's enclosed winery." Planting of Cabernet Sauvignon, Merlot, and Cabernet Franc vines began in the spring of 1972 on land where plums, alfalfa, and walnuts had grown. But Portet realized that the first Clos Du Val Cabernet would not be on the market for years if he waited until all the grapes came from their own vineyard and the fermentation and aging were done in their own win-ery. So Clos Du Val followed the path that was becoming standard for new Napa Valley wineries: buy grapes from local growers for the first year or so and ferment and age the wine at another winery. Portet, though, main-tained total control over the wine's development from grape to bottle, vis-iting the vineyards regularly during the growing season and carefully monitoring the winemaking.

The Frenchman was surprised by the cooperation of California wine-makers, which contrasted sharply with the guarded privacy of those in France. He asked his brother Dominique, who was also following the family wine tradition, to join him in the valley for the 1972 vintage. The Portet brothers listened to what local grape growers and winemakers told them about making wine in California, but they also had their own ideas. Everyone was telling them, for example, to pick grapes late so they would be sweet and have a high alcohol content. Bernard Portet, though, wanted to avoid a strong alcohol taste. So he had the Clos Du Val grapes picked early, when they would be less sweet and have less alcohol. The brothers were lucky because it rained heavily in September and October 1972. That made it very difficult for other Napa Valley wineries to harvest their grapes, but by then Clos Du Val had picked 80 percent of its crop.

Like his neighbor Warren Winiarski, Bernard Portet also went against the advice of local winemakers by blending. They urged him not to tone down the varietal intensity of Cabernet Sauvignon by mixing it with other wines, but he strongly believed that blending improved the wine. For the 1972 vintage Portet combined 80 percent Cabernet Sauvignon with 20 percent Merlot. The wine was then aged in French oak barrels for eighteen months. It had an alcohol level of 12.8 percent, which was a little higher than a typical Bordeaux red. The total Clos Du Val harvest in 1972 was just 5,000 cases—3,500 Cabernet Sauvignon and 1,500 Zinfandel.

In 1975, *Robert Finigan's Private Guide to Wines* gave the 1972 Clos Du Val only an "average" rating, although it held out the hope for more. Wrote Finigan: "Bernard Portet has debuted with an agreeable, rather austere wine which portends well for his future bottlings while suffering the limits of the unexciting 1972 harvest."

Clos Du Val was among the first of the new boutique Napa wineries to sell in the important New York City market, and in September 1974 Portet made a promotional trip there. Given his background and training, Portet knew his wines were good, with a French style of balance, complexity, and elegance. It was tough, though, to get the attention of wine buyers. Portet consciously played up his French accent, but wine buyers were still not interested in California wines—even if a French-trained winemaker made them.

Freemark Abbey Winery, 1969

Freemark Abbey was the only winery to have two wines in the Paris Tasting: a 1972 Chardonnay and a 1969 Cabernet Sauvignon. This Cabernet Sauvignon was the first bottling of a wine that Freemark Abbey has since marketed as its top of the line Bosché. The 1972 wine was a blend of 88 percent Cabernet Sauvignon and 12 percent Merlot from the Charles Carpy and Laurie Wood vineyards.

Heitz Cellars Martha's Vineyard, 1970

Like many American GIs born around the country and stationed in California during World War II, Joe Heitz decided when hostilities ended to stay in the land with beautiful weather and lots of opportunity. He had grown up on a farm in Princeton, Illinois, and served in the Army Air Corps in Fresno, the center of California's jug-wine business. Heitz got his first job in wine doing pick-up work at an Italian Swiss Colony plant outside Clovis. His boss there suggested he get a degree in winemaking from UC Davis, so he could get a better job when he graduated.

Heitz took that advice and went to Davis on the GI Bill, graduating in 1948. There were less than a half-dozen enology graduates in his class but no work for any of them. The next year Heitz finally landed a job at Gallo doing quality control. After only nine months, he left to work for the Wine Growers Guild, a trade group. From 1951 to 1958, Heitz worked at Beaulieu Vineyard, starting at $325 a month as the lab assistant for André Tchelistcheff and eventually moving up to the post of manager.

Heitz realized he could not advance further because Tchelistcheff would not be retiring anytime soon. So just before the 1958 harvest he accepted an offer to establish a new viticulture program at Fresno State College. After three years there, he decided he wasn't meant for academic life or the quiet town of Fresno. Then with the help of a $5,000 loan from an East Coast friend, Heitz made the down payment on an eight-acre vineyard and winery south of St. Helena. He called his new place Heitz Cellars. The full price was $45,000, and the property included two houses, a small winery, and about five thousand gallons of wine inventory. Four years later, he bought an additional 160 acres on the eastern side of the Napa Valley, just as the wine business began to pick up.

Heitz made a potpourri of wines—more than a dozen different kinds ranging from Sherry to Cabernet Sauvignon. His first Cabernet sold for $1.63 a bottle and was soon doing well. Heitz discovered that when he increased the price he charged wholesalers or at his tasting room, he sold even more. Although he was always a little incredulous that people were willing to pay that much, Heitz kept gradually pushing the price to $1.79, $1.99, $2.20, and higher. Heitz never apologized for his prices, saying, "If you've got a good product, people want to pay for it." He was one of the first winemakers to believe that California wines of French quality should also get French prices.

In 1965, Heitz bought some Cabernet Sauvignon grapes from Tom

May, a former schoolteacher in Ojai, a town north of Los Angeles. The fruit came from a vineyard May had planted in Oakville and named after his wife, Martha. Heitz blended the wine from Martha's vineyard with that from his other Cabernet grapes in 1965 and sold it under the generic Heitz Cabernet Sauvignon label. But the next year he kept the wine separate, and as a gesture to Tom and Martha, Heitz released it under the name Heitz Cellars Martha's Vineyard. It cost $7 a bottle, a price only the top French wines were then getting. The wine, which had a hint of minty eucalyptus taste, was a hit. Heitz was not the first winemaker to name a wine after the vineyard where the grapes were grown, but the success of Martha's Vineyard soon led others to do it. Heitz said later, "By a stroke of what turned out to be genius, but was pure luck, we put the vineyard name 'Martha's Vineyard' on the label. The wine writers liked it, the connoisseurs liked it, the restaurants liked it."

There have long been questions about the unique taste of the Martha's Vineyard wine. Heitz made no attempt to explain it, saying that if he knew how to do it, he'd repeat it in his other vineyards. Some speculated that it came from eucalyptus trees growing near the vineyard, since prevailing winds can carry oils from the leaves of those trees to grapes that are ripening, leaving a minty residue on the skin. But such trees grow all over the valley, and Martha's Vineyard wines had a special taste. Heitz said it was like growing different types of tomatoes in different soil. The hint of mint, Heitz believed, came from both the clone used for the Cabernet Sauvignon grapes grown there and from the Oakville soil where they were planted.

Heitz was a purist. His Cabernet Sauvignon wines were 100 percent varietal without a touch of Merlot or other wines. Heitz argued that California Cabernet did not need to be a blend because of the conditions under which the grapes grew. Unlike in Bordeaux, where the weather varies greatly from one year to the next, in the Napa Valley, "We can get Cabernet ripe here almost every year," he said. "They never get it as ripe as we do here. So they need those other varieties that develop more sugar, or sugar sooner, to make a sound wine." Heitz greatly admired Bordeaux wines, but he didn't want to just copy them. He wanted to make a world-class Cabernet Sauvignon that would be judged on its Napa Valley merits. Frequently he said, "If you always imitate, then you're going to be second best."

In his October 1975 review of California Cabernets, Finigan wrote of the 1969 Martha's Vineyard, "Rich minty Cabernet aromas and flavors with that unmistakable Martha's Vineyard eucalyptus much in evidence." Finigan also wrote that the wine was "unconscionably priced" at $21 a bottle, twice the price of other top-of-the-line California wines.

Although Joe Heitz had disdain for wine tastings, Martha's Vineyard did very well in them. For its October 1975 issue, the *San Diego Grapevine* newsletter had twenty-eight experienced wine tasters rate eight Bordeaux wines and two California Cabernets from the 1970 vintage. The Martha's Vineyard, the vintage that would later be in the Paris Tasting, came in first. Château Latour and Château Mouton Rothschild tied for second. It was a small event and the judges were Americans, however, so few people paid much attention.

Mayacamas Vineyards, 1971

A native Californian, Bob Travers hoped to get into oil exploration when he picked engineering as his major at Stanford University. Travers became interested in wines just before graduating in 1959, and by then he had also decided that he liked stocks and bonds better than engineering. He spent the next eight years doing investment research in San Francisco, primarily on the new electronics firms popping up in what would later be called the Silicon Valley. While working in San Francisco, Travers was deepening his knowledge of wines with courses at the University of California campuses in Berkeley and Davis.

Both of his parents came from farming families, which was perhaps why Travers started to think about a life on the land. He looked at raising cattle or sheep, but quickly turned to the more promising possibilities of wine. Just before the 1967 harvest, winemaker Joe Heitz lost one of his day laborers at the same time Bob Travers was looking for a job where he could get some hands-on experience. Travers stayed with Heitz just a year, but it was long enough for him to confirm his plans to buy a winery.

Fortunately, there was one for sale. John Henry Fisher, a German immigrant and sometime sword engraver and pickle merchant, in 1889 built a beautiful stone winery at about two thousand feet near the top of Mount Veeder on the western side of the Napa Valley. The region was known as the Napa Redwoods since the heavy rains made it a good area for those trees. Fisher sold both wine and pickles by the barrel, which horse-drawn wagons took to Napa, where they were loaded onto ferry boats that carried them to San Francisco.

Fisher went bankrupt at the turn of the twentieth century, and the J. H. Fisher Winery stood abandoned for nearly forty years, although bootleggers are believed to have made illegal wine there during Prohibition. Jack Taylor, a British chemist, and his American wife, Mary, bought the property in 1941 and restored the winery, which they named Mayacamas Vineyards after the mountain range where it is located. Mayacamas means "cry of the mountain lion" in the language of the Wappo Indians who once lived there. The first Mayacamas vintage was 1946.

The Taylors worked hard on the land for the next twenty years, bringing back some of the vineyard and fencing it in to keep out wandering deer and other animals. They were also good promoters, starting a newsletter and in 1958 selling stock in the winery at ten dollars a share, with dividends promised in bottles of wine. Some five hundred people put their money down. In the late 1960s, however, the Taylors retired and moved away, leaving the management to hired hands. In the fall of 1968, Travers and his wife, Elinor (Nonie), bought Mayacamas Vineyards from the Taylors. Bob Travers was thirty years old, and at the time he counted only seventeen active wineries in the Napa Valley. As far as Travers knew, Mayacamas was the only one then for sale.

The vineyard and property needed lots of work. The Taylors had planted quality Cabernet Sauvignon and Chardonnay grapes, but they had not been maintained after the couple moved. Travers brought back about twenty-five acres of the abandoned vines with careful pruning and cultivating and planted another thirty acres. The antiquated equipment in the winery was also replaced piece by piece, as cash flow permitted.

When Travers bought the property, Mayacamas was producing about 2,500 cases a year and had twenty different wines for sale, far too many for a small winery to produce properly. Nearly all the wines were made from grapes bought from local farmers. Travers discontinued the poorer-selling wines and began concentrating on the more popular ones. By the mid-1970s, annual production was up to 5,000 cases, and he was now selling only two wines—Cabernet Sauvignon and Chardonnay.

Growing grapes and making wine near the mountaintop at Mayacamas was far different than doing it on the valley floor. As far back as the first flowering of wine in the Napa Valley in the late nineteenth century, mountain grapes sold at a premium because their yield was lower and they were believed to produce better wine. And while Travers was still getting most of the grapes from other growers, he bought mountain ones so that his wines, from the beginning, would have the intensely flavorful mountain character. About three-quarters of the Cabernet Sauvignon grapes Travers used in the early years were bought, largely from the Draper Ranch on nearby Spring Mountain.

Travers called his Cabernet "aggressive" because of its heavy tannins. In view of that, he held it back from the market longer than other winemakers did in order to give the tannins time to mellow. Most vintners begin selling their Cabernet about two years after the harvest, having aged it about a year in oak and then another year in the bottle. Mayacamas wines were released after five years—aging a year and a half in large oak tanks, another year in small oak barrels, and finally two-and-a-half years in the bottle.

When he visited the Mayacamas winery, Steven Spurrier was very impressed with its Cabernet and wanted to include the 1970 vintage in his tasting. Travers, though, was sold out of it, and Spurrier left thinking it would not be part of the tasting. Upon further reflection, though, he decided he really wanted Mayacamas in the contest and called Travers back to see if he could find a solution. This time Travers offered him the still unreleased 1971 wine, even though he did not consider it ready to drink. So Spurrier made a long trip back up to Mayacamas and bought three bottles of the 1971 wine.

Ridge Vineyards Monte Bello, 1971

Wine has been made in the Santa Cruz Mountains south of San Francisco since the early days of California vineyards, and some of the new ambitious amateur winemakers started returning there in the late 1950s. In 1959, four scientists from the Stanford Research Institute with Ph.D. degrees in engineering, Hewitt Crane, Charles Rosen, David Bennion, and Howard Zeidler, bought a winery in the Santa Cruz Mountains. It dated back to the 1890s and was located at 2,300 feet on Monte Bello Ridge.

An elderly theologian who lived there alone surrounded by his books and dogs owned the property, and his only requirement of the new owners was that they take care of the grapevines. The scientists paid six hundred dollars an acre for eighty acres, although only twenty-five acres were planted with grapes. Most of the vines were Cabernet Sauvignon, with only a little Chardonnay and Pinot Noir, and an obscure Ruby Cabernet that had been developed by a professor at UC Davis.

Only because they had agreed to keep up the vineyard, the scientists soon became weekend farmers and vintners. David Bennion was designated winemaker, even though he had never tasted wine before leaving his Mormon family in Utah to move to California. The engineers figured that since he had grown up on a farm, he knew at least something about growing things. Bennion made a few gallons of wine from the first crop in 1959, crushing the grapes by foot. Most of the six tons of grapes harvested, though, were sold to the nearby Gemello Winery. The scientists delivered the grapes in three station wagons.

Although at their regular jobs the four were doing research on the outer edges of science on topics like magnetic-logic computers, on the weekend they had a simple, totally natural approach to winemaking. They didn't filter their wines or use many chemicals, making the most of the quality grapes already planted. The early Ridge wines were simple, big, and very tannic. The men's natural winemaking philosophy was strongly influenced by Martin Ray, who had vineyards and a winery nearby. In an obvious allusion to the famous Côte d'Or region of Burgundy, Ray told Bennion that the land above the Santa Clara Valley was the Chaîne d'Or (Golden Chain).

The winery was bonded in 1962, so the operation was now legal, but they were still only making small amounts of wine, just 187 cases in 1963. Once they began selling it, they needed a name and a label. They named the winery Ridge Vineyards, and a commercial artist designed the label, taking his payment in wine. In 1967, Bennion left the Stanford Research Institute to work full time at Ridge, whose wines were developing a strong and loyal following, especially among the academic community at Stanford University.

At a Palo Alto wine tasting in the late summer of 1968, Bennion met Paul Draper, a man with an eclectic wine background to match his own. Draper had grown up on a forty-acre farm in Illinois, graduated from the Choate prep school in Connecticut, and then picked up a degree in philosophy from Stanford. Following graduation in 1959, Draper went into the army and was stationed in Italy, working in intelligence. He rode around the country on a motorcycle just like the hero in his favorite movie *La Strada* and fell in love with the Italian lifestyle, especially the wine. As he said years later, "Wine in a sense is a sacrament of nature and takes the meal to another level."

After the army, Draper continued his European experience with a year in Paris, where he studied at the Sorbonne. It was while working with Fritz Maytag, a member of the appliance family and a Stanford friend, in a venture in Latin America that promoted family planning, better nutrition, and other social changes that Draper first thought about getting into wine. The two were looking into for-profit ventures that could provide money to let them do their not-for-profit work. Before opening a wine business, however, Draper realized he needed to learn more about winemaking. So for two months in the summer of 1967, he worked at Souverain Cellars in the Napa Valley. The following summer he went to France, where he stayed with a friend whose family owned a winery in Bordeaux and picked up still more knowledge watching the harvest and wine crush. Draper produced two vintages of Chilean Cabernet Sauvignon, but growing economic chaos in the country and the political struggle between right and left forced him to abandon his work in Latin America to return to the U.S.

After they had first met in Palo Alto, Bennion contacted Draper to see if he might be interested in joining him at Ridge, since he needed some help. The Ridge partners had expanded their operations by buying the abandoned Monte Bello winery, located one mile farther up the mountain on a single-lane, winding dirt road. An Italian-born doctor had founded Monte Bello in 1886, and its first commercial vintage was in 1892.

Draper came aboard in August 1969, a time when the winery was a counterculture outpost on the West Coast. David Darlington described the scene in his book *Zin*: "On spectacular, supernal Monte Bello Ridge, psychoactive drugs proved quite popular; one Ridge acolyte—a full-bearded red-headed individual named Jerry—reportedly ate LSD sixty-four days in a row, and bottling was frequently performed by someone who held a 750-ml glass vessel with one hand and a joint of primo sinsemilla with the other. Though Bennion himself was not a druggie, the winery's operations had to conform to this altered state of reality."

Ridge was best known for its Zinfandel wines, but Paul Draper's pride was the Ridge Monte Bello, a blend of primarily Cabernet Sauvignon and Merlot, plus, in some years, a small amount of Petit Verdot and Cabernet Franc. Ridge labels carry long descriptions of their wines, and on the bottle of the 1971 Monte Bello wine that went to Paris, Draper wrote, "Our Cabernet grapes reached their balance in 1971 at slightly lower sugar than usual and produced a wine with more elegance and finesse than we have yet seen. The wine was fermented dry on the skins and from completion of its malolactic [fermentation] in November, was aged in small cooperage until bottled. Softer than the 1970, but with the same fine Cabernet character, the 1971 will need at least six years in bottle to approach its plateau of maturity."

Steven Spurrier had his pre-tasting favorites among the American wines. He expected that the Chalone Chardonnay would do best among the California whites and that the Ridge Monte Bello would score highest among the California reds.

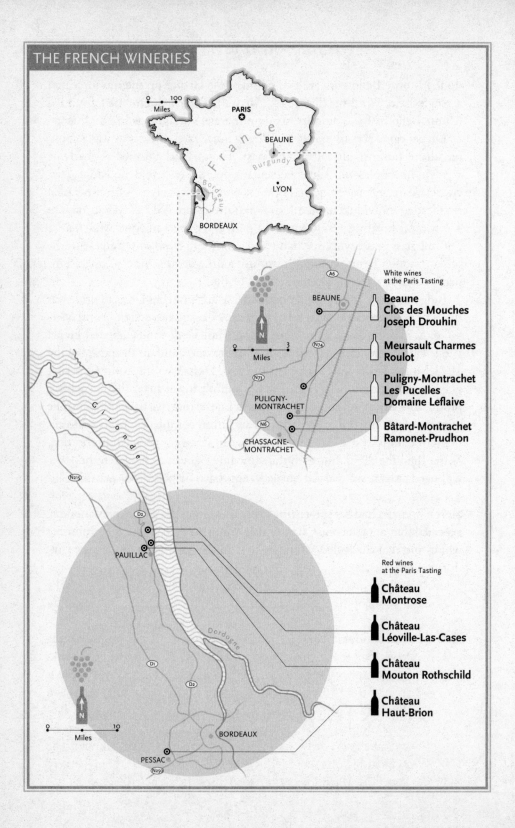

THE FRENCH WINERIES

PARIS

France

BEAUNE

Burgundy

LYON

Bordeaux

BORDEAUX

0   100
Miles

White wines
at the Paris Tasting

A6

BEAUNE

Beaune
Clos des Mouches
Joseph Drouhin

N74

Meursault Charmes
Roulot

N73

Puligny-Montrachet
Les Pucelles
Domaine Leflaive

PULIGNY-
MONTRACHET

N6

Bâtard-Montrachet
Ramonet-Prudhon

CHASSAGNE-
MONTRACHET

0   3
Miles

N

Gironde

N215

D2

PAUILLAC

Red wines
at the Paris Tasting

Château
Montrose

Château
Léoville-Las-Cases

Dordogne

D1

Château
Mouton Rothschild

D2

Château
Haut-Brion

BORDEAUX

0   10
Miles

N

PESSAC

N250

CHAPTER EIGHTEEN

French Wines at the Tasting

The flavor of wine is like delicate poetry.
—LOUIS PASTEUR

Steven Spurrier selected French wines that he thought would easily outshine the American ones at his event. The objective was first to get some publicity for the Caves de la Madeleine and the Académie du Vin and second to make the French aware of the interesting developments in California. Spurrier was certainly not out to humiliate the French wine business. After all, he was a wine merchant in Paris and wanted to continue working there. He had no plans to import and sell the California wines. His business was selling French wines—the ones in the competition and others. All of the French wines came from the stock of Spurrier's shop.

He selected four French red Bordeaux wines to be tasted with six California Cabernet Sauvignons, and four white Burgundies to be tasted with six California Chardonnays. Since this was to be just an interesting afternoon tasting and not an event that experts would be arguing about three decades later, Spurrier didn't think anything about the fact that having six California wines in each part of the competition but only four French ones would give the Americans a statistical advantage. Since he wanted to make the French aware of the unknown California wineries, why not add an extra two to the mix?

As he went about picking the French wines to face off with the California ones, Spurrier looked for close French matches. The French wines should be from vintages approximately the same as the American ones, and the reds had to be two or three years older than the whites since they take longer to develop. The new California winemakers since Hanzell Vineyards had been slavishly modeling their Chardonnays after Burgundy's best, so he chose wines that any expert would name as top-rated white Burgundies. The four whites included one Grand Cru (Great Growth) and three of the very best Premiers Crus (First Growths) from three different *appellations*.

Since the California reds were either pure Cabernet Sauvignon or Cabernet blends, Spurrier opted for the best predominately Cabernet Sauvignon Bordeaux blends. His four French reds included two First Growths and two Second Growths from the 1855 classification. He thought the First Growths, Château Mouton and Château Haut-Brion, were the best Bordeaux wines then being made, and the two Second Growths, Château Montrose and Château Léoville-Las-Cases, were his personal favorites in that category. All the French reds had the taste, structure, and finesse of classic Bordeaux.

Vintages are more important for French wines than for California ones because year-to-year variations in weather are greater in France. All the French Chardonnays came from the 1972 and 1973. The 1973 vintage was quite good for white Burgundies, while the 1972s had a high acidity and aged well for years. Both of those vintages were better for white Burgundy than either the 1971 or the 1974, which were also readily available. In addition, Spurrier had to play the card nature dealt. Chardonnays are ready to drink three or four years after bottling, and it wouldn't have been fair play to compare young California Chardonnays with much older French ones. The French and California Chardonnays in the tasting were all basically the same age.

The four red Bordeaux wines came from 1970 and 1971. The quality of a red wine vintage is often not known with certitude for many years, but at the time both were considered outstanding. Alexis Lichine wrote in 1979 of the vintage 1970 Bordeaux reds: "A great vintage. Unquestionably the best since 1961, with an abundance not seen since the beginning of the century." Three of the four reds were from 1970. The 1971 vintage was smaller in size and a modest step down in quality, but was nonetheless very good.

French reds take longer in the bottle to reach their peak than California reds, and an ideal tasting might have been between twenty-year-olds from both places. But that couldn't be since the new California wineries didn't yet have that kind of history. In any case, both the French and California wines were available in stores at the time and were already being drunk.

CHARDONNAY

Bâtard-Montrachet Ramonet-Prudhon, 1973

Montrachet in the Côte de Beaune section of Burgundy has been the reigning sovereign of white Burgundies for centuries. The name means "bald hill," and the Montrachet vineyard straddles the two villages of Puligny-

Montrachet and Chassagne-Montrachet. This is the wine that Alexandre Dumas said should be sipped only while kneeling and with head bowed.

There are no less than five wines with the highest Grand Cru ranking that have the word Montrachet in their names, and it's difficult even for dedicated wine amateurs to keep track of all of them. The five: Le Montrachet, Bâtard-Montrachet, Chevalier-Montrachet, Bienvenues-Bâtard-Montrachet, and Criots-Bâtard-Montrachet. Wine connoisseurs have spirited discussions about which of the five is best. The most famous is the simple Montrachet, but the other wines are sometimes better made, depending on the particular vintner. The defining factor of all is their scarcity, since they come from relatively small areas. Bâtard-Montrachet covers only twenty-nine acres. As a result, all the wines are much in demand and expensive.

The origin of bâtard (bastard) in Bâtard-Montrachet is lost in the mists of time. According to legend, a medieval lord of Montrachet had an illegitimate child by a local maiden. After the lord's only legitimate son was killed in the Crusades, the father adopted the other son. Many years later, the lord's château was destroyed and a variety of names from family history were given to his vineyards. One vineyard was named for the crusading son (Chevalier-Montrachet) and another for the bastard son (Bâtard-Montrachet).

Domaine Ramonet was founded by Pierre Ramonet, the son of Claude Ramonet, a vineyard worker in the village of Chassagne. Pierre was born in 1906 and quit school at the age of eight to help his father in the fields. He married Lucie Prudhon, the daughter of the vineyard supervisor at the nearby Domaine de l'Abbaye de Morgeot. Thus the name Ramonet-Prudhon. Pierre Ramonet was a man of the earth who rarely traveled outside his village of Chassagne-Montrachet. The year of the Paris Tasting, Fanny Deschamps, a French journalist, wrote of him: "In his vineyard, Ramonet seems as much at home as if he were planted next to a vine." In a 1988 book entitled *Montrachet,* Jean-François Bazin described Ramonet in the fields wearing "a big old sweater, galoshes, black pants, a cap pulled down on his head, his hands encrusted with brown from the juice of the vine."

The Montrachet knoll produces such outstanding wines that scientists have long struggled to understand the factors that contribute to their greatness. Climatologists have studied the weather; geologists have analyzed the composition of the soil and subsoil, and vintners have pondered over why Chardonnay has adapted so well to that particular place. Sun is certainly part of the answer. The vineyards face east and enjoy sunlight from early in the day to dusk.

As in all great Burgundy properties, ownership is divided among many wineries, and Ramonet owned just over an acre of the Bâtard-Montrachet vineyard, which he acquired in 1955.

After the end of Prohibition, Ramonet-Prudhon wines became very popular in the United States when Frank Schoonmaker began importing them. World War II interrupted that trade, however, and Ramonet was not paid for the hundreds of cases Schoonmaker bought until after hostilities ended.

When Spurrier was selecting the Burgundies for the Paris Tasting, he had trouble deciding whether to include the 1972 or the 1973. Finally he telephoned Ramonet to ask him which of his recent vintages he recommended for a tasting, but without explaining the event.

"All my wines are wonderful," replied Ramonet.

"Yes, but would you recommend the 1972 or the 1973?" asked Spurrier.

"Take any one you want. All my wines are brilliant."

Left to his own devices, Spurrier picked the 1973, the vintage that he thought best matched the other Chardonnays.

Beaune Clos des Mouches Joseph Drouhin, 1973

The Beaune wine region covers 1,023 acres west of the city of the same name. Ninety percent of the wines that come from those vineyards are red, but the Chardonnays are also highly regarded. A large portion of the vineyards located on what is called the "kidney of the slope" west of the town of Beaune, including those of the Clos des Mouches, are owned by the city's prominent *négociants*.

Clos des Mouches is the best known of all the subdivisions of the Beaune region. The vineyard, which produces both red and white wines and occupies sixty-two acres, is in the southernmost section of the Beaune area, along the border with Pommard. The vineyard is situated on a small hill that has a direct southern exposure. The soil is light and stony, over a layer of chalky marl.

The word *clos* means enclosure, and refers to a Burgundian tradition of building stone walls around vineyards. The word *mouches,* which means flies, was also a local word for bees in the Middle Ages, and it is presumed that the fertile southern-facing slopes where flowers grew so abundantly were a good location for bee-keeping.

The Maison Joseph Drouhin is one of the oldest and most respected wine firms in Burgundy. Based in Beaune, the company not only makes wine from its own vineyards but also buys grapes from growers that it uses to make wines sold under its label. Drouhin ages its wine in historic cellars, some of which were Gothic church vaults in the thirteenth century.

The company was founded in Beaune in 1880, when Joseph Drouhin bought a wine-trading business established in 1756. Right after World War I, Joseph's son Maurice took over the family business and bought the firm's first vineyards, including part of the Clos des Mouches vineyard. After the phylloxera epidemic in the nineteenth century, the Clos des Mouches was replanted with Pinot Noir grapes and was producing only red wine when Drouhin bought it. Maurice, though, discovered some old documents showing that Clos des Mouches had once produced excellent white wine, so in 1925 he began to replant some of his land with Chardonnay.

In 1957, Maurice's nephew Robert Jousset-Drouhin, who was only twenty-four at the time, took over as head of the firm after his uncle was partially paralyzed by a stroke. Born in Paris in 1933, Robert was the son of Maurice's sister Thérèse and the physician André Jousset. Both of his parents died before Robert was seven, and he and his two sisters were sent to Beaune to live with their uncle Maurice, who later adopted them. Robert was already tasting and comparing wines by the age of fourteen, and he claimed that the 1929–1947 vintages that he tasted in his youth remained among his most vivid memories and set his standard for Burgundy wines. From 1951 to 1953, he studied law in Paris, then literature in Heidelberg, Germany. In 1954 Robert Drouhin was drafted into the French army and served in North Africa with the French Foreign Legion. After being discharged, he took over the family enterprise.

Maison Joseph Drouhin produces wines from some eighty different *appellations* in Burgundy, including Chambertin, Corton, Bâtard-Montrachet, and Grands Echézeaux. The Drouhin Clos des Mouches is a highly revered Burgundy First Growth. British writer Clive Coates wrote that Drouhin wines are "lighter in color than some, and may seem, to the uninitiated, at first somewhat lighter on the palate. Delicate is the word used, and feminine. But this is deceptive. Underneath there is a lot of intensity. Above all there is great integrity of *terroir*."

Meursault Charmes Roulot, 1973

On his visit to Burgundy in 1787, Jefferson noted: "They only make white wines in Meursault, because it's too rocky for reds." Jefferson also reported that Burgundy's white wine producers ate inexpensive dark bread, while the wealthier red-wine producers could afford the more costly white bread. Today, however, the prices of some Meursault whites approach those of Burgundy's famous reds.

Meursault turns out the largest quantity of white Burgundies, with one-third of all the white wines of the Côte d'Or coming from the 900 acres of Meursault. There are seventeen First Growth wines among them, but none of the higher-rated Grand Cru. Among the Meursault First Growths, those of Perrières, Clos des Perrières, Charmes, and Goutte d'Or (Thomas Jefferson's favorite) are considered the best.

The origin of the name Meursault is uncertain. Some historians say it comes from the Latin *muris saltus* (the rat's leap) or the French *murs hauts* (high walls). Another guess is that it comes from the French *saule marsault* (willow tree) since many willows once grew in the area.

While the vineyards in Meursault date back to the eleventh century, Domaine Guy Roulot is younger than some California wineries. The family has been in the town of Meursault since 1830, but Guy Roulot's ancestors were modest grape growers. He married into another Burgundy wine family and expanded Domaine Guy Roulot during the 1950s by buying several parcels of vineyards and adding them to those his wife had inherited, for a total of thirty acres.

Guy Roulot was a low-keyed producer who avoided the limelight and let his wines speak for him. In the 1960s he was still selling inexpensive rosé wine in barrels to the Troisgros restaurant, a Michelin three-star eatery in nearby Roanne, but soon he was producing some of Burgundy's leading wines. A pioneer, Roulot gave vineyard names to some of his lesser properties and began producing on them First Growth quality wines. Among his most prized possessions were a small section of Meursault Les Perrières and about a half acre of Meursault Les Charmes. He also cleared an abandoned field and planted the highly regarded Meursault Les Tessons vineyard. Wine from Roulot's properties was considered among the very best white Burgundies.

Soil in the Charmes vineyard is stony limestone and clay debris. The wine's defining feature was its intense flavor that came from vines about seventy-five years old that produced small grape clusters and small berries. The Charmes was held for a relatively short eleven months in oak. It was a classic Meursault that was a little more full-bodied and richer than a Chassagne-Montrachet or a Puligny-Montrachet.

Puligny-Montrachet Les Pucelles Domaine Leflaive, 1972

The village of Puligny-Montrachet is considered by many to produce the world's greatest white wines. The Puligny-Montrachet Les Pucelles vineyard is a First Growth from the Côte de Beaune section of Burgundy. The 513-acre vineyards of Puligny-Montrachet are planted on gently sloping land facing east, at an altitude of between 759 and 957 feet. To the east of the town and covering a scant seventeen acres is the small vineyard known as Les Pucelles. Its limestone and chalky soil is stony and well drained. It is directly north of five Great Growth vineyards and the proximity shows. Wine writer Hugh Johnson calls it one of the "superior First Growths."

The name Leflaive in Burgundy can be traced back to Marc LeFlayve in 1580, who lived at Gissey, near Beaune. Domaine Leflaive was founded in 1717, when Claude Leflaive married a girl from Puligny, planted vineyards, and settled down in the stone house that still serves as the family firm's headquarters.

Because of French inheritance laws, the vineyards were gradually divided up among several generations of children, and when Joseph Leflaive (1870–1953) inherited his share in 1905, he got less than five acres. Joseph was a maritime engineer by training and helped design France's first submarine. His real love, though, was wine, and he gradually built up his vineyard holdings, taking advantage of the post-phylloxera bad times when many landowners were anxious to sell. Wherever he found lesser Aligoté and Gamay vines growing, Leflaive replanted the area with Chardonnay. He bought parcels of land in Chevalier-Montrachet, Bâtard-Montrachet, Les Pucelles, and Les Clavoillons. He also acquired nearly seven acres of Les Pucelles, a huge amount of land by Burgundy standards. By 1926, his holdings had increased to more than sixty acres, and Joseph gave up his engineering business and devoted himself entirely to wine.

Joseph's four children, Anne, Jeanne, Vincent, and Joseph, inherited Domaine Leflaive in 1953 upon their father's death and decided to keep the property intact and manage it jointly. Vincent made the wines, while Joseph handled business matters. Vincent is generally credited with turning the Domaine Leflaive into one of the best white Burgundy producers. He used to say that he sought "elegance and harmony" in his wines, while avoiding high alcoholic levels. Britain's Clive Coates thought that Pucelles in the Leflaive hands should be ranked a Great Growth, calling it "a ballerina of a wine, with enormous elegance, great depth and magnificent fruit."

CABERNET SAUVIGNON

Château Haut-Brion, 1970

Château Haut-Brion was founded in the fifteenth century and is the second-oldest Bordeaux château after its neighbor Château Pape Clément, which dates to 1299. One of the four original Premier Cru Classé or First

Growths, Château Haut-Brion was the only wine from the Graves district included in the 1855 classification. The others were from the Médoc. The red-wine vineyards of Château Haut-Brion cover 107 acres located in the suburban Bordeaux town of Pessac. The winery also makes a small amount of white wine. The soil is deep gravel, hence the name Graves. The vineyards are planted with 47 percent Cabernet Sauvignon, 43 percent Merlot, and 10 percent Cabernet Franc, which is substantially more Merlot than the other red wines in the competition. Winemakers vary the composition of their blends from year to year depending on the quality of the harvest, but the size of plantings is a good rule of thumb for the amount of each grape used.

The famous estate's history begins with the conclusion of the Hundred Years War in 1453. Arnaud de Pontac, a Bordeaux wine merchant, founded the family fortune during the fifteenth century. His son Jean de Pontac married Jeanne de Bellon, whose dowry included a part of the land that would become Haut-Brion. He enlarged the vineyards of Haut-Brion by buying parcels of the surrounding land, and in 1550 began construction of the property's château. François-Auguste de Pontac (1636–1694) was the last Pontac to own Haut-Brion through direct inheritance.

The estate's wine was originally known under the family name Pontac, and the first written mention of it as Haut-Brion is found in the writings of the English diarist Samuel Pepys in 1663. Château Haut-Brion then, as now, was a favorite with the British, as with Thomas Jefferson who visited it in 1787 and sent some home from the 1784 vintage, calling it "the very best Bordeaux wine."

The childless François-Auguste de Pontac lived a life so flamboyant and careless that the château was twice repossessed and then passed to various extended-family members. Throughout the eighteenth century Haut-Brion was one of France's most highly regarded wines. But after the French Revolution, the owner Joseph de Fumel was arrested and guillotined, as were the owners of the three other châteaux that were to become First Growths in 1855.

Napoléon's minister of foreign affairs, Talleyrand, bought Haut-Brion in 1801, but sold it three years later. Joseph-Eugène Larrieu acquired the château at auction in 1836 and brought in new technology. The château, though, fell into decline starting with the phylloxera epidemic in the late nineteenth century and was taken over by the Banque d'Algerie in 1923. The owner of the rundown property offered it to the city of Bordeaux in 1934, on the condition that the town fathers promise to maintain it intact forever.

After negotiations for that failed, Clarence Dillon, a Francophile American financier, bought Haut-Brion in 1935 for $2.3 million. Dillon restored both the château and the vineyard. The property is still owned by the extended Dillon family, and Dillons make up seven of the eight board members that control the estate. The property and its wines, though, are very much French.

Château Léoville-Las-Cases, 1971

Château Léoville-Las-Cases is a Second Growth wine from St.-Julien, which lies along the western bank of the Gironde River just south of Pauillac. The soil is composed of deep, sandy, gravelly dunes.

St.-Julien is the smallest of the Médoc communes, with only 2,250 acres of vineyards, but it nonetheless has eleven classified wines. In style the wines of St.-Julien are a middle ground between the elegant wines of Margaux and the powerful ones of Pauillac. Léoville-Las-Cases is generally considered the best wine of St.-Julien, and among the best of the Médoc. Many wine connoisseurs consider it the equivalent of a First Growth, and it has often been called the "Latour of St.-Julien."

The Château Léoville-Las-Cases vineyards cover 240 acres, part of which are picturesquely walled. The centerpiece is an arched-stone gate, topped by a reclining lion, which appears on the wine's label. The vineyards are planted with 65 percent Cabernet Sauvignon, 19 percent Merlot, 13 percent Cabernet Franc, and 3 percent Petit Verdot. The château used somewhat less Cabernet Sauvignon in its wine than its Médoc counterparts, adding only a little Cabernet Franc and Petit Verdot for finesse and color.

In the mid-eighteenth century, Léoville-Las-Cases was part of a much larger estate that belonged to Blaise Alexandre de Gasq, the ruler of Léoville, who had acquired the vineyards by marriage. In the 1820s, the estate was divided into three separate domains: the largest parcel went to Jean de Las-Cases; the second was bought by the Irish wine merchant Hugh Barton, whose descendants still run Château Léoville-Barton; and the third section went to the Baron de Poyferré when he married Jean de Las-Cases's daughter, creating Château Léoville-Poyferré. All three wines were classified as Second Growths in 1855.

In 1900, the Marquis Las Cases sold the property to a company that appointed Théophile Skawinski, a renowned winemaker, as manager, and his descendants remained in charge of winemaking for decades. Starting in the 1920s, the Léoville-Las-Cases vineyards fell into decline, but a new owner, Michel Delon, took over the property in 1950. He brought in as a consultant Émile Peynaud, the eminent professor of enology at the University of Bordeaux. Peynaud urged Léoville-Las-Cases winemakers to increase the length of fermentation and use more new oak barrels for aging. He also had Delon replant vines that were long past their prime.

Château Montrose, 1970

Château Montrose is a Second Growth in the 1855 ranking and comes from St.-Estèphe, the northernmost of the great Médoc communes. St.-Estèphe's heavy soil has less gravel and more clay, which results in slower drainage than elsewhere in the region. Since the vineyards are a little farther north where it is slightly cooler, the grapes, particularly Cabernet Sauvignon, ripen more slowly. St.-Estèphe wines are generally more full-bodied than other Médocs. They also have more acidity and more intense flavors, but somewhat less aroma. The 1970 Montrose in the Paris Tasting was considered one of the half dozen best vintages of the previous quarter century.

The vineyards of Château Montrose are in a single contiguous expanse that overlooks the Gironde River, sloping from a gravelly ridge right down to a highway that flanks the river bank, just northeast of Château Cos d'Estournel, another Second Growth. The nineteenth-century château is surrounded by workers' housing and winery buildings, forming a small village, with a row of palm trees testifying to the mild climate.

The soil in Montrose's 168 acres is made up of gravel mixed with black sand over a subsoil of clay and marl. The vineyards are planted with 65 percent Cabernet Sauvignon, 25 percent Merlot, and 10 percent Cabernet Franc. Montrose wines generally take a long time to develop.

On March 6, 1778, Etienne Théodore Dumoulin bought the land on which Château Montrose was later planted. The property was then covered with bushes, reeds, and heather, whose rosy-pink blossoms gave the château its name, Montrose—rose hill. Dumoulin's son, who was also called Etienne Théodore, planted the vineyards in 1815, then built the winery, and started constructing the château in about 1825. Château Montrose remained in the Dumoulin family until 1866, when Mathieu Dollfus bought it. He enlarged the vineyards and renovated the buildings, but when he died in 1887 his heirs sold the property to Jean Hostein, the owner of Cos d'Estournel. In 1896, Hostein sold Montrose to his son-in-law Louis Charmolüe, who put the Charmolüe family coat of arms on the label, where it still remains. Since then the property has been in the Charmolüe family, run by Louis Charmolüe until 1925, by his son André until 1944, and then by Madame Yvonne Charmolüe until 1960, when Jean-Louis Charmolüe became the master of Château Montrose.

Château Mouton Rothschild, 1970

The best known French wine at the Paris Tasting was Château Mouton Rothschild. This was due largely to its owner, Baron Philippe de Rothschild, a wily entrepreneur, marketing wizard, and lover of fast cars. The baron was passionate about art and literature (he translated Elizabethan poets and Christopher Marlowe into French), a high-society playboy in his youth and a notorious ladies' man until his advanced old age. He was also something of the black sheep of his famed family, and maintained a long-standing quarrel with his neighboring cousins at Château Lafite Rothschild.

Only three years before the Paris Tasting, Baron Philippe achieved his life-long goal of having Château Mouton Rothschild reclassified from a Second Growth to a First Growth under the historic Bordeaux classification. It is the only wine to have been reclassified since 1855. The change was due to his persistence, negotiating skills, and financial clout—not to mention the mystique of the Rothschild name.

The commune of Pauillac stretches along the banks of the Gironde Estuary in the central Médoc, between St.-Estèphe and St.-Julien. Pauillac is the jewel in the Bordeaux crown. Eighteen Pauillac wines are among the 1855 classified wines, and three of the five First Growths come from Pauillac: Château Latour, Château Lafite Rothschild, and Château Mouton Rothschild.

The vineyards of Château Mouton Rothschild rise on gravelly land that is the highest in the Pauillac area. They cover 203 acres and are planted with 80 percent Cabernet Sauvignon, 8 percent Merlot, 10 percent Cabernet Franc, and 2 percent Petit Verdot. The wines are fermented in oak vats for twenty-one to thirty-one days, then aged in mostly new oak barrels for eighteen to twenty-two months. Mouton, in old French, meant either a sheep or a small hill, and referred to the vineyard's terrain. The flamboyant Baron Philippe for some time appropriately wore mutton-chop sideburns.

Until 1730, Château Mouton, as it was then called, belonged to the Marquis Nicolas-Alexandre de Ségur. In addition to Mouton, he owned two other properties that would later be named First Growths, Château Lafite and Château Latour, as well as the respected Château Calon-Ségur and Château Phélan-Ségur. Not surprisingly, King Louis XV nicknamed Ségur "The Prince of Vines."

In the early nineteenth century, Mouton came into the hands of Baron Hector de Brane, another proprietor of large estates in Bordeaux, who renamed it Brane-Mouton. Paris banker Isaac Thuret bought Château

Brane-Mouton in 1830 and sold it in 1853 to Baron Nathaniel de Roth-schild, a member of the English branch of the family.

There are many theories about why Château Mouton was classified as a Second Growth, while the other four were ranked First Growths. Perhaps the vineyard's recent purchase by a nefarious Englishman is explanation enough. In its ruling the classification committee cited, perhaps in its own defense, the "pitiful state" of the vineyard's buildings.

When Nathaniel de Rothschild died in 1870, neither his son James nor his grandson Henri was interested in running the winery, and the property gradually fell into decline. By the end of World War I, Mouton was in sham-bles. In 1922, though, Henri de Rothschild's youngest son, Philippe, took over Mouton on his twentieth birthday, and set out to restore it to more than its former glory. In protest to Mouton being considered second rate, Baron Philippe adopted as his estate's motto a variation of the ancient one used by the princes of Rohan as a sign of their fierce local pride: *"Roi ne puis, prince ne daigne, Rohan suis."* ("King I cannot be, I do not deign to be Prince, I am Rohan.") Mouton's read: *"Premier ne puis, Second ne daigne, Mouton suis."* ("First I cannot be, Second I disdain, I am Mouton.") After the 1973 reclas-sification, Baron Philippe changed the estate's motto to *"Premier je suis, Sec-ond je fus, Mouton ne change."* ("First I am, Second I was, Mouton does not change.")

During his sixty-five-year reign, Baron Philippe made many innovations, including the policy of bottling the wine at the château as a way of guar-anteeing authenticity and reducing fraud. This led to the notice *mis en bouteille au château* (bottled at the château) found today on the corks or labels of many French wines.

In 1945 Rothschild had a local artist design a special *V* for Victory label for that year's wine. Each year thereafter he commissioned renowned artists to design that vintage's label. Among the artists who have painted the Mou-ton Rothschild label are Picasso, Miró, Braque, Chagall, Dalí, Kandinsky, and Warhol.

Among the white wines, Steven Spurrier expected Burgundy's Bâtard-Montrachet to place first overall in his tasting. He thought that by putting Château Haut-Brion and Château Mouton Rothschild among the red wines, he had guaranteed a French winner among the Cabernet Sauvignons.

CHAPTER NINETEEN

A Stunning Upset

A bottle of good wine, like a good act, shines ever in the retrospect.
—ROBERT LOUIS STEVENSON

*Patricia Gallagher, Steven Spurrier,
and Odette Kahn at the Paris Tasting*

M ay 24, 1976, was a beautiful, sunny day in Paris, and Patricia Gallagher was in good spirits as she packed up the French and California wines for the tasting at the InterContinental Hotel. Organizing the event had been good fun and easy compared with other events she and Steven had dreamed up. The good thing about working for Spurrier, she told friends, was that he was so supportive of her ideas. Many of their conversations began with her saying, "Wouldn't it be fun . . ." To which he always replied, "Great. Let's do it." The two weren't looking for fame or money. They were young people doing things strictly for the love of wine and to have fun.

Gallagher packed the wine and all the paperwork into the back of the Caves de la Madeleine's van and headed off with an American summer intern to the hotel. After the California wines had arrived on May 7 with members of the Tchelistcheff tour, they were stored in the shop's cellar at a constant 54 degrees alongside the French wines for the event and the rest of Spurrier's stock.

Gallagher and the intern arrived at the hotel about an hour and a half before the 3:00 p.m. tasting was due to start. The event was to be held in a well-appointed room just off a patio bar in the central courtyard. Long, plush velvet curtains decorated the corners of the room. Glass doors opened onto the patio, and a gathering crowd watched the event from the patio. People sitting at small tables under umbrellas became increasingly curious about what was transpiring in the room, and some of them walked over to gaze through the windows much like visitors looking at monkeys in a zoo. The waiters set up a series of plain tables covered with simple white tablecloths, aligning the tables in a long row.

Spurrier and Gallagher had previously decided that this would be a blind tasting, which meant that the judges would not see the labels on the bottles, a common practice in such events. They felt that not allowing the judges to know the nationality or brand of the wines would force them to be more objective. The two did not perceive the tasting as a Franco-American showdown, but it would have been too easy, they believed, for the judges to find fault with the California wines while praising only the French wines, if they were presented with labels.

The hotel staff first opened all the red wines and then poured them into neutral bottles at Gallagher's instructions. California wine bottles are shaped slightly differently from French ones, and this group of knowledgeable judges would have quickly recognized the difference. Gallagher was also giving the wines a chance to breathe a little by opening and decanting them, since the reds, in particular, were still relatively recent vintages. This practice helps young wines, which can sometimes be too aggressive, become more mellow and agreeable.

An hour before the event, the hotel staff opened all the white wines, poured them also into neutral bottles and put them in the hotel's wine cooler. Aeration was less important for the whites than it had been for the reds, but it would do no harm to have them opened in advance. Then a few minutes before the tasting, the waiters put the whites in buckets on ice, just as they would have done for guests in the dining room. The wine would now be at the perfect temperature for the judges.

Only a half-hour before the event was to begin, Spurrier arrived. He wrote the names of the wines on small pieces of paper and asked the summer intern to pull the names out of a hat to determine the order in which the wines would be served. Then Spurrier and the others put small white labels on the bottles that read in French, for example, Chardonnay Neuf (Chardonnay Nine) or Cabernet Trois (Cabernet Three). With that done, everything was ready.

The judges began appearing shortly before 3:00 p.m. and chatted amiably until all had arrived. Most of them knew each other from many previous encounters on the French wine circuit.

Standing along the wall and acting self-conscious were two young Frenchmen in their mid-twenties. One was Jean-Pierre Leroux, who was head of the dining room at the Paris Sofitel hotel, an elegant rival, although not at the same level as the InterContinental. The other was Gérard Bosseau des Chouad, the sommelier at the Sofitel, who had learned about the tasting while taking a course at the Académie du Vin. Bosseau des Chouad had told Leroux about it, and the two of them had come to the hotel uninvited on a lark. They were quiet in awe of the assembled big names of French wine and cuisine. Since no one asked them to leave, they watched the proceedings in nervous silence.

Shortly after 3:00, Spurrier asked everyone to give him their attention for a minute. Spurrier thanked the judges for coming and explained that he and Patricia Gallagher were staging the event to taste some of the interesting new California wines as part of the bicentennial of American independence and in honor of the role France had played in that historic endeavor. He explained that he and Patricia had recently made separate trips to California, where they had been surprised by the quality of the work being done by some small and unknown wineries. He said he thought the French too would find them interesting. Spurrier then said that although he had invited them to a sampling of California wines, in the tasting that was about to begin he had also included some very similar French wines. He added that he thought it would be better if they all tasted them blind, so as to be totally objective in their judgments. No one demurred, and so judges took their seats behind the long table, and the event began.

The judges wore standard Paris business attire. Odette Kahn of the *Revue du Vin de France* was very elegant in a patterned silk dress accented with a double strand of opera-length pearls. Claude Dubois-Millot was the most casual with no tie or jacket. The other men were all more formally dressed, and Aubert de Villaine, who sat at the far right end of the table, wore a fashionable double-breasted suit. Patricia Gallagher and Steven Spurrier sat in the middle of the judges and participated in the tasting. Spurrier was next to Kahn.

In front of each judge was a scorecard and pencil, two stemmed wine glasses, and a small roll. Behind them were several Champagne buckets on stands where they could spit the wine after tasting it, a common practice at such events since it would be impossible to drink all the wines without soon feeling the effect of the alcohol.

Spurrier instructed the judges that they were being asked to rank the wines by four criteria—eye, nose, mouth, and harmony—and then to give each a score on the basis of 20 points. Eye meant rating the color and clarity of the wine; nose was the aroma; mouth was the wine's taste and structure as it rolled over the taste buds; harmony meant the combination of all the sensations. This 20-point and four-criteria system was common in France at the time and had already been used by Spurrier and the others in many tastings.

Despite Spurrier's and Gallagher's attempts to get press coverage, it turned out that I was the only journalist who showed up at the event. As a result, I had easy access to the judges and the judging. Patricia gave me a list of the wines with the tasting order so I could follow along. And although the judges didn't know the identity of Chardonnay Neuf, for example, I did and could note their reactions to the various wines as they tasted them.

The waiters first poured a glass of 1974 Chablis to freshen the palates of the judges. Following the tradition of wine tastings, the whites then went first. I looked at my list of wines and saw that the first wine (Chardonnay Un) was the Puligny-Montrachet Les Pucelles Domaine Leflaive, 1972.

The nine judges seemed nervous at the beginning. There was lots of laughing and quick side comments. No one, though, was acting rashly. The judges pondered the wines carefully and made their judgments slowly. Pierre Tari at one moment pushed his nose deep into his glass and held it there for a long time to savor the wine's aroma.

The judge's comments were in the orchidaceous language the French often use to describe wines. As I stood only a few feet from the judges listening to their commentary, I copied into the brown reporter's notebook that I always carried with me such phrases as: "This soars out of the ordinary," and "A good nose, but not too much in the mouth," and "This is nervous and agreeable."

From their comments, though, I soon realized that the judges were becoming totally confused as they tasted the white wines. The panel couldn't tell the difference between the French ones and those from California. The judges then began talking to each other, which is very rare in a tasting. They speculated about a wine's nationality, often disagreeing.

Standing quietly on the side, the young Jean-Pierre Leroux was also surprised as he looked at the faces of the judges. They seemed both bewildered and shocked, as if they didn't quite know what was happening. Raymond Oliver of the Grand Véfour was one of Leroux's heroes, and the young man couldn't believe that the famous chef couldn't distinguish the nationality of the white wines.

Christian Vannequé, who sat at the far left with Pierre Bréjoux and Pierre Tari at his left, was irritated that those two kept talking to him, asking him what he thought of this or that wine. Vannequé felt like telling them to shut up so he could concentrate, but held his tongue. He thought the other judges seemed tense and were trying too hard to identify which wines were Californian and which were French. Vannequé complained he wanted simply to determine which wines were best.

When tasting the white wines, the judges quickly became flustered. At one point Raymond Oliver was certain he had just sipped a French wine, when in fact it was a California one from Freemark Abbey. Shortly after, Claude Dubois-Millot said he thought a wine was obviously from California because it had no nose, when it was France's famed Bâtard-Montrachet.

The judges were brutal when they found a wine wanting. They completely dismissed the David Bruce Chardonnay. Pierre Bréjoux gave it 0 points out of 20. Odette Kahn gave it just 1 point. The David Bruce was rated last by all the judges, and most of them dumped the remains from their glasses into their Champagne buckets after a cursory taste and in some cases after only smelling it. Robert Finigan had warned Spurrier and Gallagher that he'd found David Bruce wines at that time could be erratic, and this bottle appeared to be erratically bad. It was probably spoiled.

After the white wines had all been tasted, Spurrier called a break and collected the scorecards. Using the normal procedure for wine tastings, he added up the individual scores and then ranked them from highest to lowest.

Meanwhile the waiters began pouring Vittel mineral water for the judges to drink during the break. The judges spoke quietly to each other, and I talked briefly with Dubois-Millot. Even though he did not yet know the results, he told me a bit sheepishly, "We thought we were recognizing French wines, when they were California and vice versa. At times we'd say that a wine would be thin and therefore California, when it wasn't. Our confusion showed how good California wines have become."

Spurrier's original plan had been to announce all the results at the end of the day, but the waiters were slow clearing the tables and getting the red wines together and the program was getting badly behind schedule, so he decided to give the results of the white-wine tasting. He had been personally stunned and began reading them slowly to the group:

1. Chateau Montelena 1973
2. Meursault Charmes 1973
3. Chalone 1974
4. Spring Mountain 1973
5. Beaune Clos des Mouches 1973
6. Freemark Abbey 1972
7. Bâtard-Montrachet 1973
8. Puligny-Montrachet 1972
9. Veedercrest 1972
10. David Bruce 1973

When he finished, Spurrier looked at the judges, whose reaction ranged from shock to horror. No one had expected this, and soon the whole room was abuzz.

After hearing the results, I walked up to Gallagher. The French word in the winning wine's name had momentarily thrown me. "Chateau Montelena is Californian, isn't it?" I asked a bit dumbfoundedly.

"Yes, it is," she replied calmly.

The scores of the individual judges made the results even more astounding. California Chardonnays had overwhelmed their French counterparts. Every single French judge rated a California Chardonnay first. Chateau Montelena was given top rating by six judges; Chalone was rated first by the other three. Three of the top four wines were Californian. Claude Dubois-Millot gave Chateau Montelena 18.5 out of 20 points, while Aubert de Villaine gave it 18. Chateau Montelena scored a total of 132 points, comfortably ahead of second place Meursault Charmes, which got 126.5.

Spurrier and Gallagher, who were also blind tasting the wines although their scores were not counted in the final tally, were tougher on the California wines than the French judges. Spurrier had a tie for first between Freemark Abbey and Bâtard-Montrachet, while Gallagher scored a tie for first between Meursault Charmes and Spring Mountain.

As I watched the reaction of the others to the results, I felt a sense of both awe and pride. Who would have thought it? Chauvinism is a word invented by the French, but I felt some chauvinism that a California white wine had won. But how could this be happening? I was tempted to ask for a taste of the winning California Chardonnay, but decided against it. I still had a reporting job to finish, and I needed to have a clear head.

As the waiters began pouring the reds, Spurrier was certain that the judges would be more careful and would not allow a California wine to come out on top again. One California wine winning was bad enough; two would be treason. The French judges, he felt, would be very careful to identify the French wines and score them high, while rating those that seemed American low. It would perhaps be easier to taste the differences between the two since the judges knew all the French wines very well. The French reds, with their classic, distinctive and familiar tastes would certainly stand out against the California reds. All the judges, with the possible exception of Dubois-Millot, had probably tasted the French reds hundreds of times.

There was less chatter during the second wave of wines. The judges seemed both more intense and more circumspect. Their comments about the nationality of the wine in their glass were now usually correct. "That's a California, or I don't know what I'm doing here," said Christian Vannequé of La Tour d'Argent. I looked at my card and saw that he was right. It was the Ridge Monte Bello.

Raymond Oliver took one quick sip of a red and proclaimed, "That's a Mouton, without a doubt." He too was right.

Because of delays in the earlier part of the tasting, the hour was getting late and the group had to be out by 6:00 p.m. So Spurrier pushed on quickly after the ballots were collected. He followed the same procedure he had used for the Chardonnay tasting, adding up the individual scores of the nine judges.

The room was hushed as Spurrier read the results without the help of a microphone:

1. Stag's Leap Wine Cellars 1973
2. Château Mouton Rothschild 1970
3. Château Montrose 1970
4. Château Haut-Brion 1970
5. Ridge Monte Bello 1971
6. Château Léoville-Las-Cases 1971
7. Heitz Martha's Vineyard 1970
8. Clos Du Val 1972
9. Mayacamas 1971
10. Freemark Abbey 1969

This time the stir in the room was even more pronounced than before. A California wine had won again! Who would have believed it! The judges sat in disbelief. To confirm that I had heard Spurrier correctly, I walked up to Gallagher again and asked, "A California wine also won the red?"

"Yes," she replied.

The results for the Cabernet wines were much closer than for the

Chardonnays. Château Haut-Brion got the most first place votes of all the reds: three. French wines were rated first, in some cases tied for first, by seven of the nine judges. Stag's Leap was rated highly by most judges, but only Odette Kahn put it first and Raymond Oliver had it in a tie for first. In sharp contrast to the results in the white wines, the French red wines also rated much better overall than the California reds. French wines took three of the top four positions, while California wines were relegated to the last four slots.

Based on the overall scores, the results were very close for the red wines. There was only a five-and-a-half-point difference between the top four finishers. Stag's Leap won by just a point and a half, with a total of 127.5, over second place Château Mouton Rothschild. But as the old saying goes, close only counts in horseshoes. Stag's Leap was the winner that day. It was the judgment of Paris.

Spurrier's suspicion that the judges would attempt to identify the French wines and score them higher while rating the California ones low appears to have taken place. In the Cabernet competition the judges had a significantly wider scoring range than with the Chardonnays. The judges may have honestly felt the quality differences were that great, but they may also have been out to make sure a French wine won. Odette Kahn, for example, gave two wines (Clos Du Val and Heitz Martha's Vineyard) only 2 points out of 20, one (Freemark Abbey) 5 points, and one (Ridge) 7 points. All her other Cabernet scores were double digits. But if she was trying to score California wines low, she didn't succeed. Her first two highest scores went to California: Stag's Leap and Mayacamas. Four other French judges also had the same pattern of rating several California wines in single digits, which is unusual in a fine wine tasting.

The California reds did very well on Spurrier's and Gallagher's scoring cards. Spurrier in a moment of indecision had a four-way tie for first: Château Montrose, Château Mouton-Rothschild, Ridge, and Stag's Leap. Gallagher gave first place to Heitz Martha's Vineyard.

After the final results were announced, Odette Kahn marched up to Spurrier, gathering together all the force of her strong personality, elegant presence, and aristocratic demeanor. As an editor, she realized better than probably anyone else in the room did the importance of what had just happened and the impact this wine tasting might have.

"Monsieur Spurrier, I demand to have my scorecards," she said.

"I'm sorry, Madame Kahn, but you're not going to get them back."

"But they are *my* scores!"

"No, they are not *your* scores. They are *my* scores!"

Spurrier and Kahn continued the sharp exchange over the ownership of the scorecards, until she finally demurred, realizing there was no way to force him to give them to her. Spurrier then shoved the pieces of paper into the hand of his summer intern and told her to take them immediately back to the Académie du Vin.

The judges lingered for a while longer, sharing a glass of Champagne and talking freely about the results of the tasting. I spoke with five of the nine. Their immediate reactions were candid. They were generally complimentary about the California wines they had just tasted. Most said they had heard that winemakers in California were doing interesting things, but they had little firsthand experience with the wines. Said Aubert de Villaine, "I tasted my first California wines in 1964, and since then there have been more and more good wine houses there."

Pierre Bréjoux told me, "I went to California in July 1974, and I learned a lot—to my surprise. They are now certainly among the top wines in the world. But this Stag's Leap has been a secret. I've never heard of it."

Pierre Tari said, "I was really surprised by the California whites. They are excellent. We clearly saw that the California whites can stand up to the French whites. They are certainly the best—after France. They have come a long way, but they have a long way to go."

Christian Vannequé told me, "The white wines approached the best of France without a doubt. California can almost do as well producing something like a Chassagne-Montrachet. The reds, though, were not as good and don't have the character of a Bordeaux. They are a bit minty, very strong in tannin and lack finesse."

There were also a few sour grapes among the judges. Tari complained, "French wines develop slower than California wines because of the climate, so the test was not completely correct." Added Aubert de Villaine: "In general there is still quite a difference. The French wines are still superior." Snipped Odette Kahn, "It was a false test because California wines are trying to become too much like French wines." Said Michel Dovaz, "In five or ten years, when the wines have properly matured, I'm sure the French red wines will do much better."

The InterContinental staff then hurried the group out of the room so they could get on with preparations for the wedding-party guests who would soon be arriving. As the judges walked out, Spurrier gave Dovaz the extra bottle of the winning Stag's Leap wine, which had not been opened. Dovaz thanked him and took it back to his apartment in Montparnasse on the edge of the student section of Paris. He opened the bottle a few weeks later, when a friend came for dinner. They each had a glass, but then Dovaz went to the kitchen and opened a bottle of French wine to serve with the meal. The

Stag's Leap, he felt, was an admirable wine that had tested well, but it didn't quench his thirst.

After the tasting, Spurrier and Gallagher walked together back to the Académie du Vin. They chatted about the unexpected results, but didn't think much beyond that. From their trips to California, they knew Americans were making some good wines. After spending an hour or so at his business, Spurrier went home for dinner with his wife and two children. He told her about the interesting tasting they had held that afternoon and the unexpected outcome, but soon the conversation moved on to more mundane topics.

The day after the event, I called Gallagher at the Académie du Vin, looking for help in finding some of the Californians whose wines had been in the tasting. She had told me that the group was currently touring French wineries. Among them was the owner of Chateau Montelena, which had come in first among the whites. I asked if she could get a phone number where he could be reached, and a short while later she called back with the number. The Californians that day were supposed to be at the Château Lascombes winery in the Margaux region of Bordeaux. She couldn't guarantee anything, but perhaps I could track him down there.

At that exact moment at Château Lascombes, the California winemakers were having a glass of Champagne as an aperitif before lunch. One of the Château's staff members came up to group leader Joanne Dickenson and said that Monsieur Barrett was wanted on the phone. Dickenson's immediate reaction was that something must have happened at home to one of his children. Why else would anyone be trying to reach Jim Barrett in southern France in the middle of a wine tour? The only person in France who knew the group's itinerary was the travel agent in Paris.

Dickenson spotted Barrett across the room, walked over, and told him that he had a phone call. He also thought it must be bad news. The two Americans then followed the Château Lascombes staff member to another building and into a tiny office. The room was so small that Barrett had to kneel down on the floor to talk. All Dickenson heard was Barrett's end of the conversation, as he said, "No . . . Yes . . . Okay . . ." Barrett finally flashed Dickenson the okay sign and mouthed the words that everything was all right, so she went back to her hosts and the reception.

Once Barrett identified himself, I asked him, "Have you heard that your wine came in first in the tasting that was held on Monday in Paris?"

"No, I haven't. That's great."

"Well, you won in the white wine part of it. And a California red wine also won. So it was a California sweep. What's your reaction to beating the French at their own game and in Paris?"

Barrett's mind started racing, but the careful lawyer came to the fore. He thought quickly, "If I open my big mouth and say the wrong thing, it's going to seem arrogant, and they won't let me back into the Napa Valley." After a second's hesitation, Barrett said, "Not bad for kids from the sticks." He went on to add, "I guess it's time to be humble and pleased, but I'm not stunned. We've known for a long time that we could put our white Burgundy against anybody's in the world and not take a backseat."

I asked Barrett a few questions about his winery and the price of his wine in California. He said his winery was still a very new venture but that his "balance sheet has gone from a Pommard red to something like a rosé."

Following a few more exchanges, I knew I had a good reaction quote—"kids from the sticks"—and so I ended the conversation.

After talking with Barrett, I turned back to my old, gray manual typewriter to write my report. In those days, *Time* correspondents sent long files that gave the full story of an event, which was much more than ever appeared in the magazine. A report was then cut down to a much shorter piece by the magazine's New York staff. My report went on for eight pages and nearly two thousand words. It started: "Nine of France's top wine experts swirled and sniffed and sipped and spit Monday for over two hours at the Hotel InterContinental in Paris and rolled Bacchus over and awarded top prize in both red and white wines to two noble upstarts from California—Chateau Montelena for the white and Stag's Leap Wine Cellars for the red." I ended my report with a comment from the scorecard of Christian Vannequé about the Chateau Montelena Chardonnay, which he had ranked as the best white. I thought it summed up the attitude of the French judges toward all the California wines: "A very agreeable wine, which will blossom pleasantly and has a good equilibrium. To be followed."

After our conversation ended, Barrett returned to the pre-luncheon reception, which was just ending. He immediately told his wife about the call, so that she wouldn't be thinking the worst, as he had originally. Before sitting down he sidled up to Dickenson and said, "That was *Time* magazine. A reporter told me we won Steven Spurrier's tasting."

Barrett then sat down for lunch. Bob Travers, the owner of the Mayacamas winery, which also had a wine in the Spurrier competition, was sitting across the table and asked, "Is everything okay?" Travers also thought that something was probably wrong at home. Barrett looked at Travers with a smile as wide as a bottle of Chardonnay and said, "Yes, everything's fine."

The results of the Spurrier tasting soon began spreading quietly but quickly from Californian to Californian around the room.

Some ninety people attended the formal lunch, which was done in the best French style. Dickenson was seated to the right of Alexis Lichine, a part owner of Château Lascombes, while André Tchelistcheff was on his left. After lunch Lichine made a gracious, though condescending, speech, saying how nice it was that the Americans had come to learn from the French how to make great wine and how if they worked hard, someday they too might be successful. To Dickenson it was hard to take that speech, all the while knowing that California wines had just beaten some of the best French ones in Spurrier's tasting.

After lunch the California delegation politely thanked their hosts and got back into their bus. Everyone waved good-bye as the vehicle pulled away from Château Lascombes. As soon as it had passed the last pine tree and was safely out of sight of the main building, the group erupted like football fans whose team had just won the Super Bowl. Everyone was screaming; Barrett hugged Tchelistcheff. There were two more wine tastings that afternoon to bring the number of wines the Californians had tried in nearly three weeks in France to more than 250, but the group walked through the event in a dream. They were more excited about what had happened in Paris.

Once they arrived at their next hotel, Barrett sent a telegram to the staff at Chateau Montelena:

STUNNING SUCCESS IN PARIS TASTING ON MAY TWENTY-FOUR STOP TOOK FIRST PLACE OVER NINE OTHERS WITH LE PREMIER CRU WINE STOP TOP NAMES IN FRANCE WERE THE BLIND TASTERS STOP

When the telegram arrived at Chateau Montelena, the staff wasn't sure what Barrett was referring to. They learned it was something important, when Grgich got a call from *Time* asking to send a photographer to take his picture. After that call, Grgich still didn't know what to do. So he started dancing around the winery shouting in his native Croatian, "I'm born again! I'm born again!" No one could understand a word he said, but who cared? Barrett's son Bo watched Grgich from a second-story window and thought he had gone bonkers.

The next day the Tchelistcheff group flew back to San Francisco. It was near dinnertime when André Tchelistcheff and his wife, Dorothy, reached their home in the city of Napa. Dorothy thought it might be a good moment to call Barbara Winiarski and tell her about the results of the

Spurrier tasting. Barbara and the Winiarski children were already having dinner when the phone rang. When Dorothy Tchelistcheff told her that Stag's Leap had won the competition for the red wine, Barbara wasn't sure exactly which wine tasting that was, but thanked her for the message anyway. The children, though, became excited when they heard they had won something, and Barbara motioned to them to be quiet. Once her mother hung up the phone and told the children, Kasia and her younger sister Julia danced around the table with elation. They couldn't remember ever winning a wine contest before.

After dinner Barbara talked by phone with Warren, who was at his old family home in Chicago wrapping up some matters involving the estate of his mother, who had recently died. Barbara casually mentioned that their wine had won "that wine tasting in Paris." Warren also had a tough time remembering which tasting it was. Without realizing the profound impact the Paris Tasting would have on his life and his winery, he said simply, "That's nice."

PART FOUR

THE NEW WORLD OF WINE

The Paris Tasting destroyed the myth of French supremacy and marked the democratization of the wine world. It was a watershed in the history of wine.

—ROBERT M. PARKER JR., 2001

CHAPTER TWENTY

The Buzz Heard Round the World

Wine is sunlight, held together by water.
—GALILEO

The June 7, 1976, issue of *Time* magazine hit newsstands in New York City and a few other major metropolitan areas on Monday morning, May 31. The cover story was about a scandal involving the honor system at West Point. Back on page 58 in the Modern Living section was a modest story entitled "Judgment of Paris." The lead story of the section was about a new theme park in Atlanta, and my article about the wine tasting filled out the last column. No photograph accompanied the Paris article, the normal sign of a significant story. In fact, the page it was on was overwhelmed by an ad for Armstrong tires. The last sentence of the first paragraph told it all: "Last week in Paris, at a formal wine tasting organized by Spurrier, the unthinkable happened: California defeated all Gaul."

The day after the *Time* story appeared, something unusual was happening at Manhattan's Acker Merrall & Condit, America's oldest wine shop, then located on the Upper West Side on Broadway between West Eighty-sixth and West Eighty-seventh streets. Acker was one of the few liquor stores in the city at the time to carry a good selection of quality California wines. Owner Michael Kapon had been introduced to them in 1972, when a friend raved to him about the 1969 Robert Mondavi Cabernet Sauvignon. Kapon tried the wine, liked it, and began carrying several Mondavi wines.

The Mondavi Cabernet moved well at $4.99 a bottle, and Kapon always kept it in bins just under the displays of his top French wines such as Burgundy's Romanée-Conti that sold for much more. His big sellers among California products, though, were still the Gallo and Almaden jug wines. Kapon sold five hundred to six hundred cases of those per month, compared with only a few cases of premium California wines.

Acker Merrall & Condit carried both Chardonnay and Cabernet Sauvignon from two of the eleven California wineries that had taken part in the

Paris Tasting: Chateau Montelena and Freemark Abbey. The price for each: $5.99 a bottle.

At midmorning the store manager went to the back room where Michael Kapon was working and told him that the supply of Chateau Montelena and Freemark Abbey wines was running out. The manager had asked one customer why he was interested in those wines. The person told him about the *Time* story. By noon Acker Merrall & Condit had sold out of the five cases of wines it had from the two California wineries at the Paris Tasting.

The scene was repeated in countless wine stores around the country. One New York City shop reportedly received four hundred calls asking about the winning wines the day after the article appeared. Napa Valley folklore tells of a desperate man rushing into the Wine and Cheese Center in San Francisco and imploring, "Have you got any Montelena?"

The appearance of the story in *Time* magazine was important for the future impact of the Paris Tasting. If no journalist had been there that day, the tasting would have been like the tree falling in the forest that no one heard. As Spurrier said later at the time of the twentieth anniversary of the event, "If we hadn't had a reporter from *Time*, there would have been no fuss at all."

Time had a readership of 20 million and talked directly to the American middle class, the exact group that was becoming more interested in wine. It was those people who read the story, told their friends about it, and suddenly had a new respect for California wines. Had the news been reported only in one of the new American wine newsletters or magazines, it might have attracted attention among wine connoisseurs, but would have been little noted by the general public.

If no one from the press had been present, it would have also been much easier for the French and others simply to deny or distort what had happened. As it was, a whole mythology about the tasting grew up as people in both California and France embellished the event. In fact, my major objective in writing this book was to set the record straight once and for all about what transpired that day in Paris. Nearly three decades later, it is still constantly cited as the turning point in the development of California wine.

The most influential wine writer at the time was Frank Prial of the *New York Times,* who four years earlier had started a weekly column entitled "Wine Talk," which appeared on Wednesdays. Prial took the unusual step of devoting two columns in a row to the Paris event, which got the news out to the public perhaps even more than the original *Time* story. At the time, New York City was the major wine-consuming market in the U.S., and his articles brought home the importance of this event in Paris, with French judges, to many consumers who cared what happened in France and had previously paid scant attention to California wine.

On June 9, Prial discussed the Chardonnay wines in the tasting. He noted that in similar events in the U.S., "the latest only six months ago in New York," California wines had outscored top French Chardonnays, but "champions of French wines" argued that the American tasters were biased toward American wines and the French wines were perhaps damaged in shipment. Since the judges in Paris were French and the California wines had the disadvantage of travel, Prial asked, "What can they say now?"

In his second article—this one on June 16—Prial dealt with the Cabernet Sauvignon part of the event. This time he was more skeptical about the results, implying they may have just been a fluke. That was an explanation that appeared in several American publications at about the same time. The source for that view was probably Steven Spurrier, who was quoted in an article in the *Minneapolis Star* saying, "You can't expect 10 people drinking 20 wines to come out with the same answers twice." Just after the event Spurrier appears to have become concerned, probably with some justification, about the impact it was having and what that might mean for his future as a wine merchant in Paris. Spurrier's early comments to reporters dwelled on the randomness of blind tasting as if to play down what had happened. Gallagher was also unhappy that press stories, starting with the *Time* one, emphasized Franco-American wine competition, rather than the discovery of new California wines, which had been their goal in staging the tasting.

In his second article Prial also wrote: "Only the most naïve reader would conclude anything other than that on a certain day a certain group of French wine specialists agreed that California turns out some fine wines." He added that the variables in the tasting were too great and that it was unfair to compare the early-maturing Stag's Leap with Château Mouton Rothschild, which would reach its peak in perhaps twenty years. Nonetheless, Prial added, "The results were of course an enormous compliment to little Stag's Leap Wine Cellars."

Soon food-and-wine writers were doing their own stories about the Paris Tasting in papers all across the country under headlines like "U.S. Triumphant in French Tastings." For the Napa Valley's *Weekly Calistogan* the news was front page, above the banner, and carried the headline "'Kids from the Sticks' Place First." Most of the stories lamented that the California wines were hard to find. The *Seattle Times* reported that Stag's Leap was selling for $7.20 "but little is left." The *New York Times* noted that the winning red was unavailable in the New York City area.

There was a lot of flag waving in much of the American coverage. A column in the New Orleans *Times-Picayune* on June 16 headlined "California Wines Beat French Wines!" The new *Wine Spectator* newsletter noted the event in its sixth issue in June under the headline "California Wines Top French." The *Los Angeles Times* headline: "Three Cheers for the Red, White and Cru."

Since reporters were writing about the event on the basis of secondhand knowledge, some resorted to descriptions that are best classified as fiction. Such stories helped spread a myriad of myths that have built up about the Paris Tasting. In the June 13 issue of the *Los Angeles Times,* Paris-based reporter Mary Blume, for example, wrote that the area where the tasting took place was "draped out in French and American flags," while the assembled journalists covering the event "drank French Champagne" and the judges gave interviews "for the benefit of American TV." In fact, none of those things took place. Neither, according to Spurrier, did an exchange when Spurrier supposedly told judge Odette Kahn that he was going to send the results "straight to California."

The American wine industry quickly grasped what had happened: the world's most esteemed experts—French experts and in Paris—had recognized that California vintners could produce world-quality wines—not just plonk. In his autobiography Robert Mondavi wrote, "The Paris tasting was an enormous event in the history of California wine making. It put us squarely on the world map of great wine-producing regions. I saw the impact everywhere I went. Suddenly people had a new respect for what we were doing. They saw we could make wines as good as the best in France."

That added prestige allowed the California wineries to begin pushing up prices, although very slowly at first. At the time of the Paris Tasting, the Chateau Montelena Chardonnay was selling in Chicago for $7.00, while the competing Bâtard-Montrachet was $12.50 and the Puligny-Montrachet was $13.00. The winning Stag's Leap Wine Cellars Cabernet was $7.49 at a store in Chicago, but the Mouton Rothschild there was $25.00 and the Haut-Brion was $23.00. The victorious American wines sold out quickly in the rare markets where they were even available. Warren Winiarski's partners urged him to pull back the remaining bottles of the 1973 vintage that were still on retail shelves, but it was too late to get many of them back. Stag's Leap had a suggested price of $6.00 for its winning 1973 Cabernet but raised the price on the 1974 to $7.50. Chateau Montelena had already posted its suggested retail price for its 1974 Chardonnay when the Paris results were announced. It was the same as for the prize-winning 1973: $6.50. It did not later raise the 1974 price.

*   *   *

In France the first reaction was to blame the judges. Baron Philippe de Roth-schild, whose Mouton Rothschild had placed second, phoned one of the judges and asked haughtily, "What are you doing to my wines? It took me forty years to become classified as a First Growth!"

Claude Terrail, the owner of La Tour d'Argent, called his sommelier Christian Vannequé on the carpet when the restaurant's clipping service began sending dozens of articles from around the world about the Spurrier tasting that noted Vannequé's role as a judge. Vannequé says Terrail sternly told him never to do that kind of thing again. Vannequé tried to explain that it was a blind tasting and had been totally on the up-and-up. Terrail replied, "Christian, you don't understand. This is very bad for the French wine business."

According to Spurrier, Lalou Bize-Leroy, the codirector in the Domaine de la Romanée-Conti, told her codirector Aubert de Villaine, another of the judges, that he had personally put back the progress of their great vineyard by a hundred years!

There were many calls for Pierre Bréjoux to resign as Inspector General of the Appellation d'Origine Contrôlée Board. More than twenty-five years after the tasting, several judges still refused to talk with me about the event, saying it was still too painful. One French wine official in 2003 told me it was "our Waterloo," referring to the battle where Britain's Wellington defeated Napoléon and sent him into exile.

Judge Odette Kahn got her side of the story into print in the *Revue du Vin de France* under the title "On the Subject of a 'Small Scandal.'" Her report was partly factual but mostly defensive. She labeled the reports in American publications that California wines had outscored the French ones as "a nasty, slanted, and, I may say so, false conclusion." Kahn also spotted a conspiracy. She claimed that California wines that received high marks were always served just after a California wine that received poor marks, thus making the better wine score higher. In reality, as noted earlier, the wines were tasted in random order. She also said it was unfair that the wines were from various vintages and that the only valid comparison would be to taste wines from several years and several châteaux against each other. In con-clusion, Kahn wrote, "The only lesson to be drawn from this tasting, in my opinion, is that certain winegrowers in California can produce (in small quantity, if my information is correct) wines of good quality, agreeable to taste . . . I believe it is interesting for the French wine world to know this, but from this to proclaim (or to fear it to be proclaimed) that the Califor-nia wines 'beat' our great wines, that is a leap, a very great leap."

A month after the tasting, Spurrier ran into Kahn at a reception for the first time since the event. The exchange was chilly, as a roomful of people watched.

When Spurrier greeted her, Kahn haughtily replied, "I'm not speaking to you."

"I'm sorry about that."

"Of course, my dear sir, we all know you completely falsified the scores."

"That's not true, and you know it."

After the Paris Tasting, Steven Spurrier in his own words was *persona non grata* in Bordeaux and Burgundy. Many French people dragged out a thousand years of bitter history and wars between France and England and blamed the results of the Paris Tasting on the fact that Spurrier was English. Even Bernard Portet, the French-born winemaker at California's Clos Du Val, told me, "My first reaction was that only a Brit could do this to the French."

One Bordeaux winemaker told Spurrier, "You've spat in our soup. We allowed you into our country, and you've done this to us—perfidious Albion!"

Nearly a year after the tasting, Spurrier and his shop manager Mark Williamson visited Domaine Ramonet-Prudhon in Burgundy to buy some wine. Its Bâtard-Montrachet had placed seventh in the tasting. As they were looking at the bottling operation, the owner's son André Ramonet approached and said, "You're the one who did that tasting. Never darken our door again. Get out!"

While the American press was gloating about the Paris results, the French press all but ignored the event. It wasn't until August 18, nearly three months later, that *Le Figaro,* one of France's leading dailies, took note of it. The article was entitled "Did the War of the Cru Take Place?" With heavy sarcasm, the article reported that they were "crying in the thatched cottages of Burgundy," but that the results were laughable and "cannot be taken seriously." The story went on to quote Charles Quittanson, an eminent enologist, as saying that he had been very surprised to learn of the results. He dismissed the event, saying that it only goes to show what "silliness" can take place in a blind tasting.

It was not until November that *Le Monde,* France's most prestigious paper, reported the tasting. Continuing the fiction that was growing up around the event, the writer, Lionel Raux, began his story by saying it had taken place under a portrait of Thomas Jefferson. Outside of that, Raux's article was a straightforward piece, based almost entirely on the *Time* and the *Los Angeles Times* stories. In an opinion piece entitled "Let's Not Exaggerate!" that accompanied the main article, Raux condescendingly wrote that Spurrier didn't know how difficult it is to stage an impartial blind tasting, adding that in any case the French wines were too young and had not yet matured to their full flavor.

The results of the Paris Tasting have been the subject of more discussion and debate than any wine event since the Bordeaux classification of 1855. They have even been the topic of high-level scientific interest. Three leading international experts, two economists and a statistician, examined the results on a strictly technical basis in two separate studies.

Orley Ashenfelter and Richard E. Quandt are professors of economics at Princeton University and also wine connoisseurs. Ashenfelter publishes the wine newsletter *Liquid Assets: The International Guide to Fine Wine,* which now has an Internet Website, www.liquidasset.com. Ashenfelter and Quandt recalculated the results for only the Cabernet Sauvignon part of the tasting, using more rigorous academic methodology that is undoubtedly statistically superior to Spurrier's simple 20-point system that just added up all the scores. The Ashenfelter and Quandt approach takes into account the differing scoring styles of each judge. Some of the judges, for example, gave a wide range of scores, while others scored in a much narrower one. Ashenfelter and Quandt eliminated any distortion in the results caused by the differing scoring styles. The study, which promised to "rigorously analyze the famous 1976 Paris tasteoff," was published in the summer 1999 issue of the statistical magazine *Chance* and is also available at the Liquid Assets Website.

The Ashenfelter and Quandt results, though, turned out to be very similar to those of Spurrier. As they wrote in their paper, "It was no mistake for Steven Spurrier to declare the California Cabernet the winner." In their scoring, Stag's Leap places first followed by Château Montrose, Château Mouton, and Château Haut-Brion. So the winning wine is the same and the top four are also the same, although there was some shuffling in second, third, and fourth places. There is also juggling in the finishing order of the next six wines.

This analysis of the 1976 tasting is somewhat flawed, however, because they took the tasting scores, as they state, from the July 1976 issue of the *Connoisseurs Guide to California Wine* newsletter. That article included the scores of Spurrier and Gallagher in the final results even though their ratings were excluded in scoring on the day of the tasting. The results sent to the two winning wineries after the event clearly gave the "Official Jury Results" separately from the "Results Including Mr. Spurrier and Miss Gallagher." The results Spurrier announced on the day of the tasting and the ones he used later in talking with the press were only those of the "Official Jury."

The official results and those including the Spurrier and Gallagher scores, however, vary little. In the Chardonnay competition, the first four wines are in exactly the same position. There is some minor variation among the next four, and the final two are in the same position. In the Cabernet Sauvignon tasting, the top two wines are the same; the next two are the same but in reverse order; the next five vary a little, and the last wine is the same.

The other academic study was done by Dennis V. Lindley, one of the world's preeminent statisticians and a pioneer in an obscure field known as Bayesian statistics. Lindley taught at the University College London, and an international award in statistics is named in his honor. His analysis of the Paris results has not been published, but it is also available at www.liquidasset.com. Lindley too included the scores of Spurrier and Gallagher, perhaps to increase the number of judges used to assess the wines or perhaps in the belief that they had been used in the official tabulation.

Looking first at the Chardonnay tasting, Lindley classified three wines, two of them California, as standouts at the top, and one, the David Bruce wine, as a standout at the bottom. The rest he noted were closely grouped in the middle. Wrote Lindley: "The first conclusion is that the American Chardonnays did as well as the French, but that there are real differences between some wines. If the French were expecting to give high marks to their own wines in comparison with those from Napa, they failed." Lindley concluded that overall the California Chardonnays did better than the French ones.

As for the Cabernet Sauvignon results, Lindley determined that the judges scored the French wines as a group higher than the California ones. He wrote, "The French reds are really judged better than the Americans with a mean score that is higher by 2.0." After weighing other factors, he concluded that there was a statistical dead heat for first place between Stag's Leap and Château Mouton.

Lindley, though, takes a little magic out of the wines when he renders the results into such equations as $E(h_i) = 0.76_i + 024x_{..}$, $s.d.(h_i-h_j|data) = 1.10$.

Any critique of the Paris Tasting must start with the realization that no one, certainly neither Spurrier nor Gallagher, thought they were about to make history. This was just supposed to be an amusing afternoon of tasting interesting wines. If they ever dreamed that the international wine world would still be picking over the details of the event nearly thirty years later, they would have undoubtedly done many things differently.

Keeping this in mind, there are—beyond the myths, the outright falsehoods, the complex statistical equations trying to take a more academically rigorous approach to the results—four basic complaints that have been made against the Spurrier tasting.

Charge One: The 20-point system was too limiting, and there were six California wines but only four French wines in each category, thus statistically stacking the competition against the French and in favor of the Americans.

The 20-point method was then the standard procedure of judging wine in Europe and the U.S. But on having the six California wines? Guilty as charged. Spurrier never thought of the tasting as a face-off. Since he had the extra wines, he simply wanted to show more of them to the French judges. Naïve? Absolutely. A plot? Hardly.

Charge Two: Spurrier didn't choose the best French wines or the best French vintages.

It was impossible at the time to stage a fair comparison of aged French wines and aged California wines because the Californians didn't have any old wines. These were still very young wineries. It was only the second vintage the two winners had ever made. Spurrier selected recent wines from both sides that were being sold at the time. That was what people could go into a store and buy. He said then, and still says today, that he chose French wines that would be similar to their California counterparts. The Meursault Charmes, he felt, was the "fattest" of the Burgundies and a lot like the California Chardonnays. Joe Heitz had said that was his model. Spurrier thought the Ridge Monte Bello Cabernet was similar in style to the Léoville-Las-Cases, which is why he selected it. No one can deny the quality of Spurrier's French selections: two First Growths and two Second Growths among the reds, and one Great Growth and three of the most highly praised First Growths among the whites. Finally, Spurrier has always maintained that he consciously picked French wines he thought would win.

Charge Three: The French wines were too young.

All the wines, both French and Californian, came from the five vintages 1969 through 1973, with the majority from 1970 to 1973. The American wines were equally as young as the French. It was widely assumed that the French wines would improve with age; no one knew what would happen to the California wines in the bottle since the wineries had no track record. They too could improve with time. Also the vast majority of wine, even in France, is drunk soon after release. Only a few connoisseurs drink twenty- and thirty-year-old wine. The comparison of equally young wines is closer to the consuming public reality. And even in its youth, a great wine shows its greatness.

Charge Four: Blind tastings like the Paris one are inherently flawed and capricious.

This is undoubtedly true. There have been countless embarrassing cases of stupendous errors in blind tastings. But the alternative is even worse.

Spurrier and Gallagher were concerned that the French judges, whether willfully or accidentally, would score their own wines high and the California ones low if they knew the origin. And they were probably right. British wine writer Jancis Robinson in her classic book *How to Taste* wrote: "It is absolutely staggering how important a part the label plays in the business of tasting. If we know that a favorite region, producer, or vintage is coming up, we automatically start relishing it—giving it every benefit of the tasting doubt."

The most definitive answers to some of these charges can be found in the many reenactments of the Spurrier tasting that have taken place since 1976. The results have been surprisingly similar to the original. Granted these were mostly done with American judges who were not always wine experts. Unfortunately, there does not appear to have ever been a retasting— at least not again in public—done by French judges.

In 1979, three years after it had passed up the opportunity to have a reporter at the Spurrier tasting, France's *GaultMillau,* the food-and-wine magazine, staged the Wine Olympics in Paris. The magazine didn't want to just repeat the earlier event; it had to take things to a whole new level. It wasn't going to be just California versus France; this tasting was going to put on display the entire panoply of international wine. Spurrier had shown that France was no longer alone in producing great wine. Now *GaultMillau* wanted to take things one giant step further with the Wine Olympics.

A total of 330 wines of thirty-three countries were tasted by sixty-two experts from ten nationalities. France dominated in the number of wines selected to compete and the number of judges, although the wines came from as far away as China and the judges included representatives from Australia and Britain.

The wines were selected in a somewhat bizarre way and were divided into twenty-two categories. The French wines came mainly from the stock of Nicolas, the largest French wine chain. They included some of the very best French wines but also some modest ones. The California wines were from a variety of sources including the American embassy and Spurrier's Caves de la Madeleine, which by then carried a few of them. The selection of California wines also included both high-quality ones such as Stag's Leap Wine Cellars and lesser ones like Gallo.

The Wine Olympics resulted in another surprisingly good showing by California wines in Paris, particularly among the whites. In the Chardonnay tasting the 1976 Trefethen Vineyards from the Napa Valley came out on top, and California wines picked up six of the top ten positions. Among the Sauvignon Blancs, two Napa Valley wines, a 1977 Sterling Vineyards and a 1976 Spring Mountain, finished first and third.

In the red-wine tastings, the California wines did not do quite as well, although they placed six of the top ten among the Cabernet-Merlot blends, while France got the remaining four spots. A California wine, 1975 Hoffman Mountain Ranch, placed third in the Pinot Noir competition. California wines also did well in the Petite Sirah competition.

GaultMillau concluded in its story reporting the results, "There exist in California today a few properties or companies whose wines—although very expensive—can be considered among the best in the world."

The closest to a rematch took place twenty months after the original tasting on January 11 and 12, 1978, at the Vintners Club in San Francisco. Spurrier flew in from Paris to participate in the event, and many of the California winemakers were present on the night their wines were tasted.

The Chardonnay competition was held on January 11. While the club normally had thirty or so tasters for one of its regular weekly wine samplings, on this occasion there were ninety-eight. In that blind tasting the overwhelmingly American judges ranked the 1974 Chalone first, just one-tenth of a point higher than the Chateau Montelena that had won in Paris. The consensus comments of the judges on the Chalone wine: "deep gold; perfumed oaky nose; rich, buttery, powerful, long ripe, youthful." In Paris Chalone had scored third. In third position in San Francisco was the 1973 Spring Mountain, and in fourth was the 1972 Puligny-Montrachet Les Pucelles.

The following night ninety-nine tasters showed up for a similar blind tasting of the Cabernet Sauvignons. The 1973 Stag's Leap again walked off with first place, a half point ahead of the 1970 Heitz Martha's Vineyard. The consensus comments of the judges about the Stag's Leap: "deep cherry color; vanilla nose, fruity; fat, chocolate, round, supple." In third place was the 1971 Ridge Monte Bello, and in fourth the 1970 Château Mouton Rothschild.

As the crowd left the Cabernet tasting, Joseph Heitz, whose Martha's Vineyard wine had come in ninth in Paris but second at the Vintner's Club rematch, walked over to Stag Leap's Warren Winiarski and said good-naturedly, "I'm catching up with you."

The tenth anniversary of the Paris Tasting in 1986 offered a good occasion to see how the wines were aging. Early that year, the *Wine Spectator*, an American magazine, staged a retasting of just the Paris Cabernet Sauvignons. Chardonnay wines were not considered on the grounds that they would be past their prime. The judges, all Americans, were four *Spectator* staffers and two outsiders. The results were published in the magazine's April 1–15 issue. Using the *Wine Spectator*'s 100-point system, rather than Spurrier's 20-point one, the judges placed the 1970 Heitz Martha's Vineyard first with 93.5. It was followed by the 1971 Mayacamas, the 1971 Ridge Monte Bello, the

1973 Stag's Leap, and the 1972 Clos Du Val. The highest-rated French wine, the 1970 Château Montrose, placed sixth followed by the 1970 Château Mouton Rothschild, the 1971 Château Léoville-Las-Cases, the 1969 Freemark Abbey, and the 1970 Château Haut-Brion.

Spurrier helped put together a tenth anniversary rematch in September 1986 at the French Culinary Institute in New York City. The tasting this time was again limited to the reds for the same reason as at the *Wine Spectator* rematch. This time all the wine came directly from the producers except for Château Haut-Brion, which refused to have anything to do with it, and Freemark Abbey, which also declined to participate. Spurrier bought a bottle of Haut-Brion on the open market for the retasting, but Freemark Abbey was not included. The judges were eight Americans, mostly from the New York City wine trade. Just as in Paris in 1976, the wines were treated carefully, being decanted an hour before the tasting.

Spurrier's results this time were different, but California won again. The tasters commented that the 1973 Stag's Leap seemed to be over the hill, and it finished sixth. The winning wine was the 1972 Clos Du Val from the Napa Valley, which had placed eighth in Paris. Second place also went to another California wine, the 1971 Ridge Monte Bello. Then came the French in third, fourth, and fifth positions: 1970 Château Montrose, 1971 Château Léoville-Las-Cases, and 1970 Château Mouton Rothschild. The 1970 Château Haut-Brion rated last among the nine wines. Several of the judges said that they had difficulty distinguishing between the French and California wines—just as their Paris counterparts had ten years earlier.

It was difficult by the tenth anniversary, or thereafter, to take seriously the French objections that they had been robbed or tricked by Spurrier in 1976. The California wines had stood the test of time. Now all the red wines, both French and Californian, were coming up to fifteen years of bottle aging and were at or near their peak. The results of the two most highly publicized retastings showed that the California wines were probably aging better than the French ones were. Said James Laube, a *Wine Spectator* judge: "The extra decade of bottle age was kinder to California Cabs than to the Bordeaux."

At the thirtieth anniversary of the Paris event in May 2006, Steven Spurrier organized a two-continent rematch, with judges both in London and in Napa. There were nine judges at each location and only red wines from the original vintages were blind-tasted. The results in 2006 were even more stunning: California wines took the top five positions. The winning Cabernet Sauvignon this time: 1971 Ridge Monte Bello. The 1976 winner, 1973 Stag's Leap Wine Cellars, was second. All the arguments that the French wines would show better as they aged were finally and conclusively laid to rest.

CHAPTER TWENTY-ONE

A Dream Fulfilled

Anyone who knows his history must surely know his wines.
—ARNOLD TOYNBEE

Shortly after the results of the Paris Tasting in 1976 became known, Mike Grgich's phone at Chateau Montelena started ringing with offers for him to move to other wineries to be the winemaker. Relations at Chateau Montelena between managing partner Jim Barrett and Grgich had gradually been deteriorating. Both Lee Paschich and Barrett had been increasingly taking a more active role in the business, while Grgich wanted to run his own operation. He felt that too many people who didn't know anything about making wine were telling him what to do. So the winemaker listened closely to the offers and had follow-up conversations with many people. Most of the proposals, though, were only for Grgich to do the same job at a better salary than he was getting at Chateau Montelena. Grgich wanted more than that. He had worked for others for long enough; now he wanted his own winery.

Ever since he had arrived in the Napa Valley in 1958, Grgich had dreamed of being the master of his domain. Originally he thought that within a year he would have saved up enough money to buy one of the more run-down ghost wineries. But as time passed, he saw the prices—and the interest rates—gradually climb. So he told himself that he'd buy something as soon as they came down. But they never did, and by the mid-1970s his dream had all but evaporated. After the Paris Tasting, though, Grgich returned to the goal of having his own place.

The first thing he had to do was raise some money. He informed Barrett that he would be leaving at the end of his five-year agreement. His contract with Chateau Montelena gave him the right to cash out his 5 percent ownership position for $50,000. In addition, he sold the stock Ernie Hahn had given him for $45,000.

The parting was bitter on both sides. Grgich told people that he didn't think Barrett had treated him right. "When I left Robert Mondavi, we were friends," he told people. "When I left Chateau Montelena, we were not friends. There was no friendship." At the same time, Barrett was unhappy that Grgich was taking advantage of the Paris publicity to strike out on his own, leaving him without a winemaker.

With the new money in hand, Grgich set out to buy two acres of land in Rutherford. That would be just enough land for a winery and sales room, where he could sell directly to tourists. He would start with only two thousand cases a year. He would buy all his grapes and focus on what he did best: make wine. That plan died quickly, however. Grgich had been unaware of the 1968 regulation that required him to buy a minimum of twenty acres of land. Upon learning of this, he put down the $95,000 from his two stock transactions plus another $5,000 to buy twenty acres in Rutherford along Route 29. But that left him with no money to start a winery.

After on-and-off talks with several potential partners, in late 1976 came an offer from Austin E. Hills of the Hills Bros. coffee family, who already owned two vineyards in the Napa Valley. Following undergraduate work at Stanford and then getting an MBA from Columbia University, Hills had gone into the family business in San Francisco. In the early 1970s he had bought land and began growing grapes in the Napa Valley. He eventually established Hills Vineyard. In 1975 and 1976, Hills had Chardonnay and Riesling wines made with his grapes at the Souverain Cellars winery in Rutherford but sold them under his label.

The foreman who managed the Hills vineyards arranged a meeting between Grgich and Hills at the foreman's home in Calistoga. The conversation began with generalizations but soon got down to the tough issue: ownership. Grgich politely explained that he wanted to control 51 percent of the winery. His experience at Chateau Montelena had shown him that minority owners didn't have any control, even if they were star winemakers. "Under no circumstances am I going to work for anybody again, Mr. Hills," Grgich said. "I've worked for eighteen years for other people, and I've learned a lot from every place I've worked. But for once in my life, I want to work for myself. You can't change my mind."

Hills, though, also wanted majority ownership. He pointed out that he had 155 acres of land in two vineyards and could also contribute $400,000 to build a winery and help get the business started. The two men left without any agreement but on pleasant terms.

Shortly thereafter, Grgich went to San Francisco to see Ted Kolb, a lawyer who had also been on the board of directors at Beaulieu Vineyard, where Grgich had met him. Kolb and Grgich did a quick business plan for a winery that would produce ten thousand cases a year, the smallest level of production that was considered economical. Kolb calculated that it would require $750,000. Grgich would contribute $100,000 in the form of the land he had already bought, and Hills would put up his $400,000 in new capital.

"So we can make it," said Grgich.

"Mike, I don't think you're good at math," responded Kolb. "You're $250,000 short."

"Mr. Kolb, you know American business. But you don't know Mike Grgich." The winemaker then told the lawyer about meeting the Canadian businessman on the train that took him to Vancouver as an immigrant years ago. His fellow traveler had urged him to start a business and build it from the ground up by doing most of the work himself. If an American needed $750,000, Grgich felt he could do it with half that, following the old European style of scrimping and saving he had learned as a child.

Grgich returned to the Napa Valley and met again with Hills. Grgich discussed the business plan he had in mind, and Hills liked that Grgich was a frugal person who would not pay a dollar more for something than he had to. Hills believed that quality would be vital for someone starting a new company. This time the meeting went well, and shortly before the end of 1976, the two men agreed on a 50-50 partnership. Grgich would own 50 percent, while Hills and his sister, Mary Lee Strebl, would each have 25 percent. Hills would be chairman; Grgich would be CEO and winemaker. Grgich contributed his twenty acres in Rutherford, while Hills and his sister put up $400,000 with the agreement that it would be paid back over ten years.

Immediately Grgich set to work, with the goal of making his inaugural vintage in the fall of 1977. The first thing he had to do was come up with a name. Grgich wanted to call their venture Chateau Hills since the term chateau implied the quality wines that he intended to produce, and the company registered that name with the state. Hills, though, thought that the moniker was pompous since their chateau would be just a cement-block building they were going to construct on Route 29. The two men finally agreed to call it Grgich Hills Wine Cellar. Cellar, not cellars, because Grgich didn't want to promise too much. It was designed to produce ten thousand cases a year, and the founders hoped to achieve that level of production within a decade.

In the spring of 1977, while on Easter vacation at Yosemite Park, Grgich contracted to buy his first sixty tons of Chardonnay grapes in the fall from a Napa grower, closing the deal on a pay phone outside the motel where he was staying. Grgich also hired an architect to do five sketches for twenty dollars each of a combined winery and tasting room. He selected the simplest design: a rectangular building with the tasting room on the side facing the highway.

Grgich got lots of help from the local wine fraternity in his venture. Margrit Biever, the special promotions director for Robert Mondavi who three years later would become his second wife, helped Grgich design his first label. It shows a cluster of Chardonnay grapes and has a symbol for each partner: a horse from his family coat of arms for Hills and the Croatian flag for Grgich.

Getting all the legal and regulatory work done took until late spring, but finally on July 4, 1977, Hills and Grgich invited some of their friends to a groundbreaking for the new winery. The date wasn't an accident. Grgich considered American Independence Day to be his own independence day. It was a beautiful hot day, and a priest blessed the site. In the four corners of the foundation for the winery were bottles of four wines on which Grgich had worked and that played a major part in his life: a 1958 Souverain Cabernet Sauvignon, a 1968 Beaulieu Vineyard Georges de Latour Private Reserve Cabernet Sauvignon, a 1969 Robert Mondavi Winery Private Reserve Cabernet Sauvignon, and a 1973 Chateau Montelena Chardonnay. In only four months the winemaking was due to start, but there was nothing on the property. No winery, no vines, no grapes. Nothing except wild grass.

Grgich eventually signed contracts to buy 100 tons of Chardonnay grapes, 60 tons from Napa Valley and 40 from Sonoma County. He bottled the two batches separately, labeling them Chardonnay Napa and Chardonnay Sonoma. In addition, he bought 30 tons of Riesling and also made that wine. Just as at Chateau Montelena, he was going to concentrate on white wines that would quickly be on the market. The Riesling would be for sale in six months; the Chardonnay within a year.

In mid-August and shortly before the harvest was due to start, Grgich went to see Robert Mondavi. The two men had remained friends, and the new owner needed help. Grgich explained that he had gotten a late start building his winery and wasn't sure that all the equipment at his winery would be in place in time for the crush.

"Mike, you don't need my help. I started construction on my winery on July 17 and we still made the crush. You started two weeks earlier than I did. You'll make it."

Grgich was shattered. But Mondavi was only joking and pulled out a sheet of paper on which he wrote that he would crush Grgich's grapes if his own equipment was not ready. In the end, the construction was completed just before the crush started on September 5. Nonetheless, Grgich was relieved to have the Mondavi commitment on paper in his pocket just in case.

The Grgich Hills tasting room opened to visitors and buyers on November 1, selling at first only the remaining stock from Hills Vineyard, which Grgich bought from his partner at wholesale. Grgich's conservative approach to building a business is best seen in the way he expanded sales of his wines. Initially they were only available at the winery, then he sold some in St. Helena thirteen miles north, and after that he sold wines in the town of Napa thirteen miles south. Only after he had been successful in stores in those three places did he venture to the distant San Francisco market, sixty miles away. That first partial year in operation Grgich Hills lost $49,000 primarily because it was open for only a few months. In 1978, the winery's second year in operation, it made more money than it lost in the first year. Normally it takes a winery five to ten years to become profitable. Grgich did it in a year and a half.

In the fall of 1980, three Chicago wine stores and the wine columnist for the *Chicago Tribune* staged the "Great Chardonnay Showdown." At the time, that was by far America's favorite wine, and the organizers gathered 221 Chardonnays from around the world for the competition. There was heavy representation from France and California but also entrants from other countries from as far afield as Australia and Bulgaria. Five panels of five judges each first selected 19 finalists. Then ten of the original judges reviewed the finalists a second time. The wine hailed as the best in the world: the 1977 Grgich Hills Sonoma County Chardonnay, the new winery's very first vintage.

Almost from the first day it was sold, Grgich Hills Chardonnay was on allocation, and consumers couldn't buy more than three cases a year. It took the winery fifteen years before production satisfied demand and the allocation system was dropped. During that time, Mike Grgich and Austin Hills easily moved into their respective roles at Grgich Hills Wine Cellar. They had a 50-50 partnership that worked.

CHAPTER TWENTY-TWO

The Globalization of Wine

Wine brings to light the hidden secrets of the soul.
—HORACE

The Paris Tasting shattered two foundations of conventional wisdom in the world of wine. First, it demonstrated that outstanding wine can be made in many places beyond the hallowed *terroir* of France. Sure the French have great *terroir,* but maybe there are other places that are equally amenable to growing grapes that can make equally outstanding wine. If the soils of the Napa Valley could produce wines that bested the best of Burgundy and Bordeaux, what could be done in Australia, South Africa, or Chile? Obviously no one can make wine at the North Pole or in the Gobi Desert, but vintners around the world realized after the Paris event that there are many other places besides France where they could make great wine if they used the latest technology and the best practices.

Second, the Paris Tasting showed that winemakers did not need a long heritage of passing the wisdom of the ages down from one generation to the next to master the techniques for producing great wine. Newcomers could cut the discovery time dramatically if they did good research and followed French and now California procedures. Only twenty-three years transpired between the breakthrough developments at James Zellerbach's Hanzell, the first California winery that set out to make quality wines in the French style, and the Paris Tasting. But Chile in just the decade of the 1990s totally remade its antiquated wine business and brought it up to global standards.

The Californians had demystified wine, and after Spurrier's event, winemakers in many other countries saw that they could replicate the American experience. They simply had to experiment and find out what they could produce from their land with careful craftsmanship. From Canada to South Africa winemakers began to rethink the way they practiced their art. They convinced themselves that if the Californians could produce wines

230

that would make the world take notice, then they could perhaps do the same thing in Italy, Spain, or even further afield in Australia or Chile.

The result has been a globalization of wine from its European roots to many other parts of the world. Today wine is made in more than fifty countries. As wine critic Robert Parker told me, "The Paris Tasting opened the door for anyone, whether he is in California or Australia or New Zealand, to say, 'If we forget about any food-processing mentality and cut yields and pick ripe fruit and do everything we should to make a natural wine and achieve the greatest expression of our vineyard, we can make world-class wines that will be recognized as such.'"

An early result of the Paris Tasting was the increase in exchange of information among wineries and winemakers around the world. Vintners who had never strayed far from home, whether they were from France, Italy, Australia, or California, began traveling to see what was happening elsewhere. Many of them journeyed to the Napa Valley, the new happening place. French winemakers sent their children on vacations to northern California, and a few parents even enrolled them in the wine program at the University of California, Davis, or at Fresno State College.

Winemakers, then as now, are generally a very collegial group who welcome people from other countries. After the Paris Tasting, California winemakers were more than anxious to show off their new stainless-steel tanks, explain their techniques, and let visitors taste their wines.

As a result of this exchange of people and information, innovations made in one region quickly migrated to other areas. Oregon's Scott Henry, an aeronautical engineer, in the 1970s developed a new system for controlling excessive vegetation in vineyards, thereby concentrating growth in the grapes in order to improve the wine's flavor. He trained four, rather than the normal two, shoots of the plant upward along the trellis in order to increase crop level. Below those he trained four shoots downward to control vigor. The Scott Henry Trellis System, as it is known, is now used in many vineyards worldwide.

The equipment used in wineries has also become internationalized. When I visited Paul Ullinger, the winemaker/director of Redgate, a small winery in western Australia, he proudly showed me his French-made grape crusher, Italian pumps, German presses, and French and American oak barrels. Wineries in the Napa Valley or in Stellenbosch, South Africa, are likely to have the same mélange of international equipment.

After the Paris Tasting, winemakers in many countries also began concentrating on France's leading grape varietals just as the Californians did during the 1960s and early 1970s. Eight types of grapes now dominate global wine production. Among the reds, they are Cabernet Sauvignon, Merlot, Pinot Noir, Shiraz/Syrah, and Cabernet Franc. For whites, the noble grapes are Chardonnay, Sauvignon Blanc, and Riesling. Wine drinkers today can enjoy and compare Californian, Italian, South African, and Australian Chardonnays with the original Burgundy Chardonnays. With the exception of Riesling, whose roots go back to both France and Germany, all of the great eight have their origins in France.

Clones, the genetic raw material used to plant a new vineyard, generally come from the best plants that have been developed by researchers at the University of California, Davis, or at the University of Bordeaux. It should not be surprising that, *terroir* aside, a good South African Cabernet Sauvignon tastes much like a good Bordeaux, since the wine is probably made with grapes that come from Cabernet Sauvignon clones originating in Bordeaux.

Some traditionalists lament globalization, claiming that wines were more interesting when consumers could discover wines made from unusual grapes like Aligoté, Burgundy's other white wine, or Chasselas, which is grown in Switzerland. In truth, such wines are more appealing for their eccentricity than for their quality. Burgundians in the 1960s came up with a way to save the thin-flavored Aligoté wine by adding a little *crème de cassis* to it and calling the drink a Kir after a local prelate who was also mayor of Dijon. Fendant, a wine made from Chasselas grapes, may be romantic when it accompanies a hot pot of fondue on a skiing trip to Zermatt, but it's hardly an exciting wine. The international grapes have become popular around the world because they make outstanding wine, and consumers enjoy them. And traditionalists need not fear, unusual wines will continue to be made. In fact, global competition has become so intense that many small winemakers are now trying to find their niche in the market by making special wines. They are often very expensive and since production is small they are usually hard to find, but there will always be a market for out-of-the-way wines and there will always be vintners making them.

Other symbols of internationalization are the viticulturists and winemakers roaming the world as consultants, bringing along with them techniques developed in France, California, Australia, and elsewhere, improving the quality of wine wherever they work. France's Michel Rolland is perhaps the best known of the flying winemakers, as the footloose experts are called. He has consulted, among many others, for South Africa's Rupert & Rothschild, which not surprisingly produces a French-style Cabernet Sauvignon, and for Chile's Casa Lapostolle. Australian Richard Smart has consulted with more than 200 wineries worldwide. American Paul Hobbs, who started out working at the Robert Mondavi Winery and Stag's Leap Wine Cellars in California, now has his own winery in Sonoma County and also consults regularly with wineries in Chile and Argentina. Daniel Schuster, a viticulturist who is also the owner of a winery in Canterbury, New Zealand, was trained in France but has also made wine in South Africa as well as Australia and has long consulted for Stag's Leap Wine Cellars in California.

Go into a winery anywhere in the world today at harvest time, and you're likely to find workers from several countries. It's very common for young winemakers to work at various places around the globe, and many take advantage of the seasonal differences to do two harvests a year, working in the Southern Hemisphere in March and April and then in the Northern Hemisphere in September and October. Some university wine programs even require students to spend an internship in a foreign country. It is not uncommon to meet a winemaker in New Zealand or South Africa who has spent a couple of harvests in France, one in Italy, and still another in California. When the peripatetic wine scholars return home and run into a problem, they are not shy about telephoning the winemaker where they worked for the last harvest to ask for help.

The technological breakthrough of drip irrigation played a major role in spreading grape growing to new areas. This is the water-saving system of installing polyethylene tubing in farm fields to bring precise amounts of water and nutrients right to the base of the plant, rather than spraying them inefficiently across a whole field. As a result, there is less water runoff and very little evaporation from leaves and soil. The Israelis led the development of the technology starting in the 1950s and made their deserts bloom. Vineyards have been planted during the past two decades in arid parts of Australia, Chile, and the U.S. that would never have seen a grape without drip irrigation.

As a result of all these developments, cosmic change has taken place in the world of wine. Global wine production and consumption during the past quarter century has been modestly declining, but behind those overall numbers is an historic shift between the Old World and the New World.

For most of human history the wine trade was very stable. From 5500 BC, when wine began migrating along with trade from Iran and Egypt to areas of the northern Mediterranean, to relatively recent times, almost all wine was made in Europe, especially after the Prophet Mohammed outlawed it in the Muslim world in the seventh century. Countries like France, Italy, Spain, and Portugal consumed more than 90 percent of their own production, while the remaining 10 percent, usually high-quality wine, was

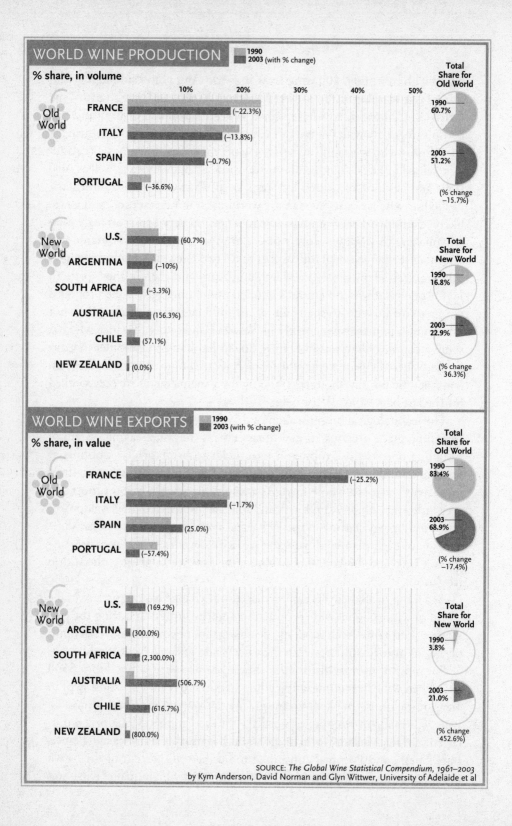

WORLD WINE PRODUCTION

■ 1990
■ 2003 (with % change)

% share, in volume

Total Share for Old World

Old World

FRANCE	(−22.3%)	
ITALY	(−13.8%)	
SPAIN	(−0.7%)	
PORTUGAL	(−36.6%)	

1990 60.7%

2003 51.2%

(% change −15.7%)

New World

U.S.	(60.7%)
ARGENTINA	(−10%)
SOUTH AFRICA	(−3.3%)
AUSTRALIA	(156.3%)
CHILE	(57.1%)
NEW ZEALAND	(0.0%)

Total Share for New World

1990 16.8%

2003 22.9%

(% change 36.3%)

WORLD WINE EXPORTS

■ 1990
■ 2003 (with % change)

% share, in value

Total Share for Old World

Old World

FRANCE	(−25.2%)
ITALY	(−1.7%)
SPAIN	(25.0%)
PORTUGAL	(−57.4%)

1990 83.4%

2003 68.9%

(% change −17.4%)

New World

U.S.	(169.2%)
ARGENTINA	(300.0%)
SOUTH AFRICA	(2,300.0%)
AUSTRALIA	(506.7%)
CHILE	(616.7%)
NEW ZEALAND	(800.0%)

Total Share for New World

1990 3.8%

2003 21.0%

(% change 452.6%)

SOURCE: *The Global Wine Statistical Compendium, 1961–2003*
by Kym Anderson, David Norman and Glyn Wittwer, University of Adelaide et al

exported to European countries such as Britain and Holland that made little or no wine. A small amount was also sold to more distant countries like the U.S. or Australia, which produced little wine and even that was of poor quality. As recently as the late 1980s, European exports accounted for 96 percent of wine sold around the world.

In the last decade, however, that historic pattern of wine production and trade has changed substantially. Wine consumption in the old major producing countries has dramatically declined. In France, Italy, Spain, and Portugal people are drinking only about half as much wine annually as their parents or grandparents did. French consumption dropped by nearly 20 percent during the decade of the 1990s and that trend continued into the new century. Similar declines took place in Italy, Spain, and Portugal.

The fall-off has been concentrated in the lower-end table wines, the mainstay of the business and the product that paid the bills for millions of peasant producers. At the same time, though, Europeans are now drinking better wines. If there's a bottle on the table, it's likely to be an *appellation*-quality wine. That, however, cannot save the millions of producers whose families have been making low-quality table wines that have been consumed with meals in Latin countries for centuries.

The worldwide area given to grape cultivation declined by 10 percent in the 1990s, but that drop-off was almost exclusively in Europe. Thousands of acres of poor quality vines were pulled up on the Continent over the past two decades, with the land often turned over to vacation homes. Total grapevine area fell in France nearly 10 percent in the 1990s, and Italy saw a 20 percent decline.

As a result of lower domestic consumption, European producers have become more dependent on exports to new wine consuming countries like the U.S. and Australia. In 1990 France exported only 20 percent of its production, but by 2003 it was exporting 33 percent. In Italy the numbers jumped from 22 percent to 32 percent during the same period.

A great deal of those exports comes from the demand for French and Italian trophy wines that sell for $100 or more a bottle and are usually produced in small quantities. Those sales are likely to remain high because there are now so many more wealthy consumers around the world willing to pay high prices for superpremium wines. Trophy wines, however, make up less than 5 percent of wine consumption by volume, even though the profit margin on them is large.

The dynamic part of the world wine business today is not in Europe, but in the New World—Argentina, Australia, Chile, New Zealand, South Africa, and the United States. Winemakers there have been planting new vineyards almost as fast as Europeans are pulling out old ones. U.S. grapevine area rose from 292,000 acres in 1990 to 954,000 acres in 2003, and Australian vineyards increased during that same period from 146,000 acres to 356,000 acres.

Chile has been increasing the size of vineyards even though its domestic wine consumption has been declining following the European pattern. Its vineyard area went from 161,500 acres to 415,000 acres between 1990 and 2003. Moreover, those overall numbers hide the fact that Chilean winemakers have been pulling out thousands of acres of low-quality grapes and replacing them with such international grapes as Chardonnay and Cabernet Sauvignon.

Wine consumption has also been growing in the New World countries, albeit from a much lower base. In the U.S. annual per capita consumption rose sharply in the 1960s and 1970s, but fell off in the early 1990s and has been coming back strongly in recent years. Nonetheless, the world's winemakers continue to look at the U.S. with enthusiasm because the market is so large and because wine consumption is still relatively low compared with the rest of the world at only 2.4 gallons per capita in 2003. In the 1990s, many Australians turned from beer to wine and annual per capita consumption reached 5.5 gallons in 2003. In New Zealand it rose 30 percent between 1990 and 2003 to 5.1 gallons.

New World wine producers increased their share of world wine exports from 3.8 percent in 1990 to 21 percent in 2003, and that trend is likely to continue, as they grab market share from European producers. France's percentage of world exports dropped in value terms from 51.9 percent in 1990 to 38.8 percent in 2003, while Australia's share rose in that period from 1.5 percent to 9.1 percent, and Chile's part of world exports increased from 0.6 percent to 4.3 percent.

The country setting the pace in world wine today is Australia, a producer unlike any the world has ever seen. Australia is the first major wine country that has focused on exports rather than on its domestic market. French, American, and Italian winemakers primarily serve their local markets, and exports are only an added plus. Australia, with a national market of only 18 million, depends vitally on sales abroad. In 1990 Australia exported just 11.8 percent of its production; it now exports nearly half of its much larger output. Total Australian exports worldwide went from $126 million in 1990 to $1.5 billion in 2003.

Old World wine producers such as France, who are seeing their domestic market decline and their dependence upon exports increasing, watch this Australian wine juggernaut with concern because it has already started taking over important markets. Just three countries—Germany, the United States, and Britain—import half of the entire world's wines, with much of that coming from Old World producers. In 2000, Australia became the biggest supplier of wines to Britain, replacing France, which had held that honor since the Middle Ages. France's loss of its number one position was all the more painful because of the sharp increase in British wine consumption. The British drank just 2 gallons of wine per capita in 1982 but now consume 5.8 gallons annually. Much of that growth, though, has been in Australian wines. France's share of the British wine market dropped from 37 percent in 1994 to 23 percent in 2003.

A similar story transpired in the American market. Australia passed France in 2002 to become the second-largest exporter behind Italy. It seems only a matter of time before Australian wines top U.S. wine imports.

Australia has been making wine since the late eighteenth century, but until the 1980s most of it was of poor quality and rarely left the country. Big producers such as Penfolds and Rosemont long dominated the business there, and mergers in recent years have put even more power in the hands of a few companies that offer wines in a broad range of style, price, and quality.

This consolidation and strong brands made it easier in the mid-1980s for major Australian producers, in conjunction with the government and with the support of the country's wine-research institutes, to begin going after the international market in an aggressive and systematic way. With a hearty disregard for the established way of doing things, in particular for the French concept of *terroir*, Australia's wineries now turn out consistently competitively priced, easy-to-consume wines that fit the tastes of younger, less experienced oenophiles.

The international wine business has never had brands that could compare with other alcohol products such as Budweiser beer, Johnnie Walker scotch, or Smirnoff vodka. Australian producers, though, are in the process of changing that, thanks to intensive branding and marketing campaigns. These please both consumers, who are often confused by the numbing number of choices in any wine outlet, as well as retailers, which in many countries are grocery stores mainly interested in moving merchandise.

Australia's Yellow Tail, which sells several different varietals specifically blended to American tastes, is the quintessential example of this Australian approach to the world market. Yellow Tail wines are not even widely sold in Australia. They are made by Casella Wines, a company started in 1969 by Italian immigrants Filippo and Maria Casella who began exporting Yellow Tail to the U.S. in June 2001. Only two years later it sold 4 million cases, replacing Chile's Concha y Toro as the largest imported brand. Yellow Tail sold some 7 million cases in 2004. It has even gone upmarket with more expensive reserve wines.

The increasing importance of brands has led to a series of international mergers in recent years that have involved all the major wine-producing countries. In 1989 France's Pernod Ricard bought Orlando Wines, maker of Jacob's Creek, a major Australian producer and the leading wine brand in Britain. In 2001 Britain's Allied Domecq bought Montana, New Zealand's largest wine company. The following year Foster's, a leading Australian beer company, took over Napa Valley's Beringer Wine Estates. In 2003 Constellation, an American wine company, bought BRL Hardy, one of Australia's leading wine producers. The following year Constellation also gobbled up the giant Robert Mondavi empire in California. Diageo, a British company, has been buying up wineries around the world, including California's Beaulieu Vineyard and Sterling Vineyards as well as France's Barton & Guestier. In early 2005, Diageo outbid an international group lead by France's Domaines Barons de Rothschild to capture California's Chalone Wine Group. In the summer of 2005, France's Pernod Ricard took over Allied Domecq to form the world's second largest spirits company after Diageo, which resulted in more wine business consolidation. At nearly the same time, Foster's bought Australia's Southcorp, owner of Penfolds and that country's largest wine producer.

The driving force in all those deals was the recognition of the globalization of wine and the growing importance of brands. They also all involved beer or liquor companies with strong, established products looking for better profits than they could get from their traditional fields alone, where consumption was stagnant or falling. The companies were seemingly undeterred by the bad experience that liquor companies like Seagrams and Heublein had in the Napa Valley in the 1960s and 1970s, when they got into wine with big investments and left only a few years later after big losses. So far, at least, the mergers generally seem to be working.

American wine companies have generally been content to live off their large domestic market. One exception is Gallo, which has gone after the British market with big advertising budgets and is also trying to get into the French market. Interestingly, Gallo abroad sells its middle-range brand, Gallo of Sonoma, rather than the jug wines that gained it fame in the U.S.

Before it was sold, the Robert Mondavi Winery went abroad by doing joint ventures in countries such as Chile and Australia. Mondavi in 2001 attempted to start a winery that would make a superpremium Syrah in the Languedoc region of France, but was stopped by an ugly grassroots movement against what was seen as the American takeover of French land. In the late 1990s when Mondavi ran short of wine for its Woodbridge brand, it gave new meaning to the globalization of wine by importing Chardonnay from southern France to blend with its California wine.

Growing up along with the globalization of wine has been the power of the global wine critic. Wine writers such as Hugh Johnson in Britain and James Halliday in Australia have long chronicled developments in the business, usually with a friendly approach that rarely, if ever, spoke ill of any winery. A new type of wine writer appeared in 1978 in the person of Robert M. Parker Jr., a lawyer from Monkton, Maryland, and his publication *The Wine Advocate*.

Parker didn't just write pleasant platitudes; he scored wines using a new 100-point scale with a candor that infuriated wineries but appealed to consumers. The Parker method, which resembled the scoring system used in U.S. schools, was easy for Americans to understand. Neophyte wine consumers could suddenly justify paying $100 for a bottle of wine simply by saying, "Parker gave it a 98." Other wine publications, such as the widely read *Wine Spectator* magazine, soon adopted the 100-point system.

In a field where many wine critics and magazines shade their opinions to please advertisers, Parker has been highly ethical. His newsletter carries no advertising, and plays no favorites except on Parker's personal basis of taste.

Parker has an incredible ability to taste, rate, and remember wines. He is most avidly a fan of Bordeaux, although he also reviews wines from some other regions and countries. His opinions are widely followed, and his judgment can make or break a winery. The saying in the wine trade is that if Parker gives a wine a score of below 80 it can't be sold at any price, but if he gives a wine above 90 it's too expensive for most consumers.

His detractors complain that Parker gives a degree of artificial statistical accuracy to a process based on subjective personal taste. They also note that his world is limited. The more than 1,600-page *Parker's Wine Buyer's Guide* gives short shrift to the Loire Valley, one of France's largest wine-producing areas, and only two paragraphs to all of South Africa's wines. Nonetheless, Parker and his system remain popular.

President Jacques Chirac in 1999 made Parker a knight in the Legion d'Honneur, France's highest award, calling him the "most followed and influential critic of French wines in the world." Winemakers around the world told me privately that they couldn't understand how one critic came to have such a sway over their business and complained bitterly that no one should have that kind of clout. As a new generation of wine drinkers gathers more experience, people are likely to develop confidence in their own tastes and depend less on the counsel of any critic. For now, however, a large group of fans look for a guide to help them find their way through the wine thicket, and the critic that stands out far above all others is Robert Parker.

Some connoisseurs complain that the development of the global wine scene risks producing a bland, international, McWine style, where an Italian Chardonnay tastes much like one from California or Australia or France. Parker is one of the loudest critics of this international standardization even though he, more than anyone, has helped foster it, because so many winemakers are styling wines to win high marks from him in order to get the resulting higher prices and greater sales. Knowing that Parker likes massive, dark-colored, intense-flavored, high-alcohol wines, that is exactly what they try to produce.

Sometimes this can lead to grotesque procedures or shortcuts that might produce so-called Frankenstein wines. Some vintners remove liquid from the must, the mixture of grape skins, juice, and seeds, to intensify the wine's tastes. The French developed a procedure called micro-oxygenation that puts oxygen into the juice while fermentation is taking place to speed up the transformation of hard tannins into soft and mellow ones, making poor quality wines seem like long-aged ones. The Australians discovered that they could get some of the same effects of aging in oak barrels by putting oak chips into holding tanks of nondescript white wine and then stirring them furiously. The final product had the vanilla and clove tastes that oak provides, although sometimes to an excessive degree.

No one can deny, though, that this is the golden age of international wine. Never before in history have consumers enjoyed such high-quality wines at generally good prices. It is easy to romanticize about a glorious past when peasants wearing baggy pants and berets turned out supposedly wonderful wine in caves with straw-littered floors. I doubt, however, that today you'd really want to drink a lot of that wine. Now from California to Italy in the Northern Hemisphere and from New Zealand to South Africa in the Southern Hemisphere, winemakers are producing better and better wines. The 100-point rating system introduced by Robert Parker has become a rigorous international standard for all quality wines, and thousands of winemakers are striving to produce wines that win high scores from him. The consumer is now indeed king.

One of the most spectacular celebrations of the globalization of wine took place twenty-one years after the Paris Tasting, and again in Paris. In September 1997, Jean-Claude Rouzaud, the managing director of Champagne Louis Roederer, celebrated his thirtieth anniversary in that position by hosting a dinner at La Tour d'Argent for the makers of what he decreed to be the world's thirty greatest wines. A non-competitive tasting of their thirty wines was held the following day at the Louvre Museum, which was fitting since all the wines are museum pieces.

A generation earlier, all thirty wines would have come from France, and even in 1997, this Frenchman chose exactly half—fifteen out of thirty—from France. Nine came from Bordeaux, starting with all five First Growths. The nine Bordeaux wines: Haut-Brion, Lafite, Latour, Margaux, and Mouton, plus Yquem, Cheval Blanc, Ausone, and Pétrus. Four wines were from Burgundy: Romanée-Conti, Faiveley's Clos des Cortons, Leflaive's Chevalier-Montrachet, and Joseph Drouhin's Montrachet Marquis de Laguiche. There was also one Champagne, Roederer Cristal naturally, and one Côte du Rhône, Etienne Guigal's Côte Rôtie La Turque.

Nonetheless, Rouzaud also recognized the rest of the world.

Four California wines were invited: Diamond Creek Volcanic Hill, Heitz Martha's Vineyard, Ridge Monte Bello, and Stag's Leap Wine Cellars Cask 23.

Four wines also came from Germany, all Trockenbeerenauslese, a sweet dessert wine made with late-harvested grapes that have undergone the same process the French call "noble rot" as Sauternes: Maximin Grünhaüser Abtsberg, Schwarzhofberger Riesling, Joh. Jos. Prüm Wehlener Sonnenuhr Riesling, and Schloss Johannisberger Riesling.

Two Super Tuscans, quintessential examples of globalization that are Bordeaux-style wines made in Italy, made the list: Sassicaia and Solaia.

Five countries had one wine each: Australia (Penfolds Grange), Chile (Lapostolle Merlot Cuvée Alexandre), Hungary (Tokaji Aszú Eszencia Diszńokö), Lebanon (Chateau Musar), and Spain (Vega Sicilia Unico).

The selection seemed a little too much like a United Nations of wines, with some questionable ones selected for geographical balance. Nonetheless, it was a good stab at naming the International First Growths.

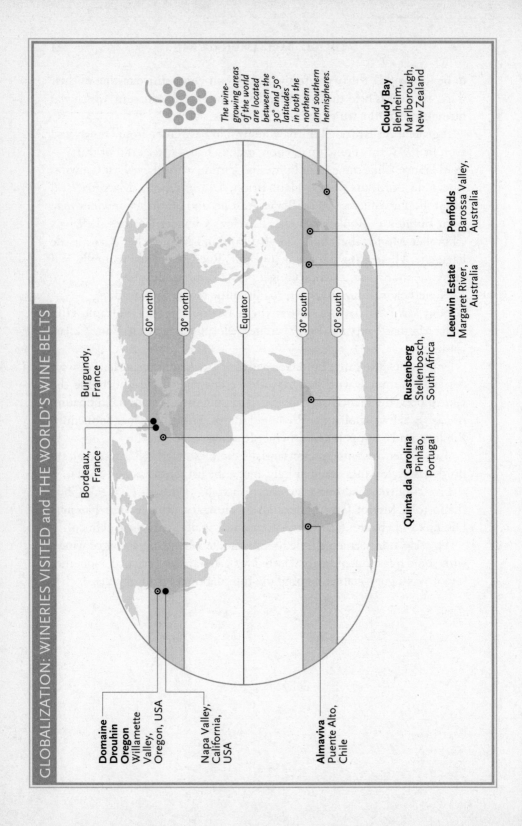

GLOBALIZATION: WINERIES VISITED and THE WORLD'S WINE BELTS

The wine-growing areas of the world are located between the 30° and 50° latitudes in both the northern and southern hemispheres.

50° north

30° north

Equator

30° south

50° south

Cloudy Bay
Blenheim, Marlborough, New Zealand

Penfolds
Barossa Valley, Australia

Leeuwin Estate
Margaret River, Australia

Rustenberg
Stellenbosch, South Africa

Quinta da Carolina
Pinhão, Portugal

Almaviva
Puente Alto, Chile

Burgundy, France

Bordeaux, France

Domaine Drouhin Oregon
Willamette Valley, Oregon, USA

Napa Valley, California, USA

CHAPTER TWENTY-THREE

Dispatches from
the International Wine Trade

Wine is a bride who brings a great dowry to the man who woos her persistently and gracefully.
—EVELYN WAUGH

While writing this book, I roamed the world in search of wines that reflected the new globalization of viticulture. These travels took me from vineyards near the surfer's promised land of western Australia to those of Chile in the shadows of the Andes. I found an American woman making wine for a French company in New Zealand and a Frenchman making wine in Chile. Some of the wineries I visited had a direct connection to the Spurrier tasting, having been built after the event. Others predated it, although they came to international prominence only after the judgment of Paris stimulated interest in non-European wines. All of them, however, reflect the revolution that started in Paris on that day in May 1976, and are six examples of the outstanding wines being made today in great *terroirs* around the world. All of them have brilliant futures and one day may have earned a place among a new ranking of the world's greatest wines.

Blenheim, Marlborough, New Zealand

David Hohnen is an Australian who studied winemaking at Fresno State in California, and worked for the French-owned Taltarni Vineyards in Australia and then for the French-owned Clos Du Val in the Napa Valley before starting the Cape Mentelle winery with his brother Mark in western Australia. He is also the father of what many people consider to be the world's best Sauvignon Blanc, New Zealand's Cloudy Bay.

Winston Churchill said of his political rival Clement Attlee that he was a modest man who had much to be modest about. The same might have been said about Sauvignon Blanc wine. Until recently, it would have been better described as Sauvignon Bland. The most famous Sauvignon Blanc is France's Sancerre, but even much of that lacks any personality and is often too acidic. In the 1960s, Robert Mondavi tried to change the wine's style and name to Fumé Blanc, which he hoped would make it easier for Americans to pronounce and enjoy. It didn't help.

The world's view of Sauvignon Blanc changed dramatically in the late 1980s, however, when a new version came roaring out of New Zealand. The Kiwi Sauvignon Blanc was alive with flavors of cut grass and fresh fruits. The wine has its detractors, who claim it's too much in your face, but no one ever forgets the taste of a well-made New Zealand Sauvignon Blanc. One wine critic compared drinking Cloudy Bay to hearing Glenn Gould playing Bach's *Goldberg Variations*. Another said drinking your first New Zealand Sauvignon Blanc was like having sex for the first time. Winemakers in other countries have tried to match the New Zealanders but with only modest success. No other region in the world can match Marlborough, the northeastern corner of New Zealand's south island, which seems to be the best place in the world to grow Sauvignon Blanc grapes. While many New Zealand companies now produce the wine, Cloudy Bay in the town of Blenheim set the world standard for Sauvignon Blanc and now demands premium prices around the globe.

The story of Cloudy Bay begins in the spring of 1983, when four New Zealand winemakers, who had been attending a conference in Perth, Australia, drove three hours south to visit the Cape Mentelle winery in Margaret River. They wanted to meet David Hohnen, a hot winemaker there who had just won the Jimmy Watson trophy, Australia's top wine honor, for the second year in a row.

Hohnen was proud to show off his wines, in particular his new Sémillon, which sparkled with lots of herbaceous flavors. The guest winemakers, though, were unimpressed. If Hohnen wanted to experience something really exciting, they said, he should try a New Zealand Sauvignon Blanc. One of them went out to their car and got Hohnen a bottle, but he only got around to opening it after the visitors left. With the first sip, he was stunned. The wine was like nothing he had ever experienced. Its taste exploded in his mouth and demanded attention.

A year later, Hohnen went to New Zealand, ostensibly to attend a wine show in Auckland, but his real purpose was to check out the country's wine scene, especially what was happening with Sauvignon Blanc. He had been successful at producing red wines in Australia, but was looking for something new and interesting in white wines. Ever since the visit of the Kiwi winemakers, Hohnen hadn't been able to get that New Zealand Sauvignon Blanc out of his mind. While driving a rental car around the country and trying various wines, he started to zero in on the Marlborough area as having the best Sauvignon Blancs. The town of Blenheim in particular looked interesting. Montana, New Zealand's largest winemaker, had planted major vineyards there in 1973 and a few other wineries were also producing some interesting Sauvignon Blancs. The area enjoyed hot days and cold nights— just the ingredients to give wines the intense aromas and lively, but not over-powering, acidity. The soils were geologically young and rich in minerals.

At the Auckland wine show Hohnen, a serious, focused person when on a mission, sampled every single Sauvignon Blanc on display and concluded that the ones he liked best all came from Marlborough. While he was tasting, Hohnen noticed another winemaker also zeroing in on the Sauvignon Blancs. His name was Kevin Judd. He was also Australian and was currently the winemaker for Selaks, one of New Zealand's quality producers. Hohnen and Judd met briefly and talked in general about the potential of the country's Sauvignon Blanc.

Hohnen returned to Australia with plans to start a new company in New Zealand to make the wine. In late 1984 and early 1985, he began putting the pieces together. Despite interest rates that were then a rapacious 24 percent, he assembled a group of investors who put up a total of $1 million. Hohnen then hired Judd to be the winemaker, even though he had to stay at Selaks to finish the 1985 vintage. Hohnen also made a deal with Corbans, another big New Zealand winemaker, to buy its surplus Sauvignon Blanc grapes from Marlborough for the next three years. Reflecting the new global wine business, the clone used to grow the grapes had been developed at the University of California, Davis. In August 1985, Hohnen and company broke ground on a winery on Jacksons Road on the northern side of the Wairau Valley just outside Blenheim. The sandy loam soil seemed to make it an ideal location for a vineyard that they wanted to plant later.

Everything for the first vintage was done on the fly and involved lots of phone calls between New Zealand and Australia. Hohnen, whose greatest strength is in viticulture, hovered over the Corbans grape crop and had frequent phone conversations with Judd, who was working in Auckland. After the grapes were picked, they had to be trucked twelve hours across the Cook Strait to the Corbans winery at Gisborne on New Zealand's north island. Still running the operation by phone, Judd directed the Corbans winemaking staff on how he wanted things done.

Judd's goal was to keep the production simple—stainless-steel fermentation and no aging in oak. The goal was a simple, pungent dry wine. Judd had been making a successful oak barrel–fermented Sémillon for Selaks, so he bought some of that from Corbans thinking it would give the wine a more interesting taste. Sémillon made up about 15 percent of the final wine, although it was not enough to require him to call it a Sauvignon Blanc–Sémillon blend. The production of the 1985 vintage was only 2,800 cases.

In addition to making the wine, Judd also played a key role in developing the wine's label, which has been cited by industry experts as one of the reasons for its great success. A gifted amateur photographer, Judd has published a book of vineyard pictures entitled *The Colour of Wine*. He had taken a shot of the Richmond Ranges, which rise majestically behind a vineyard in Marlborough in a three-tiered silhouette. An artist turned Judd's photo into a label. Then the founders needed a name. Hohnen's Cape Mentelle was named after a spit of land located near Margaret River in Australia, and he wanted another maritime connection for his new place. Captain James Cook, who had claimed New Zealand for Britain, named the bay near Blenheim Cloudy Bay because of the ethereal way that clouds, fog, and mist softly embrace the land and sea. Hohnen and Judd were reluctant to call a wine cloudy, a quality winemakers eschew. Someone quipped that they could call the wine Farewell Spit in honor of a jut of land to the west, but the idea was dismissed with a laugh. Finally the company's marketing advisors carried the day, and it was Cloudy Bay.

Now that he had a wine, a label, and a name, Hohnen had to sell the product. Since New Zealand was going through a wine glut and prices were low, he decided that the larger Australian market, where he already had a distribution system in place, would be the primary focus. The heavily indebted company had no money for a marketing campaign, so Hohnen was forced to be creative. Starting in Sydney, he made promotion trips to Australia's leading cities. At each stop he sent out a gift package to restaurateurs, wine writers, and retailers that included a wine glass, a bottle of Cloudy Bay Sauvignon Blanc, a can of New Zealand mussels, and a note that said, "Before you open this box, get a corkscrew and some fresh crusty bread."

The reaction in Australia was overwhelming. Consumers had never tasted a Sauvignon Blanc like Cloudy Bay. There was something about the *terroir* of Marlborough that gave it a unique taste. The response was similar when the wine was released into the British market the following year. Cloudy Bay entered the U.S. market in 1991 to little critical attention or press notice, but it soon had a cult following among consumers.

French winemakers watched the developments in New Zealand and the world wine market with attention. Only four years after Cloudy Bay hit stores, Veuve Clicquot, the French Champagne producer that is part of the

LVMH Group, bought land in Marlborough with the intention of producing Sauvignon Blanc. At the same time, Hohnen's investors, who were anxious to reap the rewards of their runaway success, wanted to cash out of the company and were pressuring him to find a buyer. Eventually Veuve Clicquot bought not only land in Marlborough but also controlling interest in Cape Mentelle and Cloudy Bay. Hohnen retained 20 percent of his company, but eventually sold his share in 2001.

Another French company has also made a major investment in Marlborough. Domaine Henri Bourgeois, one of France's leading producers of Sancerre and Pouilly-Fumé, two Sauvignon Blanc wines, in 2000 bought 173 acres of Marlborough land after first looking at making wine in California, South Africa, Chile, and Australia. New Zealand appeared to offer the best place for them to practice their Sauvignon Blanc skills. Their first vintage was in 2003, and the winemaker was Sally Denious, an American who had gotten her wine training in Australia. To help celebrate the first harvest, Domaine Henri Bourgeois invited forty-six French winemakers to look at its operation, and the company expects eventually to produce as much Sauvignon Blanc in New Zealand as it now makes in the Loire Valley.

As employees of Veuve Clicquot, Hohnen and Judd these days try to keep up with demand for one of the world's most popular wines. Hohnen works out of Margaret River, traveling to New Zealand four times a year, and Judd controls day-to-day affairs in Blenheim. Production is now approaching 100,000 cases a year. Unfortunately, many American wineshops run out of their allocation a few weeks after it arrives each spring. Despite large unmet demand, however, Hohnen is only increasing production by about 10 percent annually in order not to compromise its quality. Judd fine-tunes the taste of his international success, but is not making significant changes. Now that Cloudy Bay grows about half of its own grapes, Judd has more control over the viticulture side of the process. He's using riper grapes to give the wine more tropical fruit tastes, and blends Sémillon into it only in rare years. His goal remains to make a Sauvignon Blanc that continues to make the world say, "Wow!"

Barossa Valley and Margaret River, Australia

At the Paris Tasting of 1976, California wines had bested the best French red Bordeaux and white Burgundy wines. Three years later at the *Gault-Millau* Wine Olympics, another icon of French winemaking fell. A 1971 Penfolds Grange Hermitage, an Australian Shiraz, walked away with a first prize in Shiraz, a field long dominated by the French. Shiraz is the Australian version of the French grape Syrah, which is widely used in Rhône Valley wines.

It took another sixteen years before the *Wine Spectator* magazine declared the 1990 Grange the Red Wine of the Year in December 1995, and British wine critic Hugh Johnson has since called Grange the only First Growth from the Southern Hemisphere. Those international accolades for Grange marked not just the success of one particular Australian wine but also the recognition that the land down under has become one of the world's leading producers of quality wine.

Max Schubert, the determined chief winemaker at Penfolds, Australia's largest wine company, literally willed Grange into existence more than a half century ago. Schubert had to overcome a long and loud chorus of criticism, and it took years for this wine to find its place in the pantheon of world wines.

In 1950, the Penfolds board of directors sent Schubert on a trip to Europe to study the making of Sherry in Spain and Port in Portugal. At the time, Australians drank mainly those fortified wines rather than dry table wines. After finishing his work in Spain and Portugal, Schubert went on to Bordeaux to check out French winemaking. In Bordeaux he met Christian Cruse, one of the leading figures of the wine trade, who introduced Schubert to the wonders of aged Bordeaux. Just as the new breed of Americans starting with James D. Zellerbach returned from Europe with dreams of making wines as good as the French ones, Schubert came home with the goal of producing in Australia a wine that would be as rich and intense as those of Bordeaux and would also last twenty or more years. He called the wine Grange in honor of the Adelaide homestead where his company's founder, Christopher Rawson Penfold, had lived. Schubert had grand ambitions for Grange and he later wrote that his objective was "to lift the rather mediocre standard of Australian red wine in general at that time."

Even though he was chief winemaker, Schubert had to make lots of compromises in his ambitious project, for starters in the type of grape he would use. The classic Bordeaux grapes—Cabernet Sauvignon, Cabernet Franc, Merlot, and Petit Verdot—were unavailable in sufficient quantities in Australia, so he used the country's most widely available grape, Shiraz. Schubert called the wine Grange Hermitage in honor of the best-known French Syrah.

Aging in oak is the centerpiece of Bordeaux winemaking, but Schubert couldn't get enough French oak in Australia, so he used more readily available, although very different, American oak.

In 1951, Schubert launched his project with an experimental vintage.

His objective, he later wrote, was "to produce a big, full-bodied wine, containing maximum extraction of all the components in the grape material used."

By today's standards, or even those of Bordeaux in 1951, Schubert's methods and equipment were primitive. Unlike most great wines, which come from a single vineyard to assure uniformity, he selected grapes from two different Penfolds vineyards located in the Adelaide region. Schubert, though, had exacting demands for ripeness and acidity for the grapes. They were fermented in a wax-lined, open concrete tank. Schubert wanted to achieve maximum contact between the fermenting juice and the grape skins and other material in order to produce the rich color and taste intensity he desired, so he put wooden planks on top of the tank to keep the skins and seeds immersed in the fermenting juice.

Schubert also introduced some other innovative procedures. He wanted the fermentation to last much longer than normal in order to get a richer taste—twelve days rather than the customary three or four—and so he used a heat exchanger, a device like a car's radiator, that drew off heat, thus lowering the temperature of the juice and prolonging fermentation. Before the process was complete, the liquid was pumped into five 300-gallon American oak tanks, where the process was finished. By continuing fermentation in oak, the fruit and oak flavors integrated more completely: the wine took on a more concentrated taste but did not pick up additional green, harsh tannins from the grapes. That gave the Grange a soft and rich flavor. The first batch of wine remained in the oak barrels for eighteen months before bottling. The total output in 1951 was just 160 cases.

While this experimental Grange was maturing in bottles, Schubert turned out additional vintages each year. The first two Granges, 1951 and 1952, were 100 percent Shiraz, but starting in 1953 he blended in a small amount of a particularly good Cabernet Sauvignon that provided additional aromas, tannins, and flavor and improved the wine's structure. Cabernet has since been added in most, but not all, years.

Schubert believed that he had created a great wine that lived up to the objectives he had set, but just about everyone else thought he had produced a monster. A tasting of Granges from 1951 to 1956 turned into a humiliating experience for Schubert. One respected critic called the wine "a concoction of wild fruits and sundry berries with crushed ants predominating."

Shortly before the 1957 vintage, the top management at Penfolds gave Schubert written instructions to halt the Grange project and cut off all funding for it. Undeterred and unbowing, the sometimes-cantankerous Schubert stealthily continued his work. The 1957, 1958, and 1959 vintages were stored in a cellar behind a false wall, and since he couldn't get the money to buy new oak barrels, he reused old ones.

The Grange wines from the early 1950s eventually started to mature nicely and some of the rougher edges smoothed out in the bottle. They were now less aggressive and more refined. The Penfolds board of directors in 1960 retasted the early wines and told Schubert he could start making Grange Hermitage once again. He was also finally given the money to support the project properly.

Two years later, Penfolds decided to enter Grange in the Sydney Wine Show in the Open Claret classification even though it was not that type of wine. Schubert chose the 1955 vintage, which was much older than other wines in the category, because Grange takes longer than other wines to mature. The 1955 Grange won a gold medal at the show, one of more than fifty golds it eventually won before being retired from the wine show circuit in the late 1970s.

After those early victories in Australia, Grange slowly rose in stature on the international wine scene until today, when it is now recognized as perhaps the world's greatest Shiraz. In 1990, the company dropped the word Hermitage from the name, calling it simply Grange. The Australian wine no longer needed the support of an association with a famous French wine; Grange could stand on its own.

Grange is the world's best Shiraz because the Barossa Valley north of the city of Adelaide has perhaps the best *terroir* in the world for growing Syrah or Shiraz. Although it's called a valley, Barossa is at an elevation of about a thousand feet that varies between undulating hills and flat ground. The annual rainfall is about twenty inches. The soil is red and brown, with sandy loam over deep clay. Summer temperatures regularly hit 85 degrees and sometimes top 105. There is never any problem about the fruit ripening, and the grapes are always rich in flavor and deep in color. It rarely rains during the February–March harvest.

Selecting Shiraz grapes from a variety of vineyards has also been a hallmark of Grange and remains so today. Steve Lienert, who is something like the chief operating officer of Grange, works with more than a dozen growers whose grapes have shown the greatest potential to be used in Grange. All the grapes are fermented separately and then only the best go into the Grange blend. About two-thirds of the finalists make it. Lienert says he has never had a case where all the finalists were selected.

One of the most important sources of Grange fruit is the Kalimna Vineyard, which is located in Nuriootpa in the northern end of the Barossa Valley. Grapes from Block 3C, which has a heavy clay soil and produces less than a half ton per acre, consistently go into Grange. Block 42 has gnarly Cabernet Sauvignon vines that are said to be more than a hundred years old. Until a recent string of drought years, the Barossa Valley Shiraz was dry farmed, but drip irrigation has now been installed for emergencies. It is used sparingly.

Grange has always been a very expensive wine, but after it began receiving recognition the price reached the almost unthinkable. The 1976 Grange was the first one to top twenty Australian dollars a bottle upon release. At the time the average Australian red wine was selling for about two Australian dollars. The 1999 vintage, which was 100 percent Shiraz, was released on May 1, 2004, at a recommended price of $225 in the U.S. market. There is also a strong market of old Grange vintages and oversized bottles both in stores and on the Internet. The highest price ever paid for a bottle of Grange was $46,080, which went for a six-liter bottle of the 1998 vintage. The highest price for a regular bottle was $27,100 for a 1951 vintage.

Grange is expensive, in part, because of its scarcity. Penfolds makes only from 5,000 to 10,000 cases a year depending on the availability of quality grapes. Château Lafite Rothschild, a Bordeaux First Growth, produces about 20,000 cases. Despite the temptation, the company has not pumped up production to meet demand. The 2000 Grange, released on May 1, 2005, consisted of only 2,000 cases because poor growing conditions limited the amount of grapes deemed of Grange quality.

Only four winemakers have had the final authority over Grange since the wine was first made in 1951. Max Schubert made it until 1973. Don Ditter, his longtime assistant, made it from 1974 to 1986, when he retired. John Duval made it between 1986 and 2002. Peter Gago took over as the chief Penfolds winemaker in July 2002. He had worked for the company since 1989 and reached the top via a circuitous route. Originally trained as a science-and-math teacher, he taught and was a school administrator for nearly nine years. A man of eclectic interests, Gago sprinkles his conversation with musical references or song lyrics ("As Joni Mitchell says, 'You don't know what you've got till it's gone.'").

Gago told me he would "love to make five, ten, thirty times the volume," but there are simply not enough quality grapes to enable them to do it. "We could still do it and lower the quality, but bit by bit it would come back to bite us." Gago knows he is carrying a heavy historic burden, but does it with a light touch. He says his goal is to make the exact same wine Schubert originally made, while realizing that no two vintages of any wine are ever identical.

A few changes in the name of modernization have been made in the way

Grange is made. Fermentation has not been done in wax-lined concrete tanks since 1973. It now takes place in stainless-steel tanks. Over the years the length of the process has been cut from twelve days to five or six.

But there is more Australian wine than just from the Barossa Valley and Grange. The Australian wine business is highly concentrated. Only 4 companies produce 60 percent of the country's wine and 20 turn out 95 percent. Some 1,500 wineries make up the last 5 percent, but today they are the most interesting part of the Australian wine business. The country's small wineries produce some of their finest products in the Margaret River area, a region 180 miles south of Perth on the country's southwestern coast.

In 1973, Robert Mondavi traveled with Rev Cant, an Australian who had worked for him at the Charles Krug Winery, to Australia hoping to buy some land there for a vineyard and winery. At the time Margaret River was virtually unknown except to a small band of enthusiastic international surfers in search of the perfect wave. The town of Margaret River had the highest unemployment in the country, and local farmers existed mainly on dairy farming.

Mondavi honed in on Margaret River as an area of great wine potential and in 1973 met with a Perth lawyer to see who owned the tract of land there that he wanted to buy. The lawyer thought that Denis Horgan, a local thirty-two-year-old accountant more interested in drinking beer and surfing than in balance sheets, owned the 1,650-acre property. Horgan had bought it four years earlier from a man with health problems who was trying to clean up his business affairs. The lawyer telephoned Horgan to see if he were interested in selling. Horgan said he wasn't but invited Mondavi and the American lawyer who accompanied him to drop by for a drink at the end of the day. Horgan then sent his office boy out to buy the most expensive wine available in Perth and asked his personal assistant to go to the local library to find out anything she could about Robert Mondavi.

Mondavi and his lawyer arrived at Horgan's modest office located on St. George's Terrace, the city's main street, and the three men adjourned to a courtyard to talk about wine. Mondavi was enthusiastic about the potential he saw in the Margaret River area, which seemed ideally suited to the New World wines he was producing. Horgan was still not interested in selling, although they reached an agreement under which Mondavi invested in the property and directed the development of the vineyards and winery that would be called Leeuwin Estate.

Mondavi was not the first person to spot the special characteristics of Margaret River, a hunk of land that juts out from the Australian mainland into the Indian Ocean, stretching sixty-six miles from north to south and sixteen miles from east to west. John Gladstones, a researcher in plant breeding at the University of Western Australia, in 1965 published a study that showed a strong resemblance between Bordeaux and Margaret River. Water on three sides moderates temperatures and provides almost perfect conditions for grape cultivation—forty inches or so of rain annually, but 85 percent of it in six months of the year and almost none during the grape-growing season and harvest. Margaret River's clay subsoil is topped by gravelly loam rich in minerals. Pockets of broken-down granite and limestone also provide an ideal foundation for viticulture.

When Mondavi arrived, wineries were already slowly growing up in Margaret River, the first four having been financed by three doctors and a mining engineer, mirroring the amateur development of northern California winemaking in the 1960s. Young Australian winemakers began gravitating to Margaret River in the 1970s, attracted by the area's promise. The early leader of the group was Bill Hardy, whose family was a major player in the wine business and who had studied winemaking in the 1960s at the University of Bordeaux under the famed Émile Peynaud.

Keith Mugford, who became the winemaker and owner of Moss Wood, remembers hearing the results of the Paris Tasting while a student at the Roseworthy winemaking program at the University of Adelaide. That convinced him that great wine could be made outside of France and inspired him to try to do it in Margaret River. In December 1978, he went to the Napa Valley to visit wineries including Robert Mondavi and Stag's Leap Wine Cellars. Winemakers at both facilities opened their doors to him and explained their philosophies of bringing balance and complexity to Cabernet Sauvignon, which strongly influenced Mugford when he returned to Australia.

In the late 1970s and early 1980s, Mugford was part of group of about two dozen Margaret River winemakers who got together once a month on a Thursday night at the Transit Inn in Perth to sample some of the world's great wines. Since Bill Hardy had a French orientation, the group tasted mostly French wines, although they also tried California's Stag's Leap Wine Cellars and Spring Mountain, two of the wines at the Paris Tasting. Just as Napa Valley winemakers had done in the 1960s, the Australians a decade later tasted great wines—now from France and California—and then tried to match them in what would become a period of great experimentation and sharing of winemaking experience.

The joint venture between Robert Mondavi and Denis Horgan began in 1975. The following year Mondavi told Horgan about the Spurrier tasting in Paris and how it had showed that the wines of the New World such as they were going to produce could rank with the best of France. In 1980 Leeuwin Estate bottled its first Chardonnay, the wine that has made it famous around the world. Leeuwin now produces seven wines under its Art Series label, all of which have original pieces of art on the label in the style of Château Mouton Rothschild. For a decade Mondavi and Horgan worked together, but eventually they went their separate ways after Horgan refused to let Mondavi buy him out of the Margaret River winery.

In 1999, Jean-Claude Vrinat, the owner of the Taillevent restaurant and one of the judges at the Spurrier Tasting, published the book *100 Vins de Légende* (100 Legendary Wines). In it he identified "the 100 most prestigious wines in the world." They included two Australian wines: Penfolds Grange and Leeuwin Estate Art Series Chardonnay.

Stellenbosch, South Africa

While serving his obligatory military duty in the South African army in 1977, Simon Barlow, whose family owned a winery dating back to 1682, first heard about the results of the Paris Tasting, and he still recalls the impact that had on him. The French had been knocked off their pedestal, he thought, and a new world of wine was opening. At the time, South African wines were also-rans on the international scene and could not be imported into the many countries that had trade embargoes against the country because of its apartheid racial policies. Barlow had been making plans to go to France to study winemaking, but after finishing his military service he decided to go to California to see what was happening in the area that had just stunned the wine world. He got an internship at Hacienda Wine Cellars in Sonoma County in 1980, working from June through the fall harvest.

South Africa's vineyards predate some of the oldest in Bordeaux. The Dutchman Jan van Riebeeck planted the first grapes in South Africa in 1655. Dutch immigrants had noticed that sailors on Portuguese and Spanish ships that docked at the Cape of Good Hope at Africa's southern tip were not as susceptible to scurvy, an illness caused by a lack of vitamin C that could kill half the crew on the voyage from Europe. The Dutch surmised that the wine the Spanish and Portuguese sailors drank on board was perhaps the reason. Since the Cape of Good Hope area had a Mediterranean climate and soil similar to that found in Europe, the Dutch settlers planted grapes in the foothills of the towering mountains outside Cape Town, the colony's principal city.

South African wines, especially its sweet ones, soon earned a wide following. The most famous in Europe starting in the late eighteenth century was Constantia, the same wine Napoléon had asked to be comforted with on his deathbed. Wines from the Cape of Good Hope region flourished in the British market during the nineteenth century, while the country was a British colony. After London lowered tariffs on French wines in 1861, however, South African wine sales there plummeted and a slow decline began.

In 1918, after an overproduction of grapes made prices plummet, ruining many grape growers, farmers formed the Ko-öperatiewe Wijnbouwers Vereniging (KWV), a state-run cooperative that dictated everything down to how much wine could be produced and where. The government in power was looking to win the votes of the big, rich grape farmers and established a policy of production quotas for each grower that favored the mass-produced, high-yield but low-quality grapes that they grew, the same grapes that go into sweet wine and brandy, rather than premium wine. Smaller producers of quality wines were given very low quotas. South Africa thus became known mainly for cheap wines and brandies, and even those sales abroad were blocked starting in the 1960s because of the country's racial policies.

The Barlow family was part of the white establishment that ruled South Africa for more than four hundred years and ran one of its few quality wineries. Peter Barlow, the head of Barlow Rand, a huge multinational corporation, in 1940 bought Rustenberg, a then rundown estate outside the university town of Stellenbosch. The three-thousand-acre property was located on the side of Simonsberg Mountain, which looked down toward False Bay and the Cape of Good Hope far in the distance. Settlers from Germany's Rhineland built the winery in the late seventeenth century, planting the vineyard on the mountainside like an amphitheater, which gave it excellent sun exposure. Conditions for wine-grape growing were almost ideal. The deep red soils were made up of decomposed granite, clay, and alluvial material washed down from the mountain. At the lower level the ground became sandy. Rainfall totaled some thirty inches annually. Temperatures were moderate, ranging from lows of 43 degrees in the coldest months to highs of 84 degrees in the hot season.

For Peter Barlow the estate was a rural retreat from the cares of a demanding business life in Cape Town, and he ran the winery as something of a hobby. Vintages from the mid-1960s to mid-1970s were well regarded, and Rustenberg was considered one of South Africa's leading wineries in the years of apartheid isolation. After Peter Barlow's death in 1975, his wife ran the Rustenberg estate and winery with professional managers.

Their son Simon, who was born in 1956, studied at Britain's Royal Agricultural College, returning home in 1979 to go into the family business. He started off selling Caterpillar farm equipment but began drifting toward wine while working for Distillers, a large South African liquor company, and then went to California for his internship. Just before leaving, Barlow bought his own property on the Helderberg Mountain a few miles south of Stellenbosch. He already had plans of turning the 378-acre farm that he named Nooitgedacht into a vineyard and winery upon his return.

Back in South Africa after the California harvest, Barlow set out on his winery project. In effect, it became a test-run for what he would later do when he inherited the family winery at Rustenberg. He planted international grape varietals, specifically the Chardonnay that he had worked with in California. The rigid KWV, though, still ruled the country's wine business and he had to smuggle the Chardonnay cuttings past its restrictions. Barlow experimented at Nooitgedacht to see which grapes grew best in various parts of his property and built a small winery from the ground up in 1982, equipping it with all the newest technology.

Barlow took over Rustenberg in 1987 at the darkest hour for both his country and its wine business. The country was diplomatically isolated and its apartheid system was collapsing amid violence. The trade embargo was crippling the country's economy, and many feared that South Africa was on the brink of civil war. Thousands of white professionals were emigrating, primarily to Europe and Australia.

At the center of the racial struggle was Nelson Mandela, who had been in prison since 1962 after leading a campaign to topple the white-led government. Whites feared that if he were released race riots would break out, but there could be no peace in the land as long as he was imprisoned. Barlow watched and waited to see what would happen to his tense country. He told friends that his fate was like that of the pig in a bacon-and-egg breakfast. The chicken lays its egg and moves on, but the pig has to stay. He couldn't pack up and move on; he was committed.

To the surprise of experts both inside and outside South Africa, Nelson Mandela's release on February 11, 1990, did not set off a race war. Radicals on both sides were controlled, and South Africa slowly began moving toward a resolution of its tortured racial conflict.

While calm was taking hold in the country, Barlow was growing increasingly concerned about what he saw happening at Rustenberg: the winery and its reputation were declining. The equipment was so dated that Barlow felt it was like making wine in a museum. The facility was too small and too old. Bottling was done from a 1,022-gallon wooden tank that mixed up dozens of batches. There hadn't been any new vineyard plantings in years. Barlow was worried that the Rustenberg winemaker, who had been doing the job for twenty-two years, didn't seem open to new thinking or international developments. Rustenberg was selling a dozen different wines, too many to do well. The last really outstanding Cabernet Sauvignon vintage had been in 1982. In short, Rustenberg was living on its past reputation.

Everything, though, began coming together in 1992. The white-controlled government started making the changes that would eventually lead to black rule. The KWV dropped its quota system for wine production and began loosening its control over the business. And late that year Barlow reached the conclusion that nothing less than a total makeover of Rustenberg would save the winery.

The job was massive, would take several years, and required millions of dollars of Barlow's own money to accomplish. One of the first steps was to get a new vintner. Kym Milne, the winemaker at Villa Maria Estate in New Zealand and one of the international flying consultants, led Barlow to hire fellow New Zealander Rod Easthope. Employing a Kiwi winemaker did not go down well with the South African wine press or trade. They were used to the days when South Africa rarely went out of its own tightly knit, isolated society.

Wine tastings are a lagging indicator of quality in part because the vintage being tasted is at least a couple of years behind developments due to the time required for barrel aging. In the early 1990s, Rustenberg was still bringing home a good number of awards, and so in public things seemed fine. Reality hit home, though, at the annual South African Airlines wine tasting in December 1994. With the 1992 vintage on display, Rustenberg drew low scores, and wine writers told Barlow privately that his wines seemed to be slipping. Barlow was getting similar reports from friends in South African wine clubs.

A sense of urgency began to take hold. Barlow had decided to build a new winery in the old dairy, but since the building was an historic site he needed government approval of the plans, which involved gutting the insides and putting in totally new equipment. After removing the cows, construction started in 1996. Under the thatched roof of the classic white Cape building, Barlow put up a shining new, four-story, gravity-fed winery that used the natural flow from higher to lower levels to avoid mechanical pumping of wines between tanks, a process that can sometimes damage them. Picked grapes come into the winery at the first level and drop down to the second level for crushing and fermentation. Then the new wine goes to the third level for barrel aging and finally to the fourth level for bottling. An Italian-built bottling line was followed by French presses, South African fermenters, and French oak barrels. Another sign of going first-class all the way were the Riedel glasses in the tasting room.

Meanwhile, Barlow continued looking around the world to pick up people, equipment, and new winemaking techniques. In mid-1997, he felt that by studying both old Rustenberg records and the latest international developments he had an idea of what he wanted to do with his red wines, but he was still struggling with the whites. In September he traveled to Burgundy with Kym Milne and Rod Easthope for three weeks to see what was going on there with Chardonnay. Out of that trip came plans for a new, single-vineyard Chardonnay that is now marketed as Rustenberg Five Soldiers, named for five Stone Pines that Barlow thought looked like they were standing as sentinels over the estate.

Rustenberg's old vineyards got both new vines and new technology. Barlow imported more than two hundred thousand vines from France for planting. He also installed forty-two weather stations to identify changes in microclimates around the property. Aerial photography and satellite surveys helped determine when the harvest, particularly of grapes for red wine, would take place. For three centuries, Rustenberg had been dry-farmed, but a new drip irrigation system was installed starting in 1997. New soil studies confirmed that Rustenberg was indeed an exceptional place to make wine.

With so much going on, Barlow decided to take the Rustenberg label off the market for 1994 and 1995. He didn't want to go through this high-wire act in public and perhaps damage the Rustenberg name. Instead the wines were sold under the new Brampton brand, which was named after the estate's prize-winning Jersey bull Brampton Beacon Bloomer. Rustenberg, however, did not disappear entirely from the market. Old Rustenberg wines came out of South African cellars and began appearing in wine auctions. At the end of 1998, Barlow relaunched Rustenberg with the 1996 vintage.

Then in late 1999, he brought in a new South African winemaking team. South African Ari Badenhorst was named winemaker, while Nico Walters took over as viticulturist. Badenhorst was twenty-seven; Walters was thirty-two. Badenhorst is typical of the new international winemaker. He has worked harvests in New Zealand as well as at Château Angélus and Chateau de La Colline in France.

Despite Rustenberg's more than three-hundred-year history, Barlow, Badenhorst, and Walters are still searching their vineyards to find the best slopes or microclimates to grow particular grapes. The three believe in *ter-*

roir and envy the French and other Europeans who centuries ago discovered what did best where and now can get on with the job of producing the best wine possible from areas that have already proven themselves. They know they have great *terroir* on their mountainside, but they're still uncovering the mysteries of their vineyards.

Rustenberg today has two lines of wines and two styles of winemaking—Rustenberg and Brampton. Rustenberg wines are made in a classical French style. The top-of-the-line Rustenberg red wine, named Peter Barlow in honor of Simon's father, is a single-vineyard, 100 percent Cabernet Sauvignon made from grapes grown high on the main estate's mountainside vineyard. It is aged in French oak for twenty-two months and has French-style, artisanal handling. Only about a thousand cases of Peter Barlow are made each year. The winery also sells a Merlot blend named John X Merriman after a Cape Prime Minister. The top-of-the-line Rustenberg white wine is the Five Soldiers. The grapes are grown without sulfur and aged about fifteen months in French oak. Walt Disney World in Florida bought some fifty cases of 2000 Five Soldiers, the entire U.S. allocation, to serve in its restaurants. Other Bordeaux-style reds and Burgundy-style whites also carry the Rustenberg label.

With the Brampton label, the winery markets a variety of New World–style wines at less expensive prices. These include a Cabernet-Merlot blend, a Sauvignon Blanc, and an unusual Chardonnay that is not aged in oak.

Great changes have been taking place in South African wine in recent years, as the country catches up with international developments. When trade embargoes were removed in the early 1990s, the quality of many of the South African wines that reached new markets was poor and set back the whole field. More recently, however, a half dozen or so South African wineries are in competition to turn out their country's first international icon wine. Rustenberg is on everyone's short list of wineries that could do it. Vintages of the top-of-the-line Peter Barlow Cabernet have been receiving ratings in the 90s from international critics.

In December 2002, Barlow hired a boat and took all of his eighty-six employees to Robben Island, seven miles out to sea from Cape Town. It was here that Nelson Mandela spent most of his years in prison, breaking rocks in a limestone quarry. The prison has now become a South African national monument and Barlow wanted his white and black employees to share the experience of visiting it. Some of his white staff warned Barlow that the trip could cause trouble in view of the country's tortured racial history. Barlow, though, had been promoting a racially mixed staff. His assistant winemaker, who had an internship at France's Château Margaux, is black, and another black employee studied in Burgundy. Instead of splitting apart employees, the visit brought them together around a particularly poignant time in their shared history.

Pinhão, Portugal

Jerry Luper made not one but two of the wines that participated in the Paris Tasting. He produced both the 1972 Freemark Abbey Chardonnay and the 1969 Freemark Abbey Cabernet Sauvignon. Nearly three decades later, Luper is the chief winemaker at Real Companhia Velha in Porto, Portugal. This is one of several Portuguese companies striving to upgrade the quality of their country's table wines. Portugal is known to American wine drinkers mainly for its Port and Lancers, the sweet, fizzy rosé wine. With Luper the New World of wine has come back to the Old World.

Since he graduated from the wine program at California's Fresno State College in 1969, Luper has been bouncing around the global wine scene, so it's not surprising to find this American now making wine in Portugal. When he first went to the Napa Valley, the protest movement against the Vietnam War was going strong and because he wore a beard he couldn't get a job until Louis M. Martini offered him one at three dollars an hour. The following year—and a shave later—Luper was making wine at Freemark Abbey as the protégé of Brad Webb. He soon grew back the beard.

In the summer of 1976, though, Luper and his wife pulled up stakes and moved to France, where he did some consulting work and learned more about European winemaking. The following year he was back in the Napa Valley and the successor of Mike Grgich as winemaker at Chateau Montelena. In 1978 Luper started the estate Cabernet Sauvignon production there that had always been the dream of owner Jim Barrett. Three years later, Luper moved on to Bouchaine Vineyards, a winery in the Carneros region of the Napa Valley, where he stayed for four years before going to Rutherford Hill, another valley property.

From 1972 until 1993, Luper was also the winemaker of the Napa Valley's Diamond Creek Vineyards, a boutique winery that won widespread critical acclaim—and high prices—for its Cabernet Sauvignons. Diamond Creek was the first California wine to sell for more than $100 a bottle—to the eternal lament of wine drinkers everywhere.

By the spring of 1993, Luper was ready to move again. He had grown tired of producing, as he said, "just another Cabernet and just another Chardonnay." He and his wife, Carolee, also didn't like what they saw happening in the valley, as big money and snobbish society moved in and a lot of the spirit of adventure and cooperation moved out. The Napa Valley, for them, wasn't fun any longer.

While in the army in the early 1960s, Luper had learned Czech at the Army Language School in Monterey, California, before being stationed in West Germany. So in 1993 he moved his family to the Slovak Republic, where the post-Communism era was blooming and he thought he could do some consulting and exporting of wines back to the U.S. That project fell apart in less than a year, and Luper left for a job in Portugal, consulting with a winery based in Lisbon.

In 1996, he joined Real Companhia Velha in Porto. The company was founded in 1756 by royal decree and had long been a major producer of Port, but the market for that fortified wine was growing very slowly. Under the strict rules of the Douro region, whose *appellation* system dates back to the mid-eighteenth century, nearly two hundred years before the French one, about half of all grapes grown there have to go into making Port. The rest have traditionally been made into jug wine, which rarely found its way out of Portugal. After a market study of Portuguese wines done for the government by Harvard's Michael Porter, Real Companhia Velha decided to start production of quality table wines. Luper was brought in to lead the project. He also oversees the Port production, but his focus is more on table wines.

For Luper making wine in Portugal was like his first days back in the Napa Valley working for the Louis M. Martini Winery and Freemark Abbey. Everything was again new and interesting. Real Companhia Velha owns 1,360 acres of prime Douro Valley vineyards and was ready to make the investments necessary for the upgrading project to succeed.

Luper, though, was shocked by what he found in both the winery and the vineyards. The winemaking was primitive. White wines often turned bad because of oxidation, and malolactic fermentation took place by chance, rather than by design. The equipment was old, and there was little coordination between the winemakers in the cellars and the viticulturists in the fields.

Portuguese wines were a whole new world for Luper. Although Real had started replanting some vineyards with international varietals like Chardonnay and Sauvignon Blanc, the vast majority of its vineyards were covered with Portuguese grapes that bore names like Touriga Nacional, Tinta Barroca, and Touriga Francesa, which were totally new to him. Some forty red-wine grapes, most of them little known outside Portugal, are authorized to be grown in the Douro. Luper quickly concluded that red wines were the Douro's strength and would be its future.

With management's backing, Luper set out to remake the line of table wines. He hired two winemakers and two viticulturists, all straight out of school, so that he could, as he said, "teach them from square one the right kind of attitude and the right kind of approach to making world-class wines." Luper also had to teach his people how to taste—how to recognize the new easy-drinking, international style in wines that emphasized rich fruit and mellow oak flavors. "If you don't recognize it, you can't make it," he told his staff. Luper installed thirty-five new fermentation tanks and seventy-two new storage tanks plus small oak barrels for aging.

While the bulk of Real Companhia Velha's business is still in Port, with 70 percent of that being exported, table wine production has grown to more than 300,000 cases a year since Luper arrived. About 70 percent of the table wine is still consumed domestically, but the company is looking abroad for growth, primarily to Western Europe. One 370-acre vineyard has been planted with international grapes—Chardonnay, Sauvignon Blanc, Sémillon, and Cabernet Sauvignon.

The more interesting Luper wines from Portugal, however, are those made primarily with local grapes that are grown nowhere else in the world. These are sold under six brands: Evel, Grantom, Grandjó, Quinta de Cidrô, Quinta dos Aciprestes, and Porca de Murça. All of the wines are from the Douro district. Luper thinks that two Portuguese grapes, Touriga Nacional and Touriga Francesa, have the greatest potential. All of the red wines and most of the whites are aged in oak.

Dating back to his Napa Valley days, Luper has always been someone who holds down more than one job. He made the Diamond Creek wines for more than twenty years, while also having full-time jobs at other wineries. Now in addition to making wines for Real Companhia Velha, he also has his own small winery in Pinhão, an hour-and-a-half's drive east of Porto in the Douro Valley area known as Trás-os-Montes or Behind the Mountains.

While he was still consulting in Lisbon, Luper started looking to buy land in Portugal for a winery. Like so many other Napa Valley winemakers, Luper and his wife had always dreamed of having their own place. For two years, he visited Portuguese vineyards and became better acquainted with local grapes. Finally in 1995, he returned from a trip and told Carolee that he thought the Douro was "the place where we can spend the rest of our lives." Finally they found the right property in the village of Pinhão. The vineyard was located high above the Douro River on a north-facing slope, where he believes growing conditions are ideal for his grapes.

On the ten-acre property was a rundown house that hadn't been occupied for several years but had a rudimentary winery in the basement. The property also included 6.4 acres planted with a hodgepodge of Portuguese grapes and 264 olive trees. Luper later found a 1758 map that showed that the property received an "A" rating under the ancient Douro system, which meant that the grapes from there received the highest prices. Luper named the winery Quinta da Carolina in honor of his wife.

Production at the winery had to be limited because of the Douro regulations requiring that half the grapes be used for Port. Luper had to sell off those grapes to Port producers. Only with the rest could he make his wine. At the beginning, Luper couldn't make more than 400 cases annually, but he reminded himself that at Diamond Creek the first vintage had been only 175 cases and that some of the prized Burgundy wines have similarly low production.

"One family, one vineyard, one wine" was Luper's motto for this new passion. His goal, he said, was to make a "superpremium wine from the old vines planted with the traditional Douro varietals." Quinta da Carolina is a handcrafted wine. Grapes have to be picked manually because the vineyard is too steep for any equipment to be used. His first vintage in 1999 was made with ten grape varieties, and each grape, according to Luper, brought something to the final product. The 25 percent Tinta Barroca, for example, provided good body and mild tannins. The 20 percent Touriga Francesa gave floral and slightly herbaceous aromas. After picking, the grapes were crushed in a basket press, fermented in shallow, open, epoxy-lined tanks, and then aged for seventeen months in French, American, and Portuguese oak. The wine had a relatively high 13.9 percent alcohol. The entire 1999 harvest produced 350 cases, which he bottled on September 10, 2001, and released in late 2002.

As a blend of ten varieties of grapes, Quinta da Carolina is different from most other ultrapremium wine on the market. Its French, American, or Australian competitors are made from perhaps three or four of the same noble international grapes. Luper, though, says that the flavor profile for the Quinta da Carolina has been "tested and proven in centuries of making vintage Port." It is indeed a unique wine whose intense and complex, but different, flavors stand out in the crowded world of First Growth wannabes. Steven Spurrier, writing in the British wine magazine *Decanter,* gave Luper's first vintage high praise: "The berry fruit flavors come bursting through and the finish is long and succulent." The 1999 Quinta da Carolina was marketed in Europe and the U.S. mainly through the contacts Luper had built up from his decades in the wine business. It quickly sold out for about $50 a bottle on the U.S. East Coast.

Since that initial vintage, Luper has slowly been building a market for the first wine in a long career to carry his name. "You have to prove yourself and produce consistently high quality for several years before your wine can be called an ultrapremium and get 97 points from one of the prestigious wine magazines." He is already receiving 90-plus scores.

Puente Alto, Chile

The Rothschild clan, the first family of international finance, has always been a global enterprise. Its banking business was started in Frankfurt, Germany, in 1750 and soon developed both an English and a French wing in addition to operations in other major financial centers around the world. So it is not surprising that the family has also embraced the globalization of wine.

Château Mouton Rothschild came in second at the Spurrier tasting. A Rothschild isn't used to coming in second in anything, and soon after the event Baron Philippe de Rothschild began seriously exploring the possibility of doing a joint venture in the newly respected Napa Valley. In 1978, he invited Robert Mondavi to visit him at his château in Bordeaux. The baron gave Mondavi and his daughter Marcia the royal treatment during a tour of his winery and wine museum. The baron left nothing to chance, and the wines served at dinner in the family library included a century-old Mouton plus a bottle of the fabled 1945 Château d'Yquem.

The next morning the two men agreed to form a 50-50 partnership. The winery would be located in California and would draw on the technology and experience of both parent companies. Mondavi wrote in his memoirs that the goal was "to create a wine like no other, a great wine with its own style, character, and breeding." Rothschild and Mondavi named the winery Opus One, and the label carried the silhouette of both men, back to back. The inaugural vintage was in 1979, and the first case sold to the public went for $24,000 at the 1981 Napa Valley Wine Auction, a charity event. The wine was released to the general public in 1984 at $50 a bottle.

· After Baron Philippe's death in 1988, his daughter, the Baroness Philippine de Rothschild, took over the family business and began looking abroad to where she too could launch another joint venture and produce another wine that would gain international recognition. Her attention soon centered on Chile, a country with old ties to French winemaking and one that was beginning to produce quality wines.

As in other parts of the New World, wine followed the flag and the Roman Catholic Church to Chile. Missionaries accompanying the conquistadors encouraged grape planting to make wine for religious purposes, and the first Chilean vintage was in 1551. Early in the nineteenth century

Chile won its independence from Spain and soon after, a close relationship in wine production developed between France and Chile. Vine cuttings of the great Bordeaux grapes—Cabernet Sauvignon, Carmenère, Merlot, Sauvignon Blanc, and Sémillon—were brought to Chile, where they prospered. Many of today's leading Chilean wineries were started in the second half of the nineteenth century with French cuttings.

Chile's geographical isolation in the mid-nineteenth century turned out to be its salvation. The phylloxera epidemic never reached its distant plants, and even today most of its vineyards do not have grafted vines like those prevalent in almost all the rest of the world. The old French grape Carmenère, which was widely used in Bordeaux blends in the nineteenth century to smooth out the harshness of Cabernet Sauvignon, disappeared in France after phylloxera because it did not successfully graft. Carmenère, though, survived in Chile and is still widely grown today.

Despite Chile's French connection and old vineyards, the country's wine business remained a backwater until the last two decades. A few of its better wines were exported to Europe, but most were mediocre and consumed locally or in neighboring Latin American countries. Chile's warm and dry climate favored wine production, but the country gets little grape season rainfall and had only a primitive irrigation system that relied on snow runoff from the Andes Mountains, which form the country's long eastern border. In the international wine trade Chile was known as a producer of cheap wines with little finesse.

In addition to being isolated geographically, Chile was a political and economic outcast after the 1973 *coup d'etat* led by General Augusto Pinochet that toppled the elected leftist president Salvador Allende. After that no politically correct person in Europe or the U.S. would drink Chilean wines, no matter how attractive the price. The Pinochet government, though, introduced free-market economic reforms that removed government restrictions on business and encouraged Chilean companies to look abroad for their future expansion after identifying wine as a product with great export potential.

A renaissance started in Chilean wine in the mid-1980s and gathered force after Pinochet's rule ended in 1990 when drinking Chilean wines again became politically correct abroad. No country in the world has ever gone through such a rapid transformation of its wine sector. In the fifteen years between 1985 and 2000, Chile's vineyards and wine companies moved from the nineteenth century to the twenty-first century. With the help of foreign investment and the encouragement of the government, Chilean wineries threw away ancient equipment and imported state-of-the-art grape crushers, stainless-steel fermentation tanks, and oak barrels from Europe. For five years in a row in the 1990s, Chile was the biggest importer of European winemaking equipment. Farmers undertook a massive planting of new vineyards, pulling out low-quality grapes like País, the Chilean version of the old Mission grapes once grown widely in California, and developing new areas like the Casablanca Valley. Viticulturists put in the popular international varietals such as Cabernet Sauvignon, Chardonnay, and Merlot. Between 1985 and 1997 the area of Cabernet Sauvignon planting increased from 20,122 acres to 39,525 acres, while Chardonnay went from 605 acres to 13,747 acres and Merlot/Carmenère jumped from 2,471 acres to 14,187 acres.

While Chile's own domestic wine consumption was dropping more than 50 percent in those years, going from 9.9 gallons per capita in 1984 to 4.7 gallons in 2000, Chilean wine exports exploded. They grew from $9 million in 1984 to $267 million in 2000, and the number of foreign markets during that time went from thirty-six to ninety-five. Just as Australia before it, Chile has a laser focus on exports.

All of this would not have happened without drip irrigation, which was introduced starting in the 1980s. The country's arid conditions and primitive irrigation system had held back the growth of quality grapes for centuries. The new irrigation system opened the way to growing not only better grapes but also in areas where grapes had never been cultivated, such as the Casablanca Valley. Water from the Andes was too far away from that valley located forty-five miles west of Santiago and twenty miles east of the port city of Valparaíso. Casablanca Valley today is dotted with vineyards producing some of the country's best Chardonnays and Sauvignon Blancs.

The leader of the Chilean wine revolution was the country's largest producer, Viña Concha y Toro. Founded in 1883 by Don Melchor Concha y Toro, who imported vine cuttings from France, the company exported its first wines in 1933 and slowly became a major producer, shipping mainly to Latin American countries. Starting in the 1980s, Concha y Toro launched a program to go for both better quality wines and more exports. It began experimenting with a new top-of-the-line Cabernet Sauvignon, Don Melchor, and in 1985 sent samples to France to get the reactions of wine experts there. They were good, and the first Don Melchor was released in 1989.

In 1991, Concha y Toro started a major investment program, buying land in both Chile and Argentina and installing new equipment and increasing storage capacity. Three years later, the company raised $50 million when it became the first foreign winery to be traded on the New York

Stock Exchange. All the money was plowed back into the business, and the payoff soon followed. The company now owns more than nine thousand acres of vineyards in eighteen locations in Chile plus an additional thousand acres in Argentina. Concha y Toro exports 75 percent of its production. Its greatest market is the U.S., where it was the largest imported brand from 2000 to 2002, selling 2 million cases annually.

Foreign winemakers had started showing interest in Chile before Pinochet left power and that movement gathered force when he stepped down. Spain's Miguel Torres was the first of many Europeans to use his winemaking skills and new equipment in Chile. Several French wineries made investments, usually with local partners. Chile also became a stopping-off spot for the flying winemakers who consult around the world. The French, who seem more comfortable in a Latin country like Chile than in the Napa Valley, led the way. Bordeaux's Michel Rolland was a very active consultant at Casa Lapostolle, which was founded as a joint venture between France's Alexandra Marnier-Lapostolle, part of the Grand Marnier family, and a Chilean partner. France's Jacques Lurton consulted with Viña San Pedro, while his compatriot Jacques Boissenot worked for Veramonte, and Australia's Ron Potter was instrumental in the design of the J. Bouchon winery.

Robert Mondavi made two joint ventures with the Eduardo Chadwick family, a leader of Chilean wine. The first venture was Viña Caliterra in 1989, which in 2001 started a second label, Arboleda. The partners also launched the ultrapremium brand Seña in 1995. The Mondavis have shown particular interest in Chilean Carmenère.

With all the wine activity going on in Chile, it was natural for the Baron Philippe de Rothschild company to look closely at that country in the mid-1990s. It was also natural that Rothschild would team up with Concha y Toro, the country's largest producer. The precedent of its 50-50 deal with Mondavi had already been established. With its eighteen vineyards around Chile, Concha y Toro offered Rothschild the greatest choice of locations.

Discussions began in 1995, and the next year the two companies made a test vintage to see what they could produce together. The 643-acre Concha y Toro vineyard in Puente Alto, where grapes used in the Don Melchor wine are grown, was selected for the experiment. Concha y Toro winemakers told their Rothschild counterparts that they thought that vineyard was the best place in Chile to grow Cabernet Sauvignon grapes, which would be the backbone of the new wine. The vineyard is located in the shadow of the snow-capped Andes. According to an old Bordeaux truism, poor soil makes great wine, so Puente Alto should do well. The vineyard's soil is very rocky, with some stones the size of footballs.

The test vintage of 1996 was considered a success. The wine was not yet on a par with Mouton, but the taste of *terroir* that French winemakers always look for was clearly present. The wine had great potential, and in the right hands both sides thought it could be outstanding. A joint-venture deal was signed in 1997. As at Opus One, it would be a 50-50 partnership. The winery's name would be Almaviva after a character in *The Marriage of Figaro* by Pierre de Beaumarchais, a play that Mozart later made into an opera. A descendent of Beaumarchais was a close friend of Philippine de Rothschild. Concha y Toro brought to the joint venture ninety-nine acres of Puente Alto vineyards, and Rothschild brought its name as well as its knowledge of wine-making and connections in the wine trade. Thanks to the Rothschild pull, the new wine would be distributed through the Bordeaux *négociant* system, the first non-French wine ever to be accepted into that very private club.

With the exception of the *maître de chai,* Philippe Bujard, who had pre-viously worked for Mouton Rothschild in France, everything at Almaviva is shared in the spirit of the joint venture. There are co–general managers, one from Concha y Toro and one from Rothschild, and co-winemakers, one from each side. Rothschild had one specific request of its partners. It wanted someone from one of the two families that have controlling inter-est in Concha y Toro, the Guiliasastis and Larraíns, to have a prominent role in the new venture to assure harmony at the top. Thus Filipe Larraín is the Chilean co–general manager. Even the label for the new wine is 50-50. The names of both partners appear on it. The brand name is written in a style imitating the handwriting of Beaumarchais, and the label contains several examples of pre-Hispanic native art.

Bujard says his goal is to "make a Mouton in Chile"—a Médoc-style red wine but on the basis of Chilean *terroir*. The ninety-nine acres of vineyard that Concha y Toro gave Almaviva were eighteen years old at the time and contained nongrafted vines planted at a density of about 800 vines per acre, far less than the 3,200 vines per acre at Mouton. It was impractical to pull that vineyard out and start all over, but slowly Bujard is making changes. Almaviva has since bought 111 additional acres and has been planting grafted vines on the new property. Eventually Almaviva will have only grafted vines. Bujard thinks the quality of the grapes from such vines is bet-ter and will protect the vineyard against any future outbreak of phylloxera. Even though Chile avoided the nineteenth-century epidemic, it will likely hit the country someday since modern transportation makes the country less isolated than before. The new vineyards are also being planted at the Mou-ton density.

Harvests in the Southern Hemisphere, of course, are in April, rather than

October as they are in the Northern Hemisphere, but Bujard says the biggest difference between winemaking in Bordeaux and in Puente Alto is the climate. Almaviva enjoys steady sunshine from September to May, with less than an inch of rain during the entire growing season. Bordeaux winemakers dread rain during harvest because it can bloat grapes and dilute the natural flavors, but in arid Puente Alto rain during harvest is never a problem. Bujard irrigates the vines about twice a week from November to March, but never in the last month before picking when the grapes are ripening in the sun. Given the warm, dry climate the wine reaches a 13.5 to 14 percent level of alcohol very quickly.

The heritage of Almaviva may be ancient, but the winery is the epitome of modernity. Designed by a Chilean architect and encompassing myriad examples of native culture, the large wooden structure is packed with the latest European-made equipment. The stainless-steel tanks are from the same French producer that makes them for Mouton and Opus One. The press is of Swiss-French construction, and the five hundred aging barrels come from the same eight French producers that supply them to Mouton. During my visit to Almaviva, red lights flashed the temperatures from each tank in the fermentation room, and the spotless stainless-steel scene reminded me more of a hospital operating room than a French country winery.

The winemaking process at Almaviva is almost a carbon copy of that at Mouton, with only a few minor changes because of differing climatic conditions. Grapes are handpicked and placed in twenty-two-pound plastic boxes that are exactly like the ones used at Mouton. Just as with all classic Bordeaux red wines, Almaviva is a blend of several varietals. The amounts vary slightly from year to year depending on the weather, but the blend is generally about 75 percent Cabernet Sauvignon, 20 percent Carmenère, and 5 percent Cabernet Franc. The wine is aged in 100 percent new barrels for sixteen to eighteen months before bottling and then released two years after the vintage.

Almaviva currently produces thirteen thousand cases annually, and the wine has its largest following in France, Switzerland, Germany, Japan, and the United States. When the winery's new property is in full production in about a decade, Bujard expects it to be producing thirty thousand cases a year.

Tasted side by side, anyone would easily note differences between a Mouton Rothschild and an Almaviva, although both are excellent examples of a winemaker's artistry. A Mouton is more tannic and the flavors more intense than an Almaviva of the same vintage. To be appreciated at its fullest level of perfection, the Mouton is best enjoyed at least five years after its vintage, and perhaps even longer. The Almaviva wine, on the other hand, reaches its peak more quickly and can be enjoyed earlier.

Willamette Valley, Oregon

A Beaune Clos des Mouches from Maison Joseph Drouhin, one of the leading wineries in Burgundy, placed fifth in the Chardonnay part of the Spurrier tasting. Three years later at the Wine Olympics staged in Paris by *GaultMillau,* Drouhin got another shock from the New World. A 1975 Eyrie Vineyards Reserve Pinot Noir from Oregon caught the attention of French winemakers, although it came in only tenth in its category. By now they were familiar with wine from California, but most French winemakers were not even aware that wine was being produced in Oregon, and almost no one had ever heard of Eyrie Vineyards.

Robert Drouhin, who ran the family firm Maison Joseph Drouhin, was not as surprised as many others and took the Oregon challenge seriously. He had already been introduced to the state in 1961, when he was on a promotional tour of the West Coast to market his wines. One day his local sales representative suggested that he take a day off and visit the Willamette Valley, an area about an hour's drive southwest of Portland. Drouhin was struck by the similarity between the Red Hills region near the small town of Dundee and the area outside Beaune, where Drouhin is located. Both had gently rolling hills, and both are surrounded by two mountain ranges. In Burgundy they are the Alps and the Jura, while in Oregon they are the Cascade and Coast ranges. The amount of annual rainfall in the two places was about the same, although in Burgundy the rain is spread throughout the year while in Oregon it is largely concentrated in the winter months.

The most significant difference between the two regions, Drouhin concluded, was the soil, which to a French winemaker steeped in *terroir* was crucially important. The soil in Burgundy, for the most part, is limestone. In Oregon it is a mixture of ancient volcanic and alluvial soils left from the giant Missoula floods that swept through the area some fifteen thousand years ago during the last Ice Age. So Drouhin noted the similarities of the two places, but never thought at the time of making wine there, perhaps because no one was then doing that in Oregon.

Drouhin's interest in Oregon, though, deepened after the Wine Olympics, and he staged an informal blind tasting for some of his employees and friends between his own best Pinot Noirs and several of the new Oregon wines. The company's 1959 Grand Cru Joseph Drouhin Chambertin won first place, but only a few tenths of a point ahead of a 1975 Eyrie South Block Pinot Noir.

What was Eyrie Vineyards? The story by now had a familiar ring. Its owner David Lett, who had grown up on a farm near Salt Lake City, had studied enology at the University of California, Davis, worked for Lee Stewart at Souverain Cellars, and then spent a year in France learning more about his passion: Pinot Noir. After returning to the U.S., Lett concluded that the temperatures in California's wine country were too hot for Burgundy-style wines, so he headed north to the cooler Willamette Valley, where he started his winery in 1966. A year later he planted the first Pinot Noir in the valley. Lett seemed to have discovered something that overcame the differences in soil that bothered Drouhin during his 1961 visit.

At the time of Drouhin's Pinot Noir tasting, his daughter Véronique was studying enology at the University of Dijon. When she graduated in 1986, Véronique asked her father if he could arrange to get her an internship in California. She knew Burgundy well, having grown up there, and had already had an internship in Bordeaux, so she was interested in going to a New World winery. Her father said that he could easily get her a summer job at the Robert Mondavi Winery or Beringer Vineyards in the Napa Valley, but suggested that she go to Oregon, where he thought the best Pinot Noir outside Burgundy might someday be made. Drouhin's local distributor arranged for Véronique to spend the 1986 harvest at three top Oregon wineries—Eyrie, Adelsheim, and Bethel Heights.

Both the quality of the wines she found in Oregon and the openness of the local winemakers impressed her, as they did her father when he visited during her stay. Oregon winemakers quickly realized that their credibility would be greatly increased if a Burgundy winemaker with the renown of Drouhin were to begin making wine there. For his part, Robert Drouhin was open to the idea of starting a winery in Oregon because of the limited possibilities he had for expansion in Burgundy, where good vineyard land rarely comes up for sale and when it does the price is usually astronomical. If he wanted to expand, he would have to do it outside France, and the wine potential of Oregon since that initial visit in 1961 had always intrigued him. Before leaving Oregon that summer of 1986, Drouhin told some local winemakers to let him know if any good property came on the market.

Things began to move quickly. In the early summer of 1987, Drouhin received a phone call from David Adelsheim of the Adelsheim Vineyard, telling him that some interesting property was indeed now on the market. It was located near David Lett's vineyards and perhaps had great potential for making Burgundy style wines. Lett already had enough property and wasn't interested in buying it.

A month later, Drouhin went to Oregon to attend the second annual International Pinot Noir Celebration and to inspect the property. He liked what he saw. The land was located on a gently rolling hill facing southeast—just as in Burgundy. The difference in soil, though, was still an issue. Drouhin was intimately familiar with Burgundy's limestone, but this was entirely new *terroir* to him. Drouhin walked the land, looked over all the vegetation, and had soil samples analyzed. Finally, in late 1987, he wrote the check to buy 225 acres that had previously been covered with Christmas trees, hazelnut trees, and wheat.

At the conclusion of her studies, Véronique arrived in the Willamette Valley as the winemaker for the new Domaine Drouhin Oregon. Realizing it would take several years to get their own vineyards into production, she bought Pinot Noir grapes in 1988 and produced a first vintage at a nearby winery.

At the same time, the Drouhin family began to design and build a winery and vineyard from scratch. In contrast to Burgundy, where land is at a premium, the new Oregon property stretched out as well as down into the ground. A decade earlier Drouhin had built a new winery in Burgundy, and he used what had been learned there for the new four-floor, gravity-flow structure in Oregon.

Véronique's older brother, Philippe, who oversees the vineyards for all the family company's properties, directed the planting, which soon totaled seventy-eight acres of Pinot Noir. The viticulture department at the University of Burgundy in Dijon had been developing the so-called Dijon clones from the best Burgundy vineyards, and in 1990 those were brought into the U.S. through Oregon State University at Corvallis. Until that point French clones had always been brought into the U.S. via the University of California at Davis, but the Drouhins were anxious to show their support for the Oregon university. They eventually imported a total of eight Pinot Noir clones and three Chardonnay ones.

The vineyard is very much Burgundian in style, with a much higher acreage density than other Oregon wineries. The Drouhin vineyard has 3,100 plants to the acre, about twice that of other local wineries although still not as dense as in Burgundy. The goal is to force plants to drive their roots deep into the soil, where they can capture the most minerals and produce the best wines. The vines are also pruned lower to the ground than is the custom in American vineyards. Drip irrigation was installed in the vineyard and was used for the first three years to get the new vines started. But since then, there has been no irrigation. Watering vines is outlawed in Burgundy, and Drouhin believes dry farming will also eventually produce better wines in Oregon.

The original business plan was to grow only Pinot Noir at Domaine Drouhin Oregon, but in view of the popularity in the United States of Burgundy's other great grape, the company planted twelve acres of Chardonnay. Oregon vintners had faced problems with the widely used Davis 108 clone, which was developed for California's warm weather and produces fruit that ripens late in the season but was inappropriate for Oregon's climate. The University of Dijon clones, however, have worked much better in Oregon than the Davis one.

The biggest challenge facing Véronique Drouhin is to discover which sections of the Oregon property can produce the best wine, a process of *terroir* study, she says, that could easily take another thirty years. To help speed the research along, small blocks of grapes are picked and fermented separately. The vineyard has been divided into thirty-two blocks, and each has its own fermenting tank, so there is no mixing of grapes or wines. Other wineries would have far fewer fermenting tanks, but Drouhin says the extra equipment is necessary so that the staff can study the product from each block of land more closely.

While American winemakers embraced the use of French oak in the 1960s, Drouhin Oregon uses oak modestly. Barrels are used for six years, meaning that only about 16 percent of the wine is aged each year in new barrels. Chardonnay is aged about nine months in barrels, while Pinot Noir is aged one year. The cellar is kept at a constant temperature of 55 degrees and 85 percent humidity. The Chardonnay is stored in a separate section of the cellar, where the temperature is slightly higher.

Domaine Drouhin Oregon now produces annually about 15,000 cases of wine. Pinot Noir makes up about 85 percent of output, of which 10,000 cases are labeled Willamette Valley Pinot Noir. As befitting a family business, Véronique has named three of her most prized wines after her children. In 1992, she produced her first vintage of Laurène Pinot Noir, named after her first daughter, which is made from a selection of the ten best vineyard blocks. Only 2,000 cases are bottled each year. Louise Pinot Noir, named after her second daughter, is even more selective, coming from the eight best barrels of the year and producing 200 cases. The first vintage of Louise was 1999, and with it Véronique is trying to create a wine that approaches the quality of Burgundy's Chambolle-Musigny, her favorite wine. Willamette Pinot Noir is released two years after vintage, while Laurène and Louise are released after three years. Drouhin also produces

2,000 cases of Chardonnay, which is named Arthur in honor of Véronique's only son. It is released one year after vintage.

About 80 percent of Domaine Drouhin Oregon's production is sold in the U.S., with a large share of the rest going to Japan, Britain, and Canada. A small amount is shipped back to France, where it is sold as a novelty by the large wine chain Nicolas.

Véronique Drouhin spends about three months of the year in Oregon, with the biggest concentration of time in the fall during harvest and wine-making. Throughout that always tiring, always tense time of year, she can be seen on the first and second levels of the winery with folder in hand, carefully keeping track of the progress of the wines. She writes a large letter *P* on the tank's control sheet when it's time to punch down the cap, a hard crust of skins and seeds that forms during fermentation.

The goal of Véronique Drouhin is to produce in Oregon the same style wine that made her family famous in Burgundy. She eschews the powerful wines popular with some local winemakers. Her Oregon Pinot Noir, however, has a spicier taste with more black fruit flavors—black cherry, black currant—than Drouhin's Burgundy counterpart. The alcohol level rises more quickly in Oregon, and only once since she started making wines there—in the wet 1997—did she have to chaptalize or add sugar to the must to increase the alcohol level. Chaptalization is much more common in Burgundy. Drouhin says her Oregon wines today are closest to Burgundy's Vosne-Romanée.

"Elegance" is a word Drouhin uses frequently when talking about her wines. When I noted after tasting her Chardonnay that the oak flavors were subtle, she replied with a sly smile, "I take that as a compliment."

CHAPTER TWENTY-FOUR

France Revisited

Wine makes every meal an occasion, every table more elegant, every day more civilized.

—ANDRÉ SIMON

At 3–5 Boulevard de la Madeleine in the heart of the right bank in Paris, and only a few hundred yards from where Steven Spurrier's Caves de la Madeleine used to be located, is Lavinia. In the jargon of the American retail trade, it is a category-killer store like Home Depot or Toys 'R' Us, a place that stocks an exhaustive offering of products in the store's particular field and thus dominates that market niche. Lavinia has everything to do with wine.

The airy shop with lots of space around product displays carries some 3,000 French wines, 2,000 wines from forty-two other countries, plus 1,000 kinds of brandies, whiskeys, and other spirits. There's also a bookstore with volumes on wine in several languages, an exhaustive collection of corkscrews and other ways to open a wine bottle, plus glasses of every size and shape. The price of wines starts at less than $4 a bottle, and the wines come from not only all of the world's major producers but also such unexpected places as Cuba and South Dakota. Lavinia has fifteen sommeliers on staff to help customers make their selection. In the cellar, which is precisely maintained at 57 degrees and 70 percent humidity, the most prized wines are kept behind a locked gate. There can be found a six-liter bottle of 1991 Romanée-Conti Pinot Noir selling for €36,000 ($47,000), or a standard-sized bottle of Bryant Family Vineyard Napa Valley Cabernet Sauvignon at €1,097.92 ($1,430). Visitors can buy a bottle of wine and then enjoy it—without any markup—in the Lavinia restaurant. The eatery also has a daily luncheon special with a recommended wine to accompany it, and the wine bar offers wine by the glass. And just as at Steven Spurrier's old place, wine-appreciation courses are also available. Lavinia epitomizes the globalization of wine and the range of offerings available to today's oenophile.

The presence of this international wine superstore in the heart of Paris also exemplifies today's changing French wine scene.

As part of my tour of the world's major wine regions, I also returned to France. I met winemakers and policymakers and spent nearly a week at Bordeaux's Vinexpo, the biannual bash of the international wine business. The picture that emerged was of a country thrown on the defensive in the domain it once dominated. A quarter century after the Paris Tasting, all those wines on display at Lavinia are challenging France, now just one of many countries making outstanding wine. France has been forced to fight to hold on to its traditional markets in Britain and the United States. France today retains many strengths, but it is now struggling and worried about its own wine future.

The first two decades after the Paris Tasting, however, were a period of unprecedented prosperity for French wine. A new generation of consumers around the world was enjoying ever-higher standards of living and making wine an integral part of its affluent lifestyle. Huge new markets in wealthy countries like the United States, Japan, and Canada were discovering wine, and they turned to France for quality. The Italians or Spanish or even those new upstart Californians might make wine, but when the new wine drinkers wanted a show-off bottle they looked to France, especially to Bordeaux's classified growths and Grand Cru Burgundy wines.

The 1982 vintage in Bordeaux and the growing popularity of Robert Parker and his publication *The Wine Advocate* that had been started four years earlier set off a boom in French wines. Parker called the 1982 Bordeaux the "vintage of the century" and rated many of the wines in the high 90s using his 100-point scoring system. Consumers immediately rushed out to get their share of the great wines.

All the planets were aligned for Bordeaux during the 1980s. In addition to the new Parker effect, the dollar was strong, making French wines attractive buys for Americans, and the weather cooperated to produce several great vintages during the decade. In this golden period for Bordeaux, newly prosperous winemakers doubled the size of vineyards in only twenty years.

The 1980s were also a period of great technical progress in French wine, especially in the vineyards, where new and improved growing techniques were introduced. Just as California winemakers looked to research centers at UC Davis and Fresno State to help them make better wines, French winemakers turned more and more to their own wine institutes in Bordeaux, Dijon, and Montpellier for training and innovative research. Bordeaux's Émile Peynaud had a significant impact on French winemaking in the second half of the twentieth century, although not as great as Davis professors had on the American wine scene. While the Americans knew they were amateurs and readily accepted help, many French winemakers were confident in their traditions and disinclined to take recommendations from a professor. French wine for centuries was largely made by a world of peasants, with the exception of the few noble houses at the top. In the 1980s many of those peasants, though, were sending their children to school to learn the technical side of a craft that previously had offered little academic training.

Domaine Comte Senard in Burgundy is typical of that changing French winery. The property has been in the Senard family for seven generations, but the current owner Philippe was the first member to have a formal wine education, which he obtained at the viticulture institute in Beaune. "The wisdom of the ages was passed along to the next generation, but the mistakes were also," Senard told me. His daughter Lorraine, who is now making the white wines at the *domaine* and will eventually take over the winery, also studied at Beaune.

New French wine consultants also appeared on the scene in the 1980s to help winemakers. The most famous of these is Bordeaux's Michel Rolland. Born in 1947, his family owned Château Bon Pasteur in Pomerol, where he went to work at an early age. Later Rolland expanded the family holdings in Bordeaux and built up a laboratory and consulting business that has worked with more than a hundred wineries from Chile to South Africa with stops along the way in the Napa Valley. Acting as a critic as well as a coach, he visits each winery several times a year at the most crucial times of harvesting and fermentation.

Innovation flowed from the institutes and consultants into French vineyards and cellars. A better understanding of grape clones and soil structure led to higher yields, while growers learned to thin out their crops to increase the flavor intensity of the remaining grapes. Following Rolland's strictures, growers left fruit longer on the vine. In the winery new stainless-steel tanks, pneumatic presses, and innovative bottling units replaced outdated equipment. A new emphasis was also placed on hygiene, and once straw-strewn wine cellars were now spotless.

Perhaps the most important effect of all those changes was a new consistency in French vintages. In the old days the vagaries of French weather and the limited technical skills of winemakers meant that there might be only two great vintages in a decade. Better vineyard management as well as new winemaking techniques and equipment now made it possible for French winemakers to rescue the lesser vintages, while still enjoying the great years when nature smiled on the French countryside.

In the 1980s, an important movement toward ecological viticulture also gained momentum. Known as biodynamics, its advocates, such as Nicolas Joly in the Loire Valley and Olivier Zind-Humbrecht in Alsace, rebelled against excessive use of insecticides, artificial fertilizers, and herbicides in favor of organic farming. Practitioners interfere as little as possible with nature. Only small amounts of organic material such as manure and composts are used to stimulate growth or control insects. French viticulturists today openly admit that in the early decades after World War II their predecessors overused the newly available artificial fertilizers. The man-made products left behind harmful residues that required years of remediation to rid them from the soil. While only a few French winemakers practice biodynamics in its most extreme form, the vast majority of French wineries now adheres to what they call "reasonable biodynamics" and follow its broad tenets at least to some degree. A few French wineries market themselves as pure organics, and at Vinexpo there was a small section devoted to organic wines.

The French during this time also became more open to what was happening outside their country. Christian Vannequé, one of the judges at the Paris Tasting, told me that the event "made French winemakers more modest and they began looking at themselves differently." Steven Spurrier has said his tasting actually had a greater impact on France than it did on California because it was a "wake-up call."

The leaders of some large estates like the famed Domaine de la Romanée-Conti had already been aware before the Paris Tasting that work needed to be done in France's vineyards, but now other wineries were more prepared to accept non-French ideas. In November 1982, Domaine Guy Roulot, whose Meursault Charmes had come in second at Paris, did something that would have been unthinkable only a few years earlier. It hired Ted Lemon, an American winemaker! Jean-Marc Roulot, who was taking over the Domaine from his father who had died suddenly of cancer, had already learned something of what was happening outside France during an apprenticeship at the Joseph Phelps Vineyards in the Napa Valley. Lemon, though, knew both California wine from a harvest spent at Calera, a winery in the Gavilan Mountains south of San Francisco, and also French wine from studying enology at the University of Dijon and working at Burgundian wineries. Lemon stayed at Roulot for two years before moving back to California and eventually opening up his own Littorai Wines, which has vineyards in western Sonoma and western Mendocino counties.

The style of many French wines changed during this time and became more aligned with international wine norms. For French reds this meant bigger, bolder, fruitier wines with sometimes a higher alcohol content than the traditional 12.5 percent. Most French reds are now ready to be drunk shortly after release, which is two years after the vintage. In the nineteenth century, it was nothing for a great Bordeaux to need an unbelievable 50 years in the bottle before it was considered ready to be consumed. Even in the 1960s, great wines were expected to be aged in the bottle for a decade, if not longer. Today's consumers, especially in New World markets, are impatient and will simply not accept tannin-heavy wines that still need several years of bottle aging to mature. For French white wines, especially Chardonnays, the new style meant a stronger oak taste and perhaps leaving some residual sugar in the bottle. Both of these characteristics had previously been anathema to French white-wine vintners.

Then in the mid-1990s came roaring out of Bordeaux's St.-Émilion the *garagistes,* a group of innovative and irreverent winemakers who were not satisfied to just do things the way they had always been done. Instead of working out of ancient châteaux covered with ivy and steeped in tradition, they operated in unpretentious environs, often even in garages. The *garagistes* ran very small wineries that annually produced perhaps 250 cases of handcrafted wine. Often they practiced their art in vineyards that had not been previously noted for producing great wine. These perfectionists, though, performed miracles by carefully watching every step of the winemaking process and treating their product as the nectar of the gods. In the winter they pruned their vines severely to reduce the number of grape bunches. In the summer as the grapes began maturing they pulled individual leaves off the vines to expose the fruit to the sun. They left the fruit on the vine much longer than normal in order to eke out as much flavor as possible. At the last conceivable moment, and shortly before the grapes might begin to turn to raisins, they handpicked the crop, discarding any inferior or damaged fruit. The process was completed with plenty of aging in new oak barrels.

The result was very concentrated, darkly colored, and deeply flavored wine. Because the production was usually very small, garage wines are generally very expensive and they are often hard to find in stores. Robert Parker became a huge fan of the *garagistes* and regularly gave them high marks. He called La Mondotte "the ultimate garage wine" and described it as "ultraconcentrated, frightfully expensive, and worth every cent." He routinely ranked Mondotte wines in the high 90s.

Not everyone—not even some French winemakers—liked these new-style wines. Philippe Senard, for example, complained that many Burgundy wines are no longer as "subtle and delicate" as they used to be. Marc Beyer, whose Alsatian winery Maison Léon Beyer has been handed down from father to son since 1580, told me that some winemakers were using so much oak that they drove out the natural fruit tastes. He said that slightly sweet wines might score high in tastings but do not go well with food. Many French winemakers said privately that they worried about the impact Parker has had on French wine, although they would never say anything in public. Parker was criticized in particular for his high praise of the *garagistes*. A Parker-style wine, though, resembles in many aspects the Michel Rolland–style of wine, and the international wine-drinking public has shown clearly that it likes the big Parker/Rolland wines.

French wine got another enormous publicity boost on November 17, 1991, when the CBS news magazine *60 Minutes* broadcast a segment entitled "The French Paradox." It recounted how the French, despite their diet heavy in cheese, cream, and fatty foods like duck, have much lower levels of heart disease than Americans. How can you explain this paradox? Reporter Morley Safer answered with scientific research that had found a correlation between drinking red wine and low heart disease.

The cry could almost be heard across America: "*Voila!* I'll drink to that!" Americans who might have thought that wine was bad for them now saw that it might actually make them healthier. U.S. imports of French red wine soared 30 percent shortly after the broadcast. The French wine industry jumped all over the French Paradox, financing new research in countries as far flung as Scandinavia and Chile to substantiate the earlier conclusions that moderate wine consumption, especially of red wine, is beneficial to your health.

Starting in the late 1990s, however, the French wine business began running into trouble. As Jean-Luc Dairien, the general manager of Onivins, the French Wines Council, told me, "French winemakers, sitting on their little cloud and not worrying about what the world was doing, had fallen behind."

The clearest cause of concern has been changing French drinking habits. France has always been its own biggest customer. At the beginning of World War II, French soldiers had a ration of a liter (1.06 quarts) of wine per day, and for centuries during harvest workers were given a bottle of wine each day. Annual per capita French wine consumption peaked in 1926 at 35.9 gallons. But today the average French adult drinks less than 13 gallons per year and the number keeps falling. Wine no longer plays such a central role in the country that so identifies with it. While taking a cab to visit a winery in Beaune, the heart of Burgundy, I got to talking with the driver, who told me that he and his family no longer drink wine every day. Wine, he said, was now mainly for Sundays and holidays. Even Burgundians are not supporting their own business the way they once did.

The biggest drop-off has been in red table wine called *"gros rouge qui tâche"* or "big red that stains," which got its name from the red marks it left on tablecloths and anything else it touched. This reflects social change taking place in France. The number of hard-drinking blue-collar workers and peasants has been declining, while the number of office workers has been increasing. I remember from my time living in France in the 1970s how armies of workmen wearing blue manual laborer's jackets walked up to the bar in cafés and brasseries around France several times a day to order *"un ballon rouge,"* the slang expression for a large, balloon-shaped glass of red wine. Today the sons of those workers may be white-collar executives and are more likely to order a draft beer in a nearby bistro. Studies show that young people in the country that epitomizes wine now regard it as old-fashioned—something that belongs to their parents' generation.

In the decade of the 1990s, total French consumption of wine dropped just 2 percent, but the decline in the lower-quality wines that are drunk daily was much more severe, falling 19 percent. The number of French people drinking wine daily or almost daily fell from 46.9 percent in 1980 to 23.5 percent in 2000. And people in their early sixties are four times more likely to drink wine daily than those in their early thirties.

Some wine officials try to find solace in the fact that on average the French are drinking better wines. *Boire Moins, Boire Mieux* (Drink Less, Drink Better) has become the mantra of French optimists who hope that the business can make up in quality what it is losing in quantity. The higher-quality wines governed by the Appellation d'Origine Contrôlée system accounted for only 14 percent of domestic sales in 1950 but are nearly 50 percent today.

Fierce global wine competition centers around several price points: at the low-end, under-$10-a-bottle market, at the $10-to-$20 level and at above $50 a bottle. At the top end, France remains strong. Bordeaux's Château Latour or Château Lafite as well as leading Burgundies like Romanée-Conti or Chevalier-Montrachet and Rhône Valley's Hermitage or Côte Rôtie are able to demand—and get—high prices. With a large and growing world of wine consumers and the limited supply from those often very small, storied vineyards, those wines will always be scarce and expensive. But the classified wines make up only 5 percent of total Bordeaux production, and France cannot have a healthy wine business based solely on icon wines.

France, at the same time, is very poorly positioned at the low end, where it has to compete not only with European countries such as Italy and Spain but also with New World mass marketers from Australia or Chile. They all have both the favorable weather and now the production facilities to turn out huge volumes of inexpensive wines.

The most important part of the global market, where the coming battle in international wines will be fought, is in the $10-to-$20 range. New consumers in that segment reside largely in non-European countries where the market has been growing rapidly. These people are affluent and willing to pay more for quality wine, and if a producer can capture them at this point they are likely to stay with that company as they move up to still higher-priced wines. Australia's Penfolds and Chile's Concha y Toro have built powerful brands that are known throughout the world for offering a broad array of wines at a wide range of prices. They have become formidable competitors to the French in international markets where consumers tend to have little national loyalty.

By 2004, with both domestic consumption and exports continuing to fall, the French wine business was in a state of crisis. That year French exports declined in value by some 10 percent over the previous year, while Bordeaux sales abroad dropped some 25 percent. In the summer of 2004, the French government almost simultaneously put out a White Paper entitled "French Viticulture: The Role and Place of Wine in Society" and adopted several measures that would have been unthinkable only a few years before, to make French wines more competitive both at home and abroad. The White Paper was an academic treatise on the place of wine in French culture, describing it as "part of our history, our identity, our civilization." The paper proposed, among many other things, defining wine as a food as a way to get around laws that ban the advertising of alcoholic beverages. At nearly the same time, the French Agriculture Ministry changed several wine regulations, although none involving *appellation* wines. These made it possible for Vins de Pays wines, for example, to use inexpensive wood chips to add flavor, like the Australians do, rather than costly oak barrels. The ministry also allowed winemakers to make labels more consumer friendly.

While the White Paper signaled that France is focusing on its troubled wine industry, it is questionable whether these modest measures will be enough to bring back domestic and foreign consumption of French wines to their former levels. Looking out at the very competitive international wine scene, the French have many obstacles to overcome just to hold onto the market positions they now enjoy.

One of the largest hurdles is that the French are, in a sense, competing against themselves. The world has adopted France's noble grapes such as

Chardonnay and Cabernet Sauvignon. Consumers looking for a good Chardonnay can buy the Burgundy original or an Australian or California version, often at a better price for similar quality. In the Cabernet Sauvignon market they can buy a French First Growth or perhaps a Super Tuscan, Italy's answer to red Bordeaux. I personally believe that New Zealand today makes the world's best Sauvignon Blanc and Australia now sets the international standard for Syrah/Shiraz.

As they struggle to compete, France's winemakers are held back by the excessive regulations of the Appellation d'Origine Contrôlée system. In today's fiercely competitive markets, producers must be flexible and ready to adapt quickly to changing situations. The *garagistes* in recent years have introduced many innovative new products and procedures, but those developments took place outside the *appellation* rules. Indeed, it was done in direct opposition to them. More flexibility in the types of grapes that can be grown or greater use of irrigation are not going to be the downfall of the country's wine culture. They could even improve it. But French winemakers looking to experiment are locked in an often-archaic system, which the government stubbornly remains reluctant to overhaul.

When it comes to marketing, the French are handicapped by their confusing wine names that international consumers find difficult to pronounce and nearly impossible to remember. While millions of people around the world know the expensive wine stars like Château Latour, they are lost among more affordable wines in a morass of Château This and Château That. Christian Moueix, owner of the prestigious Château Pétrus, notes that in Bordeaux alone there are 14 Châteaux Belairs and 151 châteaux with Figeac in their names. There are no less than fifty-seven *appellations* in Bordeaux, but consumers in Chicago or Singapore are unlikely to know more than the most famous two or three.

The U.S. market provides a good example of how quickly France can lose its market position because it lacks strong brands. In the early 1990s, five French labels were among the top twenty-five American wine imports. Now only three remain—Georges Duboeuf, Barton & Guestier and Louis Jadot—and even they are slipping toward the bottom of the list. Between 1994 and 2004, France's share of the U.S. market for imports fell from 26 percent to 14 percent, while the Australian slice jumped from 5 percent to 31 percent. As one French export expert told me in June 2005, France is now considered *"le has-been."*

Charles de Gaulle once quipped, "How can anyone govern a nation that has 246 different kinds of cheese?" Today one might wonder how France can be a major exporter of wine when it has 35,000 independent producers. A study done by the national wine group Onivins found that 72 percent of French people over the age of fourteen found it "difficult to choose a wine." If even the French can't keep their wines straight, pity the rest of the world.

French winemakers and export officials alike complain that their country will continue to slip behind in that race for the $10-to-$20 market unless they have a big company's financial resources to invest in marketing and brand building. Establishing an international brand is an expensive endeavor where only very big companies can compete. Jacques Berthomeau, a special advisor to the French agricultural minister, in 2001 published a controversial report urging the French government to foster the development of one or more global companies that would be able to build international wine brands. France has several billion-dollar companies in the wine business, including Pernod Ricard, LVMH, and the Castel Group, but none of them has developed the international brands that Berthomeau saw as essential to success in today's global wine trade. As he said ruefully, "While we philosophize, our competitors sell."

Although French companies have had difficulty building wine brands below the trophy wines, it's not impossible. Starting in the 1960s, Baron Philippe de Rothschild used his famous Mouton name to create the inexpensive Mouton Cadet brand. Although sales have slipped in the U.S., Rothschild still sells some 1 million cases of red, white, and rosé Mouton Cadet annually around the world. French companies have built strong brands in Champagne (Moët & Chandon and Taittinger) and Cognac (Hennessy and Remy Martin). In addition, France has major brands in the world market for both yogurt (Danone, sold as Dannon in America) and bottled water (Perrier). In the latter two cases French companies virtually created the global market for national products, taking brands that had grown up in France to the world. So clearly the French know how to build strong brands.

Another French problem in the global marketplace is the country's vulnerability to international political winds. French wine is easy to boycott since there are now many good wines from other countries on store shelves. In October 1995, when French President Jacques Chirac resumed nuclear testing in the South Pacific, the antinuclear group Greenpeace led a worldwide boycott of French wine. Eventually France ended the tests, and Greenpeace claimed it was because of its actions.

After the diplomatic conflict between the Bush Administration and Chirac in the walkup to the American war in Iraq starting in 2003, a spontaneous U.S. boycott of French wines broke out, and French wine exports were reported to have slumped by 50 percent in early 2003. In the spring, Robert Parker decided not to go to Bordeaux for the first tasting of the 2002 vintage. His explanation was that the war made travel more dangerous, while some thought it was in protest to French policy on the war. Wine insiders also speculated that he didn't want to comment on the disappointing 2002 vintage.

A detailed statistical study published at the Website www.liquidasset.com showed that the American boycott was much less effective than had been first believed. Moreover, much of the drop could have been caused by the declining value of the dollar against the euro, which made French exports to the U.S. more expensive. Nonetheless, the danger of boycott always remains a threat to French wine producers, and their exports to the U.S. fell significantly in both 2003 and 2004.

Finally, France is a high-cost producer in a very price-sensitive global business. French winemakers have a hard time competing in the low-cost part of the market against their counterparts in Chile and other countries because of France's high wages and generous social benefits. These make it more expensive to produce in France what is basically a very labor-intensive agricultural product.

While the decline of French wines, particularly in export markets, is a cause of great concern in Paris, France and its winemakers still retain substantial advantages in the global wine game.

The most important is the continuing ability of French vintners to be creative, despite the restrictions of the *appellation* system. Much of the recent innovation is happening outside the traditional bastions of Bordeaux and Burgundy. Languedoc-Roussillon, an area that stretches along France's Mediterranean coast from the foothills of the Pyrenees on the Spanish border to the mouth of the Rhône River, has been a particularly exciting region in recent years. Once a producer of outstanding wine, the area's winemakers in the early twentieth century made the mistake of switching their focus from quality to quantity and began concentrating on the market for *gros rouge qui tâche*. In the days when Algeria was part of France, Algerian wine was often blended with southern French wine to bulk up the taste of thin domestic products. By the 1970s, Languedoc-Roussillon was economically in decline and winemakers were in the streets demanding help from Paris. But as Jean-Luc Dairien of Onivins explains, "Difficulties make people intelligent."

French regulators in 1979 established basic rules for the new category of Vins de Pays, with the most important and largest group being the Vins de Pays d'Oc covering Languedoc-Roussillon. Winemakers made the most of the new category, and the wines they began producing are well placed in the low- and moderate-priced end of the market.

One of the big hits in the U.S. market from Languedoc-Roussillon goes under the unseemly name Fat Bastard. It's an Anglo-French project between Guy Anderson, a British marketer, and Thierry Boudinaud, a French wine-maker, and their first names are on the label. The company was started in 1995 with the goal of selling varietal wines from Languedoc-Roussillon in foreign markets. In its first year in business Boudinaud made an impressive, buttery Chardonnay that Anderson dared to compare to Burgundy's famous Bâtard-Montrachet. Using a bilingual pun, Boudinaud called it a "fat bastard of a Montrachet," a name that stuck when a British importer bought the first batch. The initial vintage was only eight hundred cases, but sales to the American market soon exploded. When Anderson and company had trouble with U.S. retailers because of the name, they said it was supposed to have a French pronunciation—Fat Bas-tarrrd. They also came up with the apocryphal story printed on the label stating that the name came from "the British expression describing a particularly rich and full wine."

No matter how you pronounce it, Fat Bastard has been a great success in the entry-level U.S. market at about $8 a bottle. It was soon selling 450,000 cases annually of Chardonnay and Syrah in the U.S. and began exporting Merlot in 2004. Anderson told me that he had concluded that name recall is the biggest problem in the wine business, especially for French wines. "Even if people love a French wine, they can't remember its name," he said. "Our solution was a daft name for a very good product."

Another interesting international collaboration out of Languedoc-Roussillon is Red Bicyclette, which got off to a strong start when it went on sale in the U.S. in the summer of 2004. The wine is a joint venture of California's Gallo and Sieur d'Arques, a wine cooperative that earlier made wines for Baron Philippe de Rothschild that sold under the label Baron'arques. The first Red Bicyclette wines were Vins de Pays Chardonnay, Merlot, and Syrah specifically tailored to the American palate. The grape varieties are prominently positioned on a colorful yellow label showing a Frenchman riding a red bike. The wines all sell for less than $10. The name Gallo is not to be found on the bottle, but the company's goal is for Red Bicyclette to be the top French wine import by 2006.

The Vins de Pays category has been so successful that even Bordeaux winemakers are considering establishing their own Vins de Pays as a way of making it easier for consumers to find their way through the thicket of labels. While waiting for that to happen, the Bordeaux Chamber of Commerce in June 2003 reclassified the Crus Bourgeois, those lesser wines below the 1855 classification of Grands Crus Classés. It was the first change in the

Bourgeois ranking since 1932, and it was hoped that consumers would start looking for Cru Bourgeois on a wine label just as they now look for the Grand Cru Classé marking. The wines were put in three categories: Cru Bourgeois Exceptionnel, Cru Bourgeois Supérieur, and simply Cru Bourgeois. Only 9 wines made it into the top ranking, while 87 were listed in the second and 151 qualified for the third. All the wines come from the Médoc region of Bordeaux. At the same time, 243 wines were dropped from the Cru Bourgeois list, making the classification more selective and reliable than it had been before.

In the absence of a giant French company marketing its wines, the country's regions are promoting their area's products. Bordeaux has the biggest advertising budget, and its ads stress the good life of drinking Bordeaux wine, with a significant appeal to female drinkers. The level of spending, though, is insignificant on a world marketing scale. Bordeaux spends only about twice as much for promotion in the British market as California's Gallo alone spends there. Rhône Valley wines have also launched successful regional promotions. In addition, many of its Syrah wines have benefited from the popularity in the U.S. of Australian Shiraz. Regional brand building, though, has only limited effect and is not a long-term solution to France's problem.

The global wine business is developing in two directions at the same time, and France is in a good position to take advantage of that if it can make its wines simpler for consumers to understand and appreciate. On the one hand, there will be global companies offering good wines at a very competitive price/quality ratio. Languedoc-Roussillon and Côte du Rhône wines do well in that market segment. On the other hand, though, hand-crafted wines will appeal to the small but affluent segment of the market, an area where France already excels. As the generation of New World wine drinkers matures, they will move beyond the familiar Cabernet Sauvignon and Chardonnay that were their introduction to wine. When they do, France will be able to offer them a broad selection of interesting wines.

A company like E. Guigal in the Rhône Valley village of Ampuis may show the way for France to be more competitive at both ends of the international wine market. Guigal is a relatively new company by French standards, having been started only in 1946 by Etienne Guigal. His son Marcel now runs the firm, which has grown rapidly to become the largest producer of Côte Rôtie wine. The family-owned company's singular achievement has been its ability to sell a range of both popularly priced and expensive wines. Winemaker Marcel Guigal has attracted an international following with a style that resembles the *garagistes* and combines late harvests and the heavy use of oak. For its mass-market products Guigal buys grapes from more than four hundred Rhône Valley grape growers, but at the same time he carefully cultivates small vineyards in Condrieu and Côte Rôtie for premium products. Guigal makes some of the world's most expensive wines, and three from the 1999 vintage (Côte Rôtie La Landonne, Côte Rôtie La Mouline, and Côte Rôtie La Turque) won rare 100-point ratings from Robert Parker, who has called Marcel Guigal "the greatest winemaker on the planet." The retail prices of Guigal wines range from less than $10 to more than $350 a bottle. The winery has been carefully building a strong brand and its wines are found in many American wine stores.

Finally, no country can match France's wine infrastructure. Even its old European rivals in Italy or Spain do not have as much technical, financial, and human capital as France does in the wine business. The New World producers totally pale in comparison to France. That bench strength makes France a formidable competitor.

It is no longer good enough, however, for France just to make great wine. It now has to do a better job of marketing and selling its products to a world awash in good and inexpensive wine. Arnaud Lesgourgues, whose family owns Laubade Et Domaines Associés, an Armanac producer that is now trying to break into the U.S. market with a line of Château Cadillac Club wines, told me at the big Bordeaux wine show Vinexpo in June 2005, "In order to make a successful wine today, you must start with a good wine, but then also have a good marketing plan and a good distribution network." Thousands and thousands of small French producers, however, lack both marketing plans and distribution networks.

CHAPTER TWENTY-FIVE

Napa Valley Revisited

A bottle of wine begs to be shared; I have never met a miserly wine lover.

—CLIFTON FADIMAN

The last stop on my tour of the wine world was in California, where this whole story began. The most striking development there since the Paris Tasting is the growth of wine from an almost cottage industry into a $45 billion business that employs 200,000 people. There are now some 1,700 California wineries and 4,500 grape growers. At the time of the Spurrier event, virtually all California wineries were located within a sixty-mile radius of San Francisco. But today a string of wineries can be found from Santa Barbara to Mendocino County five hundred miles north. Some adventurous winemakers are even working in near-desert conditions close to San Diego on the Mexican border. While almost all of the land that can be cultivated has been planted in the Napa Valley, new vineyards have been going into areas like San Luis Obispo and Clarksburg. Today's young successors to the new breed of winemakers who came to California in the 1960s are to be found in those wine-frontier areas, where land is still affordable. The stories of the new winemakers working there reminded me of people like Joe Heitz or Rodney Strong of a generation ago. The newcomers are trying out different grapes, developing new techniques, and finding their unique styles.

Wine tourism has also become a booming business, with 15 million people visiting California wineries annually. The Napa Valley alone welcomes some 5 million travelers a year, making it the state's second most popular tourist destination after Disneyland. On any given Saturday year round, traffic on the valley's Route 29 is full of cars, limos, and buses taking people from tasting room to tasting room.

American per capita wine consumption during the past few decades has been up and down and then up again. It rose steadily through the 1960s,

1970s, and into the 1980s. But after hitting a peak in 1982, it began declining until the mid-1990s. Since then consumption has again been on an upward swing and in 2003 passed the 1982 peak and then topped that again in 2004.

Many wealthy Americans, in particular those who had made their money in Hollywood and the Silicon Valley, have sought to gain the added social prestige that Napa Valley winemaking endowed. Much as the Rothschilds had done a century before in France, the new American money looked to wine to *anoblir* them—give them the esteem of nobility. Wealthy Americans who had run out of ways to spend their fortunes were entranced with the fame that came from having their own wine label. In 1978, Francis Ford Coppola, director of *The Godfather* movies, began producing wines with the help of André Tchelistcheff. Coppola eventually bought the famed Inglenook winery that had been founded by Gustav Niebaum, and renamed it the Niebaum-Coppola Estate. The Disney family also bought a winery, and racing-car driver Mario Andretti gave his name to another.

Pioneers in the 1960s and early 1970s like Bob Travers at Mayacamas and David Bennion at Ridge made their own wine. The new-money winery owners who came after the Paris Tasting hired one of the hot new consultant winemakers to do the work in the vineyard and cellar while the owners sipped the wines bearing their names. Among the best known of the enologists-for-hire in recent years is Helen Turley, who has made wines for the Bryant Family, Martinelli, and Pahlmeyer wineries.

Foreigners, including some of France's biggest names in wine, also flocked to the Napa Valley. Moët & Chandon had been the first, coming in 1973, three years before the Paris event; but after it came many others, most prominently Baron Philippe de Rothschild in 1978. The Moueix family, owners of Château Pétrus, the most famous name in Pomerol, started Dominus Estate, a low-volume, ultrapremium wine that made its first vintage in 1983. Son Christian Moueix, who ran the operation, had studied at UC Davis in 1968 and 1969.

The Napa Valley unfortunately became another proof of the maxim that nothing succeeds like excess. Million-dollar mansions soon began dotting the countryside when Silicon Valley techies and San Francisco professionals sought homes with a view of a vineyard. Marc Benioff, a multimillionaire who made one fortune at Oracle, the software company, and then a second with Salesforce.com, an Internet firm, bought a Napa Valley hilltop estate for $3.2 million and then spent millions more redoing it. Benioff, though, is more interested in valley views than valley crus. As the number of wineries kept growing, vineyards were planted on more and more pre-

carious locations on Napa's mountainsides. Every one of the new wineries
seemed to have a business plan that called for it to make two levels of wines:
$50-a-bottle Napa Valley Cabernet Sauvignon and $100-a-bottle vineyard-
specific Cabernet. No one had bothered to ask whether there was that big
a market for $100 bottles of wine. In the go-go 1990s, however, there
seemed to be no limit to expectations or expenditures. American wine sales
in that decade nearly doubled to $19 billion, even though there was only a
modest increase in annual per capita consumption. Americans were simply
willing to spend a lot more for their wine.

A good barometer of excess was the skyrocketing price of Napa Valley
land. A milestone was passed in 1999, when Gil Nickel, the owner of the Far
Niente winery and a collector of antique cars, paid $100,000 an acre for a
forty-two-acre vineyard. Only four years later, Francis Ford Coppola put up
$300,000 an acre for a vineyard in Rutherford. In 1970 Warren Winiarski
had paid just $2,000 per acre for his first Stag's Leap land, while Jim Barrett
in 1972 paid less than $7,000 an acre for the Chateau Montelena property,
which included an historic winery.

The best symbol of the excessive 1990s was the popularity of the so-called
trophy wines, which were sold in wine auctions at unbelievable prices
and garnered mountains of publicity for both the wineries and the people
who bought them. The wineries regularly win very high ratings from
Robert Parker. The first was Harlan Estate, which received a perfect 100 rating from Parker in 1994, only its fifth vintage. Others include Screaming
Eagle, Behrens & Hitchcock, and Grace Family.

These trophy wines are all Cabernet Sauvignons and similar in style.
Their detractors in the valley call them "fruit bombs." They are big, showy
wines with lots of concentrated fruit flavors. One Napa critic told me with
obvious exaggeration, "They are so thick that you have to serve them
with a spoon." Unlike classical French wines, they are not really meant to
be quaffed with meals. They are better sipped on their own. The techniques
of trophy winemakers are very similar to those of the French *garagistes*:
severe pruning, late harvests, careful grape selection, heavy use of oak. With
their extensive handwork, these are the Ferraris of wine.

Production is only several hundred cases a year, far less than the most
prestigious Bordeaux châteaux, and so the wines never find their way to anyone's neighborhood wine shop. Screaming Eagle, for example, produces only
about five hundred cases annually. The trophy wines are sold mainly by mail
order to customers willing to pay $300 a bottle or more. Screaming Eagle
buyers are limited to three bottles each and the winery no longer adds names
to its waiting list. Aficionados brag about getting onto the allocation list just

as they might boast of their daughter getting into Harvard. After being sold by the winery, many bottles find their way to Internet auctions, where the price quickly doubles or triples.

The trophy wines are also still too young for anyone to know whether they will age to true greatness with time. Tasting them, though, is not what they are really all about: these wines are meant to be placed on a mantel and admired. They are symbols of the owner's extraordinary success and are bought mainly to impress friends and guests.

One Napa Valley winery owner told me that the trophy wines also serve another role: they provide a price ceiling that makes it easier for him and others to charge more. When Screaming Eagle is selling for $300 or more a bottle untasted, any top-ranked winery can justify asking $100 for its Cabernet Sauvignon.

The apex of valley flamboyance took place at the 2000 Napa Valley Wine Auction. The event was started in 1981 by Robert Mondavi and a few other pillars of the wine establishment to be a local version of the famed Hospice de Beaune charity fund-raiser in Burgundy. The Napa Valley auction, which was recently renamed Auction Napa Valley, originally raised money for the St. Helena Hospital, but it became so successful that the proceeds were spread around to several other charities. Over the years, the auction became a place for the newly wealthy to show off their money. At the 2000 event, which raised $9.5 million, a level yet to be matched, a six-liter bottle of 1992 Screaming Eagle Cabernet Sauvignon was sold for $500,000. That works out to $22,944 per four-ounce glass. A trophy indeed.

The buyer was Chase Bailey, a dot-com multimillionaire who had made his fortune at Cisco, the company that sells the equipment that forms the backbone of the Internet. Even Heidi Barrett, the Screaming Eagle winemaker and wife of Bo Barrett, the winemaker at Chateau Montelena, found it hard to believe that any bottle of wine could be worth that much. Afterward she was quoted as saying, "It's wild. You drink it, and it's gone. My brain doesn't get it."

The bursting of the stock market and Internet bubbles in 2000 did not kill the trophy wines, although it reduced some of the ardor for them. The level of their oversubscription declined, but the supply of the wines is so limited that there will probably always be more buyers than sellers for the prestige products. Now instead of five buyers for each bottle there are perhaps two, and the prices show no sign of declining.

People had come to the Napa Valley since the 1850s because it was what Eden must have looked like. But as the last patches of pasture were turned into vineyards and the traffic jams grew longer on Route 29, a backlash against new development gathered force. Many people wanted to halt all growth. They argued that the very qualities that brought them to the valley in the first place and made wine production possible were being destroyed, especially by building vineyards and McMansions on steep mountainsides, which in a thunderstorm could go sliding down the hill. As a result, issues like the protection of streams and the Napa River became the subject of hot debates and bitter political struggles. Environmentalists also argued that concentrating all of the valley's resources into one crop—grapes—was destroying the ecological balance that the agricultural area had enjoyed for more than a century. The trouble in the late 1990s of insects like the glassy-winged sharpshooter that attacked vineyards seemed to support their case.

The opposition to more development was also directed at the new wealth that had transformed a once simple farming valley into Rodeo Drive North, a place where people spent their time and money trying to outdo their neighbors. Long-term residents resented the weekend winery owners who were driving up local real estate prices and making it impossible for the children of old-timers to afford a home. And as so often happens, people who had moved to the area before it boomed wanted to close the valley to newcomers. Some of these were not even fans of wine, the foundation for the region's economy. Peter Mennen, an heir to the Mennen toiletries fortune, was one of the many people who had moved to the Napa Valley to get out of the fast lane. For years, he lived the simpler life as the postmaster of St. Helena, but in a letter to the editor of the local paper he called wine a "bottle of arrogance."

Winery owners at first were generally divided on development issues. In the back of the minds of many loomed the specter of what had happened in Santa Clara County to the south, which had been a quality wine region in the 1950s and early 1960s when Martin Ray was turning out great wines there. But when the area became high-technology's Silicon Valley, land that might have become prime vineyards was turned into housing developments and office complexes. No one wanted that to be repeated in the Napa Valley. At the same time, winery owners have always been rugged individualists who want to do things on their land their way. They resent anyone coming in and telling them what to do, and many formed groups to wage war with the environmentalists.

Attempts to control development are an old topic in the Napa Valley. The first restrictions were established in 1968 by the Agriculture Preserve Zone, which set twenty acres as the minimum size for vineyards. The goal was to stop any growth of small wineries that would turn the area into a rural suburbia. Big vineyards were okay because that would maintain the agricultural nature of the valley, but proponents of the agricultural preserve argued that hundreds of vest-pocket vineyards, each with its own little winery, would destroy the valley. The minimum was later increased to 40 acres and is now 160 acres in the Agricultural Watershed Zone on the hillside surrounding the valley. Such measures, though, generally had the support of winery owners.

In the 1990s, however, environmentalists became more aggressive in their demands, and winemakers began regarding them as extremists out to destroy their way of life. During my last visit to the valley, some winemakers bitterly complained to me that the environmentalists were using the court system to tie up any new development in costly litigation whose real purpose was simply to stop growth. Campaigns for local elections turned into expensive and emotional confrontations between environmentalists and winery owners.

The battle between the two groups in the valley is likely to be an ongoing and heated struggle. Compromises are difficult to achieve, and both sides are quick to run to court if they lose a skirmish. The core positions of both camps are valid, although many hold extreme views.

To a degree, the environmentalists have already won. Just as in France, there is now a much greater awareness among Napa Valley winemakers of the dangers of excessive use of chemical fertilizers, and wineries now brag about being ecofriendly. The Wine Institute, a San Francisco–based lobbying group, and the California Association of Winegrape Growers in 2002 introduced the much-heralded Sustainable Winegrowing Practices program. This teaches vintners and growers how to conserve natural resources and protect the environment. Its nearly five-hundred-page workbook contains chapters on soil management and natural pest control as well as water and energy conservation.

California's winemakers in recent years have again discovered that despite its glamour, wine is still basically an agricultural product subject to the maddeningly repetitive agricultural cycle that leads to rising prices followed by falling ones in commodities as diverse as beef and tulip bulbs. Says Vic Motto, a St. Helena–based management consultant to wineries, "There are about 4,500 grape growers in California and no invisible hand tells them what to do." When wine is in high demand and grapes are in short supply, both growers and winery owners plant more vines, and fields that had been growing perhaps tomatoes are planted with grapes. Eventually there are too many vineyards, so a glut of grapes develops and prices drop. Such market collapses occurred in 1973–74, 1982–83 and 1991–92. The latest grape glut took place at the beginning of the new century after the size of vineyards increased by 33 percent between 1995 and 2001.

At the Trader Joe's grocery store in the Bel Aire Plaza shopping center in the city of Napa, the challenge facing valley wine in the early years of the twenty-first century was on full display one warm autumn afternoon in 2003. Business was brisk in the store's well-stocked wine section. The biggest action was at the stacks of Charles Shaw wines selling for $1.99 a bottle. Its ardent fans call the wine "Two-Buck Chuck." A matronly woman wearing black pedal pushers and a light green top first put two bottles of the wine into her shopping cart, then added two more and two more until she had eight bottles. A gray-haired man in chinos and a sport shirt looked at individual bottles of four types of Charles Shaw wines—Cabernet Sauvignon, Chardonnay, Merlot, and Sauvignon Blanc—and then put a case of Merlot into his shopping cart. The wine bargains at Trader Joe's in Napa were not limited to Charles Shaw. In front of a large display of Trader Joe's Napa Valley Cabernet Sauvignon selling for $4.99 was a handwritten sign reading, "Under the winery's real label it sells for about $30."

Jon Fredrickson of Gomberg, Fredrickson & Associates, California's leading wine-market watcher and consultant, came up with a new classification for Two-Buck Chuck and its clones, calling them "extreme value varietals." Fredrickson maintains that they have actually helped the California wine business by attracting new, unsophisticated consumers who will stay around, develop more demanding tastes, and graduate to better-quality—and higher-priced—wines.

Having already seen several wine cycles, Fredrickson said this one too would eventually play itself out as farmers took marginal vineyards, which had been planted with grapes only when demand was extremely high, out of production. With a glut of grapes on the market, other agricultural products suddenly look more attractive. Sure enough, in 2003 the Robert Mondavi Winery sold its Sierra Madre Vineyard in the Santa Maria Valley to farmers who pulled out the grapes and planted strawberries. In its early days, Two-Buck Chuck was largely made from high-quality grapes from the Central Coast region, Fredrickson told me, but there were soon less of those for sale and lesser ones from the Central Valley, the center of jug wine, were going into the wine. It is clear how the story ends: when the "extreme value varietals" inevitably go down in quality, they decline in popularity.

A bigger challenge to Napa Valley winemakers than that posed by Two-Buck Chuck, however, is the tyranny of time. The ambitious young winemakers like Bob Travers and Warren Winiarski, who came to the valley in their thirties during the 1960s and 1970s, are now in their seventies and face the inevitable problem of succession. The change of generation in a family business is never easy, whether the business is a winery or a car dealership.

The most public transition took place at the famed Robert Mondavi Winery. By the time he was in his 90s, Robert was no longer involved in the day-to-day affairs of the business that bears his name, and his company went adrift. Mondavi took his problems public in late 2002, when he told the *St. Helena Star,* a weekly newspaper in the valley, that his sons Michael and Tim were more interested in making money than promoting the family's wines. Eventually both sons left the company, and for the first time no Mondavis were managing the business. In November 2004, after a tense boardroom struggle, Constellation bought Robert Mondavi Corp. for $1.03 billion plus $325 million in assumed debt. Robert was given the title Brand Ambassador.

Another bumpy transfer of generations took place at the Louis M. Martini winery. Founder Louis M. Martini's son Louis P. Martini studied wine at UC Davis and took over the business in 1968. Louis P.'s son Michael Martini in 1977 became the third-generation family winemaker, but the company ran into financial trouble and had to sell off some prime vineyards. Finally in September 2002, Gallo bought Martini. The new owner preserved the brand name but soon introduced a new label and forced other marketing changes that made its products look more up to date.

Old-timers and newcomers alike in the valley were saddened by the disappearance of both the Robert Mondavi family and the Martinis. The two clans had been founding members of the valley's winemaking establishment who had helped restore the business after the damage caused by Prohibition.

There are plenty of buyers around for family-owned wineries. Major liquor companies are once again anxious to purchase Napa Valley properties. Lexicographer and wit Samuel Johnson noted that a second marriage is the "triumph of hope over experience," and the liquor companies do not seem to have learned much from the failures of Heublein and others in buying wineries during the 1970s. Big foreign companies such as Australia's Foster's Group and Britain's twin giants, Allied Domecq and Diageo, have all been buying up family wineries in California in recent years.

American companies are also rolling up smaller brands, hoping to achieve economies of scale and maximize marketing clout. Constellation Brands, a publicly held company based in Fairport, New York, has been the most aggressive and has passed Gallo to become the largest wine company in the world. In addition to owning Australia's Hardy line of wines, Constellation now also has Napa Valley's Franciscan Estates and Mount Veeder in addition to Ravenswood and Simi in Sonoma County, and the jug wines Almaden and Inglenook. After acquiring Robert Mondavi, Constellation now sells some 80 million cases annually under a wide range of brands.

Despite the romance of boutique wineries, wine is big-company business. Only about 25 of the 1,700 wineries in California produce 95 percent of the wine sold. Those wineries each sell several million cases a year, usually of low-cost wine. The flip side is that some 1,675 wineries are fighting for just 5 percent of the market, although most of them are going after the luxury, high-profit business and have actually been taking market share away from the bigger wineries in recent times. About three-quarters of the small wineries each sell less than ten thousand cases a year. Boutique wineries, though, have 70 percent of the rapidly growing market for wines selling at more than $15 a bottle. Says consultant Vic Motto: "Small and mid-size wineries are driving the changes in the market for California wine. They are the market innovators, in part of necessity."

The biggest challenge facing small wineries is that of distribution, especially since mergers have dramatically decreased the number of wholesalers that will bring their wines to retail shops. The surviving wholesalers are more interested in wineries where they can move thousands of cases a week than those that will sell only a few hundred a year. More than half of small California wineries told a 2003 Wine Institute survey that they could not get a wholesaler to carry their brand.

As a result, small wineries have been forced to be more creative in marketing, especially through direct-to-consumer sales that can eliminate both wholesalers and retailers. Purchases by visitors to the winery or through wine clubs that ship bottles to residents in states where that is legal are a high-profit business since producers can then pocket the 50 to 60 percent of the retail price that is normally split between wholesalers and retailers.

America's antiquated liquor laws, however, make it difficult to sell wine directly to customers. When Prohibition was repealed in 1933, states were given the power to regulate the alcoholic beverage business. The result is a hodgepodge of legislation under which a state like Pennsylvania runs liquor stores while another like Alabama has dry counties where no alcoholic beverages can be sold. In Arkansas local wine can be sold in grocery stores, while out-of-state wine is sold only in liquor stores. Several states, including New York, New Jersey, and Michigan, outlaw interstate wine shipments but permit them within the state. Twenty-seven states, mostly in the west, have reciprocal agreements that permit their wineries to ship direct, and most California wineries will sell to consumers in those states.

The Internet could open up a huge new market if small wineries were permitted to sell directly to consumers. Some limited Internet sales already exist, but these are usually done through large distributors that are willing to take on the complex and costly legal fight to ship wine around the country. The

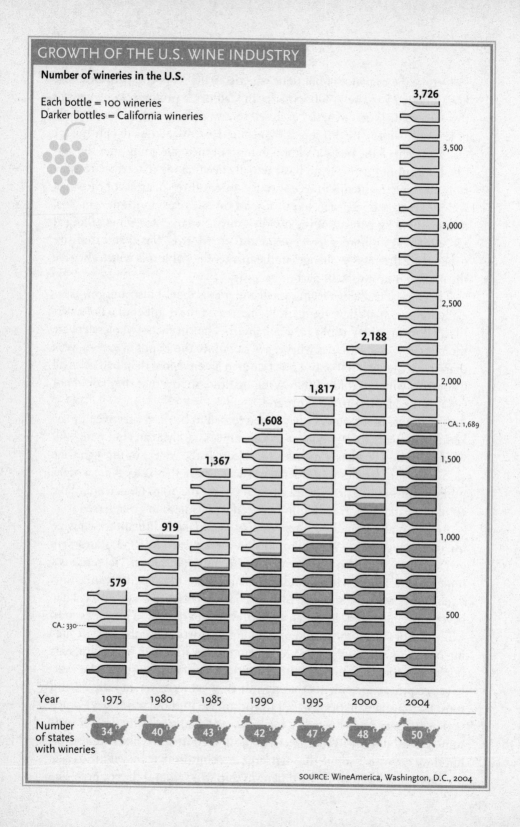

GROWTH OF THE U.S. WINE INDUSTRY

Number of wineries in the U.S.

Each bottle = 100 wineries
Darker bottles = California wineries

3,726
3,500
3,000
2,500
2,188
2,000
1,817
CA.: 1,689
1,608
1,500
1,367
1,000
919
579
500
CA.: 330

Year	1975	1980	1985	1990	1995	2000	2004
Number of states with wineries	34	40	43	42	47	48	50

SOURCE: WineAmerica, Washington, D.C., 2004

breakthrough would come if wineries themselves could operate Websites where consumers thousands of miles away could buy their wine. The Federal Trade Commission in a 2003 report called the barriers to e-commerce in wine "anticompetitive."

The tide of history, though, is slowly going in the direction of national rules to govern liquor sales. The twenty-seven reciprocal agreements were the first breach in old practices. The second was the May 2005 Supreme Court ruling that the Michigan and New York laws permitting direct wine shipments within those states but outlawing them from other states were unconstitutional. The majority of judges said the laws were discriminatory. Fifteen states still do not permit any direct-to-consumer wine shipments, and the decision does not affect them. But time and trends do not appear to be on their side, and more direct sales to consumers will be a boon to small wineries.

As they look out into the future, California winemakers can be encouraged because they have only begun to tap the huge American market, despite nearly four decades of strong growth. Just 12.5 percent of Americans, 25 million people, classify themselves as core wine drinkers, meaning that they consume wine at least weekly. And those people drink 86 percent of total national consumption. Another 28 million, or 13.9 percent, are marginal wine drinkers who have it less than once a week. A very large segment of the American public still never drinks wine. If U.S. consumption only reached the level of fellow English-speaking countries like Britain and Australia, Americans would be drinking twice as much wine as today.

Wine is also still consumed largely on the East and West Coasts, with California alone taking about one-fifth of the total. Outside of major cities like Chicago, the Midwest remains a little-tapped market for wine. Lou Gomberg, one of the early promoters of California wine, said that for wine really to take off there had to be an active winery in every state in the country. Today that goal has been achieved and wines are even made in the harsh climates of the Dakotas and Alaska. In 2004, there were 3,726 bonded wineries in the U.S., up from 1,817 in 1995. While New York, Oregon, and Washington have more than 200 wineries each, California has nearly 1,700 that produce more than 90 percent of American wine.

It's not just the United States that offers great growth opportunities for California wines; the world is also becoming a better market for its products. Between 1987 and 2003, annual American wine exports, which are almost all from California, went up ten-fold to $643 million. Britain, in particular, has become a good market for California wines.

On many fronts, the best is yet to come for California wine.

EPILOGUE

Ten of the eleven California wineries that participated in the 1976 Paris Tasting remain in operation and most are still benefiting from the worldwide publicity they received just from taking part in the event. Only Veedercrest no longer exists, having been forced out of business in 1982 after a fight with a distributor.

The three wineries that most benefited from the Paris Tasting were Chateau Montelena and Stag's Leap Wine Cellars, which placed first in their respective parts of the event, and Grgich Hills, which was started as a direct result of Chateau Montelena's victory. Today all are leading California producers, and they reinforce their market position by reminding wine buyers about their connection to the Paris Tasting. And while Steven Spurrier first thrust them into the forefront of American wine, they have all remained there by continuing to produce outstanding vintages year after year.

Jim Barrett at Chateau Montelena has stuck faithfully to his original business plan to model his winery after Bordeaux's Château Lafite. Chateau Montelena remains a small, family-owned business specializing in Cabernet Sauvignon. After winemaker Mike Grgich left to start his own winery, Barrett hired Jerry Luper, the former winemaker at Freemark Abbey, to be his vintner. Luper stayed through the 1981 vintage and then moved to another California winery. When Luper left, he urged Jim Barrett to hire his son Bo Barrett as winemaker. Bo, who had received his formal wine training at Fresno State, had only recently left the company after his father told him he didn't believe in nepotism and so he didn't have much of a future there. At Luper's suggestion, Jim Barrett changed his mind and Bo has been the winemaker at Chateau Montelena since 1982.

Chateau Montelena today produces some 35,000 cases a year. About one-third of that is its top-of-the-line Estate Cabernet Sauvignon, selling for about $100 a bottle. It still does a steady business with a Burgundy-style Chardonnay, the wine that won at Paris, and also sells less expensive Cabernet Sauvignon, Zinfandel, and Riesling. In November 1999, *Wine Spectator* magazine did a vertical tasting of twenty years of Chateau Montelena Estate Cabernet Sauvignon wines, going back to the first vintage in

1978. The title of the article: "Greatness by Design." Author James Laube wrote, "When it comes to California Cabernet, Chateau Montelena not only runs with the best of the pack, it often leads."

Stag's Leap is today the largest of the three Paris Tasting wineries, selling some 150,000 cases annually under two labels—Stag's Leap Wine Cellars and Hawk Crest. Its premium Stag's Leap line has white wines—Chardonnay, Sauvignon Blanc, and Riesling—as well as reds—Cabernet Sauvignon and Merlot. Warren Winiarski has named one of his Cabernets after the classical concept of the Golden Rectangle. The top-of-the-line Stag's Leap wine is Cask 23, a premium Cabernet that sells for some $150 and is made only in particular years when everything comes together to make an exceptional vintage.

Hawk Crest is a popularly priced line of Cabernet Sauvignon, Merlot, and Chardonnay that retails for about $14 a bottle. Winiarski started the second label in 1974, when he took advantage of one of the periodic gluts of grapes to buy fruit in Mendocino County. Hawk Crest sells about 80,000 cases annually.

Warren Winiarski steadily picked up more vineyard acreage over the years. The most important purchase was the one hundred acres of Nathan Fay's property that had been the original inspiration for him to buy the nearby Heid Ranch. Wines from the original vineyard are marketed under the label Stag's Leap SLV, while those from the Fay property carry the Stag's Leap Fay brand. The winery annually produces about 5,000 cases of Fay and 3,000 cases of SLV, plus 1,500 cases of Cask 23 in the years in which it is made.

Doubtless many wine drinkers in the past quarter century have bought a wine from Stags' Leap Winery erroneously thinking it was from Stag's Leap Wine Cellars, the winery that triumphed in Paris. In 1971, Carl Doumani, a sometime restaurant owner and sometime real estate speculator, bought the four-hundred-acre Stags' Leap ranch, which had once included a winery. The following year, and thus before the Paris Tasting, Doumani started making Petite Sirah, marketing it under the name Stags' Leap Winery. Winiarski and Doumani later sued each other for the use of the name, with each spending more than $100,000 on his case. But finally in July 1985, and after nearly twelve years of litigation, the two men agreed to disagree and settled their fight with each continuing to use its slightly different name. Stags' Leap Winery is now owned by Australia's Foster's Group. The nominal confusion, though, continues.

Winiarski, the college lecturer-turned-winemaker, has never totally left his intellectual pursuits. For more than a decade he taught a course in the summer at St. John's College in Santa Fe, New Mexico. The subject mat-

ter included Aristotle and Shakespeare as well as Machiavelli and Toc-
queville. In 2003, when he was naming a new Cabernet Sauvignon after the
Greek goddess Artemis, Winiarski got back into academic research, delv-
ing into Greek mythology in the works of Robert Graves.

Grgich Hills has expanded to a winery that now grows all its own grapes
on four hundred acres of prime Napa Valley vineyards. It currently produces
about 80,000 cases a year, and Mike Grgich says he will never go over
100,000 cases out of fear that it would be too big for him to make quality
wines. Grgich Hills produces six wines, although its flagship Chardonnay
makes up about half of total sales. The Grgich Hills Cabernet Sauvignon,
which made its way into the French book *100 Vins de Légende* (100 Legendary Wines), is about one-quarter of production. The other Grgich
Hills wines are Zinfandel, Merlot, Fumé Blanc, and a late-harvest blend of
Sauvignon Blanc, Riesling, and Chardonnay.

While Grgich still oversees production of his beloved Chardonnay, he
has set in place the succession for the winery he still owns with his original
partners, Austin Hills and Hills's sister Mary Lee Strebl. Grgich's nephew,
Ivo Jeramaz, whom Grgich brought to California from Croatia in 1986 and
trained at Grgich Hills, will take over as winemaker, while Grgich's daughter Violet has already been named general manager and sales manager. The
two will one day lead Grgich Hills.

In 1995, and after the fall of Communism, Grgich traveled back to his
native Croatia with plans to make wine there as well. He bought a stone
building in the village of Trstenik for his winery and equipped it with the
latest technology, including Californian fermentation tanks and French oak
barrels for aging. Grgić Vina, the name of the new venture, is located about
75 miles from Desne, where Grgich grew up. It now produces some 3,300
cases annually of the white wine Posip and the red wine Plavac Mali,
which sell for premium prices. The wine press that made the winning
Chateau Montelena Chardonnay at Paris is now in service at Grgić Vina.

Mike Grgich, the immigrant winemaker who arrived in the Napa Valley
with so little, takes justifiable pride in his accomplishments, saying, "We
now own all our own land plus our winery. Everything is paid off. I feel safe
going into an era where we do not need to buy another vineyard or pay off
another loan. The ship has been built, and now we just need to navigate it."

Patricia Gallagher, the person who first suggested the tasting of California
wines in Paris, has continued to be a member of the French wine world. She
remained director of the Académie du Vin until 1989 and then became a
wine writer and editor. Since 1996, she has been academic director and wine
department director at the Cordon Bleu cooking school in Paris.

Steven Spurrier, the man who brought California wines to the world's attention on May 24, 1976, has become a leading member of the international wine scene. After the Paris Tasting, his small shop and wine school grew even more popular with English-speaking visitors, and his business interests expanded to include a restaurant and wine bar also located in the Cité Berryer and a bistro in the Défense section just outside Paris. Spurrier moved to New York City in 1981 to launch an Académie du Vin there, but the venture soon failed. The following year he relocated to London so that his two children could attend British schools. His Paris businesses ran into financial problems and he finally sold them in 1989 to turn his interests to being a wine consultant, lecturer, author, and journalist. He has since written several books and become a consulting editor of *Decanter,* Britain's leading wine magazine. Although he stays firmly away from making wine, preferring to be a critic rather than a producer, Spurrier has invested in a vineyard in the Entre-Deux-Mers region of Bordeaux. The French wine establishment finally got over its anger at him for staging the Paris Tasting, and in 1999 Spurrier received the Prix Louis Marinier for his writing about Bordeaux wines. Looking back on a lifetime spent around wine, Spurrier says, "I am still totally, 100 percent in love with wine, the wine trade, and the people in it. I have been very fortunate indeed, and wine has brought me more than I could ever have imagined."

APPENDIX

SCORECARD FOR THE JUDGMENT OF PARIS

CHARDONNAY

	POINTS
Chateau Montelena, 1973	132
Meursault Charmes Roulot, 1973	126.5
Chalone Vineyard, 1974	121
Spring Mountain, 1973	104
Beaune Clos des Mouches Joseph Drophin, 1973	101
Freemark Abbey Winery, 1972	100
Bâtard-Montrachet Ramonet-Prudhon, 1973	94
Puligny-Montrachet Les Pucelles Domaine LeFlaive, 1972	89
Veedercrest Vineyards, 1972	88
David Bruce Winery, 1973	42

CABERNET SAUVIGNON

	POINTS
Stag's Leap Wine Cellars, 1973	127.5
Château Mouton Rothschild, 1970	126
Château Haut-Brion, 1970	125.5
Château Montrose, 1970	122
Ridge Vineyards Monte Bello, 1971	103.5
Château Léoville-Las-Cases, 1971	97
Mayacamas Vineyards, 1971	89.5
Clos Du Val Winery, 1972	87.5
Heitz Cellars Martha's Vineyard, 1970	84.5
Freemark Abbey Winery, 1969	78

SELECTED BIBLIOGRAPHY

The Regional Oral History Office, The Bancroft Library, University of California, Berkeley, interviews with Maynard Amerine, William Bonetti, Andy Beckstoffer, David Bruce, Charles Carpy, Charles Crawford, Jack Davies and Jamie Peterman Davies, Paul Draper, Miljenko Grgich, Joseph E. Heitz, Maynard A. Joslyn, Zelma R. Long, Louis M. Martini, Peter Mondavi, Robert Mondavi, Rodney D. Strong, Janet Spooner Trefethen and John James Trefethen, André Tchelistcheff, Warren Winiarski, and Albert J. Winkler. The Napa Valley Wine Library interviews with Maynard Amerine and J. Leland Stewart. Wines and Winemakers of the Santa Cruz Mountains Oral History interview with David Bruce and joint interview with Hewitt and Suzanne Crane, Charles and Blanche Rosen, and Frances Bennion.

Adams, Leon D. *The Wines of America*. New York: McGraw-Hill, 1973.

Bespaloff, Alexis. *The New Frank Schoonmaker Encyclopedia of Wine*. New York: Morrow, 1988.

Brook, Stephen. *A Century of Wine*. San Francisco: The Wine Appreciation Guild, 2000.

Casamayor, Pierre, Michel Dovaz, and Jean-François Bazin. *L'Or du Vin*. Paris: Hachette, 1994.

Chroman, Nathan. *The Treasury of American Wines*. New York: Rutledge Crown, 1976.

Coates, Clive. *Côte D'Or*. Berkeley: University of California Press, 1997.

Cooper, Michael. *Wine Atlas of New Zealand*. Auckland: Hodder Moa Beckett, 2002.

Conaway, James. *The Far Side of Eden*. New York: Houghton Mifflin, 2002.

———. *Napa*. New York: Avon, 1990.

Darlington, David. *Zin*. Cambridge, MA: Da Capo Press, 1991.

Deroudille, Jean-Pierre. *Le Vin Face à La Mondialisation*. Paris: Hachette, 2003.

Deutschman, Alan. *A Tale of Two Valleys*. New York: Broadway Books, 2003.

Duijker, Hubrecht. *The Wines of Chile.* Utrecht: Het Spectrum, 1999.

Echikson, William. *Noble Rot.* New York: W. W. Norton, 2004.

Gabler, James M. *Passions.* Baltimore: Bacchus Press, 1995.

Gaiter, Dorothy, and John Brecher. *Love by the Glass.* New York: Villard, 2002.

————. *The Wall Street Journal Guide to Wine.* New York: Broadway Books, 2002.

Girard-Lagorce, Sylvie. *100 Vins de Légende.* Paris: Éditions Solar, 1999.

Halliday, James. *Classic Wines of Australia and New Zealand.* New York: HarperCollins, 1997.

Hands, Phyllis, and Dave Hughes. *New World of Wine from the Cape of Good Hope.* Somerset West, South Africa: Stephan Phillips, 2001.

Heintz, William F. *California's Napa Valley.* San Francisco: Scottwall Associates, 1999.

Jefford, Andrew. *The New France.* London: Mitchell Beazley, 2002.

Johnson, Hugh. *Story of Wine.* London: Mitchell Beazley, 1989.

————. *Wine.* London: Thomas Nelson and Sons, 1966.

————. *The World Atlas of Wine.* London: Mitchell Beazley, 1971.

Johnson, Hugh, and Jancis Robinson. *The World Atlas of Wine.* 5th ed. London: Mitchell Beazley, 2000.

Jordan, Ray. *Wine.* Osborne Park, Western Australia: The West Australian, 2002.

Judd, Kevin. *The Colour of Wine.* Nelson, New Zealand: Craig Potton, 1999.

Lapsley, James T. *Bottled Poetry.* Berkeley: University of California Press, 1996.

Lichine, Alexis. *Wines of France.* New York: Knopf, 1951.

Littlewood, Joan. *Baron Philippe.* New York: Crown, 1984.

Lukacs, Paul. *American Vintage.* New York: Houghton Mifflin, 2000.

Lynch, Kermit. *Adventures on the Wine Route.* New York: North Point Press, 1988.

Lyon, Richards. *Vine to Wine.* Napa: Stonecrest Press, 1999.

MacNeil, Karen. *The Wine Bible.* New York: Workman Publishing, 2001.

Maino Aguirre, Hernán. *Chilean Wines for the Twenty-first Century.* Santiago: Libros Antártica, 2001.

Markham, Dewey, Jr. *1855.* New York: John Wiley & Sons. 1998.

Marty, Alain. *Ils Vont Tuer le Vin Français!* Paris: Éditions Ramsey, 2004.

McInerney, Jay. *Bacchus & Me.* New York: Lyons Press, 2000.

McPhee, John. *Assembling California.* New York: Farrar, Straus and Giroux, 1993.

Mondavi, Robert. *Harvests of Joy.* New York: Harcourt Brace, 1998.

Muscatine, Doris, Maynard A. Amerine, and Bob Thompson. *Book of California Wine.* Berkeley: University of California Press, 1984.

Nicklès, Sara. *Wine Memories.* San Francisco: Chronicle Books, 2000.

Osborne, Lawrence. *The Accidental Connoisseur.* New York: North Point Press, 2004.

Parker, Robert M., Jr. *Burgundy.* New York: Simon & Schuster, 1990.

————. *Parker's Wine Buyer's Guide.* 6th ed. New York: Simon & Schuster, 2002.

Platter, John. *South African Wines 2003.* Hermanus, South Africa: John Platter SA Wine Guide, 2003.

Perdue, Lewis. *The Wrath of Grapes.* New York: Avon, 1999.

Philips, Rod. *A Short History of Wine.* New York: Ecco, 2000.

Pinney, Thomas. *A History of Wine in America.* Berkeley: University of California Press, 1989.

Prial, Frank. *Decantations.* New York: St. Martin's Press, 2001.

Robinson, Jancis. *How to Taste.* New York: Simon & Schuster, 1983.

Rousset-Rouard, Yves, and Thierry Desseauve. *La France Face aux Vins du Nouveau Monde.* Paris: Albin Michel, 2002.

Schoonmaker, Frank, and Tom Marvel. *American Wines.* New York: Duell, Sloan and Pearce, 1941.

Schuster, Danny, David Jackson, and Rupert Tipples. *Canterbury Grapes & Wines.* Christchurch, New Zealand: Shoal Bay Press, 2002.

Stevenson, Robert Louis. *The Silverado Squatters.* London: Chatto & Windus, 1883.

Sullivan, Charles L. *A Companion to California Wine.* Berkeley: University of California Press, 1998.

————. *Napa Wine.* San Francisco: The Wine Appreciation Guild, 1994.

Teiser, Ruth, and Catherine Harroun. *Winemaking in California.* New York: McGraw-Hill, 1983.

Turnbull, James. *Burgundy.* Paris: Hachette, 1999.

Waugh, Alec. *In Praise of Wine.* New York: William Morrow, 1959.

Waugh, Harry. *Bacchus on the Wing.* London: Wine & Spirit Publications, 1966.

————. *Diary of a Winetaster.* New York: Quadrangle Books, 1972.

————. *Harry Waugh's Wine Diary.* Vol. 6 and 8. London: Christie's Wine Publications, 1975 and 1977.

————. *Pick of the Bunch.* London: Wine & Spirit Publications, 1970.

Wagner, Philip M. *American Wines and Wine-Making.* New York: Knopf, 1933.

Weber, Lin. *Old Napa Valley.* St. Helena, CA: Wine Ventures Publishing, 1998.

———. *Roots of the Present.* St. Helena, CA: Wine Ventures Publishing, 2001.

Wilson, James E. *Terroir.* Berkeley: University of California Press, 1998.

ACKNOWLEDGMENTS

While this book was a personal labor of love for nearly five years, it could never have been produced without the help and cooperation of many people. First and foremost were the book's four main characters: Steven Spurrier, Jim Barrett, Mike Grgich, and Warren Winiarski. Spurrier, the man who made it all happen, was as enthusiastic about the project as I was from the beginning and always responded to my inquiries, even the ones that must have seemed off the wall.

All three of the winery owners gave me hours and hours of their time, sharing with me the stories of their lives and adventures in wine. Equally important were their assistants, who were always willing to set up new interviews or to handle requests for answers to just a few more questions. Lynne Norton at Chateau Montelena, Maryanne Wedner at Grgich Hills, and Victoria Taylor and Sandra Tovrea at Stag's Leap Wine Cellars were essential in putting the story together and they have my deepest appreciation.

California libraries became my home for weeks of research. In particular, the Napa Valley Wine Library and the Sonoma County Wine Library were treasure chests of information that helped me put the Spurrier tasting into the context of what had happened to California wines during a century of successes and failures before the Paris Tasting. The raw material in the California Wine Industry Oral History Project of the Bancroft Library at the University of California, Berkeley, was priceless in learning about developments in California prior to the Paris event. The staff of the American Food and Wine Project at the Smithsonian Museum in Washington, D.C., was endlessly helpful.

Although I did the vast majority of the interviews myself, others helped me locate people and in some cases did interviews for me. The most important of these was Judy Fayard in Paris, an old colleague from *Time* magazine who still lives and works in the city she loves. She tracked down the French judges who would talk about the tasting and suffered the rebuffs from those who would still not discuss the event. Judy was also very helpful in researching the histories of the French wines at the tasting.

Elisabeth Kaiser, a friend and former colleague, found the German family with whom Mike Grgich lived for two years after leaving Yugoslavia and before he got a visa to move to Canada, providing an important glimpse of the winemaker at a crucial, but difficult, time in his life.

While I was traveling the world investigating the globalization of wine, several people stepped up to help me. Mark Pownall, the news editor of the *Western Australia Business News,* spent several days introducing me to the leading winemakers in Margaret River. Jacques Thebault, the head of the New York office of Sopexa, the French food and wine promotion organization, gave me plenty of time before I went to France and set up excellent interviews for me during my stay there. Winemakers and owners including Peter Gago, the master of Penfolds Grange, Kevin Judd and David Hohnen of New Zealand's Cloudy Bay, Véronique Drouhin at Domaine Drouhin Oregon, Philippe Senard in Burgundy, Filipe Larraín at Almaviva in Chile, Jerry Luper and his wife, Carolee, in Portugal, and Simon Barlow in South Africa were all generous with their time and their hospitality. Hervé Briand of the Institut National des Appellations d'Origine in Paris was also very helpful.

Back in the U.S. the book would never have been completed without the help of three women: my agent Wendy Silbert, who helped me shape the story of a wine tasting into a book; my Scribner editor Rica Buxbaum Allannic, who first grasped the vision of the book, and then constantly encouraged me during the long and lonely writing; and my wife, Jean, who read all the early versions and provided helpful insight and course correction from time to time along the way. The three ladies have my deepest and eternal gratitude.

Finally, special thanks to Nigel Holmes, for his illustrations that help make the book come alive, and to Michael Smith, who performed digital magic on photos from the Paris Tasting.

INDEX

Page numbers of photographs and maps appear in italics.

Paris Tasting (*cont.*)

Sauvignon, 191–96, *184*; French Chardonnay, 186–91, *184*; French wines at, criteria, 185–86, 188; Gallagher at, *197*, 197–99, 203; Gallagher trip to California in 1975 and, 155–56; Heitz Cellars Martha's Vineyard, Cabernet Sauvignon, 1970, 177–79, 203, 204, 223; idea and planning of, 16, 155, 157–58; importing the California wine, 157–58, 162; Inter-Continental Hotel, Paris, *1,* 2–3, 197–205; judges, 2–3, 159–61, *197*, 199–201, 217–18, 219; Mayacamas Vineyards, Cabernet Sauvignon, 1971, 179–81, 203, 204, 223; Meursault Charmes Roulot, 1973, 189–90, 202, 221; objective of Spurrier and Gallagher, 185; press coverage, 161–63, 200, 213, 214, 218–19; pre-tasting favorites, Spurrier, 183, 196; Puligny-Montrachet Les Pucelles Domaine Leflaive, 1972, 190–91, 200, 202, 223; red wine judging, 202–3; red wine results, 203; rematch, Jan. 11 and 12, 1978, 223; rematch, tenth anniversary, 223; rematch, thirtieth anniversary, 224; Ridge Vineyards Monte Bello, Cabernet Sauvignon, 1971, 181–83, 203, 204, 221, 223; scientific review of, two studies, 219–20; scoring system, 200, 223; Spurrier at, *197*, 198–200, 202–5; Stag's Leap Wine Cellars, Cabernet Sauvignon, 1973, 165, 203, 204, 215, 223, 224; turning point for California wines, 214; Veedercrest Vineyards, 1972, 173–74, 202; white wine judging, 200–202; white wine results, 202; wine types in, 3

Parker, Robert M., Jr., 211, 231, 239, 276, 280, 281, 284–85, 288; rating system, 239, 240

Parker's Wine Buyer's Guide, 239

Parkhill, Thomas, 79

Paschich, Lee, 117–22; Chateau Montelena Chardonnay, 1973, and, 142–43, 149; partnership with Barrett, 122, 127–30; recruits Grgich, 126–28; vineyard, 129

Pasteur Institute, 41

Patchett, John, 33

Paul Masson Mountain Winery, Santa Clara, CA, 15, 37–38, 40, 76

Penfold, Christopher Rawson, 248

Penfolds Grange Hermitage, 241, 247–52, 254

Pepys, Samuel, 22, 192

Petite Sirah: grape, 59, 109, 112; Souverain vineyard, 59

Petit Verdot, Bordeaux, France, 21

Petri family, 40

Peynaud, Émile, 18, 70n, 193–94, 253, 276–77

Phylloxera: American rootstock and, 23, 34–35; in France, 23, 34, 192; St. George rootstock and, 97

Pinot Noir: Eyrie Vineyards Reserve Pinot Noir, 270; Domaine Drouhin Oregon, 272–74; Grand Cru Joseph Drouhin Chambertin, 1959, 270–71; grapes, 18, 24, 26, 39, 69, 76, 77, 232; Hanzell winery, 69

Plato, 83

Pliny the Elder, 21

Pompidou, Georges, 13–14

Pontac family, 192

Porter, Michael, 261

Portet, Bernard, 174–76, 217

Portet, Dominique, 175–76

Portugal: Douro, 262–63; grapes of, 261–63; Pinhão, 260–64; Quinta da Carolina, 263–64; Real Companhia Velha, 260, 261; wine production and export, 1990–2003, *234*

Potter, Ron, 267

Pouilly-Fuissé Louis Jadot Chardonnay, 1971, 171

Prial, Frank, 15, 42, 214–15

Prohibition, 35–37

Puligny-Montrachet, France, 24, 186; Leflaive, 172; Paris Tasting, Les Pucelles Domaine Leflaive, 1972, 190–91, 200, 202; Paris Tasting rematch, 223; price per bottle, 216

Pure Wine Law, 1887, 38

Quandt, Richard E., 219

Quittanson, Charles, 218

Rainey, Dick, 114

Ramonet, André, 218

Ramonet, Pierre, 187–88

Raux, Lionel, 218–19

Ray, Martin, 37–38, 76, 88–90, 168–69, 182

Ray, Peter Martin, 89

Red Barn Ranch, Napa Valley, CA, 171

Redwood Ranch, 129

Revue du Vin de France, Le, 11, 160, 199, 217

Rhône Valley, France, regional consumption of wine, 19

Richebourg Pinot Noir, 24, 168

JUDGMENT OF PARIS

STAGE YOUR OWN PARIS TASTING

Since 1976 there have been countless reenactments of the famous Paris Tasting. Some in the years immediately after the event involved exactly the same wines that were tasted on that day in May. In more recent times, the events have usually involved more contemporary wines and sometimes others that represented a more up-to-date view of California and French viticulture.

The most spectacular new Paris Tasting took place for the thirtieth anniversary on May 24, 2006. It involved two tastings, one at Berry Bros. & Rudd, a wine and spirits merchant in London, and one in the Napa Valley at COPIA, the American Center for Wine, Food & the Arts. The events were done simultaneously, so that the results could be released at the same time and one panel would not influence the other. In Napa it took place at 10 a.m., while in Britain it was at 6 p.m. The London event was hosted by Steven Spurrier, and the judges included the most prestigious British wine experts including Michael Broadbent, Hugh Johnson, and Jancis Robinson. Patricia Gallagher, who had first proposed the original tasting to Spurrier, was the host in California and among the judges were such eminent American tasters as Dan Berger, Anthony Dias Blue, and Andrea Immer Robinson.

The two thirtieth anniversary events included a tasting of the original Cabernet Sauvignons, contemporary Chardonnays, and recent Cabernets.

The results in 2006 were even more stunning than in 1976: California wines took the top five positions. The winning Cabernet Sauvignon this time: 1971 Ridge Monte Bello. The 1976 winner, 1973 Stag's Leap Wine Cellars, was second. All the arguments that the French wines would show better as they aged were finally and conclusively laid to rest.

Anyone, of course, can stage a Paris Tasting for a book group of people who have read *Judgment of Paris,* or simply for friends interested in wines.

First you need to select the wines. It would almost be impossible today to get the same wines as those from the 1976 event. The original vintages of the Cabernet Sauvignons would be difficult to find, and most of the Chardonnays are now over the hill. If you go with recent vintages of the original wines, be prepared to spend a lot of money. Just buying the twenty wines would cost some $2,500 at retail stores. Also two California Chardonnays from 1976 could not be duplicated today. Veedercrest is out of business, and Spring Mountain no longer makes that wine. If you wanted to substitute a California Chardonnay for one of those two, you might choose Grgich Hills, since that is made by Mike Grgich, who made the winning Chardonnay in Paris for Chateau Montelena. For the second missing one you might take another leading Chardonnay such as Kistler or Flowers.

If the price and the complexity of a full reenactment of the Paris Tasting are too daunting, you can still have lots of fun by staging a simpler one involving just one French Chardonnay paired with a California one, and a French Cabernet Sauvignon and a California one. To keep the tasting fair, pick out wines with comparable prices. Don't have a $50 French wine against a $10 California wine or vice versa. For between $10 and $15 you can find many very good wines in both categories from both California and France.

It's also a good idea to have wines of approximately the same vintage. Don't have a very old French wine paired off with a very young California one. Spurrier's red wines were just a couple of years older than their California counterparts, and the whites were all of approximately the same age.

You could select wines that have some connection to the original Paris Tasting. Stag's Leap Wine Cellars, which won in the red category in Paris, has a second label, Hawk Crest, that would be in the $10–$15 range. Chalone, which came in third in Paris in the white category, also has a Monterey County Chardonnay at that price.

Just as Spurrier and Gallagher did at Paris, be very careful that it is truly a blind tasting and that people don't know the identity of the wines. You can buy inexpensive wine-tasting kits in retail shops or on the Internet. Or you can simply put the wines in paper bags and tie them at the top. Open the wines in advance and don't forget to take off all the foil at the top of the bottle because that might tip someone off to the contents inside.

Again, just as Spurrier did in Paris in 1976, give each of the wines, whether you have ten in each category or only two, a number and ask people to score the wines. You can use either the 20-point scale as they did in Paris or the more modern 100-point scale. If you're having only two wines in each category, you could ask each taster simply to select which wine is that person's favorite.

For the Paris reenactment, you will need a bottle of each wine for about every fifteen people at the tasting. You don't need more than a splash of wine in the glasses to have enough for a person to taste.

You might have a bowl or vase available for spitting since some participants may not want to drink the wine after they have tasted it. Professional tasters almost never swallow the wine because it will dull their senses for later wines. Amateur tasters, though, often can't pass up the opportunity to drink the wine. If you have only four wines, there's no need to spit.

The traditional order of wines in a tasting is whites before reds because the whites are generally fresher and fruitier. It can throw off people's taste buds for the heavier wines to precede the lighter ones.

Tasters might appreciate having a glass of water or some pieces of bread to clean the palate between wines.

When all the wines have been tasted and the scores tabulated, pull the wines out of their bags and enjoy noting how everyone scored the various wines. You can drink what remains in the bottles as you discuss the results. It's interesting to retaste the wines now that you know the nationalities to see whether that changes your views. A new Paris Tasting is guaranteed to be very interesting—just as it was in 1976.

DISCUSSION POINTS

1. In his tour of world wines in the book, author George M. Taber visited seven wineries on five continents to investigate wine globalization. From which of those wineries would you most like to try the wines and why?

2. Which of the main characters in *Judgment of Paris* (Jim Barrett, Mike Grgich, and Warren Winiarski) do you think most profited from winning the Paris Tasting and why?

3. What role did the University of California at Davis play in the comeback of California wines in the 1950s and 1960s?

4. How did Warren Winiarski and Jim Barrett typify the new generation of wine people who arrived in California in the 1950s and 1960s?

5. How did the Paris Tasting set off the globalization of wine? Do you think globalization has been good for wine consumers? For wine producers? For the French?

6. Discuss some of the serious challenges now facing French winemakers.

7. George M. Taber's next book will explore the history of cork and the search for a new closure for wine bottles. What do you think of the various substitutes already on the market—plastic corks, screwtops, and glass stoppers?

ABOUT THE AUTHOR

GEORGE M. TABER was a reporter and editor for *Time* magazine for twenty-one years, working in Brussels, Bonn, Houston, Washington, D.C., and New York. Stationed in Paris between 1973 and 1976, he reported extensively on French cooking and wine, including a cover story on chef Michel Guérard and his *nouvelle cuisine*. Taber left the magazine in 1988 to start *NJBIZ*, New Jersey's only weekly business publication, which he sold in 2005. For twelve years, he was also the daily on-air business reporter for 101.5 FM, the radio station with the largest Arbitron rating in the state. Taber now lives on Block Island, Rhode Island, with his wife, Jean.

Read on for an excerpt of
George M. Taber's next book

In Search of Bacchus
Wanderings in the Wonderful World of Wine Tourism

Available in hardcover from Scribner

Bordeaux, France

Of the twelve countries I visited in my search of Bacchus, France was where it was most difficult to select the best region. So many interesting areas make great wine, and local people have developed innovative ways to attract visitors. Over the years, I have visited many wine regions in France and retain fond memories of them all. Champagne produces its own special wine that never goes out of fashion, and the big Champagne producers have built wonderful programs that educate people about its history and its wine. The cathedral of Reims, where French kings were once crowned, is interesting to visit again and again and makes a nice side trip when Champagne tasting.

The Route des Vins in Alsace, which runs for some 75 miles on the eastern side of the Vosges Mountains from just outside Strasbourg in the north to the city of Thann in the south, offers exciting wineries to visit and wonderful wines to taste. Residents of little towns such as Ribeauvillé, Kaysersberg, and Bergheim always seem to be smiling. Few wine experiences can beat pilgrimages to Kientzheim to visit Domaine Paul Blanck or to Turckheim to taste Olivier Zind-Humbrecht's wines. And if you get palate fatigue, you can always move over to the Route du Fromage in the Munster Valley and enjoy fresh, unpasteurized Munster cheese.

Burgundy, with its many small wineries and crazy-quilt vineyards dating back nearly two thousand years, is a perfect place for a leisurely stroll, and you can stop along the way to enjoy both great food and great wine. The region has a wonderful three-day wine festival each November built around the Hospices de Beaune auction that has been appropriately nicknamed Les Trois Glorieuses. If you ever get a chance to attend, don't pass it up.

I will never forget the Loire Valley, where I first experienced French wines as a college student. My friends and I used to ride bicycles up and down the valley from Tours, stopping to visit such magnificent châteaux as Chenonceau, Azay-le-Rideau, and Blois as well as to enjoy wines with vintners in Vouvray, Anjou, and Chinon. Sancerre and Pouilly-Fumé were also favorite destinations.

The Côtes du Rhône and its wines were popular with both Thomas Jefferson and Robert Louis Stevenson. Jefferson loved the Viognier of Château

Grillet, while Stevenson was a fan of Hermitage. The steep hillsides and ancient ruins never cease to fascinate visitors. And who doesn't love the city of Avignon?

Yet as I pondered my final choice, I kept coming back to Bordeaux, the wine capital of the world. It was here that I had to go to experience not only the best wines France produces, although Burgundians would surely challenge that, but also to see how the Bordelais are developing wine tourism.

Bordeaux is a large wine region that includes fifty-seven *appellations,* or geographic wine regions, and vines cover just over 300,000 acres, which makes it seven times bigger than the Napa Valley and five times the size of Burgundy. Bordeaux today produces 25 percent of France's *appellation* wine. About 90 percent of its wines are red and 10 percent white or rosé, but as late as the 1960s, the region was still making more whites than reds. The red wines come from Merlot, Cabernet Sauvignon, Cabernet Franc, Malbec, Carmenère, and Petit Verdot grapes. The first three, though, dominate. The whites are made with Sauvignon Blanc, Sémillon, Muscadelle, Ugni Blanc, Colombard, Merlot Blanc, Mauzac, and Ondenc, with the first three again being the most important. The great majority of Bordeaux wines, whether red or white, are blends, and it's unusual for one to be made from a single variety.

The topography of Bordeaux is different from that of the Napa Valley or Stellenbosch, where mountains dominate the landscape. Bordeaux is mainly flat with only minor variations in altitude. That difference, though, can be important, and the price of wine from a slightly higher region may be several times more than one from a nearby vineyard only a few feet lower. The dominant geographical feature is the Gironde, a muddy river that flows 357 miles from its headwaters in the Spanish Pyrenees, past the city of Bordeaux, and then joins with the Dordogne River to form the Gironde Estuary, which empties into the Atlantic Ocean, 47 miles away.

The city of Bordeaux, which only two decades ago was dirty and rundown, has gone through a major renovation in recent years and is now a UNESCO World Heritage site. City planners tore down warehouses that used to block the view of the Gironde, and the waterfront is now a broad, open promenade complete with dramatic fountains. Buildings dating back to the eighteenth century have been scrubbed clean. For the first time in decades Bordeaux again has a top hotel, the Regent, which is located on the city's main square facing the opera. In the past, one had to go to Biarritz 105 miles away to find luxury accommodations. The Regent's management has brought in a top chef from Brussels and promises to soon be collecting Michelin stars. The menu emphasizes seafood, and the *pièce de résistance* is lobster.

Bordeaux *négociants,* the dealers who for centuries have handled the sale of most wines, are based in the city. Wineries generally only produce wines and then sell them to *négociants,* who handle the marketing. Some *négociants* also buy wine in bulk and then blend it and sell it under their own brands. It's a system that exists in no other wine-producing country, but it works for the French. There are today some four hundred Bordeaux *négociants,* about the same number as there were in the nineteenth century. From the seventeenth to the nineteenth centuries, English and Irish traders were major players among the *négociants* since the main export market was England; and names such as Barton, Lynch, and Talbot are found on many famous Bordeaux châteaux. Many foreigners later married into French families and became members of the class that Bordeaux-born author François Mauriac called the "cork aristocrats."

Bordeaux was already a major port in Roman times, when its name was Burdigala, and the Roman historian Pliny the Elder in AD 71 wrote of vineyards being cultivated there, noting that they are "never liable to injury, as they do not come before the west wind of early spring and can withstand wine and rain." Bordeaux developed a special relationship with England because of the wine trade. In the twelfth century, the marriage between Eleanor of Aquitaine, the duchy in which Bordeaux is located, and the future Henry II of England united the two regions. The English looked to Bordeaux for their wine, at least when the two countries were not waging war against each other. In the fourteenth century, 75 percent of all Bordeaux wine production was shipped to England, where they called Bordeaux red wine "claret." The name may have come from the claret or clairet grape, a common vine in the Middle Ages, or more likely from the light red, almost rosé, color of Bordeaux wines up until the eighteenth century.

Vineyards surround the city of Bordeaux on three sides, and only the western side is not cultivated. The vineyards are divided into five subregions, each with its own history and style of wine. The most famous of the five is Médoc, where most, but not all, of the top châteaux are located. Driving along the generally two-lane road called the D2, a visitor feels he is riding through French wine history, passing wineries with such famous names as Lafite, Margaux, Latour, and many more. The road is informally called the Route des Châteaux. Majestic stone castles stand in silence as monuments to the glory of France. The circuit is the wine equivalent of the Hollywood homes-of-the-stars tour. The best vineyards are in the upper part of the peninsula, where winemakers in such sleepy villages as Margaux, St.-Estèphe, and Pauillac produce some of the world's best wines. Vineyards are located in a strip of land directly north of Bordeaux for about 50 miles between the coastal marshes on the banks of the Gironde Estuary and pine forests about 8 miles inland. It was only in the seventeenth century that Dutch engineers came to Bordeaux and used their dike-making technology to drain marshland used for grazing animals and turn it into vineyards. Newly prosperous wine aristocrats built the great châteaux in the eighteenth and nineteenth centuries, launching Bordeaux's modern era.

The château owners in those days didn't consider traveling to the right bank of the Gironde Estuary because of the complications of making the trip by boat. As a result, the wine growing areas of the left and right banks developed differently. While Cabernet Sauvignon grapes rule the left bank, Merlot is more prominent on the right bank. Médoc also differs from other parts of Bordeaux by the size of properties. The five First Growths of the left bank average 183 acres, while a typical Bordeaux vineyard is only about 30 acres.

It was only after World War II that the right bank began to enjoy the success it long deserved. The main wine region on the right bank is St.-Émilion, which is located 25 miles from the city of Bordeaux; but it includes much more than the village of that name that has only three hundred residents. The Benedictine monk Émilian, who had moved there from Brittany, founded the town in the eighth century. Many of its historic treasures, including an entire church, are located underground. Eleanor of Aquitaine and Henry II established the basic structure of St.-Émilion wine that still exists today. Because the area was settled so long ago and the vineyards on the right bank have been divided among many heirs over the centuries, the average winery is only 15 acres of vines. Château Ausone is only 17.3 acres and produces fewer than 2,000 cases a year. In 1999, UNESCO put St.-Émilion and its vineyards on its World Heritage list. It was the first time the organization had given the honor to vineyards. Many visitors come to St.-Émilion for the wines, without realizing the village's great cultural heritage. Unfortunately, the village has only five hotels and fewer than two dozen restaurants.

The right bank, though, is about more than just St.-Émilion. Pomerol is a nondescript little village with a single church spire rising up out of the flat countryside. Only a small ditch that a visitor would be hard pressed to find separates this appellation from St.-Émilion. But within the confines of Pomerol are such wineries as Châteaux Le Pin, Pétrus, and Lafleur. The region was long dismissed by wine connoisseurs, but gradually, starting in the 1920s, Pomerol became better known first in France and then in northern Europe. After World War II, Harry Waugh, a British wine writer and merchant, brought Pomerol to the attention of British and American sparkling Bordeaux to nonalcoholic grape juice. The blends are mainly Merlot. "We have to be like sheep with five feet and sell everything we can to survive," Labruse says. That kind of attitude and historic structures such as the ruins of the eleventh-century Sauve-Majeure Abbey make Entre-Deux-Mers an interesting place to visit. Because of its gently rolling hills, the area has become a favorite destination for bicycle tourists.

In the southern part of Bordeaux, in Sauternes and Barsac, nature plays some tricks that allow winemakers to produce the nectar of the gods. At the end of summer, grapevines turn gold in color, and in the morning thick fog and cool breezes roll in. There is also usually little rain. The conditions conspire to produce a botrytis fungus nicknamed "noble rot," which shrinks grapes on the vine and concentrates the natural sugar. Bunches of white grapes look rotten to the untrained eye, but the wine made from them is delightful. Unfortunately for Sauternes and Barsac producers, sweet wines, which before World War I were more highly priced than dry red ones, have gone out of fashion, and so prices are relatively low. A top Médoc red, for example the 2005 **Château Latour**, costs $2,000 a bottle, but an equal-rated Sauternes, **Château La Tour Blanche**, sells for less than $50.

As far back as the mid-seventeenth century, Bordeaux wine merchants had an informal system for ranking the region's wines based solely on the price the market was willing to pay. Thomas Jefferson in his diaries refers to this system, and even tried his hand at making his own variation. In preparation for a world's fair in Paris in 1855, Emperor Napoléon III asked the Bordeaux Chamber of Commerce to come up with a list of the best local wines to exhibit. The chamber passed the job along to the Bordeaux wine brokers. Using the same procedure of basing the selection on historic price, the group chose sixty-one red wines and twenty-six sweet white wines for the exhibition. The reds were put into five categories called Crus, or Growths, while the whites fell into three. All the reds, with one exception, Château Haut-Brion, came from the Médoc region. The white wines were all from Sauternes and Barsac. Since 1855, the classification has been changed only once: Château Mouton Rothschild in 1973 went from being a Second Growth to a First Growth. It took Baron Philippe de Rothschild nearly fifty years of lobbying Paris officials to get the upgrade, and the decision to correct history was justified again on the grounds of comparative prices.

The 1855 wines still command premium prices around the world even though the 1855 listings are clearly out of date. Bordeaux places heavy emphasis on the importance of *terroir*, the hard-to-define term that emphasizes the location where the grapes are grown. But there have been changes wine consumers. Dominique Renard, the general director of the *négociant* Bordeaux Millésimes and a resident of St.-Émilion, walked with me into the vineyard of **Château Pétrus** to admire the quality of the clay soil. "The soil has three types of clay that hold water better than other areas. That's the magic of the Merlot you can grow here." Vineyards in Pomerol are generally even smaller than in St.-Émilion. **Château Lafleur** has only 9.9 acres and produces just 1,000 cases each year; **Château Pétrus** has 28.2 acres and makes at most 2,500 cases.

Also on the right bank is Fronsac, once a highly esteemed wine region and still perhaps the prettiest part of Bordeaux. Charlemagne and Cardinal Richelieu both loved Fronsac wines. In the twentieth century, the wines fell out of fashion with consumers, but that may be changing. Patrick Leon, the former winemaker at Château Mouton Rothschild and Napa Valley's Opus One, is making wine in Fronsac at **Château Les Trois Croix**, and flying winemaker Michel Rolland has **Château Fontenil**.

South of the city of Bordeaux on the left bank of the Gironde is the region of Graves, where some of Bordeaux's oldest wineries are located. From its gravelly soils come both excellent red and dry white wines. **Château Pape Clément**, the first named winery in Bordeaux, makes both, as does its neighbor **Château Haut-Brion**. Graves has suffered over the centuries from creeping urbanization, and many vineyards are now virtually in Bordeaux city. It takes a lot of determination to make wines in this area, but Denis Dubourdieu, a Bordeaux University professor as well as winemaker, produces an excellent **Clos Floridène**, also red and white, on a 44-acre property.

If Médoc is home to the aristocracy of Bordeaux, then Entre-Deux-Mers (Between Two Seas) is working-class Bordeaux. Located between the Gironde and Dordogne rivers, it is also between Graves and St.-Émilion. Once major producers of Bordeaux white wines, vintners there switched mainly to red in the 1960s and 1970s. Entre-Deux-Mers is the main producer of simple Bordeaux appellation wines. Some 2,000 wineries make 15 million bottles a year, but the average winery has only 74 acres. Cooperatives are a big part of the business, and most wineries sell 70 percent of their production to cooperatives and keep only 30 percent to market under their own brand names. **Château du Payre** in Cardan is a typical producer trying to make a go of it far from the madding crowds of Médoc and St.-Émilion. Valerie Labruse, a member of the owner's family, studied marketing, and handles much of the promotion. The winery rents three rooms to overnight guests and welcomes drop-in visitors from 9:00 a.m. to 12:00 p.m. and 2:00 p.m. to 6:00 p.m. Its tasting room offers a full range of products from in the vineyards of Grand Cru wineries over the years, and some châteaux don't have the same land as they had in 1855. Talents of winemakers also don't remain static. Some wines are rated lower than they really should be, and some should not even be on the list. Nonetheless, the 1855 classification lives on as a convenient, if flawed, scorecard for Médoc wines.

Exactly a century later in 1955, St.-Émilion came up with its own official classification. The plan was to update the list periodically to reflect the changing quality of the wines. Being on the list is a great boon to producers, who can sell all their wine and at higher prices. The first classification came out in June 1955 and was revised in August and then again in September of that year. The final list included seventy-five wines. Revisions were made in 1969, 1985, 1996, and 2006. The last one demoted eleven properties, which appealed the decision in a battle that reached the highest court in France and the French Senate. A French Court of Appeals scrapped the 2006 classification, but in May 2009 the French government tacked a footnote onto a new agriculture law reinstating the 1996 classification and permitting eight châteaux that had been promoted in 2006 to claim their higher ranking on their labels. This revised classification will last until 2011. By that time, it is hoped that a new, and less controversial, way of updating the St.-Émilion classification will have been established. Battles over promoting—and demoting—wines, though, are likely to continue.

In 1959, Graves producers established a classification for their wines, both reds and dry whites. This list now consists of thirteen reds and nine whites, and several wineries have both reds and whites on the Graves list. Château Haut-Brion is a member of both the 1855 classification and the Graves one.

Some of Bordeaux's best wines come from Pomerol, which does not have a classified list. Château Pétrus, for example, is more expensive than the most costly Médoc. But since Pomerol winemakers quickly sell out of their wines at the high prices they demand, they have no interest in a Pomerol list or being included in any of the existing classifications.

The various Bordeaux classified wines and the leading Pomerol ones make up only about 5 percent of total Bordeaux sales, and those wineries have little problem selling all their production year after year. The other 95 percent of the business, though, faces tougher and tougher competition in global wine markets from both New World producers such as California and Australia and from surging European ones in Spain, Italy, and Portugal. Many Bordeaux wine people are concerned about the future of that 95 percent.